PLEASURE IN ANCIENT GREEK PHILOSOPHY

In this volume Professor Wolfsdorf undertakes the first exploration of ancient Greek philosophical conceptions of pleasure in relation to contemporary conceptions. He provides broad coverage of the ancient material, from pre-Platonic to Old Stoic treatments; and, in the contemporary period, from World War II to the present. Examination of the nature of pleasure in ancient philosophy largely occurred within ethical contexts but in the contemporary period has, to a greater extent, been pursued within philosophy of mind and psychology. This divergence reflects the dominant philosophical preoccupations of the times. But Professor Wolfsdorf argues that the various treatments are complementary. Indeed, the Greeks' examinations of pleasure were incisive and their debates vigorous, and their results have enduring value for contemporary discussion.

The *Key Themes in Ancient Philosophy* series provides concise books, written by major scholars and accessible to non-specialists, on important themes in ancient philosophy that remain of philosophical interest today.

DAVID WOLFSDORF is an associate professor of philosophy at Temple University, Philadelphia, where he specializes in Greek and Roman philosophy. His previous publications include numerous articles on various ancient philosophical topics as well as *Trials of Reason: Plato and the Crafting of Philosophy* (2008).

KEY THEMES IN ANCIENT PHILOSOPHY

Series Editors

Catherine Osborne *Reader in Philosophy, University of East Anglia*

G. R. F. Ferrari *Professor of Classics, University of California, Berkeley*

Each book in this new series offers a concise and accessible treatment by a single author of a topic of major philosophical importance in the ancient Greek and Roman world. The emphasis is on a discussion of those debates of real philosophical interest, placed within their historical context. Future volumes will consider topics such as virtue, knowledge, psychology, cosmology, society, love and friendship, cause and explanation, and persuasion and argument. The books are designed for use in a teaching context, where they will bridge a gap between general introductions to individual philosophers or periods and specialist monographs. They will also appeal to anyone interested in the enduring influence and significance of ancient philosophy.

PLEASURE IN ANCIENT GREEK PHILOSOPHY

DAVID WOLFSDORF

CAMBRIDGE
UNIVERSITY PRESS

CAMBRIDGE UNIVERSITY PRESS
Cambridge, New York, Melbourne, Madrid, Cape Town,
Singapore, São Paulo, Delhi, Mexico City

Cambridge University Press
The Edinburgh Building, Cambridge CB2 8RU, UK

Published in the United States of America by Cambridge University Press, New York

www.cambridge.org
Information on this title: www.cambridge.org/9780521149754

First published 2013

Printed and Bound in the United Kingdom by the MPG Books Group

A catalogue record for this publication is available from the British Library

Library of Congress Cataloguing in Publication data
Wolfsdorf, David, 1969–
Pleasure in ancient Greek philosophy / David Wolfsdorf.
   p.   cm. – (Key themes in ancient philosophy)
   ISBN 978-0-521-76130-7 (Hardback) –
   ISBN 978-0-521-14975-4 (Paperback)
   1. Philosophy, Ancient.   I. Title.
   B171.W65 2013
   128′.4–dc23
   2012025555

ISBN 978-0-521-76130-7 Hardback
ISBN 978-0-521-14975-4 Paperback

But meanwhile – is it not clear that there are several concepts that need investigating simply as a part of the philosophy of psychology and – as I should recommend – *banishing ethics totally* from our minds? Namely – to begin with: "action," "intention," "pleasure," "wanting." More will probably turn up if we start with these. Eventually it might be possible to advance to considering the concept of a virtue; with which, I suppose, we should be beginning some sort of a study of ethics.

G. E. M. Anscombe, "Modern Moral Philosophy"

Muse, tell me the deeds of golden Aphrodite,
the Cyprian, who stirs up sweet passion in the gods
and subdues the tribes of mortal men, the birds
that fly in the air, and all the many creatures
that the dry land and sea rear.

Homeric Hymn to Aphrodite 5.1–5

Contents

Acknowledgments   *page* x

1   Introduction   1
    The relevance of an inquiry into ancient Greek philosophical
        conceptions of pleasure   1
    The topic of pleasure in ancient Greek philosophy   3
    The textual evidence   6
    Concluding remark   9

2   Pleasure in early Greek ethics   10
    Prodicus   10
    Democritus' *On Contentment*   13
    Antisthenes   18
    Aristippus   20
    Socrates' "What is *F*?" question   23

3   Pleasure in the early physical tradition   29
    Empedocles   31
    Diogenes of Apollonia   33
    Pleasure in nutrition   35
    Sexual pleasure   37

4   Plato on pleasure and restoration   40
    The replenishment theory of pleasure in Plato's *Gorgias* and *Republic*   41
    Sense-perceptual pleasure in *Timaeus* (Part One)   50
    Base and fine pleasures in *Hippias Major*   53
    Sense-perceptual pleasure in *Timaeus* (Part Two)   56

5   Plato on true, untrue, and false pleasures   63
    True and untrue pleasures in *Republic* 9: The Illusion Argument   63
    More and less true pleasures in *Republic* 9: The True Filling Argument   70
    Olfactory pleasures and the absolute/gradable ontological
        truth-value distinction   73
    Introduction to the treatment of pleasure in *Philebus*   74

The first two kinds of pleasure in *Philebus*   76
False pleasure in *Philebus*: Kind 1   80
False pleasure in *Philebus*: Kind 2   84
False pleasure in *Philebus*: Kind 3   88
False pleasure in *Philebus*: Kind 4   90
Pure pleasure in *Philebus*   97
Conclusion to the treatment of pleasure in *Philebus*   99
Conclusion to Plato's treatment of pleasure   101

6   Aristotle on pleasure and activation   103
Aristotle's early conception of pleasure   106
Aristotle's concept of *energeia*   114
Sense-perceiving as a kind of psychic activation   116
Pleasure as activation in *Eudemian Ethics*   119
Aristotle's criticism of the restoration theory   123
Pleasure and the completion of activation in *Nicomachean Ethics* 10   130
Aristotle on kinds of pleasure   133
Appendix: Aristotle and the Peripatetic *Problems* on sexual pleasure   138

7   Epicurus and the Cyrenaics on katastematic and kinetic
pleasures   144
Introduction to katastematic and kinetic pleasures   147
Kinetic pleasure   152
Katastematic pleasure   158
Kinetic pleasure as activation   163
Torquatus' argument that absence of pain is pleasure   167
Epicurean wisdom   172
Epicurus' conception of pleasure   176
Attention and the problem of mixed pleasure   179

8   The Old Stoics on pleasure as passion   182
Zeno on passion   185
Passion as irrational and unnatural change of the soul   186
Impulse   189
Excess   194
Fluttering   201
The four principal kinds of passion   202
Pleasure, pain, and fresh belief   203
The Stoics' conception of pleasure and common sense   208
Good passions (*eupatheiai*)   210
Kinds of pleasure   212

9   Contemporary conceptions of pleasure   214
Introduction to philosophical examination of pleasure in the
contemporary period   214
Gilbert Ryle's account of pleasure   217

Disposition, episode, sensation 221
Enjoyment, being-pleased-that, and other hedonic kinds 228
Enjoyment in the eighties: The Warner–Davis debate 232
Pleasure and intentionality in the early contemporary period 235
Pleasure and truth-aptness in the early contemporary period 240
Pleasure, intentionality, and representation in the recent
  contemporary period 245
Pleasure, intentionality, and feeling in the recent contemporary period 253
Some conclusions and suggestions for future investigation 265

10   Ancient and contemporary conceptions of pleasure 269

Suggestions for further reading 280
General Index 288
Index of Greek and Latin Words and Expressions 293
Index of Quotations from Ancient Authors 295
Index of Quotations from Contemporary Authors 299

Acknowledgments

Soon after I came to Temple University in 2004, my colleague Charles Dyke invited me to read *Philebus*. He had a hypothesis about the influence of Eudoxus' theory of proportions on the role of the discussion of mixtures of dissimilar kinds. So far as I can tell, the hypothesis never bore the intended fruit; and overall we moved through the text too swiftly. But it was a start.

At about the same time, my colleague and friend Andrew Payne, also new to the area, invited me to read Greek together. I suggested that we include Charles Kahn and proposed that since Charles was working on late Plato, we try *Philebus*. That group, occasionally augmented by graduate students, proceeded with great care and completed the text in about two years. By that time, my appetite for ancient hedonic theory had been thoroughly whetted. Charles, Andrew, and I also attempted to compose a paper on the *dihairesis* of pleasure, but we were more successful as collaborative readers and interlocutors than writers.

Felicitously, the 2007 meeting of the International Plato Society in Dublin was devoted to *Philebus*, further cementing my fascination with this text. Meanwhile, I had also begun teaching seminars on ancient Greek conceptions of pleasure and included some relevant material in courses on ethics. Temple's tradition as a stronghold of aesthetics certainly encouraged my focus on pleasure. But it was principally my growing interests in meta-ethics and philosophy of mind that motivated me. Pleasure stands at a wonderful intersection of these vigorous domains.

About 2008 I began working on a book on Plato's curious coupling of pleasure and truth-value. I was well underway when in the spring of 2010 Michael Sharp contacted me from Cambridge University Press to ask if I would be interested in contributing a book on the topic of pleasure to a series that John Ferrari and Catherine Rowett were editing. My initial reaction was mixed pleasure. I was delighted to be invited but worried that such a book would jeopardize my work on Plato on pleasure and truth-value.

In fact, the project has been extremely salutary. I find it easy to get lost in scholarly details and debates, but the conditions, including the intended audience, for this book compelled me to think through problems and write from a different perspective. In the process I came to appreciate its value. From a bird's eye view, one can see connections that are easy to miss when one's nose is too close to the ground. The project also encouraged me to think harder about the relevance of the ancients' contributions to contemporary discussions – and this has proven to be one of the most important consequences of the undertaking.

I would like to believe that ultimately I was ripe for this project and fortunate that the opportunity to execute it came my way. For this and for their editorial investment and advice, I express my gratitude and appreciation to Drs Sharp, Ferrari, and Rowett.

In writing this book, I have also sporadically consulted several experts in the relevant areas of ancient thought. For their willingness to listen, their comments and criticisms, and in some cases for sharing unpublished work, I thank Elizabeth Asmis, Tad Brennan, Victor Caston, David Sansone, Brooke Holmes, Brad Inwood, Jeffrey Purinton, and James Warren. I would also like to thank Diana Lobel for her interest in my manuscript and for a challenging and productive exchange regarding Epicurus' conception of pleasure. Epicurus' view has been particularly difficult to work out.

Finally, I'd like to thank the editorial staff at Cambridge University Press, especially Iveta Adams, for their professionalism and assistance.

CHAPTER I

Introduction

This book principally examines philosophical conceptions of pleasure in Greek and to a more limited extent Greco-Roman antiquity. The discussion begins with pre-Platonic treatments (Chapters 2 and 3). The heart of the book is then devoted to the contributions of Plato, Aristotle, Epicurus, the Cyrenaics, and the Old Stoics, in that order (Chapters 4–8). Consequently, the book principally focuses on a stretch of about 200 years of philosophical history, from the beginning of Plato's literary career in the early fourth century BCE to the death of the Old Stoic philosopher Chrysippus at the end of the third century BCE. Chapter 9, which follows, discusses contemporary conceptions of pleasure, specifically Anglophone conceptions since World War II. Its aim is to provide perspective on and a means of assessing the ancients' contributions. The conclusion (Chapter 10) then offers some remarks to this effect. A bibliography with suggestions for further reading follows the conclusion. Among these are suggestions for reading concerning conceptions of pleasure in antiquity after the Old Stoics.

THE RELEVANCE OF AN INQUIRY INTO ANCIENT GREEK PHILOSOPHICAL CONCEPTIONS OF PLEASURE

Elizabeth Anscombe's 1958 article "Modern Moral Philosophy" is often cited for encouraging a reorientation in contemporary ethical theory, away from the dominant modern traditions of deontology, utilitarianism, and contractualism, toward a style of thought exemplified by the theorizing of the Greeks, namely, virtue ethics or the ethics of character. In her article, as the epigraph indicates, Anscombe suggests that the reorientation must in fact begin outside of ethics, in philosophy of psychology, and with basic philosophical psychological concepts pertaining to the practical life of humans such as action, intention, wanting, and pleasure.

Anscombe's short treatise *Intention*, published a year before the article, itself constitutes a seminal contribution to the reorientation of ethical theory she advocates. In one section she remarks on the impoverished philosophical psychology of her British empiricist predecessors, and she singles out their treatments of wanting and pleasure as cases in point:

The cause of blindness to these problems seems to have been the epistemology characteristic of Locke, and also of Hume. Any sort of wanting would be an internal impression according to those philosophers. The bad effects of their epistemology come out most clearly if we consider the striking fact that the concept of pleasure has hardly seemed a problematic one at all to modern philosophers, until Ryle reintroduced it as a topic a year or two ago. The ancients seem to have been baffled by it; its difficulty, astonishingly, reduced Aristotle to babble, since for good reasons he both wanted pleasure to be identical with and to be different from the activity that it is pleasure in. It is customary nowadays to refute utilitarianism by accusing it of the "naturalistic fallacy," an accusation whose force I doubt. What ought to rule that philosophy out of consideration at once is the fact that it always proceeds as if 'pleasure' were a quite unproblematic concept. (§40)

Ryle's several contributions of the mid fifties, to which Anscombe here refers and which will be our point of departure in the discussion of contemporary treatments in Chapter 9, galvanized philosophical debate over the nature of pleasure for three decades. After the waning of this strain of discussion in the eighties, the topic has once again been reinvigorated in the last fifteen or so years through the burgeoning of philosophy of mind, philosophy of emotion, and consciousness studies, in conjunction with neighboring empirical arenas such as affective psychology, cognitive science, and neuroscience.

Ryle's work, like Anscombe's, was congenial with the thought of the Greeks. Indeed, Ryle's reading of Aristotle influenced his account of pleasure. True – Anscombe criticizes Aristotle for babbling; but her criticism here is misguided. Anscombe has in mind a well-known passage from Aristotle's *Nicomachean Ethics* where, according to the standard translation on which she depends, it is claimed that "pleasure supervenes on activity like the bloom of youth." This may be babble. But there is good reason to think that the translation is inaccurate. As we will see in Chapter 6, when the Greek is properly rendered, Aristotle's thought emerges as intelligible, intelligent, and arguably true.

More generally, it is facile and unjustified to claim that the topic of pleasure baffled the ancients. When Anscombe called for a return to virtue ethics and to the investigation of the psychological concepts upon which this form of ethical theorizing depends, she did not herself undertake historical investigations into the Greeks' theories of wanting, action, or pleasure. If she had and had pursued the task in a careful and searching manner worthy of a philosopher of her stature, she would have discovered a treasure of insights. The Greeks' examinations of pleasure were incisive, their debates vigorous, and their results have enduring value for contemporary discussion.

THE TOPIC OF PLEASURE IN ANCIENT GREEK PHILOSOPHY

The topic of pleasure enters Greek philosophy in the fifth century BCE from two intellectual traditions: the ethical tradition and what the Greeks call the tradition of "*physiologia.*" I will refer to the latter as the "physical" tradition and describe it in some detail in Chapter 3. Early ethical treatments of pleasure focus on whether, how, and to what extent pleasure contributes to a good life. In this context, I discuss the contributions of Prodicus of Ceos, Democritus of Abdera, and two men associated with Socrates, Antisthenes of Athens and Aristippus of Cyrene. Among the various things these figures say about pleasure, none engages the question "What is pleasure?" For convenience, I will refer to this as the *identity question.*

So far as I know, it was Plato who first raised and earnestly pursued the identity question. He does so in the context of ethical theorizing. Precisely, he thinks that in order to determine the relation between pleasure and goodness, it is necessary to determine what pleasure itself is. My discussions of Plato and his successors principally focus on their treatments of the identity question and closely related questions.

Depending on one's conception of pleasure, the answer to the identity question may require an account of human or animal physiology, including what we now call neurology. In Greek thought, such accounts initially arise within the physical tradition of inquiry. This tradition, as we will see, overlaps with the tradition of medical theory. Once again it is Plato who is pivotal in appropriating and developing such discussions.

There are fewer physiological accounts of pleasure than accounts that occur within the contexts of ethical theory. But this disparity is a function of authorial interests and not a reflection of any theoretical commitment that physiological accounts are somehow discontinuous with other accounts. So far as evidence permits, we will discuss the complementary relation between physical and non-physical accounts of pleasure. In the next section of this introduction, I offer some general orientational remarks about the state of the evidence for ancient philosophy.

Closely related to the identity question is the question "What kinds of pleasure are there?" I will refer to this as the *kinds question*. Plato and his successors variously distinguish different kinds of pleasure. The way in which they draw such distinctions depends of course on their conceptions of pleasure itself. For example, all ancient philosophers think that pleasure somehow involves the soul (*psychê*). But some philosophers think that some pleasures essentially depend on the body. Consequently, they distinguish bodily and psychic pleasures. (Note that here and throughout I use the adjective "psychic" in the sense of "relating to the *psychê*.") Some philosophers think that there are different parts of the soul. Consequently, they distinguish different kinds of pleasure according to the different parts of the soul involved. Some philosophers think that pleasures can be true and false and, moreover, that there are different ways in which pleasures can be true and false. Thus, they draw distinctions between true and false pleasures. With respect to at least to one kind of truth-conception, some philosophers think that some psychic conditions appear to be, but are not in fact, pleasures. Thus, they distinguish between true or genuine pleasures and merely apparent pleasures.

In light of such distinctions, I should note that I am here using the term "kinds" loosely. It is not, for instance, necessarily intended to demarcate relations of genus and species. The various kinds of pleasure may be related in a number of ways, and those ways may be explained according to various theoretical commitments. A central question we will pursue in tandem with the kinds question is what motivates and, to some extent, grounds the philosophers' distinctions among kinds of pleasure.

The focus of my discussion on the identity and kinds questions is to the exclusion of two other important questions or rather domains of inquiry, both of which were central to ancient philosophical discussions that engage the topic of pleasure. One of these concerns the value, specifically the ethical value, of pleasure. Generally speaking, ancient philosophers vigorously debate the positions of ethical hedonism and anti-hedonism. According to the former view, pleasure is the good, at least for humans. According to the latter view, it is not. The other question concerns the relation between pleasure and motivation. More precisely, philosophers debate the position of psychological hedonism. According to psychological hedonism, we naturally or innately desire or are motivated by pleasure.

While the question of psychological hedonism can be viewed purely as a part of the psychology of motivation, it tends to be discussed, like the identity and kinds questions, within the context of ethical theory. For example, some philosophers examine the argument that the good is that which things naturally desire. Some philosophers distinguish different kinds of pleasure in the context of arguing that certain kinds of pleasure have greater value than other kinds. In short, the identity and kinds questions as well as questions about the nature of human or animal motivation are in fact usually and in principle always subordinate to questions about value and ethics.

Insofar as this book focuses on the identity question, then, it focuses on an aspect of what may be called hedonic theorizing that tends to arise within the contexts of psychology and ethics. The focus on the identity question is, however, justified on logical grounds. How deeply or effectively can one ascertain pleasure's value without clarifying what pleasure is? Indeed, as I mentioned before, this is why the identity question arises for Plato. Compare Socrates' reply to Meno when asked whether excellence is teachable: "If I do not know what something is, how could I know what characteristics it possesses?" (71b) The same question may be put with respect to the relation between motivation and pleasure: If we do not know what pleasure is, how can we know whether we are naturally motivated by it? In short, the identity question has a claim to methodological priority. Compare the remarks of William P. Alston in his 1967 article on pleasure from *The Encyclopedia of Philosophy*, "from the time of Plato much of the discussion of the topics of motivation and value has consisted in arguments for and against the doctrines of psychological hedonism ... and ethical hedonism. One can make an intelligent judgment on these doctrines only to the extent that he has a well-worked-out view as to the nature of pleasure. Otherwise, he will be unable to settle such questions as whether a putative counterexample, for instance, a desire for the welfare of one's children, is or is not a genuine example of desiring something other than pleasure for its own sake" (341).

A further justification for restricting the focus to the identity question is simply that the ancient treatments of this question provide more than ample material for a book of this length. In fact, in numerous cases I have had to abbreviate my discussion to conform to editorial considerations. That is to say, the Greeks had a great deal to say about pleasure and its place within human psychology and life. To be sure, our discussion of what they say will inevitably bleed into questions in ethics and other areas of psychology. But we will have our hands full just coming to grips with the identity and kinds questions.

I stated above that the book principally focuses on a stretch of about 200 years of philosophical history. To prevent misunderstanding, I should emphasize that the aim of the book is not to provide a comprehensive treatment of philosophical conceptions of pleasure even across these two centuries. My primary aim has been to focus on what I regard as the most historically and, at least from a contemporary perspective, philosophically important treatments of the identity and kinds questions from this period. As it happens, these philosophically as well as historically important treatments do make for quite a comprehensive treatment of pleasure in the latter half of the Classical and the earlier half of the Hellenistic periods.

Finally, it is helpful to recognize a distinction between what any Greek philosopher or school thinks pleasure is, including what kinds of pleasure there are, on the one hand, and why that philosopher or school holds these views, on the other hand. For convenience, I will refer to the latter as the *explanation question.* Inevitably in answering the identity and kinds questions, I engage the explanation question. But in contrast to the identity and kinds questions, the explanation question can be treated at various levels of depth. Inevitable engagement of the explanation question in the process of working out the identity and kinds questions does not require deep engagement. Indeed, very deep treatment of the explanation question is not feasible within a book of this length or character. However, in the course of my discussions I explore some of the deeper reaches of explanation. To anticipate, in part these lie in the various philosophers' conceptions of the soul. That is, a given philosopher's conception of what pleasure is, if adequately theorized, will be a function of or at least informed by that philosopher's conception of the soul. In part, still deeper reaches of explanation lie in the various philosophers' basic metaphysical commitments.

THE TEXTUAL EVIDENCE

Our study of ancient Greek philosophy depends upon texts as records of the thought of the ancient philosophers and schools. In the case of every philosopher or philosophical school we will be discussing in the following pages, our textual evidence presents a range of difficulties. More precisely, the textual evidence for different philosophers presents different kinds of difficulty. Where needed, I will clarify the particular difficulty or difficulties the textual evidence of a given philosopher or philosophical school presents. Here, I make some brief general remarks.

Our textual evidence for ancient Greek philosophy is basically of three kinds: more or less complete primary texts, fragments of primary texts, and testimonies regarding figures, schools, and their texts. Plato's *Republic* and Aristotle's *On the Soul* are examples of complete primary texts. Fragments are verbatim passages from the work of a philosopher. Testimonies are paraphrases or comments upon the work, thought, or life of a philosopher or school. For example, consider the following piece of textual evidence regarding the fifth century Pythagorean philosopher Ion of Chios:

(a) [Ion of Chios] wrote many poems and tragedies and a philosophical treatise entitled *Triad* ... In some copies it is entitled *Triads*, in the plural, according to Demetrius of Skepsis and Apollonides of Nicaea. They record this from it: (b) This is the beginning of my account: all things are three, and there is nothing more or fewer than these three things. Of each one, the excellence is threefold: intelligence and power and fortune.

I have added letters to distinguish two parts of the passage. Part (b) is a fragment; it purports to be the opening words of Ion of Chios' philosophical treatise *Triad*. In contrast, part (a) is a testimony, in this case a report about the range of Ion of Chios' literary activity and the title of his philosophical treatise. The whole passage derives from a lexicon composed by Valerius Harpocration some time during the Roman Empire. Harpocration's text is the one that survives today and thereby preserves this fragment and testimony of Ion of Chios.

As in the case of the fragment from Ion of Chios' *Triad*, fragments almost always consist of passages from other non-fragmentary or relatively non-fragmentary works. Very rarely do we actually have fragmentary texts, for example, bits of papyrus scrolls, from antiquity, that are copies of an original author's work, let alone being an original author's work.

Fragments and testimonies have distinct values. Fragments of course give us the actual words of a philosopher. In the best cases, testimonies help us to contextualize fragments or, more generally, to contextualize the contribution of a philosopher. Harpocration's passage from Ion of Chios is quite helpful insofar as it specifies the work in which the fragment occurs as well as the location of the fragment within the work. But compare the following testimonies and fragment regarding another fifth-century Pythagorean, Hippo of Croton:

(1) One would not propose to place Hippo among these men because of the poverty of his thought.

(2) (a) In the third book of his *Homeric Studies* Crates says that the later philosophers of nature also agreed that the water that surrounds the earth for most of its extent is Ocean and that fresh water comes from it. Hippo: (b) "All drinking waters come from the sea. For the wells from which we drink are surely not deeper than the sea is. If they were, the water would come not from the sea, but from somewhere else. But in fact the sea is deeper than the waters. Now all waters that are higher than the sea come from the sea."

(1) is a testimony from Aristotle's *Metaphysics* (composed in the latter half of the fourth century BCE). It is barely useful as evidence for reconstructing Hippo's life or thought since it merely records that Aristotle had a poor estimation of Hippo's intellect. (2) consists of a fragment (b), which is prefaced by a testimony (a). The passage derives from an anonymous ancient commentator on Homer's *Iliad*. The testimony derives from a lost work, *Homeric Studies*, by the Stoic philosopher and grammarian Crates of Mallos. (Hence a *terminus post quem* for the anonymous commentator is Crates of Mallos' lifetime, that is, second century BCE.) The commentator is citing Crates' idea, although not verbatim. The commentator then quotes a fragment from Hippo, which supports Crates' idea. In this case, it is unclear whether Crates himself originally quoted Hippo in support of himself. We are also not given any context for Hippo's remark. For example, was Hippo also commenting on the Homer passage? Or did Hippo refer to bodies of water more generally in the context of a natural scientific discussion?

What might be called the limiting case of a fragment is one in which the fragment is simply presented with no testimony framing it. We might call this an "unframed" fragment. Unframed fragments occur, for example, in a Late Antique anthology, a compendium of knowledge and wisdom, compiled by Johannes Stobaeus for his son Septimius. The contents are organized under chapter and sub-chapter headings. But beyond these basic points of orientation, Stobaeus simply gives the name of his source and quotes or paraphrases. For example: "Heraclitus: A man when he is drunk is led by a beardless boy, stumbling not knowing where he goes, his soul is moist." Unframed fragments, while valuable insofar as they are fragments, can of course be difficult to interpret precisely because they are unframed. If a philosopher composed several works, we may not know from what work the fragment derives, nor may we know where in a given work the fragment occurs.

Given these distinctions in forms of evidence, we can now specify, loosely, the nature of our evidence for the figures and schools that we will be discussing in the following chapters. For the pre-Platonic material, we have almost no primary texts. Occasionally, we have fragments, many of which are unframed. But most of the evidence comes in the form of testimonies. For Plato and Aristotle, we have many primary texts. In the case of Aristotle, we also have fragments from otherwise lost works. In the case of Epicurus, we have a few short primary texts. In addition, we have some fragments, most of which are unframed. Finally, we have numerous testimonies. In the case of the Cyrenaics, we only have testimony, and not much testimony at that. For the Old Stoics, we have no primary texts. We have numerous fragments, framed and unframed, and numerous testimonies.

CONCLUDING REMARK

In the ancient world, pleasure was widely associated with the goddess Aphrodite (Roman Venus). In Plato's dialogue *Philebus*, the ancient text that arguably plumbs the nature of this topic more deeply than any other, Plato's principal dramatic character Socrates begins the inquiry into pleasure's role in the good human life by invoking the goddess with reverent and cautious words:

> We must do our best, making our start with the goddess herself – this fellow claims that although she is called Aphrodite, her truest name is *hêdonê* (pleasure) ... I always feel a more than human dread over what names to use for the gods ... So now I address Aphrodite by whatever title pleases her. (12b–c)

One of the delightful facts about an inquiry into pleasure is the way that philosophical scrutiny quickly gives the lie to common sense. Untutored intuition suggests that the nature of pleasure is too obvious to be contested, let alone to warrant sustained investigation. It is often assumed that pleasure, like pain, is simply a feeling. It will therefore shock readers to learn that almost no Greek or contemporary philosopher identifies pleasure with a feeling. In fact, arguably, there is no Greek word for "feeling." Most Greek and contemporary philosophers regard pleasure as something altogether different or at least something more complex. More precisely, most Greek philosophers conceive of pleasure as an attitude toward an object. Contemporary philosophers who hold such a view debate what this attitude is: attention, absorption, liking, desire. In their investigations, the Greeks tend to focus on the proper objects of pleasure. They variously propose: a process of restoration, an activity, a state of equilibrium, a proposition. The following chapters of course explore these positions and examine their grounds. Ultimately, we will also try to explain why the Greeks tend to focus on pleasure's object, while contemporaries tend to focus on pleasure's attitude.

Socrates' studied care in the *Philebus* quotation suggests that the endeavor to provide a philosophically adequate account of pleasure should begin with humility. Fortunately, mischaracterizing pleasure will not incur the wrath of Aphrodite. However, naïve assumptions about its nature may jeopardize our broader ethical theoretical aspirations.

CHAPTER 2

Pleasure in early Greek ethics

The topic of pleasure enters Greek philosophy in the fifth century BCE. The principal site of entry is ethics. Early Greek ethical treatments of pleasure focus on whether, how, and to what extent pleasure contributes to a good human life. There is also some discussion of pleasure in the contexts of theology and cosmology, physiology and psychology, all areas explored by so-called Presocratic thinkers we refer to as "philosophers." I will discuss pleasure in some of those contexts in Chapter 3. Here I discuss the early ethical contributions.

PRODICUS

Prodicus of Ceos (*c.* 465–395) – a man often but misleadingly referred to as a "sophist" – composed a pedagogical work, one part of which is known as *The Choice of Heracles.*[1] In *The Choice of Heracles*, Prodicus presented the mythological hero Heracles as a young man at a crossroads poised to choose a path of life. Feminine figures representing Excellence and Depravity advertised their respective courses. Prodicus' *Choice of Heracles* does not survive. However, a rendition of it by the historian and Socratic philosopher Xenophon of Athens (*c.* 430–354) does. Consider the following passage from Xenophon's rendition of Depravity's exhortation:

You [Heracles] will not be concerned with wars or public responsibilities, but with what food or drink you can find to suit your taste, what sight or sound might please you, what scent or touch might delight you, which beloved's company might gratify you most, how you may sleep most softly, and how you can achieve all this with the least trouble. (*Memorabilia* 2.1.24)

The allure of the path of Depravity lies in the enjoyment of these pleasures. For convenience, I will refer to them as *depraved pleasures*.

[1] The whole work seems to have been called *The Seasons* (*Horai*), perhaps referring to stages of a man's life.

One might wonder what depraved pleasures have in common in virtue of which they are to be found on the path of Depravity. Consideration of the path of Excellence helps to formulate an answer. Excellence encourages Heracles to pursue a course of duty and service to his city-state. Yet the path of Excellence is not devoid of pleasure. Excellence emphasizes that her path offers distinct pleasures of its own:

> The young enjoy the praises of their elders. The old are glad to be honored by the young. They recall their past deeds with pleasure, and they take pleasure in doing their present deeds well. (*Memorabilia* 2.1.23)

I will refer to this set of pleasures as *civic pleasures*. Civic pleasures contribute to the well-being of society. They derive from civically minded activities or from admiration of or reflection upon such activities. It is these activities that Depravity spurns as onerous: "you will not be concerned with wars or public responsibilities." Arguably then, depraved pleasures are anti-civic pleasures. They are pleasures that involve attention to and indulgence of the individual to the detriment of society.

In addition to *The Choice of Heracles*, Prodicus was celebrated in antiquity for his contribution to a field his contemporaries called "correctness of words" (*orthotês onomatôn*). This field is akin to semantics, linguistics, and philosophy of language. More precisely, Prodicus was famed for drawing distinctions between closely semantically related words. For example, Plato (427–347), in his dialogue *Protagoras*, parodically portrays the character Prodicus rattling off a series of such distinctions:

> Those who attend a discussion are, for both speakers, a joint (*koinous*), but not equal (*isous*) audience – it's not the same thing. For one must listen to both jointly, yet not give equal credit to each, but more to the wiser and less to the less intelligent. Now I myself, Protagoras and Socrates, think that you should agree to debate (*amphisbêtein*) with each other about your arguments, but not to wrangle (*erizein*) – for friends debate with friends, indeed through good will, whereas it's those who disagree with and are hostile to each other who wrangle. And it's in this way that we might have the finest meeting, as you the speakers would gain a good reputation (*eudokimoite*) among us as listeners, yet you would not be praised (*epainoisthe*). (337a–b)

Prodicus concludes his speech with the following distinction:

> We in the audience would be wholly delighted (*euphrainesthai*), not pleased (*hêdoimestha*), for being delighted (*euphrainesthai*) is a condition of learning something and partaking of understanding with the intellect itself, whereas being pleased (*hêdesthai*) is a condition of one eating something or experiencing some other pleasure with the body itself. (337c)

If this passage accurately reflects the views of the historical Prodicus, rather than Plato's character Prodicus, then Prodicus is the first Western thinker to make this terminological and explicit hedonic distinction between pleasures of the body (*sôma*) and pleasures of the soul (*psychê*), that is, between somatic and psychic or mental pleasures. Moreover, arguably this distinction conforms to the contrast between depraved and civic pleasures that Depravity and Excellence recommend in *The Choice of Heracles*. In that case, we can explain Prodicus' introduction of the distinction by reference to its occasion and context.

Despite the neat congruence, I think the distinction between somatic and psychic pleasures is Plato's rather than Prodicus'. Plato draws a distinction between somatic and psychic pleasures in several other dialogues where Prodicus is nowhere in view.[2] More significantly, Aristotle (384–322), in his logical and dialectical treatise *Topics*, mentions that "Prodicus used to divide pleasures into *chara* (joy), *terpsis* (delight), and *euphrosynê* (good-cheer)" (112b). This distinction does not correspond in number or terms with the one from Plato's *Protagoras*. But Plato is clearly parodying a man he derogatorily identifies as a sophist, whereas there is no reason, aside from the *Protagoras* passage, to suspect Aristotle of misreporting.

Unfortunately, Aristotle does not tell us how or why Prodicus drew these distinctions. However, in a passage from his *Commentary on Plato's Phaedrus*, the Neoplatonic philosopher Hermias of Alexandria (fifth century CE) corroborates and supplements Aristotle's testimony:

Prodicus invented discrimination between words; for example, with regard to the difference between *terpsis*, *chara*, and *euphrosynê*, [he said that] *terpsis* is pleasure of fine things through the ears, *chara* is pleasure of the soul, and *euphrosynê* is pleasure through the eyes. (238.22–239.2)

Following Aristotle's and Hermias' leads, I suggest that Prodicus' hedonic distinctions pertain to a subset of pleasures, pleasures of cultivation or what I will call *refined pleasures*. Note in particular the qualification "of fine things" specified for *terpsis*. I assume that this qualification is to be understood in the cases of *chara* and *euphrosynê* as well.

In light of this, it may also be significant that the most common pleasure term in Classical Greek of the fifth century BCE, "*hêdonê*," does not figure among Prodicus' distinctions. In other words, Prodicus might have reserved this common term for what he regarded as base, as opposed to refined, pleasures. Possibly, then, this interpretation of Aristotle's and

---

[2] We will discuss Plato's distinctions in detail in Chapters 4 and 5.

Hermias' testimonies remains compatible with the idea that *The Choice of Heracles* was the occasion for Prodicus' distinctions: the path of Excellence would afford refined pleasures, whereas Depravity would offer base pleasures.

Once again, however, I suspect that the truth is more complicated. The contrast between depraved and civic pleasures resembles, but I think is not the same as, the contrast between base and refined pleasures. Bear in mind that the contrast between depraved and civic pleasures derives from Xenophon's rendition of Prodicus' *Choice of Heracles*, not from Prodicus' *Choice of Heracles* itself. The broader context in which Xenophon renders *The Choice of Heracles* concerns a dispute over the advantages and disadvantages of commitment to and disengagement from civic life. I suspect that Xenophon adapts Prodicus' *Choice of Heracles* to suit this debate. Support for the more general view that Xenophon does not strictly adhere to Prodicus' ideas relates to the use of pleasure terms in Xenophon's rendition. In addition to several other pleasure terms, Xenophon does use the terms "*terpsis*," "*chara*," and "*euphrosynê*," or at least verbal or adjectival cognates of these terms. But he does not use the Prodican terms in the way Hermias says Prodicus distinguished them. Most importantly, Xenophon does not use the Prodican terms or any pleasure terms in any systematic way. Consequently, once again, I suggest that the distinction between depraved and civic pleasures is a function of Xenophon's adaptation. Thus, I assume that the distinction between refined and base pleasures (and the distinction of *terpsis*, *chara*, and *euphrosynê* among refined pleasures), which is similar to, but not the same as, the distinction between depraved and civic pleasures, derives from Prodicus' lost *Choice of Heracles*.

DEMOCRITUS' 'ON CONTENTMENT'

The topic of pleasure recurs among the ethical fragments of Democritus of Abdera (*c.* 460–370), in particular among fragments from Democritus' work *On Contentment*. A central assumption of this work is that a life of contentment (*euthymia*) is the best life for a man. I emphasize, and we will see below, that Democritus does not identify contentment with pleasure.

In pursuit of contentment Democritus appears to make two principal recommendations. One pertains to a man's power (*dynamis*), the other to his nature (*physis*). The first recommendation derives from the following fragment, which seems to constitute the opening lines of *On Contentment*:

He who is going to be content must not do many things, either in private or in public; and in his choice of what he does, he must not exceed his own power (*dynamis*) and nature (*physis*). He must be watchful so that even when fortune seizes him and urges him further in his imagination, he sets it aside and does not attempt more than what is possible. (B3)

Worldly events are largely subject to fortune. To that extent, management of these events is beyond a man's power. Thus, a man's attempts to control or regulate his environment should be modest. This pertains both to the private sphere of a man's homestead or estate and to the public sphere in which he conducts his political affairs and discharges his civic duties.

Although in fragment B3 Democritus refers both to a man's power and to his nature, the warning he offers seems specifically pertinent to a man's power. Yet it might be supposed that Democritus does not intend to draw a significant distinction between a man's power and his nature. The power of a thing is closely related to its nature. So perhaps the phrase "his own power and nature" is being used to refer to a single thing. Plausible as this suggestion is when considering fragment B3 in isolation, as we will see, it does not seem defensible in light of other fragments that also appear to derive from *On Contentment*.

In pursuit of contentment Democritus recommends the cultivation of self-control and in particular "moderation in pleasure":

For men achieve contentment by moderation in pleasure and by proportion in their lives. (B191)

By "moderation in pleasure," Democritus seems principally to mean regulation of one's desires toward particular kinds of pleasure:

The best thing for a man is to live his life contently and with least distress. And that would occur if one did not take pleasure in mortal things. (B189)

By "tak[ing] pleasure in mortal things" I understand Democritus to mean indulging in what he elsewhere calls "pleasures of the belly." Pleasures of the belly are "mortal things," for, like humans in contrast to gods, they are short-lived. Support for this interpretation can be derived from the following fragment:

Those who take their pleasures from their belly, exceeding what is appropriate in food, drink, or sex, to all of them their pleasures are meager and brief, lasting just so long as they are eating and drinking, and their pains are many. For this desire for the same thing is always with them, even when they get what they desire; and the pleasure soon passes, and they have no profit except brief delight; and then they need the same thing again. (B235)

In one fragment, Democritus imagines the body of a man who has devoted his life to the pursuit of pleasures of the belly prosecuting an immoderate soul for having ruined it:

If the body brought a suit against [the soul] for all the sufferings and ills it had endured throughout its life, and one had to judge the case oneself, one would gladly condemn the soul for having ruined certain features of the body through carelessness and made it soft through drink and brought it to rack and ruin through love of pleasures (*philhêdoniais*), just as if a tool or a utensil were in a bad state one would blame the person who used it carelessly. (B159)

Evidently, when Democritus uses the phrase "love of pleasures" here, he specifically has pleasures of the belly in mind.

Granted this, observe that the criticism Democritus makes of one who devotes himself to pleasures of the belly is not due to a misguided or futile attempt to master fortune. Rather, the problem appears to be that such indulgence is at odds with a man's nature. That is to say, it is simply unhealthy. In other words, Democritus can be critical even when a man succeeds in controlling his environment and gaining the objects of his ambitious desires. It is precisely this point that encourages the view that in his recommendations for pursuing contentment, Democritus recognizes a distinction between a man's power and his nature.

With respect to a man's nature, Democritus recommends regulation of one's desires to conform to one's limited material needs:

One should aim at measured acquisition and measure one's troubles against what is necessary. (B285)

If you do not desire many things, a little will seem much for you; for small desires make poverty as strong as wealth. (B284)

Successful is he who is content with moderate wealth, unsuccessful who is discontent with great wealth. (B286)

Of course, Democritus' recommendations about man's power and his nature are closely related and corroborate one another: a man should not seek too much from his environment because he cannot control it. But in any case, he needs little from his environment, so that even if he could attain what his ambition seeks, it would not be to his advantage.

These ideas might suggest that Democritus views a well-lived human life as affording little pleasure. But paradoxically he suggests that a life of moderation and self-control is likely to yield more pleasure than one devoted to the pursuit of pleasures of the belly:

Self-control increases delights and makes pleasure greater. (B211)

Pursuit of modest goods is more reliably achievable. Thus, a moderate man will tend to gain what he seeks and be satisfied with what he has. But modest goods are precisely what a man needs to flourish. So what is more reliably achievable is also what is necessary for well-being. Furthermore, Democritus seems to stress that a moderate man will take pleasure in the very fact that he leads his life well:

Great delights come from beholding fine deeds. (B194)

As Democritus puts it, insofar as the moderate or contented man is responsible for the pleasures of his life, he "derives pleasure from himself" (B146). In making this point, Democritus seems to be contrasting the contented man's ability to derive pleasure from himself with the ambitious and discontented man's frustrating inability to derive pleasure from his environment.

It must also be emphasized that although Democritus makes critical remarks about the pursuit of pleasures of the belly, he recognizes that there is a place for pleasures of the belly within the contented life. For example, the contented man can take great pleasure in eating and drinking modestly:

Barley-bread and straw are the sweetest remedies for hunger and fatigue. (B246)

This is also due to the fact that the contented man conceives the value of these pleasures and their place within his life differently than the man who devotes his life to pleasures of the belly. The key, as Democritus says, is to

aim at measured (*metriês*) acquisition and measure (*metrêtai*) one's labor according to what is necessary. (B285)

Here, what is necessary is what conforms to a man's nature. In contrast:

The desire for more destroys what one has, like the dog in Aesop's fable. (B224)

As we have seen, pleasures of the belly are intrinsically short-lived and thus, as Democritus says, mortal. However, because the contented man derives pleasure from various sources, in various ways, and above all from himself, he can reliably and continually engender pleasures and thereby fill his life with pleasure. Like the path of Excellence in Xenophon's rendition of Prodicus' *Choice of Heracles*, then, Democritus emphasizes that the path he recommends, namely, the contented life, has pleasures of its own. For convenience, let's call these *measured pleasures.* Measured pleasures either derive from a contented soul or contribute to the achievement of contentment. Pleasures of the belly may be among them. Thus, the sets of measured pleasures and pleasures of the belly overlap.

Finally, Democritus maintains that immoderate men contribute to social discord, which in turn compounds their psychic distress. Those with unregulated desires are susceptible, in particular, to envy; and Democritus views envy as "the root of civil strife" (B245). In the following passage, Democritus describes how the drive to emulate the wealth or power of others, presumably concomitant with the desire to maximize pleasures of the belly, leads to criminal or at least anti-social behavior:

For he who admires those who are wealthy and those who other men think are blessed and constantly dwells upon them in his mind always feels compelled to hatch new tricks and, in his desire to achieve something, to attempt some bad deed forbidden by the laws. (B191)

Consequently, "the envious man hurts himself as much as his enemy" (B88).

In contrast, the self-controlled man lives a just life and thereby enjoys peace of mind:

The contented man (*euthymos*) who undertakes right and lawful deeds rejoices in sleeping and waking and is strong and free from care. But he who takes no heed of what is right and does not do what he should is distressed by all these things, whenever he remembers them, and is frightened and reproaches himself. (B174)

The glory of justice is confidence and an untroubled mind, but the end of injustice is fear of disaster. (B215)

Measured pleasures are compatible with and perhaps conducive to civic flourishing; however, the aim of Democritus' discussion does not appear to lie in promoting the view that measured pleasures are civic pleasures. The emphasis of *On Contentment* appears to be more egocentric; Xenophon's rendition of *The Choice of Heracles* is a more civic-minded work. Thus, Excellence emphasizes social goods such as honor as her path's benefits to the individual. In contrast, although Democritus views immoderation as socially destructive, he seems primarily concerned with the fact that it is self-destructive. Again, whereas Xenophon's rendition of *The Choice of Heracles* offers a reconciliation of the individual's desire for pleasure with the goal of civic flourishing, *On Contentment* is primarily concerned to emphasize that the individual can achieve a good life by understanding his nature, his power and thus limitations, and conjointly his place within the world.

ANTISTHENES

Socrates (469–399) and his associates also engaged the topic of pleasure. Socrates himself never composed any philosophical works, and there are no surviving credible reports of what he had to say on the subject of pleasure. However, we do have some fragments and testimonies regarding the views on pleasure of some of his associates. One such associate is Antisthenes of Athens (*c.* 445–365).

Antisthenes was one of Socrates' most prolific and celebrated disciples. Within a relatively compendious catalog of Antisthenes' writings preserved by the historian and biographer of philosophy Diogenes Laertius (*c.* late second or early third century CE) – an author to whom we will return many times in the course of this book – is a work entitled *On Pleasure*. It was uncommon for ancient authors, at least at this early date, to give their works titles. Nonetheless, this title, given by some later ancient editor or commentator, must have been justified by the fact that pleasure was the principal subject of the work. Compare Democritus' *On Contentment* – most likely not a title he gave to the text, but surely appropriate to its central topic. Assuming that Antisthenes did compose some such work, then so far as we know this is the earliest philosophical work primarily devoted to pleasure.

Unfortunately, no certain fragments from this work survive. On the other hand, a number of ancient commentators attribute sayings to Antisthenes pertaining to the subject of pleasure. Whether or not these ultimately derive from *On Pleasure*, they may be consistent with views expressed therein. The sayings fall into two apparently inconsistent sets. On the one hand, there are statements such as:

I would rather go mad than undergo pleasure. (*SSR* 122)[3]

If I could get hold of Aphrodite, I would shoot her with a bow and arrow, for she has corrupted many of our best women. (*SSR* 123)

These sayings seem to support the following testimony from Aspasius (*c.* 100–150), a Peripatetic philosopher of unclear geographical origin, who is here commenting on a section of Aristotle's *Nicomachean Ethics* in which Aristotle canvasses various of his predecessors' views of pleasure's value:

---

[3] "*SSR*" stands for *Socratis Socraticorumque Reliquiae* (*Surviving Material on Socrates and the Socratics*). This four-volume collection of fragments, testimonies, and commentary (in Italian) was composed by Gabriele Giannantoni and published by Bibliopolis in 1990. There is no English translation.

Some think that no pleasure is good. And they say that Antisthenes held this opinion. For they say that pleasure is good neither in itself nor coincidentally.[4] (*SSR* 120)

On the other hand, the following sayings are also attributed to Antisthenes:

We should prefer the pleasures after, not before, exertions. (*SSR* 126)

Pleasure is good if it does not require subsequent regret. (*SSR* 127)

Assuming these attributions are also accurate, Antisthenes' view of pleasure must be more complex than the one Aspasius reports. Presumably some division must be drawn between kinds of pleasure or between conditions of pleasure.

In the course of antiquity, Antisthenes came to be identified as a forefather or precursor of the Cynic movement. While contemporary scholars have tended to conclude that the relation between Antisthenes' philosophy and Cynicism is more complex, there are some important parallels between Antisthenes' and Cynic thought. The Cynics radically and notoriously spurned the conventions and above all comforts of traditional and conventional Greek culture, advocating an ascetic lifestyle in close adherence to nature as they conceived it. Such a life was both psychologically and physically demanding, and the Cynics extol toil (*ponos*) as essential to the achievement of excellence (*aretê*).

Like the Cynics, Antisthenes rejects the pursuit of conventional goods such as wealth, material comforts, and public honor; and like them, he emphasizes the value of *ponos* for the achievement of excellence. Like Socrates, he identifies human excellence with wisdom. Wisdom he conceives as a form of strength:

We must build walls of defense with our own incontrovertible arguments. (*SSR* 134)

Wisdom is the surest fortification. It neither crumbles nor is subject to betrayal. (*SSR* 134)

In light of this, we may view Antisthenes' threat toward Aphrodite and statement that he would rather go mad than undergo pleasure as criticisms

---

[4] The Aristotelian distinction between something's having a property in itself (*kath' hauto*) and coincidentally (*kata symbebêkos*) can be explained simply as follows. If a type of entity *X* has a property *F* in virtue of what *X* itself is, then *X* has *F* in itself. If a type of entity *X* has a property *F*, but not in virtue of what *X* itself is, then *X* has *F* coincidentally. For example, a square is a shape. Thus, something that is a square (*X*) has the property of being a shape (*F*) in virtue of what a square itself is. But a square whose side is one foot long has that property coincidentally; for although squares must have sides of some length and can have sides of one foot, no square must in virtue of being a square have a side that is one foot in length.

of those pleasures that undermine the cultivation or exercise of wisdom or reason. Let us call these *foolish pleasures.* In this respect, Antisthenes' attitude seems akin to Democritus' attitude toward one who devotes himself to the pursuit of pleasures of the belly. Consider the following fragment from Democritus:

Ease is the worst of all teachers for the young, for it is that which gives birth to those pleasures from which badness arises. (B178)

And compare the following saying attributed to Antisthenes:

When someone praised luxury, [Antisthenes] replied, "May the sons of your enemies live in luxury." (*SSR* 114)

Such criticism is, however, consistent with the view that the cultivation of excellence and a life of wisdom have pleasures of their own, pleasures that follow exertions and that do not yield regret. Let us call these *wise pleasures* insofar as they either contribute to or derive from the achievement of excellence, which is wisdom.

In conclusion, we may cautiously say that Antisthenes recognizes that certain pleasures have value, but that this value is not essential to a good life. As I have suggested, their value depends upon their contribution to or derivation from the achievement of excellence or wisdom. Consequently and finally, we can say more precisely how Aspasius' comment errs. Aspasius is correct that Antisthenes denies that pleasure is good in itself; however, Aspasius is incorrect in suggesting that Antisthenes denies that pleasure may be coincidentally good. Whether or not Antisthenes explicitly recognized a distinction equivalent to Aristotle's between goodness in itself and coincidental goodness, Antisthenes' view is equivalent to the view that some pleasures are coincidentally good.

ARISTIPPUS

In contrast to Antisthenes, Aristippus of Cyrene (*c.* 435–356), another associate of Socrates, was an ethical hedonist. That is, Aristippus held that human life is good insofar as it is pleasant. Precisely what sort of hedonist Aristippus was, however, is difficult to determine. A number of ancient thinkers vilified Aristippus for maintaining that *bodily* or *somatic pleasures* are the only things of intrinsic value. For example, the Roman politician and philosopher Cicero (106–143) criticizes Aristippus for treating human beings as though they were irrational animals:

Aristippus appears to think that we have no soul, just a body. (*Prior Academics* 2.139)

Epicurus also recognizes this pleasure, the one that Aristippus does, namely where the sense-perceptual faculty is gently and joyfully moved, the very thing that animals, if they could speak, would call pleasure. (*On Goals* 2.18)

Bodily pleasure in fact comprises a rather complex class of pleasures. For example, contrast the pleasure of slaking one's thirst with the pleasure of listening to Mozart, regardless of whether one has substantial or theoretical musical background. The former is more primitive. Yet both may be considered bodily insofar as the musical pleasure depends upon sense-perception. A subtler, but nonetheless similar, distinction may be drawn between the pleasure of slaking one's thirst and the pleasure of enjoying a fine wine. We might refer to the former as a *brute pleasure*, where brute pleasures are a species of bodily pleasure. In contrast, the latter pleasure is bodily, but not brute. I will discuss this distinction in greater detail in the context of Plato's thought. But hopefully enough has been said here to indicate why there is some distinction to be made between the claims that Aristippus was a brute hedonist and that he was a somatic hedonist.

Part of the problem is that ancient thinkers tend to collapse the distinction between brute and bodily pleasures. Cicero certainly does. In the second quotation he refers to pleasure involving the sense-perceptual faculties, and he identifies such pleasures as animal. Moreover, critics of hedonism tend to vilify their opponents by psychologically reducing them and in particular reducing them to irrational animals. However, such a reduction of Aristippus distorts him. In particular, numerous anecdotes about Aristippus' enjoyment of luxuries suggest that his hedonic interests included bodily but not merely brute pleasures. In short, Aristippus had more complex tastes and views. We can appreciate and elaborate on this point by turning to another aspect of his hedonism.

Consider the following testimony from the Roman rhetorician Claudius Aelianus (*c.* 175–235):

Aristippus spoke compellingly when he exhorted people not to belabor the past or future. For this is a sign of contentment and proof of a cheerful mind. He enjoined people to focus their thought on the day at hand and more precisely on the part of the day when they are acting or thinking. For he used to say that the present alone is ours. What has passed and what lies ahead are not; for the one has perished, and it is unclear whether the other will be. (14.6)

This passage seems to bring Aristippus' position closer to Democritus' than to the sorts of base, depraved, foolish, or belly-pleasure seeking that Prodicus, Antisthenes, and Democritus all respectively criticize. In particular, Democritus and Aristippus seem to share an emphasis on

humanity's inability or at least limited ability to control their environments and instead on the importance of adapting oneself to changing and
unpredictable circumstances. Some additional evidence in support of this
view derives from the catalog of Aristippus' works that Diogenes Laertius
cites. A number of the titles suggest a preoccupation with fortune and the
vicissitudes of life: *On Fortune, The Shipwrecked, The Exiles, To a Beggar.*
Correspondingly, Diogenes remarks:

Aristippus was capable of adapting himself to place, time, and person, and of playing
his part appropriately under whatever circumstances. He reveled in the pleasure
of the present. He did not toil in seeking enjoyment of what was absent. (2.66)

For convenience, let us refer to the following principle as Aristippus'
presentist hedonism:

One ought to derive pleasure from one's present circumstances.

The principle of presentist hedonism must be distinguished from the trivial
point that all pleasures occur in the present and thus that all pleasure must be
derived *in* the present. For example, anticipatory pleasures, that is, pleasures
derived from anticipating some future event, and memorial pleasures, that is,
pleasures derived from recollecting some past event, occur in the present.
However, they are in some sense not derived *from* the present.

More importantly, the principle of presentist hedonism suggests that
one must not "toil in seeking enjoyment of what [is] absent." Observe that
one may be a rational somatic hedonist and toil in seeking enjoyment of
future somatic pleasure, insofar as the future pleasure outweighs the
present toil. But Aristippus rejects this sort of calculus precisely, it seems,
because he accepts the view that the vicissitudes of fortune should dissuade us from relying on certain or even likely future outcomes. The
question, then, is how to combine Aristippus' somatic hedonism, assuming Aristippus' hedonism is indeed limited to being somatic, with his
presentist hedonism. The problem is that one's present circumstances do
not always seem to afford somatic pleasures.

The difficulty may be overcome, I suggest, precisely to the extent that it
is possible to derive somatic pleasure from a variety of things. Now, the
idea of being able to derive pleasure from a variety of present things is
ambiguous in at least the following way. Take the example of food. One
may derive pleasure from various kinds of food, for example, meat,
vegetables, and fish, as well as from various sub-kinds of these kinds.
But one may also derive pleasure from various preparations and various

qualities of preparation of these foods. In particular, one may derive pleasure from a simple as well as a gourmet meal. Reports of Aristippus' presentist hedonism seem to underscore this last capacity. For example, the Roman poet Horace (65–8 BCE) seems to have viewed Aristippus as a sort of aesthetic hero. Horace's now famous motto, "*carpe diem*" (seize the day), comports with Aristippus' presentist hedonism. But consider also the dialogue Horace composed between Aristippus and a Cynic in Book I of his *Epistles*:

A Cynic said to Aristippus, "If you were satisfied with cabbage for your dinner, you'd have no reason to spend your time with princes." Aristippus replied, "If you knew how to spend your time with princes, you wouldn't deign to dine on cabbage … My way is better and far more elegant" … Aristippus could suit himself to any situation. However, given the choice, he'd always choose the better. On the other hand, I wonder if the man clothed in Cynic rags would be able to handle a better circumstance. Aristippus wouldn't require a purple robe; he'd make his elegant way through the crowded streets wearing whatever there happened to be at hand. (17.17–29)

The idea of Aristippus conversing with a Cynic is anachronistic – although surely Aristippus conversed with Socratics like Antisthenes as well as others who held comparable views. But the anachronism here is beside the point. Likewise, we should not worry about the more general fact that Horace is engaged in the composition of fiction. I am not citing Horace here as evidence of Aristippus' position. Rather, I suggest that Horace's dialogue felicitously captures a central truth about Aristippus' attitude toward pleasure: its versatility. My suggestion is that if Aristippus was both a somatic and a presentist hedonist, he was so because he was able to derive somatic pleasure from various circumstances.

SOCRATES' "WHAT IS 'F'?" QUESTION

There are many lines of development from these early ethical discussions of pleasure to those of the Classical, Hellenistic, and Roman Imperial, Early Christian, or Late Antique periods. Indeed, we will engage with some of these developments in the coming chapters. The present work will not, however, be devoted to a discussion of pleasure in the broad context of ancient Greek ethics. The simple reason for this is that the topic is too massive. Instead, the focus of this work will be on the narrower question of how the Greek philosophers conceive of pleasure, including what kinds of pleasure there are – questions I have referred to in the Introduction as the identity and the kinds questions. As such, the preceding discussion of the contributions of Prodicus, Democritus, Antisthenes, and Aristippus principally serves as a point of contrast rather than continuity.

For all their interests in pleasure, what we do not find in these early treatments of pleasure are attempts to determine what pleasure itself is. For example, if Prodicus were asked what *terpsis*, *chara*, and *euphrosynê* or what base and refined pleasures have in common in virtue of which they are pleasures, there is no reason to think he would have an answer, for there is no reason to think that he engaged the question. Likewise, there is no reason to think that Democritus considered what pleasures of the belly have in common with the pleasures we get from beholding fine deeds or any of the other pleasures that the contented man enjoys or derives from himself. Democritus clearly implicitly recognizes a distinction between contentment and pleasure, but he does not explicate the distinction. One way we might clarify the distinction is that contentment is a settled disposition or condition, whereas pleasure is occurrent or episodic. In that case, one of Democritus' central ideas is that the stable disposition or condition yields a bounty of the occurrent hedonic states. We might say, then, that Democritus' treatment provides grounds for an explicit account of pleasure – but again there is no reason to think that Democritus was concerned to give such an account. Like Prodicus, Democritus seems to have taken for granted what pleasure is.

In the case of the Socratic circle, matters are a bit more complicated. It is well known that one of Socrates' signal contributions to the history of philosophy is the introduction of the problem and pursuit of definitions of ethical kinds. For example, in a review of the contributions of his predecessors Aristotle distinguishes Socrates as follows:

[In contrast to his predecessors,] Socrates preoccupied himself with ethical matters and ignored the physical world as a whole. He sought the universal in these ethical matters and was the first to focus thought on definitions. (*Metaphysics* 987a)

We see the influence of Socrates' definitional pursuits especially in Plato's early dialogues, where Plato portrays the character Socrates engaging various interlocutors in questions of the form "What is *F*?" where "*F*" stands for some ethical or axiological kind such as justice, courage, or beauty.

Although none of Plato's early dialogues pursues the question "What is pleasure?" the preceding considerations at least encourage the thought that Socrates would have motivated his associates to examine and attempt to clarify what pleasure is, particularly insofar as they centrally, if variously, engaged the topic.

In the case of Antisthenes, however, there is no evidence that he ventured any definition of pleasure.[5] Moreover, in his case we can corroborate that the reason for absence of such evidence is not merely a fluke of the spotty historical record. There is evidence that Antisthenes engaged the topic of definition itself and argued that definitions are impossible. Here is Aristotle's testimony:

> [Antisthenes and his followers] claim that it is not possible to define what a thing is ... although it is possible to convey what sort of thing something is. For example, it is not possible to convey what silver is, but it is possible to convey that it is such as tin. (*Metaphysics* 1043b)

The fact that Antisthenes engaged the topic, that is, actually developed a theory of definition, is fascinating in its own right. It demonstrates a remarkable point of resistance to Socrates' signal philosophical preoccupation. Precisely why Antisthenes reached his particular conclusion about definitions is difficult to determine, and I will not pursue the subject here. Suffice it to say that he would not have offered any definition of pleasure because he held that definitions cannot be given. Of course, Aristotle's testimony allows that he could have clarified what pleasure is like. But in fact we have no evidence that he made any claims to that effect.

Given the centrality of pleasure in his ethical views, it would seem more likely that Aristippus offered a definition of pleasure. One passage that might be adduced in support of this suggestion derives from Diogenes Laertius:

> Aristippus proposed that the smooth change transmitted to perception is the goal (*telos*). (2.85)

Pleasure is here glossed as "smooth change transmitted to perception." Recall the quotation from Cicero cited above:

> Epicurus also recognizes this pleasure, the one that Aristippus does, namely where the sense-perceptual faculty is gently and joyfully moved, the very thing that animals, if they could speak, would call pleasure. (*On Goals* 2.18)

---

[5] Note that when I speak of Socrates' pursuit of "definitions," I mean nothing more than Socrates' pursuit of answers to his "What is *F*?" question. Plato himself refers to such questions and their answers as definitional. The Greek word for "definition" is "*horos*." The word "*horos*" refers to a boundary-stone, that is, a stone or rather set of stones established at the edge of a piece of property to mark its limits. Definitions in discourse are conceived as serving some analogous purpose: to delineate or demarcate the entity whose definition is sought. There is much room here for theoretical consideration of what a definition is. For example, does Socrates' "What is *F*?" question seek the meaning of the word "*F*" so that a definition is a meaning? Does the question seek clarification of the concept *F* so that a definition is like the analysis of a concept? At this point it is wise to leave the nature of Socratic definitions underdetermined. When Socrates asks "What is *F*?" he wants to know what *F* is, and a definition of *F* effectively states what *F* is.

However, there are numerous problems with using Diogenes' statement as evidence that Aristippus defined pleasure as smooth change transmitted to perception. First, it is conceivable that "smooth change transmitted to perception" is Diogenes' way of referring to pleasure rather than Aristippus'. Relatedly, the qualification "transmitted to perception" looks anachronistic. In a couple of his late dialogues Plato discusses the point that the given physiological change constitutive of pleasure or pain must be robust so that it impacts the soul and thus is perceived or consciously apprehended. Of course, Aristippus and Plato were contemporaries, so arguably Aristippus was alive to this point as well. But the idea that Diogenes' attribution is anachronistic is compounded by the word "*telos.*" "*Telos*" here is an ethical term of art referring to the goal of life. This use of "*telos*" first becomes prominent in Aristotle (384–322) and does not become established in ethical philosophy until the Hellenistic period (third to first century BCE). So it is almost certain that Aristippus would not have conceived of pleasure as a *telos.* All this doesn't leave Aristippus much of a definition of pleasure. Rather, it seems that Diogenes' line merely amounts to the claim that Aristippus thought that the good life consists in pleasure.

This is not quite the end of the story, however. Aristippus was a citizen of Cyrene (modern-day Shahhat, Libya). He became the founder or at least figurehead of the somatic hedonistic Cyrenaic school of philosophy, which emerged in his wake and persisted perhaps through the second century BCE. We know that later Cyrenaics defined or adhered to the definition of pleasure as a smooth change and pain as a rough one. For example, the Christian theologian Clement of Alexandria (*c.* 150–215) reports:

> The Cyrenaics say that their conception of pleasure is smooth and gentle change with a certain perception. (*Miscellanies* 2.20.106.3)

And Diogenes Laertius himself attributes the following view not to Aristippus but to his Cyrenaic followers:

> Pleasure is a smooth (*leia*) change; pain is a rough (*tracheia*) change. (2.86)

One way to take this evidence vis-à-vis Diogenes' report on Aristippus is that Diogenes has misattributed the view of later Cyrenaics to the founder of the school. Alternatively, it might be claimed that the Cyrenaic view goes back to Aristippus. But can the latter view be defended?

Let's focus on contrast between smooth (*leia*) and rough (*tracheia*) change. A search, using the philological database *Thesaurus Linguae*

Graecae, for the words "*leia*" and "*tracheia*" and their cognates appearing in proximate conjunction in texts composed between the time of Homer and the fourth century BCE yields only one instance of the use of the adjective "*leia*" contrasted with "*tracheia*" in an ethical context, namely, a passage from Hesiod's epic poem *Works and Days* (eighth–seventh century).

To a large extent Hesiod's *Works and Days* consists of practical advice on farming. However, the advice is cast within broader reflections on man's place and the place of his labor within the cosmos. In one of this poem's sections, which I will refer to as the *encomium to work*, Hesiod admonishes his brother Perses to cease his idleness and injustice and to devote himself to honest toil:

It is easy to get hold of badness in abundance. The road to it is smooth (*leia*), and it dwells close by. But between goodness and ourselves the immortal gods have placed the sweat of our brows. Long and steep is the path that leads to it, and it is rough (*trachys*) at first. But when one reaches the summit it is easy, hard though it was. (287–292)

In his *Choice of Heracles* Prodicus adapted Hesiod's theme of two paths when he composed the paths of Excellence and Depravity. Xenophon makes the connection explicit, for he cites this passage from the encomium to work in Hesiod's *Works and Days* immediately before his rendition of Prodicus and then writes:

And the wise Prodicus expresses a similar view concerning excellence in his writing on Heracles. (*Memorabilia* 2.1.21)

The connection is quite obvious, and we would not need Xenophon to make the point; however, it is valuable to consider the context in which Xenophon presents his rendition. The context is a discussion between Socrates and Aristippus. Socrates encourages Aristippus to desist from his anti-civic somatic pleasure-seeking and to devote himself to a more respectable and civically minded course. As a form of admonition, Socrates then offers a rendition of Prodicus' *Choice of Heracles*.

We know that a number of Socratics discussed Hesiod's *Works and Days* as well as Prodicus' *Choice of Heracles*. For example, Xenophon reports that one of Socrates' political opponents criticized Socrates as follows:

He [Socrates] selected from the most renowned poets the most base verses and used them as evidence in teaching his associates to be malefactors and tyrants. For example, Hesiod's line "No work is a disgrace, but idleness is a disgrace" [= *Works and Days* 311]. (*Memorabilia* 1.2.56)

Generally speaking, Hesiod's *Works and Days* and Prodicus' *Choice of Heracles* provided the Socratics with a framework for ethical reflection. The two paths theme informed their examination of the question: What path of life should one pursue? Different Socratics gave different answers. There is reason to believe that Aristippus engaged the question, for there is evidence that in one of his works he discussed the encomium to work in Hesiod's *Works and Days*. We learn of this from Plutarch (46–120), who in his *Commentary on Hesiod's Works and Days*, specifically in the context of discussing a section of the encomium to work, mentions Aristippus' view on the passage.[6] I suggest, then, that Aristippus engaged the Hesiodically inspired Socratic question "What path of life should one pursue?" and answered it by advocating the smooth path.

Granted this, if Aristippus ever claimed or wrote of pleasure as a smooth path or even as smooth change, this would have been metaphorical. That is, he would have been referring to the pleasant life as a smooth path. As such, it would be misleading to suggest that Aristippus *defined* pleasure as smooth change. Consequently, I conclude that while Socrates and to some extent his associates engaged in the pursuit of definitions, there is no evidence that any of them attempted to define pleasure properly speaking. In other words, there is no evidence that any of them deliberatively posed and attempted to answer the identity question.

---

[6] *Scholia on Hesiod's Works and Days* 293–297.

CHAPTER 3

Pleasure in the early physical tradition

Let us turn now from pleasure in the early ethical tradition to pleasure in the early tradition of *physiologia*, that is, the tradition of the study (*logos*) of what the Greeks call "*physis*." Recall our encounter with the word "*physis*" in the context of the opening fragment of Democritus' *On Contentment.* Democritus there speaks of a man's "own power and *physis.*" Here and often, "*physis*" is translated as "nature." In the context of *physiologia*, then, the Greeks were concerned with the study of nature. Yet their conception of *physis* or nature may be broader than ours. *Physiologia* also includes the study of non-terrestrial objects and phenomena; it saliently includes astronomy and cosmology.

Physiologia is the field from which Socrates turned when he took his path-breaking steps in ethics. In Plato's dialogue *Phaedo*, the character Socrates describes his early intellectual interests prior to the break. The passage is often referred to as Socrates' early intellectual (auto)biography. Consider the beginning of the passage:

When I was a young man, I was wonderfully keen on that wisdom they call inquiry into *physis*, for I thought it splendid to know the factors responsible for each thing, why it comes to be, why it perishes, and why it exists. I was often changing my mind in the inquiry, in the first instance, of questions such as these: Are living creatures nourished when heat and cold produce a kind of putrefaction, as some say? Do we think with our blood or air or fire or none of these? And does the brain provide our senses of hearing and sight and smell, from which come memory and opinion? And does knowledge come from memory and opinion that has become stable? Then again, as I investigated how these things perish and what happens to things in the sky and on earth, finally I became convinced that I have no natural aptitude at all for that kind of inquiry. (96a–b)

Observe the breadth of the field of inquiry. Socrates refers to questions concerning digestion, psychology, including perception, memory, opinion, and knowledge, and finally astronomical and geological phenomena. To get a feel for one of these questions, consider the first. Socrates may be alluding here to the philosopher Empedocles of Acragas (*c.* 490–430), who seems to have explained digestion in the following way. When food is ingested, the heat of the body works to decompose its components into homogeneous elements. This decomposition is conceived as analogous to putrefaction. The elements are then transported by means of the vascular system to various parts of the body where they are appropriately reconstituted into physiological stuffs and congeal through coldness.

Loosely speaking, *physiologia* encompasses what we would now call physical science – although ancient methods of inquiry were often not scientific. Also, *physiologia* includes the field of psychology, particularly since all early Greek thinkers conceived of the soul (*psychê*) as corporeal. For convenience, I will render "*physiologia*" as "physical inquiry" and use the adjective "physical" correspondingly. (When I need to refer to something as physical in the sense of material or corporeal, I will use those two words.)

Most of early Greek philosophy was devoted to physical inquiry. Thus, some scholars have reasonably suggested that most of the so-called Presocratic philosophers would be more aptly referred to as proto-physical scientists. In addition, it must be emphasized that some Greek physicians engaged in physical inquiry. Indeed, disciplinary boundaries between early Greek philosophy and medicine are porous. This point is important for our consideration of the relevance of the tradition of physical inquiry to pleasure because some of the physical treatments of pleasure occur in medical texts. An example of this derives from a treatise on epilepsy entitled *On the Sacred Disease*, probably composed in the second half of the fifth century BCE. In one passage, the author discusses questions similar to those Socrates raises in *Phaedo* concerning the organs responsible for perception and cognition more broadly. In the context of this discussion the author refers to pleasure and pain:

Men ought to know that from nothing other than the brain come our pleasures and delights and laughter and amusement, as well as our pains and distress and grief and tears. And by means of the brain we think and see and hear and recognize the ugly and the beautiful, the good and the bad, the pleasant and the unpleasant. (17.1–2 Littré)

The author then criticizes those who attribute responsibility for cognition to the diaphragm and the heart:

The diaphragm (*phrenes*), however, has come to have its name by chance and convention, not according to reality and nature. I do not know what power the diaphragm has for thought and cognition (*phronein*). It can only be said that if a man is suddenly overjoyed or distressed, the diaphragm jumps and causes throbbing ... Some say that we think with the heart and that it is this that suffers distress and anxiety. But that is not the case; rather, it merely convulses, like the diaphragm ... Moreover, the body necessarily shudders and contracts when a man is distressed. And it suffers the same affection when one is overcome with joy. (17.2–4 Littré)

Within the early physical tradition, there is evidence that pleasure was discussed in two contexts, within accounts of sense-perception and within accounts of the processes of nutrition and sex. Evidence from the former is shaky and as we will see may lead to an exegetical dead-end; it is nonetheless instructive to pursue. I begin with this.

EMPEDOCLES

Theophrastus of Eresos (*c.* 371–287), Aristotle's student and successor as head of his school, the Peripatos or Lyceum, composed a treatise known as *On Perceptions*. This work, perhaps originally part of a much larger work known as *On Physical Opinions*, critically reviews the sense-perceptual and cognitive theories of Aristotle's predecessors. Theophrastus specifically discusses the views of Plato as well as of the fifth-century philosophers Alcmaeon of Croton, Parmenides of Elea (born *c.* 515), Empedocles (*c.* 495–435), Anaxagoras of Clazomenae (*c.* 500–428), Diogenes of Apollonia (*c.* 470–400), and Democritus. Among his discussion of their views of perception, Theophrastus attributes views of pleasure and pain to Empedocles and to Diogenes of Apollonia.[1]

Theophrastus' account of Empedocles' views of pleasure and pain is extremely condensed:

Pleasure occurs through things that are alike in accordance with their parts and blending. Pain occurs through opposites. (9)

In order to understand what Theophrastus is saying here, it is helpful to know two things: one concerns the basic principles of Empedocles' cosmology; the other concerns the general scheme of Theophrastus' treatment of his predecessors' views of perception. Empedocles held that the cosmos fundamentally consists of six entities: four so-called roots – earth, water, fire, and air – plus Love and Strife, which influence the

---

[1] Theophrastus also remarks on certain of Anaxagoras' views concerning pleasure and pain. In fact, what he has to say here is more likely to be accurate than what he says about Empedocles and Diogenes of Apollonia. But what he says about Anaxagoras is not relevant to the identity question.

behavior of the roots. Specifically, Love and Strife are antagonists who endeavor to combine and separate the roots respectively. When Strife dominates, the cosmos, which Empedocles conceives as being spherical, comes to be arranged in four concentric spheres of pure earth, water, air, and fire, from its center to its periphery. In other words, the roots are separated from one another. When Love dominates, the roots blend and the cosmos comes to consist of a single homogeneous stuff. Empedocles conceives of the present state of the cosmos as lying between these two extremes, albeit with Strife ascendant. In addition, it is important to note that Empedocles conceives of Love, Strife, and the roots not simply as inanimate physical stuffs, but as possessing psychological capacities. This point is important because Theophrastus interprets Empedocles as holding that like portions of roots, for example, fire and fire, willingly and gladly combine, whereas unlike or opposing portions, for example, water and fire, resist and so are hostile to one another. Given this, it would seem a small step to the conclusion that pleasure derives from the blending of like entities, while pain derives from the blending of unlike or opposing entities. But in order to understand the view of pleasure that Theophrastus attributes to Empedocles, it is necessary to understand more about Empedocles and sense-perception. The reason is this: in *On Perceptions* Theophrastus is not interested in the psychological states of portions of like and opposing roots as they combine or separate. He is interested in perception in humans or more generally animals. The question, then, is how we get from the preceding cosmological points to a theory of perception.

Theophrastus begins his account of his predecessors' views of perception by schematizing them in two groups: those who explain perception according to likeness and those who explain perception according to opposition. Empedocles is among those who explain perception according to likeness. This construal of Empedocles accords with Empedocles' account of vision, at least in the following respect. Assuming action at a distance is impossible, an adequate account of vision requires an explanation of how observers and observable objects come into contact. Empedocles does not appeal to light as a medium. Instead, he holds that objects release from their surfaces what he calls "effluences." Visual perception then requires that the effluences of objects enter the receptive pores of the visual faculty of the observer. More precisely, in order for vision to occur, the structures of the effluences must correspond with the structures of the pores. In this context, likeness amounts to structural conformity between effluences and pores. Contrast this conception of likeness with the one from the explanation of pleasure and pain above; in that case, likeness is understood as sameness of substance, for example, fire and fire.

Theophrastus generalizes from Empedocles' theory of vision to an Empedoclean theory of perception and experience, including pleasure and pain. But this yields an inconsistency, specifically in the case of pain. According to the general theory of perception, pain as a form of perception or experience requires likeness in the sense of structural conformity. In contrast, according to the theory of pleasure and pain as involving the blending of like and opposing elements, pain requires opposition in the sense of unlikeness of substance. Indeed, Theophrastus criticizes Empedocles accordingly:

[Empedocles'] account of pleasure and pain is inconsistent, for he makes pleasure occur through things that are alike and pain through things that are opposite ... But he assigns the same account of perception [in general] to pleasure [specifically,] [namely, blending of like elements]. And yet when we are perceiving, we often experience pain in the very act of perception. (16–17)

Theophrastus' criticism of Empedocles is unjustified. The inconsistency is rather a function of his own misunderstanding. Empedocles nowhere suggests that the blending or conjunction of substantively alike entities alone is pleasant. On the contrary, Empedocles allows that Love combines diverse roots and more complex entities in a harmonious and thus pleasant way. The sexual union of males and females is a signal example. But more significantly, Theophrastus is fundamentally misguided in wedding an Empedoclean account of perception – whether or not justifiably generalized from Empedocles' account of vision – to an explanation of the pleasure or pain accompanying perception. There is simply no evidence that Empedocles engaged this topic.

DIOGENES OF APOLLONIA

Generally speaking, we must be cautious in handling Theophrastus' treatments of the early philosophers. Theophrastus approaches the contributions of these men with strong and often anachronistic presuppositions.[2] He assumes he can make their contributions conform to his philosophical agenda, which is to assemble past views on thought, sight, hearing, smell, taste, touch, pleasure, and pain. The arrangement and focus on this set of psychological functions is largely due to Theophrastus'

[2] Generally speaking, this is the basic peril of using ancient authors as evidence of their predecessors.

mentor and colleague Aristotle, who in turn derives it from Plato. In particular, in *Timaeus* Plato presents accounts of pleasure and pain alongside those of the particular sense-perceptual modalities. Plato could be following a schema of some earlier thinker – although we have no compelling evidence that he is. But even if Plato had a model or several models, there is no reason to think that most early philosophers approached perception, let alone pleasure, as a topic in the way Theophrastus or Aristotle or Plato does.

This conclusion should at least make us suspicious of Theophrastus' account of Diogenes of Apollonia's account of pleasure. Nonetheless, let's have a look:

Pleasure and pain occur in the following way. Whenever a large quantity of air mixes with the blood and lightens it, since the air is in its natural state and pervades the entire body, pleasure occurs. But pain occurs whenever the air is in an abnormal state and does not mix with the blood. Then the blood settles and becomes weak and dense. Similarly [Diogenes] explains confidence and health and their opposites. (43)

In contrast to Empedocles' view that the cosmos consists of a plurality, albeit a small one, of fundamental entities, Diogenes held that the cosmos fundamentally consists of one substance, air. The apparent variety of entities and their properties was explained as a function of various conditions to which air is subject: compression, rarefaction, and motion of various kinds and speeds. Likewise, the distinction between animate and inanimate entities is explicable according to differences in the quality of air that constitutes them. When in his testimony Theophrastus speaks of air as being in a natural or abnormal state, he means natural or abnormal relative to the kind of entity in which it is present. We can assume that the natural state of a human being is one of health and vitality and thus that for a human to be in such a state, air of a certain quality must pervade the body in a certain way.

Granted this, there is room for doubt that Diogenes of Apollonia specifically addressed Theophrastus' topic of interest, pleasure and pain in conjunction with sense-perception. The idea of pleasure deriving from air that pervades the blood and lightens it suggests, rather, levity or buoyancy of mood or disposition. Likewise, heaviness of the blood suggests lethargy, melancholy, or depression. The last line of the testimony also encourages this interpretation. Confidence and health are dispositions rather than occurrent or active states of the sort that constitute or accompany perceptual episodes.

Granted this, Diogenes might well have explained cheerfulness or joyfulness and melancholy in terms of the conditions of air pervading the body. Moreover, he might have – although this is less plausible – identified some such positive mood with pleasure. If so, then Diogenes of Apollonia would be the earliest Greek philosopher to offer an answer to the identity question and to do so specifically with a physical account. But again Theophrastus' testimony cannot confidently be confirmed, partly because we have good reason to be suspicious of Theophrastus' reliability as a Presocratic doxographer,[3] and partly because we completely lack independent evidence on the subject of Diogenes of Apollonia's conception of pleasure. Consequently, our view of Diogenes' contribution to hedonic theorizing must remain speculative.

PLEASURE IN NUTRITION

As I suggested above, evidence for certain early Greek philosophical accounts of pleasure may lead to an exegetical dead-end – interesting though the path to that end is to follow. Somewhat more fruitful results come from the early medical literature. I turn now to two treatments of pleasure in the contexts of medical accounts of nutrition and sex respectively. The first is brief. It occurs in a text that we call *Diseases IV*. *Diseases IV* was composed in the late fifth century BCE, probably by Hippocrates' son-in-law Polybus of Cos. The context is an account of metabolism involving what for the author constitutes the four fundamental physiological humors: blood, bile, phlegm, and water. Here Polybus describes why on certain occasions we find food or drink pleasant:

Now if we are in need of food or drink, then the body will draw from the sources [that store the various humors] until the [quantities of the] humors [in these sources] are reduced below what is fitting. At that point a man has a desire to eat or drink something of a nature to fill up that [deficient] portion and make it equal to the others. This is why even after we have eaten or drunk a large amount, we sometimes still desire a food or drink and will eat nothing else with pleasure, except the particular thing that we desire. But when we have eaten and the humor in the sources [that is, those parts of the body in which the humor is stored] and in the body is equalized as far as possible, then the desire ceases. (39.5)

---

[3] The word "doxographer," coined by the German philologist Hermann Diels in the late nineteenth century, refers to an ancient "composer or compiler of (his predecessors') opinions." The practice of doxography, which in some form probably began with Hippias of Elis of the fifth century BCE, significantly developed with Aristotle and his school. Strictly speaking "doxography" refers to the assembly of one's predecessors' opinions on physical questions. However, "doxography" may be used in a broader sense to refer to compilation of opinions in any number of philosophical, scientific, or mathematical spheres.

The passage says only a little about pleasure and nothing explicitly about pain. Nonetheless, it contains elements of a view that became important in the fourth century. The desires for food and drink to which the author refers are conditions of hunger and thirst. These conditions are unpleasant, if not painful. (It is noteworthy here and generally that Greek theorists do not distinguish displeasure or discomfort from pain. In other words, they have a broader or vaguer conception of pain, one that encompasses displeasure.)[4] Accordingly – in the context of nutrition – pain, discomfort, or displeasure may be conceived as a state of depletion of nourishment. Correspondingly, pleasure is conceived as a state of replenishment of a nutritional deficit of the kind that is depleted. This is why, Polybus explains, eating or drinking something that does not replenish the particular nutritional deficit will not be pleasant or terminate the desire. I will hereafter refer to this as the *replenishment and depletion theory (or model) of pleasure and pain*.

In light of the replenishment model, it is of interest to note that in antiquity a similar view was also attributed to Empedocles and that this view also resembles the view Theophrastus attributes to Empedocles in *On Perceptions*. The complex Empedoclean view to which I am referring derives from the huge fifth-century CE anthology of philosophical and medical quotations and testimonies compiled by Johannes Stobaeus – another text to which we will make frequent reference throughout this study:

Empedocles says that like things derive pleasure from like things and that [they aim] at a refilling in accordance with the deficiency. Consequently, desire is for that which is like because of that which is lacking. And pains occur because of opposites. For things that differ are hostile to one another in accordance with both the combination and the blending of elements. (1.50.31)

This view may be summarized and clarified as follows. Subjects of desire, pleasure, and pain are composed of a set of elements. The diminution in one of the elements evokes desire in that subject. The subject desires the kind of element whose quantity is diminished. Pleasure arises as the subject regains the elemental kind in which it is deficient. More precisely, pleasure arises because the portion of the regained element mixes with the diminished portion of the same kind of element. On the other hand, if a deficient subject obtains an elemental portion that is opposite in kind to the element in which it is deficient, then pain arises. Precisely, pain arises because the portion of the acquired element mixes with the diminished portion of the opposite kind of element.

---

[4] The only exception to this of which I am aware is in the *Ethical Problems* of the Peripatetic philosopher Alexander of Aphrodisias (first to second century), which I discuss in n. 8 of Chapter 10.

Stobaeus himself derived this testimony from a first or second-century CE Peripatetic philosopher named Aëtius, who compiled an important doxographical work.[5] Stobaeus' passage occurs in a section devoted to past views of pleasure and desire. Aëtius drew heavily on Theophrastus for the views of the early philosophers, hence the resemblance to Theophrastus' passage. Encountering Theophrastus' very brief testimony on Empedocles, he must have been puzzled by it. I believe that the version we find in Stobaeus owes to Aëtius' attempt to clarify the testimony. In his attempt at clarification, Aëtius was evidently influenced by the replenishment and depletion theory, which, as we will see in the following chapter, became familiar through the influence of Plato.

SEXUAL PLEASURE

Polybus, the likely author of *Diseases IV*, is probably also the author of a treatise on sexual reproduction and embryology entitled *On Generation*. The treatise contains some passages in which features of sexual pleasure are explained. In considering these, it is helpful to note that there was a long-standing debate in antiquity over whether in sexual reproduction only men or both men and women contribute reproductive seed (*sperma*). Polybus supports the latter view. Granted this, according to Polybus' conception of the vascular system in human anatomy, certain veins descend from the head to the genital organs: the penis in males and the uterus in females. I will call these *seminal veins* because in reproduction they transmit the reproductive seed. In puberty the seminal veins widen, facilitating the flow into them of humors that constitute seminal fluid:

In the case of boys, the little veins, being narrow and congested, prevent the passage of humor ... While they are still young, girls for the same reason do not menstruate. But as boys and girls grow, the veins that extend in the boy's case to the penis and in the girl's to the uterus, expand and widen in the process of growth; and an opening is produced, and a path and conduit is created through the narrow passages ... That is why [seminal fluid] flows when the boy reaches puberty and the girl reaches her menses. (1.2–3)

The entry of humors into the seminal veins results from several factors, but principally from the rubbing of the penis or friction in the vagina, which produces warmth. For example:

When the penis is rubbed and the person is moved, the humor in the body becomes warm and it diffuses, and it is agitated by the movement and it foams (*aphreei*), just as all other liquids, when agitated, produce foam (*aphros*). (2.1)

---

[5] See n. 3.

I have drawn attention to the talk of foam (*aphros*). This is supposed to explain why semen is white, for the humors from which seminal fluid derive – phlegm, blood, bile, and water – are not. In this context, it is also noteworthy that Diogenes of Apollonia called semen a foam (*aphros*) of the blood and explained the word "*aphrodisia*," which means "sexual intercourse," as deriving from it: "*aphros*" + "*dosis*" (foam + giving).[6] In fact, "*aphrodisia*" derives from the name of the goddess Aphrodite who was, among other things, traditionally identified with sexual pleasure.

Returning now to the physiological process, Polybus seems to understand the pleasure experienced in sexual activity as a function of warmth in the genitals – warmth generated by movement, but particularly by agitation of the seminal fluid in the seminal veins or uterus, and finally by the force of the emission or ejaculation of the fluid:

[In the case of men,] veins extend from the whole body to the penis. When these are gently rubbed and heated and filled, a sort of friction occurs, and from this pleasure and heat arise in the whole body. (1.1)

In the case of women, I claim that during intercourse when the vagina is rubbed and the uterus is moved, friction occurs in the uterus and produces pleasure and warmth in the rest of the body. (4.1)

The reason that the man experiences more pleasure is that the [emission of the seminal fluid] in his case occurs suddenly and as the result of a more violent disturbance than in the woman's case. (4.2)

Finally, in one extraordinary passage Polybus seeks to explain differences between male and female pleasure in the context of intercourse:

Once intercourse has begun, she experiences pleasure through the whole time. This occurs until the man ejaculates. If her desire for intercourse is excited, she [emits] seed before the man; and for the remainder of the time she does not feel pleasure to the same extent. But if she is not in a state of excitement, then her pleasure terminates along with that of the man. What happens is this. If into boiling water you pour another quantity of water, which is cold, the water stops boiling. In the same way, the man's seed arriving in the uterus extinguishes both the heat and the pleasure of the woman. Both the pleasure and the heat reach their peak with the arrival of the [man's] seed in the uterus, and then they cease. If, for example, you pour wine on a flame, first of all the flame flares up and increases for a short period when you pour the wine on; then it dies away. In the same way the woman's heat flares up in response to the man's seed and then dies away. (4.2)

---

[6] A24, B6.

A central assumption of this passage, consistent with our prior conclusion, is that pleasure correlates with heat. So, for instance, a woman's pleasure may terminate after a man ejaculates because his ejaculate is taken, like water, to douse the heat generated in the woman. At the same time, the woman's pleasure may not terminate immediately, for the man's ejaculate, like wine poured on flame, may temporarily increase the heat.

These physiological causes of heat and so pleasure do not exhaust the author's explanation. A psychological factor is relevant as well. A woman's sexual desire is responsible for how quickly she comes to "emit seed" and so also for a concomitant degree of pleasure. How desire contributes to sexual pleasure is, however, not explained; and it may be wondered whether an explanation would remain consistent with the author's assumption of the correlation between heat and pleasure.

CHAPTER 4

Plato on pleasure and restoration

Turning to Plato (427–347), we turn away from largely fragmentary and sparse testimonial evidence to substantial primary textual evidence and to such evidence as bears directly on the question "What is pleasure?" We have more from Plato on pleasure and specifically on the identity question than from any other ancient author. Because of this, I have divided the discussion of Plato's treatment of pleasure into two chapters. The emphasis of the present chapter is on what Plato takes pleasure to be. The emphasis of Chapter 5 is on a distinction central to Plato's thinking about pleasure, namely, between true and untrue or true and false pleasures. As we will see, the two topics overlap to a considerable extent.

Plato discusses pleasure in many of his dialogues. His most important discussions occur in three: *Republic* (specifically, Book 9), *Timaeus,* and *Philebus.* Our discussion will focus on Plato's treatments of pleasure in these texts. I will also have some things to say about Plato's treatment of pleasure in two other dialogues, *Gorgias* and *Hippias Major.*

Let me make two general points about Plato's dialogues here that bear on our discussions of his various treatments of pleasure. First, Plato's dialogues are commonly divided into three chronological periods: early, middle, and late. According to this division, *Gorgias* and *Hippias Major* are early, *Republic* is middle, and *Timaeus* and *Philebus* are late. My discussions in this and the next chapter will occasionally conform to this chronological order. To that extent, then, I believe there are some important chronological developments in Plato's thinking about pleasure. However, to a greater extent, Plato's various treatments differ because he pursues different questions or problems relating to pleasure in different contexts. Consequently, in the course of our discussion we will need to recognize three distinct features of Plato's various treatments: changes in Plato's thinking about pleasure over the course of his career; differences among treatments not due to the former, but rather to the distinct philosophical interests of various occasions on which Plato engages the topic; and finally common or persistent features of Plato's treatments.

The second general point pertains to the fact that Plato's philosophical writings are dramatic dialogues. In no case does Plato represent himself as a dramatic persona, that is, as a speaker. Rather, in each dialogue he creates what may be called a "favored character" to serve as the philosophical protagonist. The views espoused or developed by this philosophical protagonist in the course of discussions with others tend to be views that it is reasonable to attribute to Plato. In most dialogues, especially dialogues whose content is primarily ethical, the philosophical protagonist is the character Socrates. In casting Socrates in this role, Plato is, among other things, acknowledging an intellectual debt and situating his own work within a certain intellectual tradition. This is the case in *Gorgias, Hippias Major, Republic*, and *Philebus*, that is, in most of the dialogues we will be discussing. *Timaeus* is the exception, for the philosophical protagonist of *Timaeus* is the character Timaeus (fashioned after the historical fifth to fourth-century BCE Pythagorean philosopher Timaeus of Locri). I will have something to say about why Plato uses Timaeus as the philosophical protagonist of that eponymous dialogue below. My main point here is that given Plato's employment of dramatic personae in his writings, there will be a tendency in my discussion to speak equivalently of Plato's views or of the views of the character Socrates or Timaeus. In addition, I emphasize that there is no reason to assume that the views of Plato's character Socrates or Plato's character Timaeus accurately reflect the views of the historical Socrates or Timaeus.

THE REPLENISHMENT THEORY OF PLEASURE IN PLATO'S 'GORGIAS' AND 'REPUBLIC'

Among Plato's various treatments of pleasure, we find the following persistent view: pleasure is a replenishment or a restoration to the natural state, where the subject that undergoes the replenishment or restoration is aware of the replenishment or restoration. Replenishment or restoration, natural state, awareness – let's clarify each of these components. Replenishment is a kind of restoration, so for the time being I will speak simply of restoration. Below I will clarify why there is reason to draw a distinction between replenishment and restoration.

The concept of the natural state of a living being is easy to clarify superficially, hard to clarify well. Let's start with two key examples. The natural state of the body of a living being is health; the natural state of the soul of a living being is psychological well-being. These are global states of the body and soul. There are also partial or rather local natural states, for example, health of the lungs or heart or eyes or ears. Thus, a man may be blind and so have a non-natural state of his eyes or visual faculty, but otherwise be physically healthy and so in a natural state.

The difficulty is to clarify what examples of natural states have in common in virtue of which they are natural. A truly satisfactory answer requires an account of Plato's conception of value and the good, to which an independent chapter or book could be devoted. My comments will therefore be restricted. The first thing to note is that the term "natural" here is normative. More precisely, the natural state of a substance, organ, or part is an intrinsically good state for that entity. It is a state that the substance or possessor of the organ or part ought to have, for its own good. The question, then, is what in general makes such a state good. In various places Plato makes various illuminating suggestions. For example, certain substances or parts have characteristic or proper functions, and the natural state of the substance or part enables it to perform its characteristic or proper function well. For example, the characteristic function of the eyes or visual faculty is seeing well. Thus, the condition of the eyes or visual faculty that enables good vision is the natural state. Elsewhere, Plato says that the goodness of substances or parts requires order or harmony. Assume that order and harmony are, loosely speaking, constituted by a proper arrangement or organization of components.[1] So, for example, bodily health might be conceived as depending upon a certain balance or proportion of physiological humors; psychic health or well-being might be conceived at least as requiring a certain distribution and delineation of roles among a set of psychic components. A crucial, perhaps the crucial, concept in Plato's theory of goodness and value is unity. A properly ordered or harmonious entity is a unified one. Such unity confers integrity, stability, or durability, and thus longevity, on that entity.

I turn now to restoration. The concept of restoration itself seems to entail wholeness, integrity, or well-being. For example, it sounds odd to speak of restoring a state of chaos or restoring a corrupt condition. If this is correct, then strictly speaking the description "restoration to the natural state" is otiose. Indeed, Plato sometimes simply speaks of pleasure as a restoration of which one is aware. However, he also takes pains to clarify that the terminus of restoration is the natural state.

As the prefix "re-" in "restoration" and "replenishment" indicates, restoration and replenishment entail or at least suggest a prior state of fullness, completion, or wholeness. Contrast this with filling or completing, which

---

[1] But observe the crucial normative work that the term "proper" is doing here.

does not. The question whether Plato holds that all pleasure entails a prior state of fullness or wholeness is actually complex. For example, Plato commonly refers to drinking when thirsty as a pleasure of restoration or replenishment. In all or at least almost all such cases, replenishment rather than mere filling occurs. The question is how Plato conceives the original state of the given substance or part. If, at their inception, all living beings possess global states of integrity and wholeness, then all pleasures are restorative or replenishing, not merely pleasures of filling or completing. But if there are global or partial cases of defective or incomplete initial conditions, then some pleasures are merely of filling or completing. I note the problem, but will not pursue it here. Suffice it to say that although it is clear, according to Plato's theory, that many pleasures entail a prior state of integrity or wholeness and thus that the term "replenishment" or "restoration" is then appropriate, strictly speaking my use of "replenishment" or "restoration" should be understood as general and not necessarily universal.

We come to awareness. I can think of at least two reasons that the subject of the restoration must be aware of the restoration. One is that entities that do not have the capacity for awareness may be restored; however, in such cases, no pleasure can occur. For example, one may restore a dilapidated house, but the house experiences no pleasure in the process. Plato does not actually address this point – no doubt because it is too obvious to warrant stating.

Granted this, it is questionable whether all animate beings have the capacity for pleasure. In particular there appears to have been some debate in antiquity over whether plants experience pleasure and pain. In his treatise *On Plants*, Aristotle reports that a number of early philosophers held that plants undergo psychic conditions such as desire, pleasure, and pain:

Before we can assert the presence of life in plants, a long inquiry must be conducted into whether plants possess a soul and a distinctive capacity for desire and pleasure and pain. Now Anaxagoras and Empedocles say that they are influenced by desire; they also assert that they can perceive and experience sadness and pleasure. (815a11–16)[2]

In *Timaeus* Plato too maintains that a certain kind of soul endows plants with the capacity for "pleasant and painful perception with desires" (77b). Aristotle disagrees with his predecessors, for he believes that sense-perception requires a certain sort of thermoregulation, which plants lack. At any

---

[2] Note that the text *On Plants* from which this passage derives was not composed by Aristotle himself, but by a later Peripatetic philosopher. However, much of the content of *On Plants* derives from Aristotle, in particular, this passage.

rate, it suffices to note here that pleasure and pain require awareness and that Aristotle and his predecessors held divergent views about which living entities are capable of awareness. Our discussion, like Plato's, will principally focus on pleasure in humans.

The second reason why an entity must be aware of the restoration in order to experience pleasure – a reason that Plato explicitly states – is that entities that have the capacity for awareness may undergo restorations, but not be aware of the restorations and thus not experience them as pleasant. I can think of at least two ways this failure to experience pleasure could occur. One is that the subject's awareness could be focused elsewhere or otherwise disabled or distracted. Plato does not address this point. The other way this could occur – one that Plato does address – is if the restoration is too subtle and thus takes place below the threshold of awareness. Accordingly, the restoration must be robust enough so that it registers psychically or consciously. As we will see, in *Timaeus* Plato specifies conditions for robustness.

Let me now return to the distinction I first introduced between replenishment and restoration. As I mentioned, the concept of restoration is broader than the concept of replenishment. Compare the process of replenishing a physiological deficit, say, a nutritional deficit, with that of restoring a physiological balance by removing an excess of some substance. For example, while it might be pleasant to slake one's thirst by drinking, it might also be pleasant to relieve a full bladder. In this respect, the restoration theory may be more satisfactory than the replenishment theory. In fact, there is reason to think that Plato first adopted the replenishment theory and later replaced it with the restoration theory.

In Plato's corpus, the replenishment theory first appears in *Gorgias*. As I mentioned above, *Gorgias* is most likely a relatively early Platonic dialogue, composed prior to *Republic*, *Timaeus*, and *Philebus*. In *Gorgias* Plato conveys the view, although without stating it explicitly, that pleasure involves a kind of filling or replenishment. In the final movement of the dialogue, the characters Socrates and Callicles, Socrates' principal interlocutor at this stage of the text, are engaged in a debate over whether pleasure is identical to goodness. Socrates argues against this view, and Callicles attempts to argue for it. In attempting to persuade Callicles of his position, Socrates employs the following metaphor: in life we each possess a set of urns; we must attend to these urns and precisely endeavor to keep them full of wine, honey, and milk.[3] An immoderate man is one whose

---

[3] *Gorgias* 493d–494a.

urns are leaky and who is constantly preoccupied with filling them. Socrates asserts that such a life is full of distress, whereas the life of a man whose urns are sound and full is a life of well-being. Against this, Callicles argues:

That man who has filled his urns can have no pleasure. Rather, his is the life of a stone ... for once he fills [his urns], he experiences no joy or pain. Living pleasantly consists of the greatest inflow. (494a)

Socrates interprets and Callicles confirms his interpretation of the advocacy of the life of attending leaky urns:

so Are you speaking of feeling hunger and eating when one is hungry ... and feeling thirst and drinking when one is thirsty?
CA Yes, and having all the other desires and being able to fill them; [that is] living well and pleasantly. (494b–c)

Although neither Socrates nor Callicles says so explicitly, it is clear from the metaphor and the following exchange that pleasure is conceived in terms of filling some sort of deficit. Correlatively, pain is conceived in terms of the emergence of the deficit. The examples of hunger and thirst suggest that the deficits and replenishments are physiological. These examples and the general model that they exemplify encourage the view that Plato's conception derives from the replenishment theory we encountered in *Diseases IV*.

Immediately before he introduces the metaphor of the leaky jars in *Gorgias*, Socrates introduces another closely related metaphor: the part of the soul in which appetites reside is itself an urn. Socrates attributes this metaphor to "a Sicilian, perhaps, or an Italian" (493a).[4] The Greek word for urn is "*pithos*," which, Socrates reports, the Sicilian or Italian had associated with the Greek word "*pithanon*," meaning "persuadable." By doing so he suggested that in foolish men the psychic urn leaks and so creates a disposition of insatiability. When Socrates offers the second and related metaphor of the three leaky urns, he says that the account derives from "the same school" (493d). Since Socrates refers both to Italy and Sicily and to a school, he seems to have the Pythagoreans in mind. Pythagoras himself had dwelt in the southern Italian city-states of Croton and Metapontum in the late sixth century, and Pythagoreanism had

---

[4] Note that during Plato's lifetime much of Sicily and southern Italy were populated by Greeks, who began to colonize these fertile regions as early as the eighth century BCE.

spread from there through Sicily. Support for this suggestion also comes from a claim Socrates makes as he introduces the first metaphor:

Perhaps in reality we're dead. I once even heard one of the wise men say that we are now dead and that our body (*sôma*) is a tomb (*sêma*), and that the part of our souls in which our appetites reside is actually the sort of thing that is open to persuasion. (493a)

The identification of the body with a tomb in which the soul is imprisoned during the period we normally identify with life is expressed by Pythagorean sources, who, like Plato himself, are committed to *metempsychosis*, the view that a single soul passes through various incarnations. If the source of the replenishment theory is indeed Greek medicine, then Plato drew the model himself either directly from medical literature or from Sicilian or Italian Pythagoreans who were themselves influenced by the medical literature. Alternatively, the medical author derived the view from the Pythagoreans. Or, finally, each may have devised the theory independently of the other. The first and third options are perhaps more plausible than the second. But I see no evidence for favoring either the first or third. Let this suffice for now as an account of Plato's source for the replenishment theory.[5]

Note that when Socrates asks Callicles whether he is referring to hunger and thirst and eating and drinking, he responds: "Yes, and having all the other desires and being able to fill them." Thus, the range of replenishments and deficits of the model in *Gorgias* is, at least implicitly, broader than the replenishment theory in *Diseases IV*. We might say that in *Diseases IV*, we encounter a replenishment theory limited to nutritional pleasure, but that in *Gorgias* the theory is at least implicitly broader. Unfortunately, we cannot clarify how it is broader because Callicles does not specify what other desires he has in mind. When we turn to *Republic*, however, we will find that Plato is more specific.

Presently, let's consider a related, but distinct, question raised by the replenishment theory in *Gorgias*: Is the replenishment corporeal or psychic or both? Clearly, eating and drinking involve corporeal replenishments, while hunger and thirst involve corporeal deficits. But according to the Pythagorean metaphor, the part of the soul in which appetites reside is an urn, and this psychic component is, in the case of fools, said to be leaky. Thus, the soul or a part of it also appears to be subject to depletion

---

[5] Below, however, I will give another piece of evidence to support the view that Plato depended on the Pythagoreans for his replenishment theory.

and replenishment. Since the identity of pleasure in *Gorgias* is both implicit and expressed through metaphors, I think that we lack adequate information to resolve the question whether pleasure as treated in *Gorgias* involves corporeal or psychic replenishment or both. Indeed, a satisfactory answer would also require clarification of the relation between body and soul. This problem is especially complicated in the context of this particular passage. First, as I have mentioned, most Greek philosophers viewed the soul as corporeal. On the other hand, Plato did not view the soul as corporeal. At least, it is clear that he did not view all of the soul as corporeal. As we will discuss shortly when we turn to *Republic*, in some dialogues Plato distinguishes multiple parts of the soul. It is controversial whether some or all of the parts are incorporeal. Yet again, in the *Gorgias* passage Plato may have the Pythagoreans' conception of the soul in mind. But it is anyone's guess what the Pythagoreans' conception of the soul is.[6] So, as I said, this is a particularly tricky passage for determining whether the replenishment is corporeal or psychic or both.

Let us turn now to Plato's *Republic* to see how the replenishment theory is there treated. The pertinent discussion of pleasure occurs in Book 9, where Socrates and his interlocutor Glaucon are considering the question whether the just life is also a pleasant life, indeed, the most pleasant life. Socrates develops three arguments to support the view that the just life is the most pleasant. The third argument is the most important for our purposes.[7] This argument depends upon a division of the soul into three parts, for which Socrates had argued previously in Book 4.

The basic argument Socrates uses in Book 4 to defend the view that the soul has various parts is that we can have simultaneous conflicting motivations. For example, one may desire to eat something sweet, but also at the same time have the contradictory desire not to eat something sweet, for example, because one is concerned about its impact on one's health. Socrates suggests that the conflicting desires must derive from distinct psychic sources. Through examination of various conflicting motivations, he concludes that there are three parts of the soul: appetitive, spirited, and rational. The appetitive part is motivated to satisfy our basic bodily needs; for example, it desires food and drink. The spirited part is concerned with our social status; for example, it desires esteem or honor.

---

[6] The best treatment of which I am aware is Carl Huffman, "The Pythagorean Conception of the Soul from Pythagoras to Philolaus," in *Body and Soul in Ancient Philosophy*, D. Frede and B. Reis, eds., de Gruyter, 2009, 21–43.

[7] This argument occurs at 583–587.

The rational part is concerned with knowledge and understanding; for example, it desires wisdom.

In Book 9, Socrates argues that there are three kinds of pleasure, each of which relates to one of the three parts of the soul. That is, there are appetitive, spirited, and rational pleasures.[8] The gist of Socrates' argument that the just life is the most pleasant is, accordingly, this: the just life is a life governed by reason or the rational part of the soul; rational pleasures are more pleasant than appetitive and spirited pleasures; thus, the just life is the most pleasant life. I will discuss why Socrates maintains that rational pleasures are most pleasant below. For now, I will consider whether the various pleasures involve corporeal or psychic replenishments.

Socrates begins the *Republic* 9 argument with the following claim:

Both pleasure and pain arising in the soul are a kind of change (*kinêsis*). (583e)

Evidently, then, in *Republic* Plato maintains that pleasure involves a certain sort of psychic change. Contrast a state of psychic calm, which Plato here also distinguishes from pleasure and pain. If one who is in pain comes to be relieved of the pain and so to have a state of psychic calm, then calm involves change in some respect. But this is not the respect in which Plato understands pleasure and pain as involving psychic change. Pleasure and pain intrinsically involve change. Hence, one might also say that they are processes rather than states.

Granted that pleasure involves psychic change, it is unclear precisely what kind of psychic change this is. It may well be a change of replenishment, but without further evidence one cannot confidently say. Later in the discussion Socrates suggests that pleasure involves filling and pain emptying. More precisely, at that point in the discussion Socrates focuses on two kinds of pleasure. He claims that hunger and thirst are conditions of bodily emptiness and that one fills the emptiness by partaking of "food, drink, relish, and all nourishment" (585b). He also says that there are psychic pleasures of filling with true opinion, knowledge, and understanding. Evidently, Socrates is here distinguishing appetitive and rational pleasures. He has a bit to say about spirited pleasures elsewhere in the argument, but his focus is on the distinction between appetitive and rational ones.

As we have seen, appetitive pleasures clearly involve corporeal deficits and replenishments. The treatment in *Republic* is consistent with this.

---

[8] The tripartition of pleasure in *Republic* 9 is also notable vis-à-vis Prodicus' tripartition of pleasure. However, the two tripartitions involve different sets of pleasures, and Plato does not distinguish the three pleasures terminologically.

Yet – given Socrates' general claim at the beginning of the argument – appetitive pleasures also involve psychic change of some kind. Indeed, at another point in the discussion, Socrates speaks of certain pleasures "extending through the body to the soul" (584c). This suggests that at least some pleasures involve both body and soul. I think that the sort of pleasure Socrates has in mind here is appetitive.

From this, it seems reasonable to infer at least the following: appetitive, spirited, and rational pleasures involve changes in the appetitive, spirited, and rational parts of the soul respectively. In the case of spirited and rational pleasures, psychic replenishments occur. For example, in the case of rational pleasure, the rational part of the soul is filled with some sort of cognitive content. In the case of spirited pleasure, the spirited part of the soul is presumably filled with some sort of spirited or emotional content; for example, the spirited part of the soul is emboldened by a sense of confidence. By parity of reasoning it would seem that in the case of appetitive pleasure, the appetitive part of the soul is also filled. However, there is no explicit evidence for this position. Moreover, the appetitive filling to which Socrates explicitly refers is clearly corporeal. Once again, for example, when a man who is hungry eats, he fills a nutritional, not a psychic, deficit. In that case, appetitive pleasure may be unlike rational and spirited pleasure.

And yet, since pleasure requires psychic change, appetitive pleasure must involve some sort of psychic change. The psychic change that appetitive pleasure involves, I suggest, is not change of replenishment, but of awareness. That is, the psychic change is the mode of awareness of the corporeal replenishment. Now, the change that constitutes the awareness of corporeal replenishment cannot be the same as the change that constitutes the awareness of corporeal depletion. Otherwise, awareness of pain and awareness of pleasure would be identical, whereas they obviously differ. Socrates does not, however, say how these changes differ. We simply must allow that they do.

This view is problematic, however. Although psychic changes constitute the awareness of pleasure and pain, psychic change cannot be necessary for awareness generally. This is because one can be aware of calm. Perhaps the nature of this awareness is of a different kind, comparable to awareness of absence. Plato does not address the problem.

The following question also arises: Do rational and spirited pleasures involve two psychic changes, one of replenishment and one of awareness? Arguably, rational and spirited pleasures do not require changes of awareness precisely because the soul will necessarily be aware of any change within it. Again, Plato does not address this question.

The preceding discussion also raises the question of what the various parts of the soul are, such that they are subject to change and in some cases at least replenishment or restoration. We will to some extent pursue this question in our discussion of the treatment of pleasure in *Timaeus*. Presently, let us summarize the transition from *Gorgias* to *Republic* 9 as follows. In *Gorgias*, the replenishment theory of pleasure is implicit. It is treated as broader than the nutritional theory we encountered in *Disease IV*, but how much broader is unclear. In *Republic* 9, the replenishment theory is extended in accordance with the tripartition of the soul, which is introduced in this dialogue. Thus, replenishments are conceived both as corporeal, as in the case of appetitive pleasure, and psychic, as in the cases of spirited and rational pleasure.

SENSE-PERCEPTUAL PLEASURE IN 'TIMAEUS' (PART ONE)

It is notable that within Theophrastus' *On Perceptions* pleasure and pain are treated among forms of sense-perception. Theophrastus' treatment of pleasure and pain among forms of sense-perception does not follow the treatments of sense-perception of his older colleague Aristotle. Aristotle discusses sense-perception, including some of the views of his predecessors, in particular in two works: *On the Soul* and *On Sense-Perception and Sensibles*. Aristotle says almost nothing in these works about pleasure and pain. Instead, Theophrastus' inclusion of pleasure and pain among forms of sense-perception owes to Plato and specifically to Plato's *Timaeus*, which Theophrastus discusses at greater length than any other figure or text.

At the outset, it must be emphasized that *Timaeus* is by far Plato's most physical-theoretical dialogue. As noted above, the main speaker in this text is Timaeus of Locri, not Socrates. This is significant. It suggests that Plato is principally drawing on a different intellectual tradition from the ethical one with which he identifies Socrates. Indeed, Plato is drawing on the tradition of *physiologia*. Thus, the account of pleasure and pain he offers here is largely physical-theoretical.

In the section of *Timaeus* that particularly concerns us, Timaeus introduces what he calls "*pathēmata aisthētika*." "*Pathēmata*" is the plural of the noun "*pathēma*." "*Pathēma*" or its cognate "*pathos*" can be translated as "affection." Both words derive from the Greek verb "*paschein*," which means "to undergo" or "to be affected (by something)." An affection is, accordingly, a condition of being affected. Thus, an affection is a passive condition; its contrary is an action (*poiēma*).[9]

---

[9] This sense of "affection," then, obviously differs from the sense of "affection" as "fondness."

The word "*aisthêtika*" is an adjective cognate with the noun "*aisthêsis*." In *Timaeus* Timaeus describes "*aisthêsis*" in the following way:

Changes transmitted through the body impact the soul; all these changes have been called *aisthêseis* (plural of "*aisthêsis*"). (43c)

Compare Socrates' description in *Philebus*:

When the soul and body are jointly affected and changed by one and the same affection, if you should call this change *aisthêsis*, you would say nothing out of place. (34a)

An *aisthêsis*, then, is a somatic affection that in turn affects the psyche.

For convenience, I will render "*aisthêsis*" as "perception." Bear in mind that this rendition is somewhat artificial. Normally, "perception" can be used to refer to a purely mental condition; for example, one can perceive, just by thinking, that a proposed solution to a problem will work. Given this, "perception" here should be understood as "somatic perception," which is to say, perception by means of the body. Note also the following distinction between two kinds of somatic perception. For example, contrast feeling queasy with sensing the warmth of a fire. The latter is more precisely an instance of sense-perception, by tactile sensation, whereas the former, whatever it is,[10] is not a case of sense-perception. Nonetheless, it is a form of somatic perception. In the context of *Timaeus* in which the phrase "*pathêmata aisthêtika*" occurs, Timaeus is in fact discussing the various forms of sense-perception. Thus, although strictly speaking "*pathêmata aisthêtika*" should be rendered as "somatic perceptual affections," Timaeus has a particular species of somatic perceptual affection in mind, again, sense-perceptual affection.

Plato's account of pleasure and pain in *Timaeus* specifically follows his account of tactile affections and precedes his accounts of gustatory, olfactory, auditory, and visual affections. This is significant. In discussing tactile affections Timaeus does not in fact use the Greek words for "touch" or "tactile." Rather, he describes tactile affections as "pansomatic." By "pansomatic" he means that these affections can occur all over the body (*sôma*). For example, one's toes as well as one's face can feel warmth or pressure. In contrast, he speaks of gustatory, olfactory, auditory, and visual affections as restricted to parts of the body. In other words, these are localized affections. For example, one can only see with

---

[10] It is a form of proprioception.

one part of the body, the eyes. The treatment of pleasure and pain is sandwiched between those of pansomatic and localized sense-perceptual affections because pleasure and pain are, in a sense, both pansomatic and localized. That is, pleasure and pain can occur throughout the body, but they can also occur in conjunction with localized sense-perceptual affections. Here is how Timaeus puts the point:

> The most important thing that remains to be said about the affections common to the whole body is the explanation of the pleasant and painful [affections] within those affections we have discussed (that is, pansomatic affections) and all the affections through the parts of the body that possess perceptions (that is, localized affections) and at the same time accompanying pains and pleasures within themselves. (64a)

Observe Timaeus' claims here that pleasure and pain occur "within" pansomatic affections and "accompany" localized affections. We will explain these locutions below.

Although Timaeus is Plato's philosophical protagonist in *Timaeus*, one should not infer that Plato thought at the time he composed *Timaeus* that all pleasure and pain accompany sense-perception. That view is hard to sustain if one considers the rational and spirited pleasures of *Republic* 9; neither of these appears to be a form of sense-perceptual pleasure. One might wonder whether at the time he composed *Timaeus* Plato had abandoned the tripartition of pleasures he introduces in *Republic*. But Plato retains the tripartition of the soul in *Timaeus* quite explicitly and elaborately. We will discuss that point shortly in order to clarify the way in which the soul is involved in sense-perceptual pleasure.[11]

Spirited and rational pleasures are, then, not the same as sense-perceptual pleasures. More interestingly, sense-perceptual pleasures also seem to be distinguishable from another sort of somatic pleasure, namely, appetitive pleasure. Consider in particular what in Chapters 2 and 3 I called "brute pleasures," in particular, pleasures of nutrition and sex. These pleasures are not discussed within the treatment of sense-perceptual pleasure in *Timaeus*, and there is a good reason for that. Pleasures of nutrition and sex are not or at least arguably not sense-perceptual pleasures – even though brute pleasures and sense-perceptual pleasures often occur simultaneously. Consider the following distinction: it is pleasant to drink when one is thirsty; the taste of Sicilian wine is pleasant. The former is a nutritional pleasure; the latter is

---

[11] Plato also discusses appetitive, spirited, rational, and sense-perceptual pleasures in *Philebus*, although, admittedly, without mentioning three distinct psychic parts.

a gustatory pleasure. It is one thing to quench thirst; it is another to savor a drink. Again, consider the following distinction: it is pleasant to feel warmth on one's body; it is pleasant – to put it mildly – to have an orgasm. The former is a tactile pleasure; the latter is a sexual pleasure. It is one thing to sense temperature by means of touch; it is another to feel sexual stimulation or release. One way the distinction between brute and sense-perceptual pleasures might be drawn is that the contents or objects of brute pleasures are limited to conditions of internal processes, whereas the contents or objects of sense-perceptual pleasures are external conditions. This is precisely because the function of sense-perception is to gather information about the environment. In other words, there are two forms of somatic perception: exteroception and proprioception. The distinction is not crisp, however. Consider touching one's own arm. Additionally, the distinction between exteroceptive and proprioceptive pleasures, to the extent that it can be drawn, overlaps the distinction between brute and non-brute bodily pleasures. As we will see in discussing Plato's *Hippias Major* below, pleasures of touch and taste are generally treated as brute.

These difficulties or lack of clear distinctions can be explained by the fact that Plato only implicitly recognizes the various distinctions; he does not explicitly theorize them. The treatment of sense-perceptual pleasures in *Timaeus* in fact appears to be a new development in Plato's thinking about pleasures and pains. Prior to *Timaeus* Plato does not segregate and thereby implicitly distinguish sense-perceptual pleasures from non-sense-perceptual somatic pleasures. Presumably the distinction arises in *Timaeus* because Plato treats sense-perceptual affections here more carefully than anywhere else in his corpus.

BASE AND FINE PLEASURES IN 'HIPPIAS MAJOR'

In the context of exploring distinctions among somatic pleasures, I would here like to make a brief excursus into the discussion of pleasure in another of Plato's early dialogues, *Hippias Major*. In *Hippias Major*, the characters Socrates and Hippias of Elis attempt to define fineness (*to kalon*).[12] The penultimate definition of fineness they consider is pleasure through sight and hearing. Socrates describes such pleasures as follows:

[12] The translation of the Greek word "*kallos*" or the equivalent phrase "*to kalon*" is difficult. In some cases, the expressions refer to physical beauty. But in other cases they have the sense of "nobility" or simply "goodness." "Fineness" is an attempt, of limited success, to capture the broad range. Likewise, the antonym of "*kallos*" or "*to kalon*" is "*aischos*" or "*to aischron*," which may mean "ugliness" as well as "baseness" or "badness."

Everything decorative, paintings and sculptures, these all delight us when we see them – if they're fine (*kala*). And fine sounds and music and speeches and story-telling have the same effect. (298a)

Socrates distinguishes pleasures of sight and sound from pleasures of "food, drink, sex, and all such things." He characterizes the latter as occurring "through other forms of perception (*aisthêseis*)" (298d–e). Socrates appears to have in mind here brute pleasures. At any rate, he regards these pleasures as base. So I will refer to them as *base pleasures*. Among base pleasures Socrates also includes olfactory pleasures:

[We would be laughable] if we called a pleasant smell not pleasant but fine (*kalon*). (299a)

Accordingly, in *Hippias Major* Plato does not distinguish brute pleasures from sense-perceptual pleasures. Instead, in this dialogue the distinction that interests him is between base and fine pleasures, and this distinction is drawn according to the conceived values of various somatic perceptual – but not necessarily sense-perceptual – faculties. Socrates views pleasures of eating, drinking, sex, as well as smell, as base because he views those perceptual faculties as base, and he views pleasures of sight and hearing as fine because those perceptual faculties are fine. Why the perceptual faculties themselves are evaluated in this way is a question we will consider in Chapter 6 when we turn to Aristotle.

Before we return to the account of pleasure in *Timaeus*, I want to make two further remarks on the relation between the treatment of pleasure in *Hippias Major* and in later dialogues. One remark pertains to the suspicion that Plato's distinction of visual and auditory pleasures from other perceptual pleasures in *Hippias Major* and specifically his distinction of the former as fine and the latter as base is indebted to Prodicus' hedonic distinctions. Recall that for Prodicus visual and auditory pleasures are among the set of refined pleasures. If this is correct, one may wonder about the absence from the treatment in *Hippias Major* of what Prodicus refers to as pleasures of the soul. In fact, arguably, these pleasures are not entirely absent. After he introduces pleasures of sight and hearing as fine, Socrates asks:

Should we say, Hippias, that fine practices and customs are fine because they are pleasing through sight and hearing, or do they have some other form? (298b)

The question is not directly answered. Instead, Hippias attempts to dodge: "Perhaps we can avoid these things" (298b). And Socrates himself subsequently does:

Perhaps fine customs and practices will not appear to lie outside of perception through sight and hearing. But let us focus on the claim that that which is pleasing through these senses [sight and hearing] is fine, and let us ignore the topic of customs. (298d)

The exchange indicates that it is questionable how pleasures relating to practices and customs should be conceived. In consideration of the fact that Plato identifies excellence or virtue (*aretê*) with knowledge in his early dialogues, my supposition is that Plato may be thinking of pleasures through fine customs and practices as being of the soul, that is, as psychic, but that he does not wish to broach the subject here or to explain the distinction between visual and auditory pleasures, on the one hand, and psychic pleasures, on the other. In this case, then, a distinct kind of pleasure may be implicit. If this is correct, then in *Hippias Major* Plato may be following Prodicus even more closely than it initially appears. That is, Prodicus and then Plato conceptualize pleasures in terms of a psychological hierarchy, with certain perceptual faculties situated lower on the hierarchy, other perceptual faculties situated higher, and reason or intellect located at the peak.

A final distinction between the treatment of pleasure in *Hippias Major* and in later dialogues is also worth noting here. The inclusion of olfactory pleasure among base pleasures in *Hippias Major* is noteworthy because later in his career Plato came to think that olfactory pleasures should in fact be distinguished from base pleasures. First in *Republic* 9 and later in *Philebus* Plato notes that olfactory pleasures, in contrast to pleasures of eating and drinking, are not preceded by a felt depletion and so by pain. Accordingly, Plato comes to refer to pleasures that are preceded by a felt depletion and so pain as impure or mixed. They are mixed pleasures precisely because they are mixed with pain, that is, antecedent pain. (The concept of mixture here is, then, precisely sequential rather than simultaneous mixture. As we will see, elsewhere Plato operates with both conceptions of mixed pleasure.) According to the replenishment theory, olfactory pleasures also involve replenishments of some sort of nasal depletion. Yet nasal depletion is not felt and thus not painful. Consequently, olfactory pleasures are distinguished as a relatively pure kind of pleasure.[13] The same point is made in *Timaeus* and once again in *Philebus*.[14] As I will discuss more fully in Chapter 5, in *Philebus* in particular Socrates' attempt to distinguish kinds of pleasure concludes with three kinds of pure and unmixed pleasure. Hierarchically ordered, the lowest

---

[13] *Republic* 584b–c.   [14] *Timaeus* 65a–b; *Philebus* 51e.

kind is olfactory pleasure; visual and auditory pleasures are jointly ranked second; and intellectual pleasure is the highest kind. In short, from *Hippias Major* to *Republic* 9 and *Philebus* the evaluation of olfactory pleasures improves.

One further, historical, point about olfactory pleasure as replenishment or restoration deserves mention. While it is clear that olfactory pleasures occur, it is strange to think that they involve olfactory replenishments. Of course, one might simply take Plato here to be extending the replenishment model with inadequate discrimination – as indeed one might criticize his view of spirited and rational pleasures in *Republic* 9. Even so, it is worth noting that Plato's conception of olfactory pleasures as restorative is most likely not his own extension. In his treatise *On Sense-Perception and Sensibles*, Aristotle criticizes a theory "held by certain Pythagoreans that some animals are nourished by odors alone" (445a). The interest of this remark for our purposes is that, taken in conjunction with the idea proposed above that certain Pythagoreans were committed to the replenishment theory of pleasure, it suggests that these Pythagoreans themselves might have already extended the replenishment theory of pleasure to olfactory pleasure. Moreover, it provides some explanation for the extension, namely, a connection between smell and nutrition. If this is correct, then it should also be noted that the view raises the objection that although we take pleasure in the smell of certain edibles and potables, we also take pleasure in scents of things that are neither edible nor potable.

SENSE-PERCEPTUAL PLEASURE IN 'TIMAEUS' (PART TWO)

So much for our excursus into pleasure in *Hippias Major* – let us return to *Timaeus*, specifically in view of the idea that certain depletions are unfelt and thus not painful. In *Timaeus* Plato presents the following description of pleasure and pain:

It is necessary to conceive of pleasure and pain in the following way. When an affection occurs within us that is contrary to nature, violent, and sudden, it is painful; but a return again to nature when sudden is pleasant. (64c–d)

Let me focus first on what Timaeus says about pain. I want to draw attention to the three descriptions attributed to the painful affection: it is contrary to nature, violent, and sudden. "Contrary to nature" glosses the idea of being a departure from the natural state. Note that this departure need not be a depletion. So here the replenishment and depletion theories have given way to broader theories of restoration and destruction. Likewise, in the case of pleasure, Timaeus speaks of a "return to nature," which refers to a broader process than replenishment (hence restoration).

The other two attributes of painful affections are violence and suddenness. Observe that in the case of pleasant affections, Timaeus only mentions suddenness. I take this to be an innocent and perhaps expedient omission. Pleasant affections must in fact be both sudden and violent. By "violent" Timaeus means that the affection must affect the body to a substantial extent. For example, a slight scrape will not be painful because too little of the body has been affected. By "sudden" Timaeus means that the affection must occur with a certain alacrity. A very gradual departure from or restoration to the natural state will also not be experienced as painful or pleasant. Timaeus gives the following examples to support his claim. When we receive a substantive wound or burn, we normally experience pain; however, we do not experience pleasure as the wound or burn heals, even though the healing is a process of restoration to the natural state. This is because the healing process is too gradual, in other words, not sudden enough. Correlatively, pleasant smells, Timaeus thinks, result from a rather sudden restoration to the natural state. However, these are not preceded by olfactory pains, which involve departures from the natural state of the olfactory faculty. This is because the departure is too gradual to notice. Here is how Timaeus puts these points:

Bodies that have only gradual departures from their [natural] states or gradual depletions but whose replenishments are violent and sudden do not perceive their depletions but do perceive their replenishments. Hence they provide very substantial pleasures to the mortal part of the soul, but not any pains. This is clear from the case of fragrances. But all those bodies whose alienations are violent, while their restorations to their [natural] states are gradual and slow, transmit changes that are entirely contrary to those mentioned just now. Again, this is clear in cases where the body suffers cuts and burns. (65a–b)

Finally, it should be emphasized that pleasant and painful affections require the conjunction of violence and suddenness. As evidence for this, Timaeus cites visual perception. Recall that we began our brief discussion of Empedocles' theory of vision in Chapter 3 with the point that a theory of vision must explain how external objects and the visual organs come into contact. According to Empedocles' theory, external objects emit effluences that impact the eye. In contrast, according to Timaeus' theory of vision, when the eyes are open a certain sort of fire naturally projects from the pupil into the external environment and contacts visible objects. Timaeus explains our inability to see in darkness as a function of the darkness severing the projected visual fire. This can occur suddenly, as when we step out of daylight into a dark enclosure. The severing of the projected visual fire is a destruction of this natural condition. However, it is not painful. Nor is the resumption of seeing in the presence of daylight pleasant. The explanation Timaeus gives is that although the destruction and restoration are extremely rapid, they do not involve violent affections. On the contrary, visual fire is a particularly subtle entity so that the affections it undergoes are normally not violent enough to engender pleasure or pain.[15]

Let us now turn to the role of the soul in the awareness of pleasant and painful affections. There are three distinct, but closely related, questions to be considered here: What is the soul? What parts of the soul are involved in sense-perceptual pleasure? And how are these parts involved in sense-perceptual pleasure? I have mentioned that Timaeus holds, as Socrates does in *Republic*, that the soul has three parts: rational, spirited, and appetitive. These parts are conceived as spatial, but not corporeal. This is a strange view, to be sure. Nonetheless, Plato holds the view. It would be illuminating to explore why he feels compelled or attracted to this position, but I cannot embark on that explanation here. At any rate, the idea of a spatial, but not corporeal, entity is at least conceivable if one thinks of space in absolute, Newtonian terms. On the other hand, the soul is not merely extended; it is also kinetic. For example, Timaeus maintains that the ideal movement of the rational part of the soul is circular, in imitation of the circular motion of the heavens (as he conceives it). The conception of the soul as both spatially extended and kinetic is evidently a physicalistic conception, sans corporeal aspect. Once again, this is weird; but Plato holds the view.

In considering Timaeus' conception of the soul, it is also important to discuss his conception of *myelos*, a term standardly but problematically translated as "marrow." In one part of the dialogue, Timaeus explains the physical composition of the body from its innermost parts to the skin. The innermost part of the body is *myelos*. The conception of *myelos* here employed is broader than our conception of marrow. Marrow here constitutes the brain as well as stuff inside the bones. Timaeus says that the soul is rooted and anchored in the marrow of the brain and spinal cord. Since the soul is spatial, but not corporeal, it is unclear how this is to be conceived. In any case, from the brain and spinal cord, veins of

---

[15] The example seems to be problematic, however; consider the fact that it can be painful when we move from a very dark space to a bright one.

marrow extend throughout the body. These veins probably correlate with nerves as well as blood vessels, for the Greeks had yet to recognize the distinction between the nervous and vascular systems. The understood function of the network of veins of marrow was to pervade the body with psychic capacities. Here are two passages in which Timaeus describes this:

[The divinities whose role it was to create the body] divided the marrow into shapes corresponding in sort and size to those which the several kinds [of soul] were originally allotted to have. And [they] molded one part into a spherical shape like a plough-land that was to have the divine seed within itself. And this part of the marrow [they] named "brain" (*enkephalon*), signifying that when each living creature was completed, the vessel containing this should be the head (*kephalē*). Furthermore, the part that was to hold the remaining, mortal kind of soul [they] divided into shapes both round and elongated, naming them all "marrow." And from these [myeloid forms], as if from anchors, casting the bonds of the entire soul, [they] produced around all of this our entire body. (73c–d)

Next, [the divinities] split up these veins in the region of the head and wove the ends so as to pass across one another in opposite directions, slanting those from the right toward the left side of the body and those from the left toward the right side ... so that perceptual affections coming from the parts on each side would be delivered to the whole body. (77d–e)

Note that in the first passage, Timaeus implicitly distinguishes an immortal from a mortal part of the soul. The immortal part of the soul is the rational part; the mortal part comprises the spirited and appetitive parts. This itself is puzzling, for it is unclear in virtue of what the spirited and appetitive parts would be mortal. Since they are not corporeal, it is not clear how they can decompose or be destroyed. Once again, I will make no attempt to resolve this puzzle. I merely note it.

The rational part of the soul is anchored and located in the brain; the spirited and appetitive parts are anchored in the spinal cord. However, the spirited part is closely related to the heart, presumably by way of veins of marrow extending from the spinal cord. Similarly, the appetitive part is closely related to the abdomen, principally the liver, and again presumably by way of veins of marrow extending from the spinal cord.

Since somatic perceptual affections involve the soul, they only occur in entities that have souls. However, even in entities with soul, not all bodily affections are transmitted to the soul and thus are not perceptual or sense-perceptual affections. Plato follows Empedocles in holding that all bodies, and thus all living bodies, are composed of one or more of four basic entities (and their compounds): earth, water, fire, and air.[16] Some of these basic entities and their compounds are intrinsically more kinetic or mobile than others. For example, Plato thinks that air and fire are the most kinetic elements, while water and earth are least kinetic. Accordingly, transmission of bodily affections to the soul requires that the bodily part affected have kinetic properties. Here's how Timaeus puts the point:

> Whenever even a small affection strikes what is naturally kinetic, it transmits [the affection] by rotary motion, [that is, by rolling and thus impacting adjacent particles or compounds], parts affecting other parts in the same way until, arriving at the rational part of the soul (*phronimon*), it reports the power of the agent. (64b)

Observe here that Timaeus refers to the bodily affections arriving at the "rational part of the soul" (*phronimon*). In contrast, in another passage we discussed above, Timaeus refers to the affections providing pleasures to the "mortal part of the soul." Here again is that line:

> [Sudden and violent restorative affections] provide very substantial pleasures to the mortal part of the soul. (65a)

Since the rational soul is immortal, these passages appear inconsistent. The inconsistency can be resolved, however, if we think that sense-perception can involve both mortal and immortal parts of the soul. Indeed it can. Sense-perceptual affections begin at the surface of the body's sense-perceptual organs, for example, skin or tongue. But the appetitive soul is the psychic site of sense-perception. Thus, insofar as sense-perceptual affections are in fact perceived, they must be transmitted to the appetitive soul. In most cases sense-perceptual affections are transmitted through the rational and spirited parts of the soul en route to the appetitive soul. For example, visual and auditory (and perhaps also olfactory) perceptual affections pass through the brain. Gustatory (and perhaps also olfactory) perceptual affections pass through the heart. However, the rational and spirited parts of the soul function in these cases merely as transmitters of sense-perceptual affections; they do not have the capacity for sense-perceptual experience, which is reserved for the appetitive soul. Granted this, once the sense-perceptual affection has registered in the appetitive soul, in the case of humans it will usually be transmitted to the rational soul (and depending on its prior course, that

---

[16] Unlike Empedocles, Plato does not conceive of earth, water, air, and fire as elemental. Hence "basic entity" should not be taken absolutely. Later in the chapter, I use the term "particle" instead of "element" to refer to the basic bits of earth, water, air, and fire.

means back to the rational soul). This enables sense-perceptual judgment; for example, the subject of experience judges that, say, the honey tasted is sweet. Additionally, the subject of experience can appreciate rational qualities of the experience inaccessible to the appetitive part of the soul. This is the case, for instance, with musical appreciation. As Timaeus says, restorative auditory affections

give pleasure (*hêdonê*) to the unintelligent and enjoyment (*euphrosynê*) to the wise through their imitation of divine harmony in mortal movements. (80b)

Timaeus is here distinguishing individuals who appreciate and enjoy the harmonic and thus rational structures of music from those who merely experience the sounds as pleasant.[17]

Let's return now to the point introduced at the beginning of our discussion of pleasure in *Timaeus* (in Part One above), the point that pleasure occurs *within* or *accompanies* the sense-perceptual affection. As I emphasized, this is only the case with sense-perceptual pleasure. It is not the case or not necessarily the case with brute, rational, or spirited pleasure. We have seen that all sense-perception involves motion transmitted by the body to the appetitive part of the soul. The bodily motions, which are affections, may have properties of various dimensions. For example, spatio-temporally, the motions may be rapid or gradual. With respect to scope, that is, the extent of the effect on the body, they may be great or small. With respect to their effect on the organization of the particles constitutive of the bodily compounds but within the parameters of natural conditions, they may variously alter these particles, both spatially and temporally. For example, Timaeus explains that one sort of pansomatic affection, warmth, derives from separation of particles, while coolness derives from their condensation. Again, one sort of auditory affection, low pitch, derives from slow motion of the particles, while high pitch derives from quick motion. Finally, with respect to their effect on the natural condition of the body, sense-perceptual affections may be restorative or disintegrative or neutral. Since a given affection will simultaneously have properties of some of these various dimensions, the affection may have both sense-perceptual properties, such as warmth or coolness or high or low pitch, and hedonic or algesic properties. Indeed, Timaeus maintains that any sense-perceptual affection that has hedonic or algesic properties will have sense-perceptual

---

[17] Observe the uses of "*hêdonê*" and "*euphrosynê*" here. These conform to the distinction Plato attributes to Prodicus in *Protagoras*. As I discussed in Chapter 2, Plato there deforms Prodicus' hedonic distinctions according to Plato's own distinction between somatic and psychic pleasure.

properties – although, as we have seen, the reverse is not true. In other words, some form of sense-perception accompanies all sense-perceptual pleasure and pain. This is because all sense-perceptual affections must occur either within the parameters of the natural state and thus be neutral or involve restorations to or disintegrations from the natural state and thus be pleasant or painful.

CHAPTER 5

Plato on true, untrue, and false pleasures

In this chapter I continue the discussion of Plato's treatment of pleasure. As I mentioned at the beginning of Chapter 4, I will be focusing here on Plato's distinction between true and untrue or true and false pleasures. Plato first introduces this distinction in *Republic* 9. It then becomes central to his discussion of pleasure in *Philebus*. In this respect, the treatment in *Republic* 9 reads like a rough draft of *Philebus*. Accordingly, I begin with the distinction between true and untrue pleasures in *Republic* 9.

Note that in the chapter title and in discussing *Republic* 9, I use the word "untrue" rather than "false." This follows Plato's usage. The distinction between an untrue and a false pleasure seems to be significant. In particular, it relates to a distinction between two truth-conceptions with which Plato operates and which I will explain in due course.[1] Basically, in *Republic* 9 there seems to be a distinction between two ways in which a pleasure can be true and untrue: representationally and ontologically. In fact, there are multiple ways in which a pleasure can be representationally and ontologically true and untrue. Again, we will come to these distinctions below.

TRUE AND UNTRUE PLEASURES IN 'REPUBLIC' 9: THE ILLUSION ARGUMENT

The third argument in *Republic* 9 for the view that the just life is the most pleasant life – part of which we discussed in Chapter 4 – is divisible into two successive arguments. For convenience, I will refer to these as the *Illusion Argument* and the *True Filling Argument*.[2] The distinction between appetitive, spirited, and rational pleasures and correlative replenishments occurs

---

[1] See n. 9.   [2] These occur at 583b–585a and 585a–587a respectively.

in the True Filling Argument. I'll discuss that in the following section. Here I focus on the Illusion Argument.

Socrates begins the Illusion Argument by distinguishing three conditions: pleasure, pain, and calm. Recall the line I cited in Chapter 4 that pleasure and pain are changes of the soul:

Both pleasure and pain arising in the soul are a kind of change (*kinêsis*). (583e)

In contrast, calm is, as the term indicates, a psychic condition of stillness. Given this, Socrates argues that there is a tendency to mistake pleasure for calm. Note that in arguing for this point, Socrates specifically has conditions of bodily pleasure and calm in mind. For example, when people who have been sick recover their health, they claim that the condition of being healthy is pleasant. Socrates argues that this is a mistake. The condition of being healthy is a condition of calm. It is the condition he describes in *Timaeus* and *Philebus* as natural or the natural state.

Socrates then proceeds to explain why people tend to mistake the condition of calm for pleasure. The mistake is due to an illusion. In explaining the illusion Socrates employs an analogy with painting. In the decades shortly before Plato composed *Republic*, a technique called shadow-painting (*skiagraphia*) had been developed in Athens. Shadow-painting involves the juxtaposition of lighter and darker shades on a two-dimensional surface in order to create the illusion of depth. Analogously, Socrates argues, when people are sick, they are in conditions of pain. When they are healthy, they are in conditions of calm. But the juxtaposition of the antecedent pain and the present calm can create the illusion of pleasure.[3] Likewise, Socrates argues, the juxtaposition of antecedent pleasure and present calm can create an illusion of pain. Here is how Socrates puts it:

[It is not that calm] is [pleasant or painful], but that it appears pleasant beside that which is painful and that calm appears painful beside that which is pleasant. (584a)

With respect to the truth of pleasure, there is nothing healthy in these phantasms, but a certain magic. (584a)

[These pseudo-pleasures] are shadow-painted and tainted by juxtaposition. (586b–c)

In considering the implications of Socrates' account here for his conception of pleasure, it is helpful to distinguish two aspects of pleasure. One is the appearance or what I will call the *appearance aspect*; Socrates' word is

---

[3] Strictly speaking, as I will explain below, it cannot be genuine calm that is occurring.

"*phainomenon.*" In the case of genuine and pseudo-pleasures the appearance is the same. Both appear pleasant. The difference between them pertains to the second aspect. The precise nature of this aspect is, however, unclear at this point in Socrates' discussion. As we have seen, Socrates initially distinguishes pleasure from calm on the grounds that pleasure involves psychic change, whereas calm involves psychic stillness. But, as I suggested in Chapter 4, these psychic conditions correspond to the character of awareness, what Plato here calls the appearance. Thus, since, according to the Illusion Argument, calm appears pleasant, the character of awareness of pseudo-pleasure will also be a form of *kinêsis*; that is, it will be a psychic change.[4] It is in the True Filling Argument that Socrates suggests that pleasure involves filling. This is what pseudo-pleasure lacks: the replenishment. For convenience, I will refer to this as the *core aspect* of pleasure. I have suggested that in the case of appetitive pleasure, the replenishment is somatic or corporeal or physiological – all equivalent terms here – whereas in the case of spirited and rational pleasure it is psychic. Since in the Illusion Argument Socrates has bodily pleasures in mind, the core aspect is somatic replenishment.

Let us focus now on the appearance aspect of pleasure and pseudo-pleasure. In speaking of the appearance as a psychic change, we are speaking of it in terms at least consonant with those used to describe physical or concrete objects. But these are not the only terms in which Plato speaks of the appearance. Indeed, the word "appearance" (*phaino-menon*) itself is not a physicalistic term, but a subjective psychological or phenomenological one. Insofar as the appearance is pleasant, it is reasonable to understand the appearance of pleasure or pseudo-pleasure to be the pleasantness of pleasure. Indeed, I think that pleasantness is constitutive of the appearance. However, below I will suggest that this does not exhaust the appearance aspect. Moreover, it is unclear what the pleasantness of pleasure or pseudo-pleasure is.

Is the pleasantness, for instance, a feeling? Is it a sensation? For the sake of analyzing Plato's conception of pleasure here, I propose to take the words "feeling" and "sensation" to have different meanings. I will take the word "feeling" to refer to a certain kind of subjective quality. Contemporary philosophers also use the Latin term "*quale.*" A *quale* is what it is like for the subject of experience or awareness to experience or undergo

---

[4] This is also the reason that the condition of calm here cannot be genuine calm. If it were genuine calm, it would not have the misleading appearance of pleasure. Granted this, for the sake of simplicity, I will hereafter refer (loosely) to calm.

something. For example, one may speak of the *quale* of an itch or the *quale* of the taste of chocolate. The sense of "feeling" on which I am relying is that of a particular kind of *quale*. For example, contrast the experience of placing one's hand over a fire with looking at the flame. In each case, there is something it is like to have that experience. So there are visual and tactile subjective qualities or *qualia* (plural of "*quale*"). However, whereas it sounds right to say that the tactile perception entails a feeling of a kind, specifically a feeling of warmth, it does not sound right to say that the visual perception entails a feeling, say, a feeling of yellow or a feeling of brightness. There is, I take it, no visual feeling per se of seeing a fire. As far as forms of exteroception are concerned, feelings seem to be limited to tactile perception. Feelings also seem to be associated with forms of proprioception. Consider, for example, feeling nauseated, ticklish, bloated, sore in one's throat, vertiginous.

Like "feeling," the word "sensation" is and has been used by philosophers in various ways. In one sense of "sensation," "sensation" is equivalent to "feeling." However, I am drawing on the sense of "sensation" that entails the sensing of something. As such, I am taking sensations to be sensings and perceptions. Sensing is information acquisition or gathering. In contrast, "feeling" in the sense I am employing it, that is, conceived simply as a kind of *quale*, does not entail the sensing of something.

Granted this, we can distinguish forms of sensing that have feelings from those that do not. For example, seeing is a form of sensing; but as I suggested, although seeing has distinctive *qualia*, it does not involve feeling. Thus, seeing is to be contrasted with forms of sensation that have feeling, namely, touch. Consequently, I will refer to felt and unfelt sensations.

Finally, let us also assume that in the case of felt sensations, the feeling and sensing are related in the following way: the mode of sensing is a feeling. In order to understand the claim that the mode of sensing, in the case of felt sensation, is a feeling, consider the distinction between sensing the presence of, say, a flower by means of sight versus by means of smell versus by means of touch. In each case, a sensing of the flower occurs. However, in each case, the mode or manner of sensing differs. That is, the way or mode or modality in which the sensing occurs differs. In one case the sense-modality is visual, in another olfactory, in another tactile. In the case of tactile sensing, touch itself entails feeling. Thus, touch is a form of felt sensation.

Given the preceding, we can now ask whether for Plato here in *Republic* 9 the appearance or pleasantness of pleasure is a felt sensation, an unfelt sensation, or merely a feeling. Plato takes the appearance of pleasure or pseudo-pleasure to be a sensing of something. In the case of genuine pleasure, the appearance entails a sensing of the replenishment. In the case of pseudo-pleasure, it entails a mis-sensing, that is, a gathering of misinformation. It is less clear whether Plato takes the appearance to have a particular feeling. Some evidence that he does comes from the fact that in certain passages Socrates refers to pleasures and pseudo-pleasures using qualitative terms such as "intense" (*sphodron*) and "robust" (*megethos*).[5] For example, in one passage – which we will discuss again later and more fully – Socrates says: "The pleasures of smell are especially good examples to note, for they suddenly become robust" (584b). But this is compatible with the view that some pleasures, which are not robust or intense, do not entail feelings. One reason to think that Plato takes all pleasures to have feelings is that a pleasure without feeling would, at least subjectively, seem to be a state of calm.[6]

Assuming tentatively, then, that the appearance aspect of pleasure or pseudo-pleasure entails feeling, I want to distinguish this sort of feeling from other kinds of feeling. For example, the feeling of heat may be pleasant. But I want to contrast the feeling of pleasure with the feeling of heat. I will refer to the former as *hedonic feeling*. Again, consider that the feeling of heat may, on certain occasions, be painful. Again, I want to contrast the feeling of pain with the feeling of heat. I will refer to the former as *algesic feeling*. I now want to subsume hedonic and algesic feelings under a common class, which I will call the class of *affect*. Note that I am using the word "affect" in the sense that psychologists use it, not in the sense of "affection" as in "*pathêma*" from Chapter 4 – and regardless of the fact that affective feelings are affections, that is, things that one undergoes. Accordingly, I will say that hedonic and algesic feelings are *affective feelings*. So I want to contrast affective feelings with other sorts of feeling such as the feelings of warmth, coldness, nausea, being tickled, and so forth. I will not attempt to classify or define this other large species of feeling beyond simply calling it non-affective. Granted this, consider again that, for example, feelings of warmth or coldness can be pleasant or painful. Thus, affective and non-affective feelings can concur. Without using these terms, I discussed the physiological explanation for the concurrence of affective and non-affective feelings as well as affective feelings and unfelt sensations at the end of Chapter 4. Finally, it will also be convenient to include calm

---

[5] Note that the term "*megethos*" needn't be used in a qualitative sense. It can just refer to size or largeness. But in this context, I interpret it to mean "robust."

[6] It should, however, also be borne in mind that there is no generic Greek word for "feeling."

(or, equivalently, the neutral state) within the class of affect. I do not assume that calm is an affective feeling, for I do not assume that calm has a feeling aspect. At least, I assume that Plato would deny that calm has a feeling aspect.

In short, then, in the context of the *Republic* 9 argument, I am suggesting that sensation and feeling are components of the appearance aspect of pleasure or pseudo-pleasure. Moreover, the sensing of the replenishment or the pseudo-sensing of calm as pleasant occurs in the mode of hedonic feeling, which is to say, in the affective mode. But sensation and feeling do not exhaust the appearance aspect of pleasure or pseudo-pleasure. The appearance aspect also has a doxastic component. By "doxastic component" I mean a "belief component"; the Greek word for "belief" is "*doxa*." Precisely what the content of this belief is, however, is unclear. For example, it could be the reflexive belief that one is experiencing pleasure; it could be the existential belief that pleasure is occurring; it could be the demonstrative belief that this is pleasure; or it could be the run-of-the-mill predicative belief that some object or activity, for example, the wine one is drinking, is pleasant. Unfortunately, Socrates does not specify what the doxastic content of a hedonic appearance is. For convenience, let us assume that the doxastic component of the appearance is the reflexive belief that one is experiencing pleasure.

In considering the doxastic component, it may be natural to think that this component *derives* from the felt sensation. That is, one senses replenishment or calm in the hedonic mode, and on the basis of the sensation one forms the belief that one is experiencing pleasure. There is, however, no evidence that Socrates conceives of the relation between the sensation, feeling, and doxastic components in this way in *Republic.*[7] In fact, there is evidence that he does not think of the relation of the doxastic component to the sensation and feeling components as derived. I will not discuss that evidence here. Suffice it to say that the appearance aspect of pleasure or pseudo-pleasure is a complex of these three components: sensation, feeling, and believing.

The view that the appearance of pleasure or pseudo-pleasure has a doxastic as well as a feeling and sensation component is significant,

---

[7] Indeed, in the discussion of the role of the various parts of the soul in sense-perceptual pleasure, I suggested that the appetitive soul is the principal site of awareness or experience of sense-perceptual pleasure and that the rational soul is the site of sense-perceptual judgment. However, this distinction between perceptual judgment and, as we may call it, bare perception is a development in Plato's thinking. It is not present in *Republic*, but is first conveyed in the later dialogue *Theaetetus.*

especially given Socrates' view that there are true and untrue pleasures. As we have seen, the Illusion Argument introduces the idea that there are illusory pleasures, and an illusory pleasure is an untrue pleasure. The question is: In what sense is the illusory pleasure untrue? There are at least two options: ontological and representational. I will use some examples to explain the difference between ontological and representational truth-conceptions.

I begin with the ontological conception of truth. Consider fool's gold. Fool's gold is not true gold. It has the appearance of true or genuine gold, but it lacks the chemical composition of true gold. Thus, fool's gold is pseudo-gold. Illusory pleasure seems untrue in just this sense: it has the appearance of genuine or true pleasure, the pleasantness of genuine pleasure, but it lacks what I have called the core aspect of genuine pleasure, that is, the replenishment. The core aspect is here analogous to the right chemical composition. In these cases, I speak of the operative truth-conception as ontological. Fool's gold and illusory pleasure are simply not gold or pleasure; they are not the real things.

Contrast this with the representational conception of truth. Take the example of belief, for instance, the belief that Santiago is the capital of Peru. The belief is untrue or false, since Lima is the capital of Peru. The falsity or untruth of the belief that Santiago is the capital of Peru is not a function of the belief's lacking some component or aspect, core or otherwise; it is a function of a lack of correspondence of the content of the belief with the world. Accordingly, if the appearance aspect of pseudo-pleasure has a doxastic component that is untrue, then it is untrue in the way that a belief is untrue, not in the way that fool's gold is untrue. The former sort of truth-value is representational.[8] It is a matter of accurately or inaccurately representing the world. The latter is, again, ontological. We said that fool's gold is not really gold; but an untrue belief really is a belief.[9]

It seems, then, that the untruth of the illusory pleasure may be explicable in two ways: in terms of what it is and in terms of what it represents. But the situation is still more complex. Why assume that it is only the doxastic component of the appearance that is responsible for the untruth of the pseudo-pleasure? The sensation may also be responsible. Sensation, we said, entails information gathering. In the case of pleasure, this

---

[8] Note that by "truth-value" is meant the property of being either true or untrue/false.

[9] Above I had mentioned that Plato evinces a preference for distinguishing the terms "false" and "untrue." This preference can now be explained. Although Plato's language is not completely consistent, he prefers the term "untrue" (*ouk alêthes*) for ontological truth-value and "false" (*pseudes*) for representational truth-value.

information gathering occurs in the modality of hedonic feeling. Thus, it could be that sensation in the hedonic mode correctly or incorrectly indicates the occurrence of pleasure. If this is correct, then we ought to draw a distinction between two kinds of representation. The distinction turns precisely on two kinds of representational content. Doxastic content, the content of belief, is linguistic. The content of sensation in the hedonic mode is feeling, which is not linguistic. Thus, we might speak of linguistic and non-linguistic representation. A pleasant appearance may be representationally true or untrue in either or both ways.

The difficulty here is that although Socrates' treatment of the appearance aspect of pleasure includes sensation, feeling, and doxastic components, he does not carefully distinguish these from one another. Consequently, he does not carefully distinguish that in virtue of which the appearance aspect is true or untrue. The problem is further compounded by the fact that Socrates does not clearly distinguish representational and ontological truth-conceptions in *Republic*, let alone different sub-kinds of these kinds of truth-conception. Plato becomes more aware of these distinctions in his later works, in particular *Theaetetus*, *Sophist*, and *Philebus*. For now, let this suffice for an account of pseudo-pleasures that are analogous to the illusions of shadow-painting in the Illusion Argument of *Republic* 9.

MORE AND LESS TRUE PLEASURES IN 'REPUBLIC' 9: THE TRUE FILLING ARGUMENT

To a large extent, the function of the Illusion Argument may be viewed as critical. Its emphasis is on what is not pleasure and so on what pleasure is not. In contrast, the function of the True Filling Argument can be viewed as constructive: to clarify what pleasure is. The True Filling Argument distinguishes different grades of true pleasure. In this context, the ontological conception of truth is operative. That is to say, more and less true pleasure is equivalent to more and less real pleasure. Precisely, Socrates distinguishes three grades of true or real pleasure: appetitive, spirited, and rational pleasure. These three grades correlate with the three parts of the soul.

Granted the trifold distinction among pleasures, the argument actually focuses on the contrast between two kinds of pleasure, appetitive and rational, and accordingly on appetitive and rational filling. Socrates argues that rational filling is truer than appetitive filling. Thus, rational pleasure is truer than appetitive pleasure. Why does Socrates think that some pleasures involve truer fillings than others? In particular, why does Socrates think that rational filling is truer than appetitive filling?

The details of Socrates' conception of more and less true fillings are rather metaphysically extravagant, but this should not obscure the fact that a mundane conception of more and less true fillings informs his account. For example, assume that a patient visits a dentist to have a cavity filled. Typically dentists completely fill cavities. But a cavity that is not completely filled may be conceived as not truly filled. Assume, further, that dentists may fill cavities with various substances and that some substances are more durable than others. In that case, a cavity might be characterized as more or less truly filled depending on whether the filling-substance was more or less durable. Admittedly, in this case it is more natural to say that the cavity has been more or less completely repaired or that the tooth has been more or less perfectly restored. But Socrates' conception of filling seems to rely on concepts such as repair, remedy, or restoration. In other words, Socrates' conception of filling does not merely entail the occupation of space, but the completion or fulfillment of something lacking.

Finally, assume that a patient might suffer from such bad tooth decay that despite the intrinsic durability of a given filling-substance, the filling will nevertheless be unstable. In that case, we might say that it is impossible to truly repair the cavity or restore the tooth. The second and third of these mundane conceptions of true filling, repair, or restoration operate within Socrates' True Filling Argument.

As I have mentioned, in his argument Socrates focuses on the contrast between appetitive, more specifically nutritional, fillings and psychic, more specifically rational, fillings. He maintains that the quality of the filling is a function of both the contents that fill a container and the container that is filled. In the case of nutritional filling, the body is the container and nutriment or alimentation is the content. Socrates maintains that the body and its nutriment are relatively untrue. They are untrue insofar as they are unstable and so short-lived. In the case of psychic and specifically rational filling, the soul is the container and knowledge is the content. Socrates maintains that the soul and knowledge are relatively true. They are true insofar as they are stable. Consequently, the relative truths of these species of filling are conceived as functions of the containers and contents.

Granted this, why are truth and untruth here associated with stability and instability? Again, the operative truth-conception is ontological. So a thing is true insofar as it is real. Now, a thing is real to the extent that it exists. Stable things perdure, that is, their existence persists. Unstable things do not perdure. They decompose or are destroyed. Accordingly,

Plato implicitly reasons as follows: the more stable a thing is, the more it perdures, the more it exists, the more it is real, the more it is (ontologically) true. This, at any rate, appears to be Plato's conception of ontological truth and reality as gradable.

As we saw in *Timaeus*, Plato thinks that the soul, at least the rational part of the soul, is immortal. Accordingly, let us grant him that the (rational part of the) soul and knowledge are more stable than the body and its nutriment and that filling the rational soul with knowledge is a more stable filling than filling the body with nutriment. I think, however, that the inference from these claims to the claim that rational filling is truer than appetitive filling is based on a mistake. The central assumption in the True Filling Argument is that true replenishment requires the stability of the container and content. A container is more or less filled depending on whether the filling content completely fills the deficit. In other words, a true filling is a matter of the relation between the quantity of the deficit of the container and the quantity of the filling content, not the durability of either the container or content.

Granted this, one might charitably suggest that although Plato speaks of filling or replenishment, he has the concept of restoration in mind. True restoration seems to require durability and stability. For example, if one glued two broken cups with two different adhesives and one cup came unglued, while the other held, it would be correct to say that the one cup had been more truly restored than the other. But this charitable move does not save the True Filling argument. In restoration, extent of durability or stability is relative to the kind of entity restored. Compare restoring a torn paper cup and restoring a broken ceramic cup. A truly restored paper cup should be as durable and stable as an intact paper cup, while a truly restored ceramic cup should be as durable and stable as an intact ceramic cup. Thus, the fact that the properly restored ceramic cup is far more durable or stable than the properly restored paper cup in no way undermines the fact that the paper cup is truly restored.

Plato misses this point. Instead, in view of the fact that the soul and its proper content, knowledge, are immortal and immutable respectively, whereas the body and its proper content are mortal and mutable, he is misled to think that what makes rational filling or restoration truer than appetitive filling or restoration is its absolute stability or durability. Thus, he falsely claims that that which is filled with what is more stable is more truly filled. The mistake is fatal to the True Filling Argument, for Plato argues that truer pleasure entails truer filling and that rational filling is truer than appetitive filling.

Let me return now to the question of the truth-conception operative in the True Filling Argument. As I have suggested, the truth-conception is ontological, not representational. A container that is truly filled is a container that is really and properly filled. Such filling does not represent anything, accurately or inaccurately. Interestingly, however, this ontological truth-conception is not precisely the ontological truth-conception that we encountered in the Illusion Argument. As we have also seen, the ontological truth-conception we encountered in the True Filling Argument is gradable. That is to say, there are more and less true fillings and so pleasures. Appetitive filling is less (ontologically) true than rational filling; rational filling is (ontologically) truer than appetitive filling. In contrast, an illusory pleasure is not less (ontologically) true than a genuine pleasure. This is because an illusory pleasure doesn't have any degree of (ontological) truth at all. An illusory pleasure is simply untrue. Likewise, fool's gold is not less true gold than genuine gold. Fool's gold is simply untrue. In this case, the operative ontological truth-conceptions are not gradable. For convenience, I will distinguish these two conceptions of ontological truth by referring to the one from the Illusion Argument as *absolute* ontological truth and the one from the True Filling Argument as *gradable* ontological truth.

OLFACTORY PLEASURES AND THE ABSOLUTE/GRADABLE ONTOLOGICAL TRUTH-VALUE DISTINCTION

In Chapter 4 I referred to olfactory pleasures in several places. One was in the course of discussing sense-perceptual pleasure in *Timaeus*. Recall that Timaeus refers to olfactory pleasure to exemplify the condition where a perceived restoration is not preceded by a perceived disintegration. Timaeus does not explicitly classify such pleasures, and he passes no value judgment on them. The other place was in the course of discussing base and fine pleasures in *Hippias Major*. There I noted that the status of olfactory pleasures improves as we turn from *Hippias Major* to *Republic* 9 and *Philebus*. The shift in status derives from Plato's observation, first conveyed in *Republic* 9, that there is a distinction between pure and impure or, equivalently, unmixed and mixed pleasures. Pure or unmixed pleasures are conceived as having greater value than mixed or impure pleasures, and olfactory pleasures are pure.

The distinction of pure pleasures and of pure olfactory pleasures in particular is introduced in the Illusion Argument of *Republic* 9 in the following way. Immediately following his explanation of illusory pleasure by analogy with shadow-painting, Socrates emphasizes that some pleasures are not illusory:

Take a look at the pleasures that don't come from pains so that you won't think in their case also that it is the nature of pleasure to be the cessation of pain ... The pleasures of smell are especially good examples to note, for they suddenly become robust without being preceded by pain; and when they cease, they leave no pain behind ... Then no one persuade us that pure (*kathara*) pleasure is relief from pain. (584b)

Socrates' contrast here between pure and impure pleasure correlates with the distinction between true and untrue pleasure. Pure pleasures are true; impure pleasures are untrue. But this correlation is complicated in two respects. First, observe that impure pleasure is not true pleasure that is sequentially mixed with true pain; rather, it is true pain mixed with the core aspect of calm and the appearance aspect of pleasure. Other types of mixed pleasure are at least theoretically possible. Indeed, as we will see in our discussion of *Philebus*, Plato proposes that there are several kinds of mixed pleasure. Second, recall that insofar as they are ontologically untrue, illusory pleasures are absolutely (rather than gradably) ontologically untrue. Accordingly, true pleasures are absolutely ontologically true. However, purity is gradable. For example, a truer or purer red is a red with less admixture of, say, blue or green. Likewise, a truer or purer Irish Setter is a more pure-bred Irish Setter. Thus, the concept of purity would be more appropriately applied in the context of gradable ontological truth and untruth than absolute ontological truth and untruth. The fact that Plato has Socrates employ the concept of purity in the context of a discussion of genuine and pseudo-pleasures is a further indication of the fact that throughout the Illusion and True Filling Arguments he lacks a firm theoretical grasp of the various truth-conceptions implicitly operating. As we will see, Plato comes more carefully to grips with this matter in *Philebus* as well.

INTRODUCTION TO THE TREATMENT
OF PLEASURE IN 'PHILEBUS'

The treatment of pleasure in *Philebus* is by far Plato's most elaborate. Indeed, it is the most elaborate ancient treatment of pleasure we have. The context of the treatment is a discussion of what constitutes the good life for humans. Initially Socrates proposes two candidates: a life of knowledge and a life of pleasure. At least in this basic and general way, the design of the dialogue is vaguely reminiscent of the treatments of the two-paths theme from Prodicus' *Choice of Heracles* and Hesiod's *Works and Days*.

Quickly, however, Socrates determines that neither the life of knowledge nor the life of pleasure can constitute the good life for humans. He claims that a life solely consisting of pleasure, that is, without any knowledge, more befits a primitive sea creature than a human. Likewise, a life solely consisting of knowledge, that is, without pleasure, more befits a god than a human. Consequently, Socrates suggests that the good human life consists of a mixture of pleasure and knowledge. Given this, the dialogue's leading question shifts to whether, relative to the mixed life, the life purely of knowledge or the life purely of pleasure is better. In other words, the question shifts to which life deserves second place in the competition for the best human life.

How is the competition for second place to be decided? The method Socrates employs is very puzzling. When the competition is originally conceived as being for first place, Socrates suggests that his principal interlocutor Protarchus and he must determine what pleasure and knowledge are. Socrates' idea seems to be this. Assume that one has clarified a set of conditions that anything that constitutes the human good must satisfy. In that case, if one well understands what some other thing, say, knowledge or pleasure, is in its own right, then one can determine whether knowledge or pleasure satisfies the conditions and thus whether knowledge or pleasure is the human good. Granted this, Socrates claims that in order to understand what pleasure and knowledge are, it is necessary to clarify their kinds and sub-kinds, indeed, to determine an exhaustive taxonomy of them. This is an interesting claim. It is by no means obvious why one should think that in order to come to know something, one must come to understand its various kinds and sub-kinds exhaustively. I will not explore this interesting point further.

When the competition shifts to the question of whether pleasure or knowledge deserves second place, however, Socrates claims that no such taxonomy is needed. On the other hand, Socrates does proceed to discuss pleasure and knowledge successively, and in the course of doing so he distinguishes various kinds and sub-kinds of each. Ostensibly, Socrates is doing precisely what he said need not be done. However, the objective of the ensuing distinctions of kinds and sub-kinds is not to achieve complete taxonomies of pleasure and knowledge. Instead, it is limited to and organized by an interest in clarifying the purest kinds of pleasure and knowledge respectively. This point is made explicit when Socrates begins his taxonomy of knowledge:

> Now, let us not subject pleasure to every possible test, while treating reason and knowledge gingerly. Let us rather strike them valiantly all around to see if there is some fault anywhere so that we learn what is by nature purest in them. And seeing this, we can use the truest parts of these, as well as of pleasure, to make our joint decision. (55c)

Since the Greek word for "pure" is "*katharon,*" I will for convenience refer to the alternative, incomplete taxonomic procedure that Socrates employs as *cathartic taxonomy.*[10]

It is questionable how the objective of cathartic taxonomy is achievable independently of achieving a complete taxonomy. This is another interesting question that I must table here. I will proceed on the assumption that the objective of cathartic taxonomy is possible independently of achieving a complete taxonomy. The upshot, then, is that Socrates thinks he can answer the question whether pleasure or knowledge deserves second place relative to the mixed good life by determining what pleasure and knowledge are in their purest forms. We must bear the motives of cathartic taxonomy in mind as we now examine the various kinds and sub-kinds of pleasure that Socrates proceeds to distinguish.

To anticipate, we will find that Socrates, with the help of Protarchus, distinguishes eleven or rather ten kinds of pleasure. I say "eleven or rather ten" because some time after discussing the second kind, which he originally construes as pure, Socrates returns to it and recasts it as impure. Ultimately, then, Socrates distinguishes ten kinds of pleasure. The first seven of these are impure, false, or untrue. The last three are pure.

THE FIRST TWO KINDS OF PLEASURE IN 'PHILEBUS'

The first kind of pleasure with which Socrates begins the cathartic taxonomy is a kind of bodily pleasure. Here is how Socrates describes it:

> When in us living beings harmony is dissolved, a disruption of nature and a generation of pains then occur ... But if harmony is again composed and brought back to its nature, then pleasure occurs. (31d)

[10] Evidently, then, I am using the word "cathartic" in its etymological sense and not in the related, but narrower and more familiar, psychological sense.

Socrates uses four examples to illustrate this description:

Hunger, I take it, is a case of disintegration and pain ... And eating, the corresponding refilling, is a pleasure. ... Once again, thirst is a destruction and pain, while the process that fills what is dried out with liquid is pleasure. And further the unnatural separation and dissolution, the affection caused by heat, is pain, while the natural restoration of cooling down is pleasure ... And the unnatural coagulation of fluids in an animal through freezing is pain, while the natural process of their dissolution or redistribution is pleasure. (31e–32b)

Observe that the first two examples are familiar from *Gorgias* and *Republic* 9, while the last two are relatively new. Notice that the last two are not expressed in terms of depletion and replenishment. Accordingly, here, as in *Timaeus*, and in contrast to *Republic* 9 and *Gorgias*, the replenishment and depletion theory has been supplanted by a restoration and destruction theory. Furthermore, as in *Timaeus*, Socrates proceeds to clarify that only those restorations robust enough to affect the soul constitute pleasure. Although Socrates explicitly identifies this first kind of pleasure as a "kind" (*eidos*), he does not give it a name. In turning from it to a second kind, however, he speaks of the second as "pleasure that the soul experiences without the body" (34c). Accordingly, Socrates surely conceives the first kind as pleasure that the soul experiences with the body. We might then simply refer to it as bodily pleasure on the grounds that it requires bodily restoration. Moreover, the bodily pleasure described here appears to encompass both brute pleasure (as in pleasure of satisfying hunger and thirst) and sense-perceptual pleasure (as in pleasure of warmth) – although Socrates does not explicitly note this. It is not correct, however, to view this first kind of pleasure simply as bodily pleasure. More precisely, it is a kind of bodily pleasure. I will clarify why once we have discussed the second kind of pleasure.

Following his account of the first kind of pleasure, Socrates turns to "pleasure that the soul experiences without the body." Given how common the distinction between body and soul is in Plato's writings, Socrates' description here might lead one to expect his second kind of pleasure simply to be psychic pleasure and thus for the initial steps in the cathartic taxonomy to involve a distinction between somatic and psychic kinds of pleasure. But that is not how the taxonomy proceeds. As I just suggested – although as yet without explaining why – the first kind of pleasure is a kind of bodily pleasure. Likewise, the second kind of pleasure is a kind of psychic pleasure:

Now accept that the anticipation by the soul itself of these two types of experience [namely, the kind of bodily pleasure or pain just described], the hope before the actual pleasure will be pleasant and comforting, while the expectation of pain will be frightening and painful. (32b–c)

Socrates' interlocutor Protarchus responds:

This turns out then to be a different kind (*eidos*) of pleasure and pain, namely, the expectation that the soul experiences by itself, without the body. (32c)

And Socrates confirms that Protarchus' "assumption is correct" (32c). Consequently, Socrates' second kind of pleasure is anticipatory pleasure – more precisely, it is a kind of anticipatory pleasure. There are many kinds of pleasure one can anticipate. For example, one can anticipate the pleasure of a philosophical lecture; one can anticipate the pleasure of being honored at an award ceremony. In the terms of *Republic* 9's tripartition of pleasures, the former is an anticipatory pleasure of a rational pleasure; the latter is an anticipatory pleasure of a spirited pleasure. Here in *Philebus* Socrates distinguishes anticipatory pleasure of a kind of bodily pleasure.

Why does Socrates move from a kind of bodily pleasure to anticipatory pleasure of a kind of bodily pleasure? Anticipatory pleasure of a kind of bodily pleasure *depends upon* the kind of bodily pleasure. Socrates takes pains to make this clear. He says:

As for the other kind of pleasure, which we said belongs to the soul itself, it depends entirely on memory. (33c)

That is, the anticipatory pleasure depends upon memory of past occasions of kinds of bodily pleasure. So the move from a kind of bodily pleasure to anticipatory pleasure of a kind of bodily pleasure is a move from what may be called an independent to a dependent kind of pleasure.

This much is clear. Yet it is not clear why Plato chose to make the cathartic taxonomy proceed in this way. One possible reason is that the cathartic taxonomy begins with what Plato takes to be the most basic or primitive kind of pleasure. This at least is consistent with the examples he uses. All of these pertain to the basic physiological functions of a living creature. In contrast, visual or auditory pleasures – which are also bodily pleasures, but which are not or at least not obviously required for survival – are not mentioned. This cannot be the whole story, however. The problem is that it is unclear how the kind of bodily pleasure at issue and the anticipatory pleasure of this kind of bodily pleasure relate to purity and impurity. In other words, it is unclear, relative to the aims of a cathartic taxonomy, what the function is of the introduction of the kind of bodily pleasure and anticipatory pleasure of this kind of bodily pleasure. The answer is supplied by a claim Socrates makes immediately after he introduces anticipatory pleasure of the kind of bodily pleasure:

In both of these cases [that is, in the cases of anticipatory pleasure of the kind of bodily pleasure and anticipatory pain of the kind of bodily pain], as I see it at least, pleasure and pain will arise pure and unmixed with each other. (32c)

In light of this claim, we can still maintain that Socrates begins the cathartic taxonomy with a certain kind of bodily pleasure because it is the most primitive kind. But he moves to the particular kind of anticipatory pleasure in order to contrast this with the former. The particular kind of anticipatory pleasure is pure – but the particular kind of bodily pleasure is not: it is preceded by a correlative bodily pain. For example, the pleasure of replenishing a nutritional lack depends upon the pain of the antecedent nutritional depletion. If the antecedent nutritional depletion were too slight to yield a pain of hunger, then, I take it, a consequent replenishment would also be too slight to be pleasant. Thus, as I suggested, Socrates does not begin the cathartic taxonomy simply with bodily pleasure. He begins with a kind of bodily pleasure. This kind is distinctive in that it is impure. It is impure because it is preceded by bodily pain. Contrast this with the pure olfactory pleasure we encountered in *Republic* 9. In that case, the olfactory pleasure is not preceded by an olfactory pain. The depletion of the olfactory faculty is subtle and gradual and thus does not register psychically. But the replenishment of the olfactory faculty is sudden and robust and thus does register psychically and thus is a pleasure. Finally, let me emphasize that impurity and mixture in these contexts are conceived as sequential, not simultaneous. Pain precedes pleasure or vice versa. The emphasis is significant for two reasons. One is that it is perhaps natural to think of mixture in terms of simultaneity. However, we have seen in *Republic* 9 that this is not naturally or necessarily the way Plato conceives of mixture. The other reason is that later in *Philebus* Socrates examines mixed pleasures in which pleasure and pain do occur simultaneously. For convenience, I will refer to the two kinds of mixture as *sequential* and *simultaneous* respectively.

Granted this, in the case of the anticipatory pleasure, Socrates is claiming that there is no correlative, antecedent anticipatory pain. For example, assume one is hungry and thus experiences a bodily pain (precisely a sequentially impure or mixed bodily pain). One can take pleasure in anticipating the bodily pleasure of satisfying hunger by eating. But this anticipatory pleasure is not or is not necessarily – Socrates is assuming – preceded by a correlative anticipatory pain.[11] Thus, it is a sequentially pure or unmixed pleasure.

In light of the preceding we can now also clarify that the kind of bodily pleasure with which Socrates begins the cathartic taxonomy is *sequentially mixed bodily pleasure*. It is also interesting to note that this kind of bodily pleasure cuts across the distinction we drew in *Timaeus* between brute or somatic, but non-sense-perceptual, pleasure, on the one hand, and sense-perceptual pleasure, on the other. Evidently, the taxonomic interests motivating the discussion in *Philebus* differ from those in *Timaeus*.

Before we proceed to the next stage of the cathartic taxonomy, let me also emphasize that we have not explained what makes the anticipatory pleasure a pleasure. We have merely admitted it as a pleasure. Indeed, Socrates does not specify what makes it a pleasure. His main interest, evidently, is to contrast it as a pure pleasure with the impure bodily pleasure on which it depends. Indeed, nowhere in *Philebus* does Socrates address the question what makes this kind of anticipatory pleasure a pleasure.

FALSE PLEASURE IN 'PHILEBUS': KIND I

Let us move on to the next stage of the discussion. Socrates proceeds to argue that there are true and false anticipatory pleasures.[12] There are two questions to consider here: How does Socrates defend this view? And what is the function of the introduction of the view relative to the aims of the cathartic taxonomy? We will address these questions in the order presented.

A simple explanation of how there can be true and false anticipatory pleasures is this. Assume you expect to win a prize. That is, you believe that you are going to win a prize. Assume further that you take pleasure in this belief and expectation. If the belief is true, then your anticipatory pleasure is true; if the belief is false, then your anticipatory pleasure is false. Indeed – simplifying considerably – this is what Socrates proceeds to argue. However, there is an obvious objection to this view: it is not the pleasure that is true or false, but the belief on which it depends. Indeed, Socrates' interlocutor Protarchus criticizes Socrates in just this way:

SO: As to pleasure, it certainly often seems to arise in us not with a correct, but a false belief.
PR: Of course – but what we call false in this case at that point is the belief, Socrates. Nobody would dream of calling the pleasure itself false. (37e–38a)

---

[11] Note that this is compatible with there being an unfelt emotional lack.
[12] 36c–40e.

Consequently, the challenge for Socrates is to show that although true and false anticipatory pleasures depend upon true and false beliefs, anticipatory pleasure itself is true and false.

Socrates attempts to meet the challenge in the following way. He claims that the soul contains something like a scribe and a painter. That is, Socrates distinguishes two psychological faculties and characterizes these metaphorically in terms of writing and painting. The scribe creates psychic or mental inscriptions. The painter creates psychic or mental depictions.[13] In illustrating how these distinctions pertain to anticipatory pleasure, Socrates uses the following example. Assume a man believes he is going to acquire some wealth and intends to use the wealth to indulge, let us say, in an expensive meal. The very condition of holding this belief entails something like a psychological inscription whose content is that the man is going to come into a great deal of wealth and indulge in an expensive meal. On the basis of this inscription, the painter in the soul then depicts the man indulging in the expensive meal.

In defense of his view that the anticipatory pleasure can be true or false, Socrates maintains that the anticipatory pleasure may be taken not in the belief, but in the depiction of the man indulging in the meal. Moreover, Socrates maintains that the depiction in which the pleasure is taken has truth-value, precisely, truth-value derived from the truth-value of the inscription on which it is based.[14]

The success of Socrates' argument depends on at least four things: the distinguishability of hedonic object (the depiction) from the doxastic object (the inscription); the depiction's being a constituent rather than a cause of the anticipatory pleasure; the depiction's capacity to bear truth-value; and the capacity of the anticipatory pleasure to bear truth-value in virtue of the truth-value of the depiction in which the pleasure is taken. I'll take these topics in order.

Clearly we can take pleasure in things we do not believe in. We do this, for example, when we take pleasure in a fantasy. In addition, there seems to be a difference between taking pleasure in a non-imagistic or non-pictorial object and taking pleasure in the image of something. Sexual fantasies seem to be a good example of this.

---

[13] Note that Socrates' focus on visual imagery in contrast to objects related to different sense-perceptual modalities may merely be a convenience. In other words, Socrates may well concede that there is something akin to a musician in the soul, something akin to a cook, and so forth.

[14] I emphasize that Socrates does not argue that all anticipatory pleasure must be taken in imaginative objects. Presumably, he would grant that some anticipatory pleasure is taken in doxastic objects. He is simply arguing that anticipatory pleasure can be taken in imaginative objects and that these are distinct from doxastic objects.

The second topic concerns the idea that the depiction is partly constitutive of the anticipatory pleasure. Consider a belief such as that Omaha is the capital of Nebraska. We can distinguish the object of the belief, which is that Omaha is the capital of Nebraska, from the attitude taken toward it, that is, the believing. Contrast this attitude with, for example, *wondering* whether or *entertaining the possibility* that Omaha is the capital of Nebraska. Although in the case of belief we can distinguish the object from the attitude taken toward it, there can be no belief without an object. Socrates clearly holds the same view with respect to anticipatory pleasure. That is, he takes it to be an attitude toward an object, and he thinks that there cannot be that particular hedonic attitude without an appropriate object. One might think, however, that the pleasure is not an attitude taken toward the object, but rather an effect caused by the envisioning or imagining. Thus, as I have said, Socrates needs to show that the depiction is partly constitutive of the pleasure, in the way doxastic objects are partly constitutive of belief (where "belief" is here understood as a complex of the attitude of believing and that which is believed). I will not attempt to defend Socrates' position here. I merely note that this aspect of his account requires more defense.

The third topic concerns the fact that the depiction must have truth-value. The inscription and the depiction are psychic, that is, mental representations. Accordingly, with respect to their bearing truth-value, the operative truth-conception is representational, not ontological. Granting this, it must also be recognized that the inscription and depiction represent in different ways. Here it may help to consider the concept of a representational *vehicle* discussed by the contemporary philosopher of mind Tim Crane:

Consider a road sign with a schematic picture in a red triangle of two children holding hands. The message this sign conveys is: "Beware! Children crossing!" Compare this with a verbal sign that says in English: "Beware! Children crossing!" These two signs express the same message, but in very different ways. I'll call this sort of difference in the way a message can be stored a difference in the *vehicle* of representation ... The most obvious distinction between vehicles of representation is that which can be made between sentences and pictures.[15]

Glossing "message" here by "content" and assuming that the contents of the inscription and depiction in Socrates' account are the same or at least overlapping, we can say that their vehicles are distinct.

---

[15] *The Mechanical Mind*, 2nd edn., Routledge, 2003, 136.

Assuming the depiction and inscription share the same truth-evaluable content, what is this shared content? Philosophers today typically take propositions to be the principal bearers of truth-value. Here a proposition is understood to be an abstract entity. Propositions are abstract because, among other reasons, multiple people may have attitudes toward the same content, for example, two people may believe that Omaha is the capital of Nebraska. Propositions are typically said to be representable as sentences or that-clauses, for example, "Omaha is the capital of Nebraska" or "that Omaha is the capital of Nebraska." In light of Socrates' argument, then, we would also have to admit that propositions may be representable pictorially or imagistically.

Accordingly, one might suggest that the depiction shares propositional content with inscription. Thus, the depiction bears truth-value in virtue of the proposition that it depicts. The problem with this interpretation is just that it requires Socrates' commitment to propositions, when there is no discussion of any such thing in the text. It is, at least, more faithful to the text to treat inscriptions and depictions as the basic truth-evaluable entities in Socrates' account. In that case, we should say simply that Socrates holds that a truth-evaluable inscription may be depicted and that the depiction then bears the truth-value of the inscription. Now, if the only defensible way in which the depiction of an inscription can bear the truth-value of the inscription is if the depiction depicts the proposition borne by the inscription, then Socrates' account would have to be regarded as inadequate precisely because it would fail to theorize and make explicit the role of propositions. So this is another open question in the interpretation and evaluation of Socrates' account.[16]

Assuming the depiction bears truth-value in virtue of its derivation from the inscription, we come to our fourth topic: how anticipatory pleasure derives truth-value from the truth-value of its object. It seems that Socrates is tacitly committed to a principle such as this: a psychological state that is a complex of a psychological attitude and a truth-evaluable object inherits the truth-value of its object. Indeed, Socrates' view is not just that pleasure can bear truth-value in this way, but that desire, fear, and a wide range of psychological states can:

And the same account holds in the case of fear, anger, and everything of that sort, namely, that all of them can at times be false. (40e)

---

[16] This problem here is very complex for at least the following two reasons. First, the nature of propositions is much contested in contemporary philosophy. Second, it is questionable whether Plato ever commits to the existence of propositional attitudes, in particular whether he conceives of belief or judgment as propositional. For an incisive discussion of this topic, see Paolo Crivelli, *Plato's Account of Falsehood*, Cambridge University Press, 2012, especially 3–4 and 221–260.

This is a peculiar position. Although we speak of true and false beliefs, we have noted that "belief" is ambiguous; and here we mean "true or false doxastic object or content," not "true or false complex of attitude and object." There are a few analogous cases for other psychological states such as "false hope." Again, it is the content or object of the attitude of hope that is false. Socrates' argument thus requires defense of his principle of truth-value derivation from objects to the complexes of attitude and object.[17] Once again, I note the problem, but will not pursue it further.

So much for an evaluation – albeit one with several loose ends – of Socrates' argument for the possibility of false anticipatory pleasure. Let us now consider the function of the argument relative to the aims of cathartic taxonomy. Recall that Socrates had previously distinguished sequentially mixed bodily pleasure from anticipatory pleasure of sequentially mixed bodily pleasure by describing the latter as pure. In light of this, one might think that the introduction of the possibility of false anticipatory pleasure serves to show that such pleasures may be impure. This can be so, however, only if Socrates is operating with a different or broader conception of impurity than mixture with pain, be it sequential or otherwise. Is there any reason to think that he is? I suggest that there is. However, it will be convenient to explain why this is so after we have discussed the second kind of false pleasure.

FALSE PLEASURE IN 'PHILEBUS': KIND 2

Although Socrates' first kind of false pleasure is anticipatory, there is no reason to doubt that his argument could be retooled to account for pleasures with past or present contents, for example, pleasure taken in recollecting a good meal or pleasure taken in imagining that one is presently eating a good meal.[18] Indeed, Socrates explicitly states that his defense of the possibility of falsity in the case of anticipatory pleasure of sequentially mixed bodily pleasure holds for the present and past as well as the future. As Protarchus says, "[these conditions] apply equally to all the

---

[17] One might think here that a complex would necessarily inherit the properties of its components. But consider the following counter-examples. A 2-inch line segment AB does not inherit the quantitative property of being 1-inch, although its sub-segment AC is 1-inch. Likewise, although AC is a proper part of AB, AB is not a proper part of AC. Possessing representational truth-value is not a quantitative property or a mereological property. But, again, more argument is needed to show that such truth-value is transitive from component to complex.

[18] There is, however, the following problem: it is harder to see how time is representable imagistically or pictorially.

times: past, present, and future" (39c). What seems to interest Socrates in particular is the fact that certain pleasures have representationally truth-evaluable content, that the object bearing this content is imagistic, and that the content of the imagistic object derives from the content of a doxastic object.

Immediately following his account of false pleasure kind 1, Socrates proceeds to explain a second kind of false pleasure.[19] False pleasure kind 2 is closely related to false pleasure kind 1. Consider what Socrates says at the conclusion of his account of false pleasure kind 2:

> This is the opposite of what occurred before [that is, in the case of false pleasure kind 1] ... In the former case, true and false beliefs filled up the pains and pleasures with their condition [that is, with their truth or falsity] ... But now it [that is, the truth or falsity] applies to pleasures and pains themselves. (42a–b)

In the case of false pleasure kind 2, the content of the pleasure is the source of truth-value, and doxastic content derives its truth-value from that. Here is how Socrates thinks this occurs. Recall from the discussion of *Republic* 9 my stipulative use of the adjective "affective" to refer generically to hedonic, algesic, and neutral or calm conditions. In other words, pleasure, pain, and calm or the neutral condition are all affective conditions. Granted this, there are occasions where we experience two affective conditions simultaneously. For example, one is hungry and thus experiences some brute pain, but also enjoys some anticipatory pleasure in expectation of a meal. In some such cases, Socrates suggests, the juxtaposition of the two affective conditions – in this case, the brute pain and the anticipatory pleasure – distorts at least one of the affective conditions. For example, the present pain makes the anticipatory pleasure appear lesser than it will in fact be. Socrates conceives such distortion as analogous to the way a proximate object visually appears larger than a distant one, even though they are actually the same size:

> Well, does it happen only to eyesight that seeing objects from afar or close by distorts the truth and causes false beliefs? Or does not the same thing happen also in the case of pleasure and pain? (41e–42a)

The account Socrates is offering actually conjoins two factors responsible for what may be called "affective illusions." One is the subject's spatial or temporal perspective relative to the object. In the case of visual illusions, this is a spatial perspective. In the case of affective illusions, the perspective

---

[19] 41a–42c.

is temporal. The other factor relates to the account we discussed in the Illusion Argument of *Republic* 9 where the mere juxtaposition of two affective conditions, rather than the temporal relation between them, creates affective distortion.[20] One might assume that the difference in temporal perspective would make the distant affective condition appear less pleasant or less painful. In the case of the mere juxtaposition of affective conditions, Socrates does not specify any principle concerning how distortion occurs. For example, one can imagine conditions where a sense-perceptual pain makes an imagined pleasure greater or lesser. Moreover, our ignorance here is compounded by the fact that there are two distorting factors.

For convenience, let us assume that in the example where one experiences a brute pain of hunger in conjunction with an anticipatory pleasure from expecting a meal, the brute pain heightens the imagined pleasure, that is, makes the imagined pleasure greater than the actual pleasure, when it comes to pass, will be. For convenience, let's assume we can precisely determine the quantities of pleasantness of both the imagined pleasure and the actual pleasure (that the imagined pleasure falsely represents). Let us say that the pleasantness of the imagined pleasure has the quantity m and that the actual pleasure has the quantity n. Since we have said that the imagined pleasure distorts by excess, it follows that $m > n$. So, again for convenience, let us identify the quantity of pleasantness by which the imagined pleasure distorts by excess as d. Accordingly, it follows that $m - n = d$. Socrates concludes:

But if you take that portion of the pleasures by which they appear greater . . . than they really are [$= d$] and cut it off from them as mere appearance and without real being, you will neither admit that this appearance is right nor dare to say that anything connected with this portion of pleasure . . . is right and true. (42b–c)

Socrates makes at least two points here. One is that the distorted portion is false; it corresponds to nothing. We might say that it is analogous to the empty names "Santa Claus" and "Pegasus." The other is that the imagined pleasure is false because it contains the distorted portion. In other words, the falsity of the distorted portion falsifies the imagined pleasure as a whole. Compare the way a portrait of, say, Winston Churchill with blonde hair might be said to be false in respect of the hair color, but also to falsify the portrait as a whole.[21]

---

[20] "It is because they are alternately looked at from close up or far away or simultaneously side by side . . ." (42b).

[21] Observe how this way of conceptualizing falsity is consistent with Socrates' view of anticipatory pleasure, that is, the complex of attitude and object, as falsified by the falsity of its component object.

Finally, a false imagined pleasure can cause a correspondingly false belief. For example, one who underwent the experience described in the example I have used might come to have the belief that the actual (future) pleasure would be more pleasant than in fact it will be. Thus, as Socrates said – and in precise contrast with false pleasure kind 1 – false pleasure kind 2 can fill up beliefs with their falsity.

Having discussed false pleasures kinds 1 and 2 and seen how they are related, let us now return to the question posed at the end of the preceding section. Recall that Socrates had distinguished sequentially mixed bodily pleasure from anticipatory pleasure of sequentially mixed bodily pleasure by describing the latter as pure. Consequently, one might think that the introduction of the possibility of false anticipatory pleasure serves to show that such pleasures may be impure. This can only be so, however, if Socrates is operating with a different or broader conception of impurity than mixture with pain, be it sequential or otherwise. I claimed that there is reason to think that Socrates is operating with a broader conception of purity.

Socrates seems to think that something's being false, in any sense, makes that thing impure. In other words, falsity of any kind spoils things. In this respect, purity is equivalent to freedom from taint or fault. Consider Socrates' remarks, which immediately follow the conclusion of his account of false pleasure kind 1:

SO: Well, then, do we have any other way of distinguishing between bad and good beliefs than their falsity?
PR: We have no other.
SO: Nor, I presume, will we find any other way to account for badness in the case of pleasures unless they are false. (40e)

Protarchus does not in fact agree with Socrates' last point. But that is inconsequential for my present point. My point is that in Socrates' view falsity corrupts pleasure.

Assuming, then, that the broader conception of purity at work in the cathartic taxonomy is freedom from fault or taint or corruption, we must now clarify how mixture is faulty. First, note that mixture is relative to a kind. When Socrates speaks of mixed pleasure, he means pleasure mixed specifically with pain. This is because pain and pleasure are construed as opposites or contraries. Accordingly, if, for instance, there were such a thing as mixed courage, it would be courage mixed with its opposite, cowardice. Given this, one might think that Socrates holds that something that is impure insofar as it is mixed is faulty because it is not fully realized as a member of the kind with which it is identified. For example, a mixed pleasure is faulty because it is not fully realized as a pleasure.

This proposal cannot be right, however, for it entails that pure pain is good insofar as it is purely painful and pure badness is good insofar as it is purely bad. Consequently, the operative concept of purity cannot simply be equivalent to uniformity. For example, pure pain is uniformly painful. Instead, the operative concept of purity must entail goodness. It is necessary, then, to draw a distinction between two senses of "purity." Again, in one sense "purity" is equivalent to "uniformity." But this is not the sense of "purity" Socrates is employing. In another sense, "purity" entails goodness. Both senses are familiar enough. Compare the following sentences: this jar contains pure alcohol; Mary's heart is pure. Socrates is employing the latter sense. Note that this commits Socrates to the view that pleasure itself is good. And indeed Socrates does think this. That is, insofar as pleasure is a restoration to the natural state, it is at least instrumentally good; for the natural state is intrinsically good and pleasure conduces to that.

FALSE PLEASURE IN 'PHILEBUS': KIND 3

Immediately following his account of false pleasure kind 2, Socrates says:

> Next in order we will find pleasures ... that are even falser (*pseudeis eti mallon*) than these, both [(a)] in appearance (*phainomenas*) and [(b)] in reality (*ousas*). (42c)

This passage is important; it orients us to the ensuing discussion of false pleasures. It should be interpreted in light of the following passage, which occurs at the end of Socrates' account of false pleasures:

> [I have tried to show that] there are [(c)] certain seeming (*dokousas*) pleasures, that are not pleasures in reality (*ousas*), and furthermore, that there are [(d)] other pleasures that have the appearance (*phantastheisas*) of enormous size and great variety, but which are in truth commingled with pain or respite from severe pains suffered by soul and body. (51a)

These two passages frame, by introducing (at 42c) and then recapitulating (at 51a), Socrates' account of false pleasures at 42c–51a. Precisely, the passages show that Socrates distinguishes two further types of false pleasure: apparent, but unreal, pleasures – (b) and (c) – and real pleasures whose appearances are distorted – (a) and (d). In other words, (b) and (c) refer to the same thing, and (a) and (d) refer to the same thing.[22]

---

[22] This second claim will be qualified below since although (a) and (d) do refer to the same kind of false pleasure, Socrates recognizes two sub-kinds: (i) those that are commingled with pain and (ii) those that are commingled with respite from severe pains suffered by soul and body.

We encountered apparent-but-unreal pleasures in the Illusion Argument in *Republic* 9. These are cases where calm mis-appears as pleasure. These cases exemplify false pleasure kind 3 in *Philebus*. They will be the focus of this section. Real-but-distorted pleasures constitute false pleasure kind 4. False pleasure kind 2 in fact turns out to be a sub-kind of false pleasure kind 4 since the imagined pleasure is a real pleasure, but with distorted imaginative content. But Socrates distinguishes three sub-kinds of real-but-distorted pleasure. These will be the focus of the next section.

With respect to apparent-but-unreal pleasure, as in *Republic* 9, Socrates distinguishes between pleasure, pain, and calm. He suggests that calm can appear, or rather *mis*-appear, as pleasant. In fact, in *Philebus* Socrates does not provide an explanation of how this occurs. He simply says it does – or, more precisely, he says:

We encounter people who ... really believe they are experiencing pleasure when they are not in pain [that is, they are merely in a state of calm]. (44a)

So, strictly speaking, what Socrates says is that people believe (*oionto, doxazousi*) they are experiencing pleasure when they are not. It would be helpful for Socrates to be explicit that this false belief derives from a false appearance, namely, the appearance of calm as pleasant. But this omission is, perhaps, explicable in light of the fact that enough has been said in the account of false pleasure kind 2 in *Philebus* itself to infer how calm might appear pleasant. The same illusory mechanism is at work – or at least one of two illusory mechanisms is at work, since we have said that Socrates conjoins two different factors. In this case, the juxtaposition of two affective conditions engenders an illusion. In short, the difference between false pleasure kind 2 and false pleasure kind 3 is that in the case of false pleasure kind 2 some pleasure is indeed occurring, whereas in the case of false pleasure kind 3, pleasure is not in fact occurring. Instead, calm is occurring, and it mis-appears as pleasure.[23]

Recall that as Socrates makes the transition from false pleasures of kinds 1 and 2 to those of kinds 3 and 4, he says that the latter are "even more false" than the former. We need, then, to explain in what sense this is so. In the case of false pleasures of kinds 1 and 2, the falsity is representational. In the present case, that is, in the case of false pleasure kind 3, I suggest that Socrates treats the falsity as ontological. Why? Because although the

---

[23] The following difference between the treatments of hedonic illusion in *Republic* 9 and false pleasure kind 3 in *Philebus* is also noteworthy. As we saw in our discussion of *Republic* 9, Socrates does not distinguish the doxastic and non-doxastic aspects of the appearance aspect of the hedonic condition. However, in *Philebus* he does. This is explicit in the distinction between the functions of the painter and the scribe. Plato first introduces this distinction within the context of a discussion of perception in *Theaetetus*.

appearance is pleasant and thus represents the occurrence of pleasure, that which in our discussion of *Republic* 9 we called the "core aspect" is not a restoration but a calm condition. False pleasure kind 3 is thus like fool's gold or a forged Rembrandt painting or a wax sculpture of Ronald Reagan. All appear to be the real thing, but none is. In contrast, note once again that a representationally false entity such as a belief or statement is, nonetheless, really and truly a belief or statement. Likewise, Socrates thinks that a representationally false pleasure is, nonetheless, really and truly a pleasure. So false pleasures of kinds 1 and 2 are really and truly pleasures, although representationally false, whereas false pleasure of kind 3 is not really and truly pleasure; and thus, as Socrates claims, it is more false than the preceding two kinds.

Evidently, then, Socrates thinks that ontological truth or falsity is truer or more false than representational truth or falsity. This raises two questions. First, what justification is there for thinking this? Second, does Socrates think that representational and ontological truth-values are related? And if so, how? For example, are both species of a common genus? Or is one derivative of the other? These are important questions, but questions that we cannot pursue in this study.

FALSE PLEASURE IN 'PHILEBUS': KIND 4

The remainder of Socrates' discussion of false pleasures, at 44a–51a, is devoted to real pleasures whose appearances are distorted. These are mixed pleasures, of which Socrates distinguishes various sub-kinds:

PR: Let us turn to the families of these pleasures.
SO: You mean the ones that have that mixed nature?
PR: Right.
SO: There are mixtures that have their origin in the body and are confined to the body. Then there are mixtures in the soul, and they are confined to the soul. But then we also find mixtures of pleasures and pains in both body and soul. (46b–c)

As Socrates indicates here, there are three kinds of mixed pleasure: somatic, psychic, and psychosomatic. He discusses them in the following order: somatic, psychosomatic, and psychic.

It is worth noting, and Socrates explicitly acknowledges, that affective mixtures come with different proportions of pleasure and pain:

Now isn't it the case that some of those mixtures contain an even amount of pleasures and pains, while there is a preponderance of either of the two in other cases? (46d)

Consequently, it would seem reasonable to speak of mixed pleasures only in cases where there is a significant portion of pleasure, precisely a greater portion than that of pain. I will proceed on this assumption.

Recall now that the first kind of pleasure Socrates discusses in the cathartic taxonomy is impure, that is, mixed bodily pleasure. In that case, as we explained, the mixture is sequential not simultaneous: bodily pain immediately precedes the bodily pleasure. At 42c–51a Socrates focuses on simultaneously, rather than sequentially, mixed pleasures, although he refers to sequentially mixed pleasures in some cases. In fact, in treatments of pleasure throughout his corpus Plato variously emphasizes simultaneous and sequential mixtures. It is interesting and difficult to explain the fact that in *Gorgias* Socrates admits simultaneous hedonic mixtures, denies them in *Phaedo*, operates with sequential hedonic mixtures in *Republic*, and then operates with both simultaneous and sequential mixtures in *Philebus*.[24] I note this fact, but will not attempt an explanation here.[25]

The simultaneously mixed bodily pleasures Socrates describes in *Philebus* share the following property: some hedonic or algesic condition is present relatively deep within the body and some opposite affective condition is present relatively superficially. For example, one may experience an itch below the surface of the skin. This itch is painful or at least uncomfortable. Simultaneously one may take some pleasure from scratching the surface of the skin:

> Take the case we just mentioned, of itching and scratching ... Now when the irritation and infection are inside and cannot be reached by rubbing and scratching, there is only relief on the surface. (46d–e)

One might wonder why Socrates conceives of the opposed hedonic and algesic conditions as mixed, since they derive from affections in different, albeit related and even contiguous, parts of the body. The answer seems to be that the psychic affections that the bodily affections engender mix. That is to say, one *experiences* a hedonic-cum-algesic condition. This view is supported by the explanation Socrates proceeds to give of mixed psychosomatic conditions:

> But now take cases where the soul's contributions are opposed to the body's, where there is pain over and against pleasure or pleasure against pain, with the result that both turn into a single mixture. (47c)

---

[24] See *Gorgias* 495e–497a, *Phaedo* 60b–c, and *Republic* 584b. Cf. *Timaeus* 65a–b.
[25] It is also noteworthy that although Socrates operates with both forms of mixture in *Philebus*, he does not explicitly distinguish them.

Assuming this account pertains to all of the mixed pleasures Socrates discusses at 42c–51a, then by mixed pleasures he means not merely simultaneously mixed pleasures, but still more precisely pleasures whose psychic aspect is simultaneously mixed with an algesic psychic aspect.

It is also important to note that Socrates links mixed psychosomatic pleasures with anticipatory pleasures of impure bodily pleasure:

> We talked about these conditions earlier and agreed that in these cases it is the deprivation that gives rise to the desire for replenishment. And while the expectation is pleasant, the deprivation itself is painful. When we discussed this, we did not make any special mention, as we do now, of the fact that in all cases vast in number where soul and body are not in agreement a single mixture of pleasure and pain results. (47c–d)

This comment is particularly significant when one recalls that after he initially introduces anticipatory pleasure Socrates contrasts this kind of pleasure with impure (in the sense of sequentially mixed) bodily pleasure by characterizing the anticipatory pleasure as "pure and unmixed." Indeed, the anticipatory pleasure is not necessarily sequentially mixed with an antecedent psychic pain. However, as Socrates emphasizes now, it is simultaneously mixed with bodily pain. For example, one is hungry and thus experiences a bodily pain, but anticipates with pleasure a meal and thus experiences a mixed psychosomatic pleasure. Accordingly, upon later examination, the second kind of pleasure turns out to be impure, once again, in the sense of being simultaneously mixed.

Socrates describes the third kind of mixed pleasure, psychic pleasure mixed with psychic pain, at significantly greater length than the preceding two mixed pleasures. Basically, he has in mind what we call "bittersweet" emotions. To begin, Socrates cites a range of painful emotions, including: anger, fear, longing, lamenting, lust, ambition, and what the Greeks call "*phthonos.*" This set is not taken to be exhaustive; it constitutes salient members of a class. Socrates also vaguely adds: "and other such things." In fact, there is no Greek word for "emotion" at this time. So the class that Socrates has in mind must be understood implicitly.

Socrates claims that these painful emotions are "full" of pleasures. What Socrates means is that there are many instances where these emotions are mixed with pleasure. He exemplifies the point by referring to a passage from Homer's *Iliad* where Achilles, lamenting and raging over his failure to protect his beloved Patroclus, describes anger as "much sweeter than soft-flowing honey" (18.108–109). I take it that Achilles and Socrates have in mind the thoughts of revenge that anger fuels. This interpretation is corroborated by Aristotle's discussion of the same passage in his treatise on rhetoric. In Book 1, section 10 of that text, within a discussion of pleasure, Aristotle suggests that "even being angry is pleasant . . . when there is a prospect of taking revenge" (*Rhetoric* 1370b). In this case, then, the pleasure is anticipatory.

In *Philebus* Socrates claims that cases of lamenting and longing are similar. In the case of lamentation – we can assume – the pain of loss is mixed with memorial pleasures concerning the lost object or person. In the case of longing, once again pain is mixed with anticipatory pleasure.

In enumerating examples of mixed emotions, Socrates now turns to the experiences of spectators at dramatic festivals. First, he refers to tragedies: the "same thing happens to the spectators of tragic dramas: they enjoy their weeping" (48a). Socrates then claims that a similar kind of mixed experience occurs among spectators of comedies. In this case, however, he claims that the mixture is more obscure (*skoteinoteron*) and so requires more careful consideration. The remainder of Socrates' discussion of mixed psychic pleasure endeavors to elucidate this case. The example Socrates constructs to convey his idea involves a number of unexpected maneuvers. In particular, the shift from the context of real interpersonal relations to dramatic experience requires explanation.

The painful emotion that serves as Socrates' point of departure in his discussion of the comic-dramatic case is one from his initial list, the one I left untranslated: *phthonos*. Common translations of "*phthonos*" are "envy" and "malice." I suggest that while these renditions are certainly in the right semantic ball park, neither is quite satisfactory. "Envy" may be defined as a painful or resentful awareness of a good enjoyed by another, which is joined with a desire to possess the same good. "Malice" may be defined simply as a desire, which may be unreasonable, to see another suffer. *Phthonos* involves a painful attitude toward another person because, one thinks, that person possesses some good. Moreover, one does not want that person to have that good because its possession elevates that person above oneself. For lack of a better expression, I will, accordingly, translate "*phthonos*" as "diminishing-desire." In short, *phthonos* is a desire, for the reason given, that another person be diminished. Accordingly, *phthonos* shares with envy pain at another's possession of a good. However, *phthonos* differs from envy in that it is not conjoined with a desire to possess the same good. Rather, it is conjoined with the desire to see the other lose that good. It has, we might say, an other-directed-diminishing-desire rather than a self-directed-elevating-desire. Again, *phthonos* shares with malice a desire, which may be unreasonable, to see another suffer. But malice needn't be painful. A sadist is malicious, but needn't experience pain at the desire to see another suffer.[26]

Phthonos or diminishing-desire is, Socrates maintains, a pain of the soul. But, he continues, a diminishing-desirous person will take pleasure in the misfortune of someone "close to him" (*tôn pelas*). It is questionable why Socrates refers to taking pleasure in the misfortune of someone "close to him." I will return to this point shortly. Presently, note that the psychological state to which Socrates is here referring is closely related to *Schadenfreude*; indeed, the Greeks had a word for *Schadenfreude*: *epichairekakia*. But the enjoyment experienced by the person of diminishing-desire is not equivalent to *Schadenfreude*. Rather, it is a kind of *Schadenfreude*. Like malice, *Schadenfreude* does not entail pain on the part of the subject. But diminishing-desire does.

Schadenfreude as well as the enjoyment experienced by one in a condition of diminishing-desire typically occurs in the context of a real interpersonal relation. Indeed, once again, Socrates refers to enjoying the misfortune of someone "close to us." But since he has targeted the context of comic drama, it is jarring or at least odd that he refers back to a real interpersonal case. We need, then, to be attentive to the function of the reference to a real interpersonal case within the context of dramatic experience.

At this point in the account, however, Socrates turns to the object of enjoyment, specifically, to an account of the "ridiculous" (*geloion*), that is, to an account of the object of ridicule. One property of the ridiculous, Socrates suggests, is that it is something bad. In other words, Socrates specifically has in mind here the kind of laughter or enjoyment directed toward human failing or weakness. He specifically focuses on self-ignorance as a kind of badness. In fact, he focuses still more precisely on a certain species of self-ignorance: a person may think he possesses a greater good than he does. Socrates distinguishes three types of such self-ignorance in terms of three types of value: external, bodily, and psychic. For example, a person may be ignorant about his wealth, thinking he has more than he does; a person may be ignorant about his physical appearance, thinking

---

[26] Compare the following testimony regarding Hippias of Elis' (*c.* 470–400) view of *phthonos*: "Hippias says that there are two kinds of *phthonos*: the just kind, when one has *phthonos* toward bad men in view of their honors; and the unjust kind, when one has *phthonos* toward good men" (Stobaeus 3.38.32). My view that *phthonos* entails the desire that the person who is the object of *phthonos* be diminished is consistent with this distinction since it is just that bad men be diminished by losing their honors, whereas it is unjust that good men lose theirs.

he is more attractive than he is; and a person may be ignorant about his intelligence, thinking he is wiser than he is.

Socrates then observes that self-ignorance in any of these forms may be combined with either strength or weakness. This distinction is crucial for Socrates' account, for, he claims, when self-ignorance is combined with weakness, it is ridiculous; whereas when it is combined with strength, it is dangerous and thus not ridiculous. The reason, Socrates explains, is that "all those who combine [self-ignorance] with weakness . . . are unable to avenge themselves when they are ridiculed" (49b).

In considering the function of this distinction between strength and weakness as it pertains to the ridiculous, it is helpful, I suggest, to underscore the dramatic context that frames Socrates' account. Compare the portrayal of tragic or terrifying scenes on stage in contrast to those we encounter in real life. The impotence of fictional events in relation to our real lives enables spectators to enjoy their horrific or tragic features. Likewise, in the case of comic dramas, we can without inhibition laugh at those who are lampooned on stage because there is no threat of retaliation. Indeed, the public context and norms of comic drama facilitate and encourage such laughter.

Granted this, Socrates is not merely interested in explaining the ridiculous. If he were, then he might as well be offering an account of unmixed hedonic emotion. It is crucial that the pleasure taken in the ridiculous here be mixed with pain. This is why Socrates focuses on the case of a spectator who has the attitude of diminishing-desire. Diminishing-desire, he claims, involves injustice. There is nothing unjust in enjoying the misfortunes of one's enemies, he says; but it is unjust to be pleased by misfortunes of those close to us. When we laugh at the shortcomings of our fellows or allies, this is a product of *phthonos* or diminishing-desire. And since *phthonos* is a psychic pain, laughter derived from *phthonos* is an emotion of pleasure mixed with pain.

What exactly is Socrates trying to convey through his emphasis on the injustice of diminishing-desire? One thing Socrates wants to convey, I suggest, is that this particular sort of bittersweet emotion, this particular form of ridicule, derives from a motivation to see one's peer, fellow, or ally reduced. Although Socrates does not make the following point explicit, it may be assumed that this motivation itself derives from a defect of character. It is one thing to be troubled by the good fortune of one's enemies, but those who are disturbed by the good fortune of those close to them suffer from a sense of inadequacy about themselves. It is important that Socrates focuses on the laughter of such a person precisely because it is an impure laughter, enjoyment fueled by the pain of inadequacy.

Compare and contrast Timaeus' remark about the beneficence of the divine creator of the cosmos in the eponymous dialogue:

Now why did he who constructed this whole cosmos . . . construct it? Let us state the reason: He was good, and one who is good can never have *phthonos* toward anything. And so, being free of *phthonos*, he wanted everything to become as much like himself as possible . . . In fact, wise men will tell you . . . that this . . . was the pre-eminent reason for the world's coming to be: the divine wanted everything to be good and nothing to be bad so far as that was possible. (29d–30a)

Consequently, another thing Socrates wants to convey is that the pleasure at issue is not only mixed and thus ontologically untrue, but also vicious. Recall the point introduced above that Socrates' operative conception of purity is not merely uniformity, but freedom from fault or taint or corruption. Of course, since pain is bad, pleasure mixed with pain will be thus tainted in value. But the present pleasure is also corrupt in that it arises from a defect of character.

Finally, before we turn to Socrates' treatment of pure pleasures, one further small point regarding mixed pleasures should be noted. Recall that Socrates regards mixed pleasures as pleasures whose appearances are distorted. We have yet to clarify how the appearance aspect of mixed pleasures is distorted. The basic explanation seems to be this. Consider false pleasure kind 3 where the neutral condition or calm appears pleasant. As we discussed in our account of the Illusion Argument in *Republic* 9, the juxtaposition of calm and antecedent pain engenders a hedonic illusion. Thus, the appearance aspect of the affective condition is also distorted. But in the case of false pleasure kind 4, that is, mixed pleasure, distortion occurs for a different reason. In contrast to false pleasure kind 3, pleasure is indeed occurring. However, the pleasure is mixed with pain. Here the simultaneous juxtaposition of pleasure and pain is responsible for distorting the hedonic appearance. Precisely how the hedonic appearance is distorted is not adequately clarified. For example, the mixture of pain with pleasure may heighten the pleasure analogously to the way that in foods saltiness mixed with sweetness can intensify the sweetness. Some reason for thinking that this is how Socrates conceives of the distortion derives from his account of the first kind of mixed pleasure, mixed somatic pleasure. There, Socrates explicitly says that when somatic pleasures are mixed with pains they are more intense (*sphodrôs*) and robust (*megalôs*). For example:

And is it the case that pleasures are greater when people suffer from an illness than when they are healthy? . . . And when people suffer from fever or any such disease, aren't they more subject to thirst, chill, and whatever else continues to affect them through the body? Do they not experience greater deprivations and also greater pleasures at the replenishment? (45a–b)

In this passage, however, the explanation for the heightening of the bodily pleasure is that greater deficit precedes greater restoration. But this suggests sequential rather than simultaneous mixture. Indeed, Socrates discusses bodily pleasures sequentially as well as simultaneously mixed with pains. My point is merely that since both hedonic conditions involve juxtaposition with pain there is some reason for thinking that the way in which the appearance of pleasure that is sequentially mixed with pain is distorted is the same as the way in which the appearance of pleasure that is simultaneously mixed with pain is distorted.

PURE PLEASURE IN 'PHILEBUS'

In contrast to mixed pleasures, that is, both simultaneously and sequentially mixed pleasures, Socrates concludes his examination of kinds of pleasure in *Philebus* with a brief, indeed remarkably brief, account of unmixed pleasure (at 51b–52b):

It is natural and necessary, following the mixed pleasures, that we proceed to the unmixed ones in turn. (50e)

Unmixed or pure pleasures are also explicitly treated as "true" (*alêtheis*). Indeed, here we have the ontological sense of "true," more precisely the gradable ontological sense. We have already discussed the purity of olfactory pleasures in the contexts of *Timaeus* and *Republic* 9. Visual, auditory, and intellectual pleasures share with them the property of not being preceded by a felt lack or deficit, in other words, by pain.

In *Philebus* Socrates distinguishes three kinds of pure pleasure: olfactory, visual and auditory, and intellectual. Even though it is conceivable that pure visual and auditory pleasures are distinct in kind insofar as they involve distinct sense-perceptual faculties, Socrates conjoins them into a single kind. This is because Socrates here ranks and so organizes kinds of pure pleasure according to their value, not according to the psychic or cognitive faculty exercised, and because he regards pure visual and auditory pleasures as being of equal value. Olfactory pleasures are characterized as least divine (*theion*); intellectual pleasures are, implicitly, treated as most divine. Note also that since pleasure requires restoration, intellectual pleasure is pleasure of learning. That is to say, Socrates cannot countenance the possibility of enjoying contemplation, if contemplation does not entail the acquisition of information or knowledge.

Socrates does not make explicit why he evaluates the pure pleasures as he does. I suggest that the answer relates to an independent metaphysical hierarchy to which Plato is committed and that relates to the respective psychic functions of smell, sight and hearing, and mind. Recall Socrates' attempt in *Republic* 9 to argue that rational pleasures are truer than appetitive pleasures, in part on the grounds that epistemic or intellectual and nutritional contents are more and less real because more and less stable. In *Philebus*, mind or intellect, that is, the rational part of the soul, clearly has the capacity to apprehend entities of a higher metaphysical order than any of the sense-perceptual faculties. Likewise, I take it that Socrates thinks that sight and hearing have greater powers of apprehension than smell. Although all of the sense-perceptual faculties are limited to the apprehension of sensible objects, sight and hearing, in humans at least, can apprehend with far greater discrimination than smell. In particular, sight and hearing can apprehend harmonious structures in sensible objects in a way that smell cannot. Recall in our discussion of *Timaeus* Timaeus' point that those without musical-theoretic knowledge take pleasure (*hêdonê*) by apprehending through mere sense-perception divine harmonies in mortal movement. Contrast this with Timaeus' remark about the limited discriminatory power of smell:

Variations among smells ... form two sets [pleasant and offensive], neither of which has an [olfactory-modality-specific] name, since they do not consist of a specific number of kinds nor of basic kinds. (67a)

Compare also Aristotle's remarks on smell in his treatise *On the Soul*:

Concerning smell and the objects of smell, it is less easy to give an account ... for it is not so clear what sort of thing smell is, as it is in the cases of sound and color. The reason is that in humans this form of sense-perception is not discriminating (*akribê*), less so than in many animals ... And the fact that humans are unable to perceive smells without pleasure and pain shows that this faculty of sense-perception lacks discrimination. (421a)

In short, then, pure olfactory pleasure is "less divine" than pure visual or auditory pleasure because the capacity of smell (in humans) has weaker powers of discrimination, and thus weaker cognitive or epistemological powers, than those of sight and hearing.

Pure pleasures, in particular pure sense-perceptual pleasures, derive from the apprehension of beautiful (*kala*) sensible objects:

PR: But, Socrates, what pleasures could one rightly grasp as true?
SO: Those that are related to so-called beautiful (*kala*) colors and shapes and most smells and sounds. (51b)

Socrates proceeds to describe the beauty of visual and auditory objects as follows:

> By the beauty of shapes I do not mean what the masses regard as beautiful, the shapes of animals or their representations in paintings. Rather, I mean – and the argument demands – straight or curved lines and plane and solid figures constructed from these using the compass, rule, and square. These things are not beautiful in relation to something else, they are beautiful in themselves, and provide their own particular pleasures ... Likewise, I am speaking of smooth and bright notes that produce a single pure song. (51b–d)

At least two points should be clarified here. One concerns Socrates' distinction between what is beautiful in relation to something and what is beautiful in itself. For example, a person might have a particular attachment to a piece of music because he associates it with someone he loves. Consequently, this person may find that piece of music more beautiful than some other piece of music whose intrinsic structure is actually more beautiful. In the former case, one finds the piece of music beautiful not in itself, but in relation to something else. (Observe, then, that this account requires and indeed Plato and Socrates assume that beauty is a mind-independent property.)

The second point in this brief account of auditory and visual pleasures lies in the rudiments of what might be called an aesthetic theory, additional information for which can be gleaned from passages in *Timaeus*. Central to the theory is the idea that normal sense-perceptual experiences tend to disorder the natural (in the normative sense of "natural") structures and motions of the human soul. This is because the vast quantity of sense-perceptual experiences to which we are subject involve non-harmonious, ill-arranged, or simply chaotic forms. In contrast, beautiful forms are precisely those whose elements and compounds are harmonious. Their apprehension thus has the effect of restoring or at least partially restoring order and harmony to the soul. This is the reason they are experienced as pleasant.

CONCLUSION TO THE TREATMENT OF PLEASURE IN 'PHILEBUS'

Given the complexity of the treatment of pleasure at *Philebus* 31b–52b, it will be helpful here to provide a summary of the foregoing discussion. In the course of the cathartic taxonomy, Socrates distinguishes ten kinds, including sub-kinds, of pleasure in the following order:

(1) sequentially mixed bodily pleasure (31b–32b);
(2) anticipatory pleasure, belonging to the soul alone, of (1), that is, sequentially mixed bodily pleasure (32b–36d);

(3) false pleasure kind 1: representationally false imagistic pleasure, where the falsity of the image or depiction derives from the falsity of belief (36c–40e);

(4) false pleasure kind 2: representationally false pleasure, where the falsity of the hedonic appearance gives rise to a false belief (41b–42c);

(5) false pleasure kind 3: absolutely ontologically false pleasure, where the neutral or calm condition mis-appears as pleasant (42c–44a);

(6) false pleasure kind 4, type 1: gradably ontologically false bodily pleasure simultaneously mixed with bodily pain (45a–47c);

(2r) false pleasure kind 4, type 2: gradably ontologically false anticipatory pleasure of bodily pleasure simultaneously mixed with bodily pain (47c–d, = item (2) re-examined);

(7) false pleasure kind 4, type 3: gradably ontologically false psychic pleasure simultaneously mixed with psychic pain (as in bittersweet emotions) (47d–50d);

(8) true pleasure kind 1: pure visual and auditory pleasures (51d–e);

(9) true pleasure kind 2: pure olfactory pleasure (51e);

(10) true pleasure kind 3: pure intellectual pleasure (51e–52b).

These ten kinds are organized according to false and true pleasures. Item (1) is not initially identified as false, but since it is explicitly characterized as mixed and mixed pleasures are subsequently characterized as (ontologically) false, item (1) is an ontologically false pleasure. Again, item (2) is not initially characterized in terms of truth-value. It is initially described as pure and unmixed. However, it is subsequently re-examined and then characterized as simultaneously mixed. Thus, it emerges as ontologically false.

False pleasures kinds 1 and 2 are representationally false, while false pleasure kind 4 is ontologically false. False pleasure kind 3 is treated as ontologically false. It could be regarded as representationally false insofar as the appearance aspect misrepresents pleasure as occurring. As such, it may be regarded as a representationally false pleasure. However, since the core aspect is calm or the neutral condition, it would perhaps be more accurate to characterize this affective condition as a representationally false calm. All of the true pleasures are ontologically true and thereby contrast specifically with the ontologically false pleasures kind 4.

Plato's aim is clearly not to provide an exhaustive taxonomy of pleasures. It is easy to identify kinds of pleasure that go untreated: for example, representationally true anticipatory pleasure. Rather, as I have suggested, since Socrates' aim is to conduct a cathartic taxonomy, he needs only to proceed in a way that clarifies where pure and impure pleasures lie.

CONCLUSION TO PLATO'S TREATMENT OF PLEASURE

Since Chapter 4, we have covered a lot of Platonic hedonic-theoretical ground. As I mentioned, we have more from Plato on the identity and kinds questions than from any other ancient author. It will be helpful to provide a few summarizing remarks regarding Plato's contribution. I have three.

First, central to Plato's conception of pleasure is the idea of filling or replenishment or restoration. Two points are noteworthy here. One is that Plato tends to focus less on the phenomenology or phenomenal character of pleasure, what I called the "appearance aspect," and more on what I have called the "core aspect" of pleasure. This holds even for purely psychic or intellectual pleasures, that is, pleasures that involve psychic restorations. A similar point can be made about the pre-Platonic physiological treatments. It is an important question why this is so. I postpone my answer to the concluding chapter of the book.

The second point I want to make about Plato's idea that pleasure centrally involves filling or replenishment or restoration is that restoration and its kin entail conditions of deficiency, even as they are remedial or therapeutic processes. This means for Plato that pleasure cannot be intrinsically, but must at best be instrumentally and extrinsically, good. Pleasure is not an end, but a means to an end. Its value derives from the forms of intrinsic goodness in relation to which it stands, principally bodily health and psychic well-being.

My second general remark concerns the appearance aspect of pleasure. While Plato focuses on the core aspect, it is of course true that he has things to say about the appearance aspect, especially insofar as these things relate to the truth-value of pleasure. Plato's principal interest in the appearance aspect or phenomenal character of pleasure has to do with the relation between appearance and what the appearance is of, and precisely the truth-value or representationality of the appearance. In other words, Plato's principal interest in the appearance aspect of pleasure is epistemological. Relatedly – and this is another crucial aspect of Plato's conception of pleasure – Plato takes the appearance aspect of pleasure to be representational. It is important here to distinguish this point from the point that certain pleasures, such as anticipatory or memorial pleasures, have linguistic or imagistic representational contents. The present point is, as I put it in discussing the Illusion Argument in *Republic* 9, that feeling is itself the hedonic mode of sensing.

Third and finally, we have seen that Plato distinguishes kinds of pleasure in various ways; and I have emphasized that the various ways in which Plato distinguishes hedonic kinds are variously motivated. For example, in *Republic* 9 Plato's tripartite distinction of appetitive, spirited, and intellectual or rational pleasures follows his distinction of the tripartite soul. In *Timaeus* Plato distinguishes sense-perceptual pleasures within the context of a physical theory of sense-perception. Sense-perceptual pleasures, I suggested, are a kind of somatic pleasure, specifically exteroceptive somatic pleasure, distinguishable from proprioceptive somatic pleasure. In *Philebus* the aims of cathartic taxonomy explain the division of pleasures into impure and pure and correspondingly into false or untrue and true. Moreover, we saw that here as well as in *Republic* 9 ontological and representational truth-conceptions operate and that there is a further distinction between gradable and absolute ontological truth. Finally, at the end of the cathartic taxonomy in *Philebus* Plato's distinction of grades of pure pleasure depends upon an implicit hierarchy of the epistemological capacities of psychic faculties. In sum, even if it is possible to unify the various ways in which Plato distinguishes kinds of pleasure within one system of hedonic classification – and I am silent on this possibility – Plato's distinctions are in fact a function of local, that is, specific dialogic interests.

CHAPTER 6

Aristotle on pleasure and activation

As in Plato's corpus so in Aristotle's, the topic of pleasure arises in numerous passages. By far the most important of these occur in Aristotle's ethical writings, specifically in *Eudemian Ethics* and *Nicomachean Ethics*, more precisely still in *Eudemian Ethics*, Book 6, sections 4–5 and sections 11–14; and in *Nicomachean Ethics*, Book 3, section 10; Book 7, section 4–5 and sections 11–14; and Book 10, sections 1–5.[1]

An ethical treatise transmitted in the Aristotelian corpus and entitled *Magna Moralia* also contains an important discussion of pleasure (precisely, at *Magna Moralia* 2.7). There has been a long-standing debate over the authenticity of this work.

One further substantial treatment of pleasure occurs in Aristotle's rhetorical treatise *Rhetoric* 1.11. Here again the treatment is closely related to ethics. At least, one of the central concerns of Aristotelian ethics is the cultivation of emotional dispositions, and one of the central concerns of rhetoric is manipulation of emotions.

There are also numerous, more cursory treatments or mentions of pleasure scattered throughout Aristotle's corpus, for example, in the following logical, metaphysical, physical, biological, and psychological works: *Posterior Analytics, Topics, Categories, Physics, On the Generation of Animals, On the Soul*, and *On Sense-Perception and Sensibles*.[2] Finally, pleasure plays an important role in a number of the surviving fragments of Aristotle's *Protrepticus*, a work whose title translates as "Exhortation" and which, in contrast to all of the other works mentioned, was intended for a relatively broad and public audience as opposed to committed students of

---

[1] For convenience, I will hereafter refer to passages excluding the words "book" and "section" simply as follows: *Title* b.s.; for example, *Nicomachean Ethics* 10.4 (= *Nicomachean Ethics*, Book 10, section 4).

[2] The discussion in *On the Generation of Animals* (1.17) specifically concerns sexual pleasure. I discuss this in conjunction with a post-Aristotelian treatment of this topic in an appendix to this chapter.

philosophy and specifically those of Aristotle's school, alternately known as the Lyceum or Peripatos.

This last point about Aristotle's *Protrepticus* warrants some elaboration. It is generally agreed that almost all of Aristotle's surviving writings are derived from or were composed for lecture courses that he gave. These lecture-based writings are polished to varying degrees, but they were not intended – as Plato's dialogues or at least most of them were – to be disseminated to a broad or relatively broad public. Again, these lecture-based writings were intended for committed students.

Scholars often refer to the distinction between writings intended for members of a school and writings intended for a broader public using the technical terms "esoteric" and "exoteric." "Esoteric" refers to texts or lectures for an inner circle; "exoteric" refers to texts or lectures for an outer circle. Often exoteric texts had an introductory or exhortatory function; they were intended to introduce people to philosophy and to encourage its practice. Such is Aristotle's *Protrepticus*. In this case, as in the case of all of Aristotle's exoteric works, mere fragments survive. In standard English, "esoteric" has the sense of "abstruse" or "cryptic"; and certainly works composed for students in a philosophical school versus a more general public may be relatively abstruse. However, in the present context "esoteric" does not entail abstruseness.

Aristotle's surviving esoteric works are plentiful.[3] But they present various interpretive problems of their own. First, because they are lecture-based, Aristotle seems to have variously used and reused them – adding and revising in the process in various ways. Thus, while any given text ostensibly represents Aristotle's culminating views on the subject therein treated – at least up to the point in his career when, for any number of reasons, he stopped revising – in fact the text also reflects, to varying degrees, a kind of accretion of ideas and treatments. It is a complex and in some respects impossible task to distinguish the various stages or aspects of the development of the ultimate version. This problem will be particularly pertinent to my discussion since I favor the view that Aristotle's conception of pleasure develops in several stages.

A further complicating feature of the esoteric works concerns the posthumous editing to which they were subject. At some point in antiquity, the texts constitutive of Aristotle's corpus were organized into three groups: logical works (*logika*), works on nature (*physika*), and works on human values, practices, and institutions (*ethika*).[4] This form of

---

[3] It is generally thought that we possess about a third of Aristotle's complete *oeuvre*.
[4] Note that this corpus also includes texts of Aristotle's school that were not composed by Aristotle.

organization reflects a certain conception of philosophy and its pedagogy that has some grounds in Aristotle's thought, but that crystallized only in the centuries after his death. Furthermore, before this broad organization of Aristotle's corpus could occur, the individual works that were regarded as falling into these three spheres of philosophy were themselves subject to editing to varying degrees. For example, it is questionable whether the fourteen books that constitute Aristotle's *Metaphysics* were, at any point, conceived by their author as a single, coherent study or lecture course. For example, the contents of Book 11 are largely quotations from another text, *Physics*. A similar, but more acute, problem concerns the ten books that constitute *Nicomachean Ethics* and the eight that constitute *Eudemian Ethics*. In particular, Books 5, 6, and 7 of *Nicomachean Ethics* are identical to Books 4, 5, and 6 of *Eudemian Ethics* respectively. This point has special bearing on our discussion: since *Nicomachean Ethics* 7.11–14 is a key passage for Aristotle's conception of pleasure, this means that *Eudemian Ethics* 6.11–14 is. But given this, it is questionable where the passage itself was originally conceived as belonging within *Nicomachean Ethics* or within *Eudemian Ethics*. Note also that the preceding assumes, perhaps dubiously, that Aristotle intended either *Nicomachean Ethics* or *Eudemian Ethics* as a unified collection of books. I will return to this point momentarily and again further below.

One further interpretive problem relates to the questionable authenticity of some of the works in the Aristotelian corpus. I noted above that the authenticity of *Magna Moralia* has been doubted. The text obviously belongs to Aristotle's school. But it is questionable whether Aristotle composed it himself. I favor the view that the work is Aristotle's.

Beyond these deep interpretative problems, the various Aristotelian treatments of pleasure throughout the corpus differ in various ways. As in the case of Plato's corpus, some differences are clearly due to the distinct interests of the texts or passages. For example, it is one thing to discuss the pleasure of sexual physiology in a treatise on animal reproduction; it is another to discuss the value of pleasure in a treatise on the cultivation of ethical character. On the other hand, there are at least two rather striking differences among the various treatments that may be attributable to changes in Aristotle's thought. The first of these concerns the question whether Aristotle was ever committed to a Platonic view of pleasure as restoration. In a few texts Aristotle discusses pleasure as such, whereas in others he explicitly argues against this view. The second concerns the relation between the treatments of pleasure in *Nicomachean Ethics* 7 and 10. In Book 7, Aristotle identifies pleasure with what he calls an *energeia*. "*Energeia*" is a technical Aristotelian term. I will translate it as "activation" and provide further clarification below. In *Nicomachean Ethics* 10, Aristotle denies that pleasure is activation; instead, he maintains that pleasure completes or culminates an activation. Since *Nicomachean Ethics* 7 is identical to *Eudemian Ethics* 6, it is plausible that *Nicomachean Ethics* 7 originally constituted *Eudemian Ethics* 6. Indeed, this is the position I endorse. But even so, one wonders why Aristotle's editors, if not Aristotle himself, employed both treatments in a single ethical work or lecture course.

ARISTOTLE'S EARLY CONCEPTION OF PLEASURE

Let me begin with the question whether Aristotle ever held the Platonic view that pleasure is a restoration. Consider the following passage from Aristotle's *Rhetoric* 1.11:

> Let us assume that pleasure is a certain change (*kinêsis*), a sudden (*athroa*) and perceived (*aisthêtê*) restoration of the soul to its prevailing (*hyparchousa*) condition, and that pain is the opposite ... Necessarily then it is, for the most part, pleasant to move toward one's natural state, and especially when things are restored naturally. (1369b–1370a)

Several points in this passage echo Plato's treatment of pleasure. Beyond the general conception of pleasure as a restoration, Aristotle's mention of "sudden and perceived change" is literally reminiscent of Plato's treatments both in *Timaeus* and *Philebus*. Recall the following *Timaeus* passage: "It is necessary to conceive of pleasure and pain in the following way. When an affection occurs within us that is contrary to nature, violent, and sudden, it is painful; but a return again to nature when sudden is pleasant" (64c–d). Consider also the following passage from *Philebus* where Socrates refers to pleasure as "the restoration to the prevailing nature" (*katastasin ... eis tên hyparchousan physin*) (42d).

Granted this, there are at least two noteworthy, if subtle, points of difference between Aristotle's description and Plato's views. First, Aristotle explicitly speaks of the change as being "of the soul." Recall that in our discussion of Plato, especially of *Gorgias* and *Republic* 9, we wrestled with the question whether, in the case of bodily pleasure, the soul was restored or whether this was only true of spirited and rational pleasures. In *Rhetoric* 1.11, Aristotle discusses various kinds of pleasure, some of which correspond to appetitive or bodily, spirited, and rational pleasures. But in the opening passage of section 11 just quoted, Aristotle's account of pleasure appears to be completely general. Thus, Aristotle appears to hold that bodily pleasures, like all other pleasures, involve psychic restoration. This may be explained in one of two ways. Aristotle may interpret Plato as holding and consequently himself hold that whenever pleasure occurs, the soul is restored. Alternatively, Aristotle may be modifying Plato's view on the grounds that Aristotle thinks that bodily pleasure, like all other pleasure, involves psychic restoration. In considering either position, it is important to make a few remarks about Aristotle's psychology or theory of the soul.

In our discussion of *Timaeus* in Chapter 4, we noted some fundamental difficulties with Plato's conception of the soul. On the one hand, Plato treats soul as a spatially extended entity. Accordingly, the soul is literally located within certain parts of the body. For example, the rational part is located in the brain. But Plato also treats soul as a substantively distinct entity from body. That is, soul is not itself a kind of body, composed, for example, of material elements, perhaps material elements distinct from those that compose lifeless entities. The soul is simply not composed of material elements. At the same time, Plato also treats certain parts of the soul as mortal, which is to say, destructible. This suggests that the parts of the soul themselves are complex. Once again, however, it is unclear what the constituents of these psychic parts are. In short, Plato's conception of the metaphysics of the soul is problematic.

Aristotle's conception of the soul largely, if not wholly, overcomes these problems in the following way. Aristotle holds that the soul is not a distinct, that is, separable substance from the body, but rather that soul is the form or structure or organization of the body or rather of parts of the body. More precisely, animate bodies are those that are formed, structured, or arranged in ways that enable them to perform specific functions, above all, growth and development through nourishment, locomotion, and sense-perception. Such forms, structures, or arrangements, conferring such functions, constitute the soul. Form and matter are, thus, two aspects of an individual living being:

> It is not necessary to ask whether soul and body are one, just as it is not necessary to ask whether the wax and its shape are one, nor generally whether the matter of each thing and that of which it is the matter are one. (*On the Soul* 412b)

As such, form and specifically soul does not and cannot exist separately from matter or body.[5] The Greek word "*hylē*" means "matter,"[6] and

---

[5] There are one or two exceptions to this last claim, which I mention in passing, but will not dwell upon. They are exceptional as instances of forms existing separately from matter. One is god; the other is intellect (*nous*). But it should also be noted that the latter case is controversial.

[6] More precisely, "*hylē*," which was widely used with the meaning "timber," was appropriated by Aristotle to mean "matter."

"*morphē*" means "form or shape." Thus, the adjective "hylomorphic" is used to refer to the Aristotelian conception of the unity of matter and form in general and specifically to Aristotle's conception of animate beings as ensouled bodies or equivalently enmattered souls.

Another, slightly less fundamental, distinction between Aristotle's and Plato's psychologies concerns the bodily location of the principal site of psychological activity. As we have seen, Plato locates the rational and thus, normatively, governing part of the soul in the brain, with the spirited and appetitive parts in the heart and abdomen or specifically liver respectively. In contrast, Aristotle identifies the heart as the principal site of all psychological activity:

The animal's ability for sense-perception, locomotion, and nutrition lies in the same part of the body ... The analogue [of the heart] in bloodless animals and the heart in sanguineous animals is such a part. (*On the Parts of Animals* 647a)

To return now to our first point about Aristotle's account of pleasure in *Rhetoric* I.11, specifically to the point that pleasure entails psychic restoration – Aristotle's hylomorphic conception entails that the soul cannot be affected without the body.[7] Thus, Aristotle's hylomorphism provides an explanation for why in *Rhetoric* he speaks generally of pleasure as involving psychic restoration.

A second notable point of difference between Plato's view of pleasure and the account Aristotle gives in *Rhetoric* I.11 is that Aristotle speaks of the soul's restoration to its "prevailing" (*hyparchousa*) condition. Aristotle does not take the soul's prevailing condition to be identical to its natural condition. The prevailing condition may be the natural condition, but it may also be a non-natural habituated condition. Consider the way Aristotle's discussion continues:

Habits are also pleasant. For as soon as a thing has become habitual, it is virtually natural. Habit is a thing not unlike nature. What happens often is akin to what happens always. Natural events happen always; habitual events happen often. (*Rhetoric* 1370a)

Aristotle's view of the relation between natural and habituated conditions is in fact complicated for the following reason. There are certain psychic conditions whose natural state can only be achieved by means of habituation. In particular, central to Aristotle's ethics is the view that excellence of character is a psychic condition that is engendered through habituation.

---

[7] Again, an exception to this may be intellectual pleasure.

Character excellence is the natural condition of the psychic faculty that is akin to Plato's spirited part of the soul. In this context, as in the context of Plato's discussion of pleasure, "natural" is intended normatively. In particular, for Aristotle "natural" here means the condition that "nature intends as the goal of development." For example, a flourishing oak tree is the natural condition of an acorn. Accordingly, various natural conditions, in this sense of "natural," may come about by various means, and some of these means are habituation. Again, this is the case with character excellence. Granted this, assume that a man's character has been habituated in such a way that it is malformed or perverse. Consequently, the prevailing state or condition of that particular man's character will not be the natural condition of man's character. However, Aristotle holds, this particular man may experience pleasure and pain relative to that prevailing, habitual, non-natural condition. Consequently, it is necessary to recognize an Aristotelian distinction between natural habituation and non-natural habituation and accordingly between natural and non-natural habituated prevailing states in relation to which pleasure, as restoration, is oriented.

Despite some important differences, the account of pleasure at the beginning of *Rhetoric* I.11 seems to be an Aristotelian variation on a dominantly Platonic theme. There are a couple of other passages where Aristotle appears to maintain a Platonic conception of pleasure. One of these occurs in *Posterior Analytics*. The context is a point of logic in argumentation, and Aristotle uses pleasure to illustrate the point:

> It is possible for there to be several demonstrations of the same thing not only if one takes a non-continuous middle term from the same chain – for example, C, D, and F for AB – but also if one takes a middle term from a different chain. For example, let A be mutating, D change, B pleasure, and again G be coming to rest. Now it is true to predicate both D of B (that is, pleasure is change) and A of D (change is mutation); for the man who is experiencing pleasure is undergoing change, and what is undergoing change is mutating. Again, it is true to predicate A of G (mutating is coming to rest) and G of B (coming to rest is pleasure); for everyone who is experiencing pleasure is coming to rest, and he who is coming to rest is mutating. (87b)

For convenience, I ignore the logical point. The pertinent content here is that pleasure is assumed to be a kind of change and precisely one directed toward rest. Aristotle does not explicitly say that the point of rest is the natural or prevailing condition of the soul or that such change is restoration, but this is the most plausible interpretation.

Somewhat similar to the *Posterior Analytics* passage is the following one from *Topics*, another treatise on argumentation, where again pleasure is used to illustrate a logical point:

If, therefore, change is stated to be the genus of pleasure, you should look to see if pleasure is neither locomotion nor alteration, nor any of the remaining species of change, for clearly [if change is not the genus of pleasure,] pleasure will not partake of any of the species [of change], and therefore not of the genus either, since what partakes of the genus must partake of one of the species as well. (121a)

Aristotle's use of the thesis that pleasure is a kind of change to illustrate logical points in both the *Topics* and *Posterior Analytics* passages is consistent with the view that he himself does not maintain the thesis. But, of course, it is also consistent with the view that Aristotle does maintain the thesis. We cannot tell simply from the illustrations. Granted this, the mere fact that Aristotle uses the thesis as illustrative provides a presumptive reason to think that he is committed to it.

Note, however, that even if we grant that Aristotle is committed to the thesis that pleasure is a kind of change, the *Topics* passage does not entail that he holds that pleasure is a type of restoration. There are other types of change. In contrast to the *Posterior Analytics* passage, the *Topics* passage says nothing about coming to be or coming to rest. Furthermore, in another passage in *Topics* Aristotle again uses pleasure to illustrate a point about argumentation. There he also speaks of pleasure as a kind of change; however, his statement entails the denial of the view that pleasure is a restorative change:

Look and see also if that in relation to which he has rendered the term is a process of generation (*genesis*) or an activation (*energeia*), for nothing of that kind is an end or completion (*telos*), for the result of the activation or process of generation is the completion rather than the process of generation or activation itself. Or perhaps this is not true in all cases, for almost everybody would rather be experiencing pleasure than have ceased experiencing pleasure, so that they would count the activation as the completion rather than the result of the activation. (146b)

Here pleasure is conceived as an end in itself. This entails that pleasure is not a restoration, for restoration has an end outside of itself. The end outside of restoration is the natural or prevailing state. This is what restoration is for the sake of; it is what restoration is for.

The second *Topics* passage comes from Book 6; the first passage comes from Book 4. Assuming that Aristotle held the same view about pleasure throughout his composition of *Topics*, the first *Topics* passage could indicate Aristotle's view that although pleasure is a change, it is not a restorative one. This is a reason to think that the first *Topics* passage does not reflect Aristotle's commitment to the Platonic view of pleasure as a restoration. Moreover, as we will see, the view expressed in the second *Topics* passage, that pleasure is an activation (*energeia*), is distinctly Aristotelian. In other words, in this case, albeit merely for illustrative purposes, Aristotle is definitely employing a thesis to which he is committed.

What conclusion are we to draw from this result vis-à-vis the *Posterior Analytics* and *Rhetoric* passages? Again, in the case of the *Posterior Analytics* passage, we might claim that Aristotle is merely employing a Platonic thesis for the sake of illustrating his logical point. Let us momentarily assume so. In that case, a similar interpretation might be advanced in the case of the *Rhetoric* passage. As two scholars of pleasure in Greek philosophy propose, "the aim of [*Rhetoric*] did not require [Aristotle's] acceptance" of the restorative conception of pleasure; instead, Aristotle merely needed "a current view."[8] After all, the study of rhetoric is supposed to teach not particular substantive theses in, say, ethics or metaphysics, but how to speak persuasively on behalf of any substantive thesis. But this pat solution does not sit well with the agenda of *Rhetoric* I.II in particular. Aristotle is not using the restorative conception merely to illustrate some other point, as he seems to be in *Posterior Analytics*. Rather, section II of *Rhetoric* I falls within a broader movement of the treatise in which Aristotle distinguishes the emotions. The correct and not merely some current or conventional account of the emotions is necessary for expertise in rhetoric precisely because rhetoric's means of persuasion involve appeal to the emotions and not merely to reason.

The current, prevailing view concerning the composition date of *Rhetoric* is that certain sections of the work, including I.II, were written quite early in Aristotle's career, specifically during his years at Plato's Academy, 367–347.[9] If this view is correct, then I think that it is likely that the restorative conception of pleasure in I.II is Aristotle's and reflects the influence of Academic thought on him. I suggest, then, that at one point in his career Aristotle did hold the view that pleasure is a kind of

---

[8] Justin Gosling and Christopher Taylor, *The Greeks on Pleasure*, Clarendon Press, 1982, 198.

[9] Consider the remarks of a recent translator and commentator on Aristotle's *Rhetoric*: "The chronological fixing of the *Rhetoric* has turned out to be a delicate matter. At least the core of *Rhet.* I & II seems to be an early work, written during Aristotle's first stay in Athens (it is unclear, however, which chapters belong to that core; regularly mentioned are the chapters 1.4–15 and II.1–17). It is true that the *Rhetoric* refers to historical events that fall in the time of Aristotle's exile and his second stay in Athens, but most of them can be found in the chapters II.23–24, and besides this, examples could have been updated, which is especially plausible if we assume that the *Rhetoric* formed the basis of a lecture held several times" (Christoph Rapp, "Aristotle's Rhetoric," *Stanford Encyclopedia of Philosophy*, available at: plato.stanford.edu/entries/aristotle-rhetoric).

restoration. *Rhetoric* 1.11 is our principal evidence for this conclusion. This conclusion is, I believe, strengthened precisely by the fact that the restorative conception of pleasure in *Rhetoric* is not simply Platonic, but, as I have suggested, an Aristotelian variation on a Platonic theme.

Finally, this conclusion in turn encourages reconsideration of the view that in the *Posterior Analytics* passage, where pleasure entails restoration, Aristotle is expressing his own view. Confirmation of that possibility depends on whether the composition of *Posterior Analytics* or at least this section of *Posterior Analytics* can be dated prior to *Topics* 4 and 6. So far as I know, there is no compelling evidence to support the view that *Posterior Analytics* was composed so early. But before drawing any conclusion about the *Posterior Analytics* passage, there is one further piece of evidence or, if you will, twist in the story of Aristotle's early conception of pleasure that we need to address. Consider the following, now third, passage from *Topics*, this time from Book 1:

Moreover, see if one use of a term has a contrary, while another has absolutely none. For example, the pleasure of drinking has a contrary, the pain of thirst; whereas the pleasure of perceiving that the diagonal is incommensurate with the side has none, so that pleasure is used in more than one way. (106a–b)

In this passage, Aristotle is suggesting to his intended audience, students of dialectic, a strategy for determining whether a term is homonymous. By "homonymous" Aristotle means something like "equivocal." The adjective "light" is equivocal since it means "being bright" as well as "having little weight." "Homonymy," more precisely, is an Aristotelian term of art, which means that a single word refers to entities that are distinct precisely in that each has a different essence (*ousia*). I will clarify what an essence is momentarily. In the *Topics* passage, the proposed argumentative strategy for identifying homonymy is to check whether in its uses the given term has or lacks one and the same contrary. Aristotle suggests that "pleasure" is homonymous, for in one of its uses it has a contrary, but in another it does not.

A term such as "bank" is also homonymous, in one sense meaning "an embankment," in another "a financial institution." But the case of "bank" is one in which the senses or the kinds of referent are radically distinct. Homonymy does not require such a radical distinction. So the pleasure of drinking when thirsty, an appetitive or bodily pleasure, and the pleasure of discerning a geometrical truth, a rational or theoretical pleasure, must be essentially distinct, but need not be radically essentially distinct. For Aristotle, things that are distinct in essence (*ousia*) have different definitions, where the definition of an entity E is given by the genus to which E belongs and its differentiating property (*diaphora* in Greek, *differentia* in Latin). A differentiating property of E is a property without which E could not exist as E and that distinguishes E from other species of the same genus. For example, human being may be defined as rational animal, that is, animal (genus) that is rational (differentiating property). In that case, the differentiating property of being rational distinguishes human beings from other animals. Thus, in the *Topics* passage, Aristotle thinks – assuming his illustration reflects his own views – that there are at least two essentially distinct kinds of pleasure.

The pleasure of drinking when thirsty appears to be a restoration. The pleasure of appreciating a geometrical truth does not. For convenience, I will hereafter refer to these two kinds of pleasure as "restorative" and "non-restorative" respectively. In that case, Aristotle's conception of pleasure in *Topics* may not simply be an outright rejection of the Platonic view. Rather, Aristotle may admit with Plato that restorative pleasure exists, but hold that something else, non-restorative, is also properly called "pleasure." As Aristotle often puts the point when he speaks of homonymy, "pleasure" is *spoken of in multiple ways*.

Since the restorative view in *Rhetoric* 1.11 is stated in a completely general way, it now appears that Aristotle's early conception of pleasure underwent development. Initially, Aristotle held a restorative view, the Aristotelian variation on a Platonic theme. Subsequently, Aristotle held that some pleasures are not restorative. As we will see below, in *Eudemian Ethics* 6.11–14 (= *Nicomachean Ethics* 7.11–14), Aristotle subsequently and explicitly rejects the view that any pleasure is restorative. Indeed, it is questionable whether the development of Aristotle's conception of pleasure ends there. First, we need to examine the concept of pleasure as *energeia* and its relation to the concept of pleasure as restoration. But before doing so, there is one more brief point to consider.

In light of the preceding results, let us return to the *Posterior Analytics* passage, where, you will recall, Aristotle illustrates a logical point with the thesis that pleasure is a restoration. So long as this passage was composed prior to *Eudemian Ethics* 6, it is consistent with Aristotle's holding either the earliest view that all pleasure is restorative or the subsequent view that some pleasures are non-restorative. Plausibly, *Posterior Analytics* is a relatively early work.[10] Accordingly, we may tentatively conclude that

---

[10] An argument for a relatively early composition date for *Posterior Analytics* can be found in Robin Smith, "The Relationship of Aristotle's Two *Analytics*," *Classical Quarterly* 32 (1982) 327–335.

Aristotle does not merely use the restoration thesis to exemplify a logical point, but that he is committed to that thesis or at least to the thesis that some pleasures are restorative. It must be emphasized, however, that this conclusion and indeed the preceding developmental account of Aristotle's early conception of pleasure are tentative. To reiterate – the main difficulties are twofold: first, sorting out the chronological relations of many of Aristotle's works is vexed; second, most of Aristotle's references to pleasure and its properties in the works we have been considering are for purposes of illustrating logical points and so extrinsic to hedonic theorizing.

ARISTOTLE'S CONCEPT OF 'ENERGEIA'

If pleasures such as those of appreciating or enjoying the contemplation of a mathematical truth are not restorative, what are they? In answering this question, let us turn to Aristotle's more distinctive conception of pleasure in *Eudemian Ethics* 6. Once again, *Eudemian Ethics* 6 is identical to *Nicomachean Ethics* 7. Yet I regard *Eudemian Ethics* otherwise as an earlier composition than *Nicomachean Ethics*. Consequently, I will refer to the treatment of pleasure in *Eudemian Ethics* 6 rather than *Nicomachean Ethics* 7.

As I have mentioned, in *Eudemian Ethics* 6 Aristotle argues that pleasure is an activation (*energeia*). In fact, we have seen that Aristotle introduces this view in *Topics*:

Almost everybody would rather be experiencing pleasure than have ceased experiencing pleasure, so that they would count the activation (*energeia*) as the end (*telos*) rather than the completion of the activation. (146b)

At some point between the composition of *Rhetoric* 1.11 and *Topics*, Aristotle rejected the view that all pleasures are restorative and, as I have suggested, replaced it with the view that at least some pleasures are activations.[11]

The term that I am translating as "activation," namely, "*energeia*," is central to Aristotle's philosophy. It is often translated as "actuality" and thereby contrasted with "potentiality" (*dynamis*). "*Energeia*" is most likely an Aristotelian coinage. If not, then some other heir of Plato coined the

---

[11] Aristotle also advances the view of pleasure as activation in *Protrepticus*. It has recently been proposed that this work was composed after Isocrates' *Antidosis* and so *c.* 350 BCE. (See Gerhart Schneeweiß, *Aristoteles Protreptikos Hinführung zur Philosophie*, Wissenschaftliche Buchgesellschaft, 2005, 28–30.) However, we don't know the relative dates of *Protrepticus* and *Topics* 6.

term in the Old Academy around the mid fourth century.[12] It is note-worthy that the term does not occur in any of Plato's works.

There has been a great deal of controversy over the etymology of "*energeia.*" But assuming that the term was coined as a technical expression by philosophers not necessarily committed to etymological principles that any modern linguist would endorse, that controversy seems to me misguided. More vociferous still has been the debate over the development of the concept in Aristotle's works. Indeed, there is development. Fortunately, we can entirely skirt that vexatious subject too, for the use of "*energeia*" in conjunction with the topic of pleasure in the texts we will be treating is, to my mind at least, rather clear.

"*Energeia*" is a noun cognate with the verb "*energein*" and the adjective "*energos.*" The verb means "to make use of"; the adjective means "active," "at work," or "in use" as opposed to "idle" or, less pejoratively, "available for use," "ready at hand," "on stand-by." *Energeia* is, then, the condition of being in use, deployed, exercised, or at work. Both something in use, deployed, or being exercised and something available for use, ready at hand, or on stand-by are in existence and thus actual. Hence, the existential implications of "actuality" in contrast to "potentiality" are misleading. At the same time, it should be emphasized that a given activation is relative to a given potential, an actual potential, for that activation.

Consideration of some Aristotelian passages will help to support this rendition as "activation" and to corroborate this sense of "*energeia.*" In particular, I have chosen passages in which Aristotle contrasts the condition of being exercised or used with the condition of being ready or available to use or exercise. Indeed, it seems that Aristotle or his Academic contemporaries coined the term "*energeia*" precisely to clarify this distinction:

Things are said to be alive in two senses, in virtue of capability and in virtue of activation (*energeiai*), for we describe as seeing both those animals that have sight and the natural ability to see, even if they happen to have their eyes shut, and those that are using this capability and are looking at something. Similarly with knowing and cognition: we sometimes mean by it the deployment of the capability and contemplation, sometimes the possession of the capability and having of knowledge. (*Protrepticus* fr. 79)

Likewise, also in the case of abilities and uses of things – for if an ability is a disposition, then also to be able is to be disposed; and if the use of anything is an

---

[12] "Old Academy" refers to the first period in the history of the school Plato founded, including Plato's first four successors as heads, called "scholarchs" in Greek: Speusippus, Xenocrates, Polemo, and Crates. The Old Academy ends with the beginning of Arcesilaus' scholarchy in 266 BCE. Another possibility is that the term "*energeia*" derives from medical theory.

activation (*energeia*), then to use it is to activate (*energein*) [it], and to have used it is to have activated (*enêrgêkenai*) [it]. (*Topics* 124a)

Again, all causes, whether they are properly so called or whether they are so called in virtue of some coincidental attribute, may be called causes either because they are able to cause or because they are actively operating (*energeiai*) as causes. For example, the cause of the building of the house may be either a builder (something able to cause) or a builder building (something actively causing). (*Physics* 195b)

Wealth as a whole consists in using things rather than in possessing them. It is really the activation (*energeia*), that is, the use of property that constitutes wealth. (*Rhetoric* 1361a)

So much, then, for a first pass at the interpretation of "*energeia*" as "activation." In an effort to clarify this concept further, I will discuss one kind of activation, sense-perception, in greater detail.

SENSE-PERCEIVING AS A KIND OF PSYCHIC ACTIVATION

As Aristotle himself notes in his treatise *On the Soul*, the term "sense-perception" (*aisthêsis*) can be used in multiple ways. In other words, the term "sense-perception" is homonymous. In particular, "sense-perception" can be used to refer to a psychic capacity or disposition as well as to the activation of this capacity. For example, an animal may possess the capacity for a certain form of sense-perception, say, vision, but not be using this capacity at a given moment, for instance, because it is sleeping. For the sake of clarity I will use the gerund "sense-perceiving" to refer to the activation of the capacity or disposition, and I will use "sense-perceptual faculty" for the capacity or disposition itself. In the case of certain sense-perceptual modalities, this distinction is clearly marked in English, whereas in the case of others it is not. Compare "vision" and "seeing" or "taste" and "tasting" with "hearing" and "hearing."

In his treatise *On Sense-Perception and Sensibles*, Aristotle claims that each specific sense-perceptual organ is principally constituted by a distinct kind of material element. For example, the eye is principally constituted by water; the nose by fire; the ear by air. These elements have properties that variously enable them to be affected by the various proper objects of sense-perception.

It is convenient to distinguish two ways in which the sensible object may be described. Aristotle distinguishes what he calls "proper" (*idion*) sensible objects from coincidental (*symbebêkos*) objects of sense-perception. Proper sensible objects are the specific objects of specific sense-perceptual modalities. For example, color is the proper sensible object of vision and so seeing, and sound is the proper sensible object of hearing. In contrast, when one sees the red surface of an apple, the apple is the coincidental object of visual sense-perceiving; likewise, when one hears the sounds of a bird, the bird is the coincidental object of auditory sense-perceiving.

Recall that in our discussion of Empedocles' theory of vision in Chapter 3 and in our discussion of Plato's theory of vision in Chapter 4 we said that a satisfactory account of sense-perception must explain how the sense-perceptual organ and the sensible object come into contact. I explained that historically theories are divisible into two main types: those of intramission and those of extramission. Empedocles' is a theory of intramission: sensible objects release effluences or emanations from their surfaces; these are transmitted through the intervening space and enter the eye of the perceiver. In contrast, Plato's is a theory of extramission: a fire-like substance within the eye projects outward and contacts objects. Aristotle holds an intramission theory. But unlike Empedocles, Aristotle explains that all contact between sensibles, that is, objects of sense-perception, and sense-perceptual organs occurs through a medium (*to metaxy*), that is, a physical intermediary. In the case of vision, this medium is identified as "the diaphanous or transparent." Since we can see by means of both air and water, the diaphanous is a property shared by both elements. Moreover, Aristotle holds that the diaphanous is activated by the presence of light. Consequently, the color of a given external object (conceived as an intrinsic property of that object) affects the diaphanous. The diaphanous transmits this affection to the perceiver, specifically, to the visual organ of the perceiver.[13]

This much of Aristotle's account is relatively clear. The theory becomes more obscure when it comes to explaining the way in which the affection on the sense-perceptual-organ, by the sensible object via the medium, is perceived. Contrast the way a stone next to a fire becomes hot or the way air next to a flower becomes fragrant. In both cases, impercipient entities are affected by coming to have tactile and olfactory properties. Likewise, a sentient creature might be so affected without perceiving the affections, for example, if it is asleep or otherwise unconscious.

In fact, it is controversial whether for Aristotle sense-perceiving requires any material affection whatsoever. One school of interpretation, which

---

[13] In the cases of hearing and smell, it is ostensibly clear that a similar medium must facilitate sense-perceiving. In the cases of touch and taste, it is less clear; nonetheless, Aristotle maintains that various media exist in all cases.

scholars refer to as "spiritualism," holds that sense-perceiving is a psychic change that entails no correlative material change or affection. Sense-perceiving simply occurs when the following conditions are met: the appropriate sensible object is accessible; there is an intervening sensory medium of the right kind and in the right condition; and the sense-perceptual organ and faculty are intact.[14]

I find spiritualism inconsistent with hylomorphism generally and with the textual evidence precisely. For example, early in *On the Soul* Aristotle explicitly states that sense-perceiving requires a material affection:

The affections of the soul present a further difficulty. Are they shared by that which possesses the soul [the body], or are some of them particular to the soul itself? . . . In most cases, it is apparent that the soul neither is affected nor acts without the body, for example, when it becomes angry, confident, desirous, and when it sense-perceives (*aisthanesthai*). (403a)[15]

The question, then, is what sort of material affection occurs. Scholars who advance this interpretation, called "literalism," construe the material affection in one of two ways: brute literally or representationally. Brute literally, the sense-perceptual organ comes to have the sensible quality of the sensible object. Compare the skin becoming hot when next to a fire. In the case of vision, when one sees a red object, the visual organ, more precisely, the aqueous "eye jelly" (*korê*), as Aristotle conceives it, is supposed to become colored red.[16]

According to a representational interpretation, the sense-perceptual organ does not acquire the sensible quality of the sensible object. Rather – to continue with the example of vision – the affection of the eye or eye jelly materially encodes or contains information. This information is transmitted to and interpreted by the sense-perceptual faculty, located in or about the heart. The information is interpreted as representing the sensible quality, and so in this case representing the color red. More precisely, the representation shares with the sensible quality information concerning the way in which the sensible quality is constituted. One

---

[14] Spiritualism has been defended, most prominently by Myles Burnyeat in a number of papers, for instance, "Is an Aristotelian Philosophy of Mind Still Credible? (A Draft)" and "How Much Happens When Aristotle Sees Red and Hears Middle C? Remarks on *De Anima* 2.7–8," both in M. Nussbaum and A. Rorty, eds., *Essays on Aristotle's De Anima*, Clarendon Press, 1995, 15–26 and 421–434.

[15] The exception, which is what Aristotle has in mind, is the activation of the intellect.

[16] A prominent brute literal interpreter is Richard Sorabji, "Body and Soul in Aristotle," *Philosophy* 49 (1974) 63–89; and "Intentionality and Physiological Processes: Aristotle's Theory of Sense Perception," in M. Nussbaum and A. Rorty, eds., *Essays on Aristotle's De Anima*, Clarendon Press, 1995, 195–225.

commentator offers the following analogy: compare a building with an architect's blueprint of the building. The blueprint represents the building by containing information concerning the way the building is constructed. Granted this, the question arises: What sort of information could there be about the way sensible qualities are constituted that could represent those qualities? In *On Sense-Perception and Sensibles*, Aristotle explains that proportions of light and dark constitute colors. Consequently, the information conveyed in sense-perceiving includes the proportions or ratio of light and dark of the proper sensible object. Some such information is supposed to be conveyed in the case of all the sense-perceptual modalities.[17]

In short, according to the representationalist-literalist interpretation, the activation (*energeia*) of sense-perception involves the reception of the form, without the matter, of the sensible object. Compare Aristotle's own words in *On the Soul*:

We must grasp that generally ... sense-perception involves that which is receptive of the sensible forms without the matter, just as the wax receives the impression of the signet ring without the iron or gold, and grasps the impression from the gold or bronze, but not as gold or bronze. (424a)

PLEASURE AS ACTIVATION IN 'EUDEMIAN ETHICS'

Let us now examine Aristotle's account of pleasure as activation. In *Eudemian Ethics* 6.12, Aristotle asserts that pleasure is an activation. More precisely, Aristotle claims that pleasure is "an unimpeded activation of a natural disposition."[18] In fact, Aristotle's view in Book 6 is still more specific than this. He maintains that pleasure is an unimpeded activation of a certain set of kinds of natural disposition. In clarifying this claim, we need to clarify each of the other three concepts involved: disposition (*hexis*), natural (*kata physin*), and unimpeded (*anempodiston*).

When elsewhere in *Eudemian Ethics* (2.2) Aristotle explicitly defines or clarifies "disposition" (*hexis*),[19] he specifically has in mind dispositions of

---

[17] This line of interpretation has been well defended by Victor Caston, "The Spirit and the Letter: Aristotle on Perception," in R. Salles, ed., *Metaphysics, Soul, and Ethics*, Oxford University Press, 2005, 245–320.

[18] 1153a. Note that here and throughout the pagination actually refers to *Nicomachean Ethics* 7. This is due to the fact that editors tend to publish only the unique books of *Eudemian Ethics*.

[19] It is worth noting that the noun "*hexis*" is cognate with the verb "*echein*," meaning "to have," and so literally means "(a) having," that is, "a condition of possessing."

ethical character. He views these as responsible for the formation of emotional dispositions that are in turn responsible for our emotional reactions:

And dispositions (*hexeis*) are the causes through which the powers [that constitute our emotional tendencies] belong to us in a reasonable way or the opposite, for example, courage, self-control, cowardice, lack of self-control. (1220b)

Aristotle puts the point somewhat more clearly in *Nicomachean Ethics* 2.5:

It is in terms of dispositions (*hexeis*) that we are well or badly disposed in relation to emotions, as for example in relation to becoming angry, if we are violently or sluggishly disposed, we are badly disposed. And if in an intermediate way, then we are well disposed. (1105b)

Despite these passages, it is quite clear that in *Eudemian Ethics* 6, Aristotle does not limit pleasures to activations of dispositions of ethical character. In particular, there are also intellectual, sense-perceptual, and imaginative pleasures, and these involve activations of intellectual, sense-perceptual, and imaginative dispositions respectively.[20] In that case, Aristotle must be using "disposition" in *Eudemian Ethics* 6.12 in a broader sense than in *Eudemian Ethics* 2.2 and *Nicomachean Ethics* 2.5.

There is textual evidence to support Aristotle's use of a broader conception of disposition. For example, in *Categories* 10, *Topics* 2.8, and *Topics* 5.6, Aristotle refers to sense-perceptual faculties such as sight and hearing as dispositions.[21] Again, in *Topics* 6.9 he refers to the possession of knowledge as a disposition;[22] and in *Categories* 8, he includes forms of knowledge as well as ethical character traits as dispositions. In such cases, "having a disposition" simply seems equivalent to "possessing a capacity or faculty." Indeed, compare a line from one of the *Topics* passages we considered above: "For if an ability is a disposition, then also to be able is to be disposed." In fact, in *Eudemian Ethics* 6.12 itself Aristotle refers to bodily health as a disposition.[23] Consequently, I suggest that in his definition of pleasure in *Eudemian Ethics* 6.12, Aristotle is using "disposition" to refer simply to a capacity, in this case, a psychic capacity.

By "natural" in "natural disposition" Aristotle means "natural" in the normative sense, namely, the goal (*telos*) or normative endpoint of development. In fact, when he speaks of bodily health in

---

[20] Aristotle regards intellect (*nous*) as a distinct psychic faculty alongside nutrition, locomotion, and sense-perception.
[21] *Categories* 12a, *Topics* 114a, *Topics* 135b.   [22] 147b.   [23] 1152b.

Eudemian Ethics 6.12 as a disposition, he uses this very phrase, "natural disposition" (*hê physikê hexis*).[24]

I said, more precisely, that Aristotle views pleasure as the activation of a certain set of kinds of natural disposition. This set correlates with Aristotle's view that the soul has various faculties or powers. Among these faculties, three are particularly relevant to this discussion: sense-perception, character, and intellect. Aristotle certainly recognizes imaginative pleasures as well, in particular, memorial and anticipatory pleasures. But he has very little to say about these.[25] Additionally, he is less clear about whether imagination constitutes a distinct psychic faculty.

We have introduced sense-perception above. Character consists of those traits, acquired through habitual action, that, as the passage above from *Nicomachean Ethics* 2.5 indicated, variously dispose us to emotional reactions. More broadly and importantly, character disposes us to various kinds of ethically relevant action. The faculty of intellect, which facilitates both practical and theoretical intellectual activity, develops through learning and study. Accordingly, these two forms of intellect are rational (*logikon*) faculties. In contrast, sense-perception and character are irrational (*alogon*) faculties – although Aristotle allows that character "participates in reason in a way,"[26] namely, by having the capacity to follow the judgment or obey the injunctions of practical intellect. For example, we may know that pursuing such-and-such a course of action is the right thing to do because it is the courageous thing to do. But we need to have the ethical character trait of courage to comply with this practical conclusion.

Normally, the dispositions of the sense-perceptual faculties are natural. For example, humans are normally born with the capacity to hear rather than deaf. In the cases of the characterological and practical- and theoretical-intellectual faculties, the condition of the disposition depends upon the kind of habituation and learning to which the individual is subject. In fact, in these cases the achievement of natural dispositions is rare. For example, only a studious philosopher or mathematician will achieve the natural disposition of the theoretical intellect, and only a well-socialized and well-habituated person will achieve the natural disposition of character. In short, pleasure entails the activation of one of these kinds of disposition when it is in its natural condition.

---

[24] Note also, then, that in his definition of pleasure in *Eudemian Ethics* 6.12, Aristotle is ignoring what we described in our account of Aristotle's early conception of pleasure in *Rhetoric* 1.11 as prevailing dispositions that are non-natural, that is, mis-habituated or perverse dispositions. Aristotle's silence here is not due to a change of opinion on this matter.

[25] But see *Physics* 247a.   [26] *Nicomachean Ethics* 1102b.

Aristotle's view that pleasure requires the *unimpeded* activation of one of these natural dispositions relates to the idea that at least characterological and sense-perceptual activations also depend upon conditions external to the respective faculties of the soul. Consider a case of seeing. Hermogenes goes to Delphi to gaze on a newly erected statue of Apollo. Hermogenes has good vision. Thus, his visual organ is disposed in a natural way. But he arrives late in the day. Not only is it dark, but it is rainy and windy. These environmental conditions impede Hermogenes from activating his vision in a complete or full way. Again, assume that Hermogenes goes to Philocrates' house to look at a statue of Apollo in the atrium. Assume that it is a sunny day and that the weather is calm. On the other hand, assume that Philocrates has invited Hermogenes to view the statue because he is angry at the manager of the workshop he commissioned to sculpt it. The manager offered him a good price, but the statue itself has been poorly executed. Hermogenes arrives to see the shoddy workmanship, the disproportions in the figure, and the crude treatment of the surface. In this case, Hermogenes beholds the object clearly and stead-fastly, but the object itself impedes the activation of his vision in a full or complete way insofar as it is not visually beautiful. In both cases, Hermogenes sees, but he does not see well. In the first case, Hermogenes fails to see well because he fails to see clearly. In the second case, Hermogenes fails to see well because the sensible object is not beautiful. "See well" is, then, ambiguous here. But the ambiguity extends to Aristotle's conception of the function of vision. Vision serves both the aim of merely living and the aim of flourishing, that is, living well. Thus, in *On Sense-Perception and Sensibles* Aristotle writes:

To all those [animals] that possess [smell, hearing, and vision], they are a means of survival, in order that they may be aware of their food before they pursue it and may avoid what is inferior or destructive; while in those that have intelligence, these sense-perceptual faculties also exist for the sake of living well. For they inform us of many distinctions, from which arises understanding both of the object of theory and of practical matters. (436b–437a)

The example of visual impediments is merely illustrative. There are different kinds of impediment for the activation of different kinds of natural disposition, sense-perceptual and non-sense-perceptual. For example, one cannot exercise certain natural dispositions of ethical character or practical reasoning, for instance, courage or practical judgment pertaining to courage, unless one is confronted with certain environmental conditions, in this case, danger. Likewise, one cannot exercise moderation or practical judgment pertaining to moderation unless one is confronted with a situation in which there is something tempting.

When in *Eudemian Ethics* Aristotle claims that pleasure is an unimpeded activation, he says more precisely:

Instead of perceived (*aisthêtê*), one should say unimpeded (*anempodistos*). (1153a)

Given this, an adequate explanation of the condition of being unimpeded that Aristotle requires for pleasure must involve an explanation of why Aristotle thinks the condition of being unimpeded should replace the condition of being perceived. One idea is that Aristotle uses "unimpeded" instead of "perceived" because there are non-sense-perceptual pleasures, again, characterological and intellectual pleasures. But this explanation is unsatisfactory for two reasons. One is that it does not explain why "unimpeded" should *replace* "perceived," only why "perceived" itself is inadequate. The other reason is that Aristotle seems to use "perceived" here in the sense of "grasped by awareness," that is, as a general term for awareness or consciousness rather than a specific term for sense-perceptual awareness.

A more satisfactory explanation of why Aristotle suggests replacing "perceived" with "unimpeded" is this. Recall the Platonic idea that some restorations are not robust or swift enough to be perceived. In that case, lack of robustness or swiftness constitutes a defeater for the realization of the pleasure. Impediments play an analogous role: pleasure will not occur if defeaters are present.

In short, in *Eudemian Ethics* 6 Aristotle maintains that pleasure is the unimpeded and thus full or complete activation of sense-perceptual, characterological, or intellectual faculties that are in their natural conditions.

ARISTOTLE'S CRITICISM OF THE RESTORATION THEORY

In light of the preceding discussion, Aristotle's conception of pleasure up to and including *Eudemian Ethics* 6.12 seems to have developed: from (a) a variation on a Platonic restorative theme to (b) the homonymy view, expressed in *Topics*, that there are essentially distinct restorative and non-restorative pleasures to (c) the view that no pleasures are restorations or processes of generation (*genesis*). What transpired in Aristotle's thinking about pleasure between his early commitment to the restoration theory and his account of pleasure as an unimpeded activation of a natural disposition in *Eudemian Ethics* 6?

One thing that occurred is that Aristotle came to accept that some pleasures are not preceded by pains or lacks and hence that there are some non-restorative pleasures. Although this view is not expressed in *Topics* 1, I assume it lies behind the view that some pleasures, namely restorative or generative ones, have contraries, namely destructive pains, whereas other pleasures have no contraries:

Moreover, see if one use of a term has a contrary, while another has absolutely none. For example, the pleasure of drinking has a contrary, the pain of thirst, whereas the pleasure of perceiving that the diagonal is incommensurate with the side has none, so that pleasure is used in more than one way. (*Topics* 106a–b)

Recall that it is in *Republic* 9 that Plato first introduces the idea of pure pleasures as those pleasures that are not preceded by pains. He uses olfactory pleasure to exemplify this: olfactory pleasure does not remedy some olfactory pain. This and like conditions do not, however, dissuade Plato from the view that olfactory pleasure involves the restoration or replenishment of an olfactory depletion. Instead, he maintains that olfactory depletion occurs, but that it is too subtle or gradual to register psychically. I suggest that at some point between the composition of *Rhetoric* 1.11 and *Topics* Aristotle ceased to find this view tenable.

Another reason for Aristotle's rejection of the restoration theory is that he came to think that so-called restorative pleasures are in fact not processes of restoration or generation. Instead, they are activations that accompany processes of restoration or generation. Assuming Aristotle is the author of *Magna Moralia* 2.7 and that he composed this text early in his career – although subsequent to *Rhetoric* 1.11 – this second criticism of the restoration theory first occurs here. Consider the following statement from *Magna Moralia*:

Since there is pleasure both when the natural condition is being restored (*kathistamenês*) and when the natural condition has been restored (*kathestêkuias*) – for example, the former includes replenishments of deficiencies, the latter includes pleasures of vision, hearing, and such things – the activations (*energeiai*) that occur when the natural condition has been restored are better. For the pleasures that are spoken of in both ways (*hêdonai kat' amphoterous legomenai tous tropous*) are activations (*energeiai*). (1205b)

Aristotle states here that both restorative and non-restorative pleasures are activations. But note that, in keeping with the homonymy view of *Topics* 1, he maintains that although non-restorative and restorative pleasures are both activations, they are still essentially different and thus spoken of in different ways. In other words, restorative and non-restorative pleasures are different kinds of activation. Given this, it is possible – and I see no reason to deny – that the view expressed here in *Magna Moralia* lies behind the view expressed in *Topics* 1.

Earlier in *Magna Moralia* 2.7, Aristotle clarifies why restorative pleasures are not processes of restoration as well as why people – presumably adherents of Plato's view, including Aristotle's earlier self – have been misled to think that they are:

On the whole, no pleasure is a process of generation (*genesis*). For even the pleasures that come from eating and drinking are not processes of generation (*geneseis*); and those who claim that these pleasures are processes of generation are mistaken. For they think that because pleasure occurs when we are being nourished, pleasure itself is a process of generation. But it isn't. For there is a certain part of the soul with which we experience pleasure at the same time as we are nourished with that in which we are deficient. This part of the soul is active (*energei*) and is changed (*kineitai*), and the change (*kinêsis*) that it undergoes and the activation (*energeia*) is pleasure. But because this part of the soul is active (*energein*) at the same time as we are nourished, or precisely because of its activation (*energeia*), they think that the pleasure is a process of generation – the nourishment being evident to them, but the part of the soul not. (1204b)

Aristotle explains here that restorative pleasures are not processes of generation, but merely co-occur with processes of generation. Given this, we should be attentive to the fact that when we continue to speak of restorative pleasure, as we will, we merely mean to refer to pleasure that occurs when restoration occurs, not to imply that the pleasure itself is a form of restoration.

Granted this, the *Magna Moralia* passage raises some significant questions. One is how Aristotle views the two kinds of pleasure, restorative and non-restorative, as essentially distinct activations. Another question relates to Aristotle's view that while the process of generation occurs, pleasure occurs in a different "part of the soul." What is the relation between the restoration and the pleasure? And, third, what part of the soul is activated in the hedonic experience? I will address the second and third questions first. In doing so, let's turn to Aristotle's criticism of the restoration theory in *Eudemian Ethics* 6.12:

Given that the good is part activation and part disposition, it is only coincidentally (*symbebêkos*) that the restorations to the natural disposition are pleasant. And the activation lies in the appetites (*epithymiais*) of the remaining disposition and nature. (1152b–1153a)[27]

---

[27] The passage continues: "For that matter, there are also pleasures unaccompanied by pain and appetite, like the activations of theorizing (*theôrein*), where there is no depletion of nature." By way of corroborating our earlier point that Aristotle came to reject the view that all pleasures are restorations, consider the claim that "there are some pleasures that are not accompanied by pain or appetite." We said that Plato holds this view as well and that he calls such pleasures "pure." But Aristotle's view is not that pleasures unpreceded by pains are preceded by unfelt lacks. Rather, as he says: "For there are also pleasures unaccompanied by pain and appetite ... where there is no depletion of the natural disposition." Moreover, Aristotle gives the pleasures of theorizing (*theôrein*) as an example of such pleasures. Apprehending or reflecting on a geometrical truth, the example he uses in *Topics*, is an example of theorizing.

As in the case of *Magna Moralia* 2.7, Aristotle here maintains that restorative pleasures are not restorations, but rather co-occur with restorations. Moreover, Aristotle explicitly describes the restorations as coincidentally (*symbebêkos*) pleasant. Again, this means that the restoration and the pleasure are coterminous, but that the restoration does not constitute the pleasure. Instead, the activation "of the remaining disposition and nature" constitutes the pleasure.

Aristotle does not specify that the restoration is bodily, but this is surely the case. More precisely, the restoration involves the exercise of the most basic faculty of the soul, namely, the nutritive faculty. This is a faculty that all living things, plants as well as animals, possess. For example, a fern as well as a foal may be dehydrated and hydrated. In contrast, I suggest that the experience of pleasure, concurrent with nutritive restoration, is a function of the appetitive part of the soul. Appetite depends upon perceptual capacities, which plants lack. In *Eudemian Ethics* 6.12, Aristotle so identifies the activated part of the soul that constitutes the pleasure that accompanies nutritive restoration: "the activation lies in the appetites (*epithymiais*) of the remaining disposition and nature." By "appetite" (*epithymia*) Aristotle means nutritive desire, specifically, hunger or thirst. While plants as well as animals can be dehydrated, they cannot experience a desire for liquid or solid nutrients. This is because desire depends on the capacity to represent the desideratum, namely, the capacity of imagination (*phantasia*). In this case, imagination is closely related to sense-perception, since the representation of the desideratum depends upon prior sense-perception:

If a living thing has the capacity for sense-perception, it also has the capacity for desire. For desire comprises appetitive desire . . . And all animals have at least one of the sense-perceptual faculties, namely, touch. For that which has sense-perception, there is both pleasure and pain, and both the pleasant and the painful; and where there are these, there is also appetitive desire, for this is desire for the pleasant. (*On the Soul* 414b)[28]

The pleasure that accompanies nutritive restoration, then, relates to appetitive desire. Precisely, one takes pleasure in certain foods and liquids. Since these sate one's hunger and quench one's thirst, Aristotle appears to commit himself to the view that restorative pleasure is appetitive desire-satisfaction. It is difficult to be sure that Aristotle in fact is committed to this view. Certainly, it must be emphasized that he does not explicitly characterize restorative pleasure as such.

---

[28] Cf. *On Sleep* 454b.

Related to this obscurity is the obscurity of the appetitive faculty itself. In particular, Aristotle here seems to conjoin or conflate the exercise of gustation with certain functions of digestion. For example, in some passages Aristotle refers to gustatory qualities such as bitterness,[29] but in others he seems to have in mind merely the consumption of nutriment. One explanation for this conflation or perhaps vagueness on Aristotle's part derives from a passage in his biological treatise *On the Parts of Animals*, where he is discussing the fact that some animals lack tongues and thus a sense-perceptual organ for taste:

In some fish … there is no appearance whatsoever of a tongue, unless the mouth is stretched open very widely indeed; while in others it is indistinctly separated from the rest of the mouth. The reason for this is that a tongue would be of but little service to such animals, seeing that they are unable to chew their food or taste it beforehand, the pleasurable sensations they derive from it occurring during swallowing. For it is in their passage down the gullet that solid edibles bring pleasure, while it is by the tongue that the flavor of fluids is perceived. Thus, it is during swallowing that the oiliness, the heat, and other such qualities of food are recognized. Now the viviparous animals also have this power of sense-perception – and in fact the satisfaction from most solid edibles and delicacies is derived almost entirely from the esophagus during swallowing; that is why the same animals are not intemperate both with regard to tasty drinks and with regard to delectable foods. But while other animals have in addition the perception of taste, tongueless animals lack it and have the other form of sense-perception only (namely, touch). (690b–691a)

In the case of tongueless animals, then, restorative, that is, appetitive, pleasures involve the exercise of tactile perception alone. For example, the heat or oiliness of food is perceived, but not, say, its sweetness or saltiness. In contrast, in the case of animals with tongues, appetitive pleasures involve both gustatory and tactile perception. Given the diversity of appetitive capacities and sense-perceptual forms among animals, it is understandable that Aristotle should leave the nature of the appetitive faculty vague when he describes appetitive pleasure.

I turn now to note an important distinction between the criticisms of the restoration theory in *Magna Moralia* and in *Eudemian Ethics*. As we saw, in *Magna Moralia* Aristotle maintains that although restorative and non-restorative pleasures are both activations, they are different kinds of activation and thus different kinds of pleasure. But in *Eudemian Ethics*, Aristotle never grants that restorative pleasure is a kind of pleasure. Consider the following passage from *Eudemian*

---

[29] I cite one such passage immediately below.

Ethics 6.12 where Aristotle attempts to support his view that restorations are only coincidentally pleasant:

An indication [that restorations are only coincidentally pleasant] is that people do not take pleasure in the same things while their nature is being restored and when it has been re-established. When it has been re-established, they take pleasure in things that are pleasant without qualification; but while it is being restored, they take pleasure even in things that are the contrary of these – even sharp and bitter things, neither of which is either naturally pleasant or pleasant without qualification. (1153a)

Aristotle maintains that restorative pleasures are only pleasures in a qualified way. Why? Because in *Eudemian Ethics*, but not in *Magna Moralia*, he maintains that pleasure is the *unimpeded* activation of the natural disposition. But the activation of the appetites that accompanies the restoration is not unimpeded. The conditions under which it operates are non-natural, a depleted rather than restored body. Thus, foods and liquids that are sharp and bitter will seem pleasant to it – even though, as Aristotle claims, these are not pleasant by nature.

   Compare Aristotle's description of restorative pleasure in *Eudemian Ethics* 6.14:

What I call coincidentally pleasant are things that are healing (*iatreuonta*). For because one happens to be healed by the action of that which remains healthy, *the healing seems to be pleasant.* (1154b, with my italics)[30]

Consequently, in *Eudemian Ethics* Aristotle maintains that the restorative pleasure, that is, pleasure that accompanies restoration, is only pleasure in a qualified way. In other words, the so-called pleasure does not satisfy all of the conditions for being pleasure. As such, there appears to be an important distinction between the position of *Magna Moralia* 2.7 and *Eudemian Ethics* 6. In *Magna Moralia* Aristotle treats both restorative and non-restorative pleasures as genuine kinds of pleasure. But in *Eudemian Ethics*, he treats restorative pleasure as not genuinely pleasure.

   In Aristotle's own words, restorative pleasure is not naturally pleasant, whereas non-restorative pleasure is naturally pleasant. When we are being restored, we take pleasure in things that are not naturally pleasant; but we take pleasure in things that are naturally pleasant when we are in a natural

---

[30] "Healing" is here equivalent to "restoration." Granted this, once again the restoration of the unhealthy or non-natural disposition and the activity or activation of the healthy or natural disposition are coterminous. The restoration of the unhealthy disposition is *coincidentally* pleasant because it coincides with the activation of the healthy disposition, and again the activation of the healthy disposition is constitutive of the pleasure.

state. The claim is partly empirical: when we are hungry, we take pleasure in certain foods; but when we are not hungry, we take pleasure in different foods. Let us assume this is true. The question, then, is why we should think that the foods in which we take pleasure when we are not hungry are the naturally pleasant ones. Aristotle's answer is that what is *naturally* pleasant is that in which we take pleasure when we are in the natural condition.

Granted this, let us return to our first question concerning the homonymy view expressed in *Topics* and *Magna Moralia*. Given that both kinds of pleasure are activations (*energeiai*), in virtue of what are they essentially distinct? My suggestion is that Aristotle views them as complete and incomplete activations respectively. Aristotle distinguishes complete (*teleiai*) and incomplete (*ateleis*) activations in several passages in his corpus. For example:

To begin, let us assume that being affected and changed (*kineisthai*) and being active (*energein*) are the same thing. For change (*kinêsis*) is a kind of activation (*energeia*), although incomplete (*atelês*) [activation]. (*On the Soul* 417a)

Change (*kinêsis*) is thought to be a sort of activation (*energeia*), but incomplete. The reason for this view is that the capacity whose activation (*energeia*) it is is incomplete. (*Physics* 201b)

Recall also one of the *Topics* passages we discussed above:

Look and see also if that in relation to which he has rendered the term is a process of generation (*genesis*) or an activation (*energeia*), for nothing of that kind is an end or completion (*telos*), for the result of the activation or process of generation is the completion rather than the process of generation or activation itself. Or perhaps this is not true in all cases, for almost everybody would rather be experiencing pleasure than have ceased experiencing pleasure, so that they would count the activation as the completion rather than the result of the activation. (146b)

While Aristotle here acknowledges that pleasure, at least one kind of pleasure, is a completion and thus a complete activation, he may regard restorative pleasures as incomplete precisely insofar as they are pleasures taken when we are in non-natural and thus defective conditions. Compare also Aristotle's remark at the end of his discussion of pleasure in *Eudemian Ethics* 6.14: "There is an activation (*energeia*) not only of change (*kinêsis*), but also of absence of change" (1154b).

Finally, consider Aristotle's explanation in *Nicomachean Ethics* 10.3 for why Plato and his adherents became attracted to the restoration theory:

This view of pleasure [the restoration view] seems to have its origins in the pains and pleasures connected with nourishment: the claim is that lack comes first, and so pain, then the pleasure of replenishment. But this does not happen with all pleasures; for there are no pains involved with the pleasures of coming to understand, or, if it is a matter of sense-perceptual pleasures, those that arise through the sense of smell; and sounds and sights, too, are often painless, as is remembering and looking to the future.[31] So, of what will they be processes of generation? For there has occurred no lack of anything for there to be a replenishment of. (1173b)

This account accords with what we saw in Chapter 4, that the point of departure for Plato's replenishment and restoration theory are the cases of hunger and thirst and eating and drinking; and the nature of other pleasures is generalized from these. In his view of restorative pleasures as coincidentally pleasant, Aristotle returns to the foundation of Plato's theory and argues that it is confused. Plato mistakes the process of restoration for the concurrent pleasure.

PLEASURE AND THE COMPLETION OF ACTIVATION IN 'NICOMACHEAN ETHICS' 10

In *Eudemian Ethics* 6, Aristotle maintains that pleasure is identical to activation of a kind, namely, unimpeded activation of the natural state of the sense-perceptual, characterological, or intellectual faculty of the soul. But in *Nicomachean Ethics* 10 Aristotle appears to offer a different account. Instead of identifying pleasure with activation so construed, he claims that pleasure completes (*teleioi*) activation:

Pleasure completes (*teleioi*) the activation. (1174b)

For these things [pleasure and activation] appear to be yoked together and not to admit separation: without activation pleasure does not occur, and pleasure completes every [kind of] activation. (1175a)

Pleasure completes the activation not as prevailing disposition does, but as a certain end added on (*epiginomenon ti telos*) to [the activation], as maturity comes to those in the prime of their lives (*tois akmaiois hê hôra*). (1174b)[32]

And more pointedly:

[Pleasures and activations] are so close together (*synengys*) and indistinguishable (*adioristai*) that it is disputable whether pleasure is activation. And yet pleasure

---

[31] Observe that this is one of the few places where Aristotle alludes to imaginative pleasures, precisely, memorial and anticipatory pleasures.

[32] It is more common to translate the simile as "the bloom of youth comes to those in the flower of their age." For an account of why this translation is unlikely to be accurate and why the one I have offered is, see Peter Hadreas, "Aristotle's Simile of Pleasure at *EN* 1174b33," *Ancient Philosophy* 17 (1997) 371–374.

does not seem to be intellecting or sense-perceiving – for that would be strange – but because of their inseparability, they seem to some people to be the same thing. (1175b)

The disparity between the accounts of pleasure in *Eudemian Ethics* 6 and *Nicomachean Ethics* 10 has stirred up considerable controversy. A basic division exists between those scholars who think the two accounts can be reconciled and those who maintain that they cannot. For instance, one way to reconcile the accounts may be to admit that Aristotle has distinct agendas in each book. In *Eudemian Ethics* 6, so far as he is concerned to account for what pleasure is, Aristotle's principal aim is to reject the Platonic view of pleasure as restoration or becoming (*genesis*) and to replace it with the view that pleasure is activation. In fact, Aristotle does hold the more precise view that pleasure completes activation, but he suppresses this precisification because its introduction and explanation would complicate and obscure his principal aim.

My view is that, between the composition of *Eudemian Ethics* 6 and *Nicomachean Ethics* 10, Aristotle altered his view of pleasure once again. In other words, I take the claims in the two books at face value. In the earlier text, Aristotle identifies pleasure with activation of a kind; in the later text, he maintains that pleasure is not identical to activation; rather, pleasure is something added on to activation, thereby completing it. We have two questions then: Why does Aristotle change his mind? And what is the meaning of the claim that pleasure completes an activation? Let us take these questions in reverse order.

First, we need a conception of activation that admits degrees of realization and that culminates with the inclusion of pleasure. Such a conception is available. Activation does not require that the disposition that is activated be in the natural state; nor does activation require the complete absence of impediments – only fully realized activation does. Granted this, the claim that pleasure completes an activation can be understood to mean that fully realized activation psychologically entails pleasure. In other words, pleasure is an aspect of fully realized activation. Now since in *Eudemian Ethics* 6 Aristotle identifies pleasure with the unimpeded activation of the natural disposition and this unimpeded activation is fully realized activation, from the perspective of *Nicomachean Ethics* 10 he must be making a mistake, the mistake of confusing the activation itself with an aspect of the activation.

Granted this, let us turn to the question of why Aristotle shifts his view in *Nicomachean Ethics* 10. At the beginning of *Nicomachean Ethics* 2.3

Aristotle discusses various ways in which pleasure relates to ethical character and its development. The first of these is as follows:

We should treat the pleasure or pain that is added to (*epiginomenê*) a person's actions as an indicator of his [ethical] dispositions.[33] For one who holds back from bodily pleasure and enjoys doing so is a moderate person, while one who is upset at doing so is self-indulgent; and one who withstands frightening things and enjoys doing so, or at least does so without distress, is a courageous person, while one who is distressed by them is cowardly. (1104b)

Aristotle implicitly acknowledges here that it is possible in a given situation to do the right or excellent thing, but without the right or excellent attitude. Accordingly, he is also implicitly claiming that part of the development of ethical character involves coming to take pleasure in excellent conduct. Indeed, Aristotle proceeds to cite Plato's endorsement of this point:

This is why we must have been raised in a certain way from childhood onwards, as Plato says, so as to take pleasure in and be distressed by the things we should. (1104b)[34]

Note Aristotle's use of the phrase "pleasure that is added" (*epiginomenê*) in the previous passage (at 1104b). This is the expression Aristotle uses in book 10 when he describes pleasure's relation to activation: it is "added on (*epiginomenê*) to [the activation]" like maturity to those in the prime of their lives. The repetition of the phrase corroborates the idea that, at least in the case of ethical conduct, pleasure is an attitude taken in or toward such activation. Indeed, I suggest that this is Aristotle's view – although I hasten to emphasize that Aristotle employs no Greek equivalent of "attitude." In other words, in answer to the question "How does Aristotle conceive the relation between pleasure and activation?" I propose that Aristotle implicitly commits to the view that pleasure is an attitude toward an activation.

This view can be applied to the activation of the intellect as well. That is, pleasure can be added to intellection in the sense that one can take pleasure in contemplation or practical reasoning. I assume that the relation between pleasure and activation can be understood similarly in the case of sense-perception; that is, one can take pleasure in seeing, hearing, smelling, and so on. From this it should also be clear why, as Aristotle says in *Nicomachean Ethics* 10, pleasure cannot be separated from the

---

[33] Note the phrase "added to (*epiginomenê*)," on which I will comment shortly below.
[34] Cf. *Republic* 401e–402a; *Laws* 653a–c.

activation: one does not merely experience pleasure, but takes pleasure *in something*. The activation is, then, the object of the pleasure.

Assuming pleasure as conceived here is such an attitude, pleasure is, then, what we might call a second-order psychic condition, that is, one psychic condition directed toward another psychic condition. Granted this, the following limitation of the account should also be noted. If one asks, "What is this thing, pleasure, which is taken in such activation?" or "What is this attitude of pleasure, which is taken toward certain sense-perceiving, ethical conduct, or intellecting?" Aristotle appears to have very little to say. For example, Plato might say that pleasure is a representation or perception of restoration. But there is no reason to think that Aristotle is committed to viewing the relation between the second- and first-order psychic conditions as representational or perceptual.

One passage from *On the Soul* suggests an intriguing consideration:

Sense-perceiving then is like bare asserting or thinking; but when the object is pleasant or painful, the soul does something like (*hoion*) affirm (*kataphasa*) or negate (*apophasa*) the object, and then it pursues or avoids it. (431a)

This passage suggests that taking pleasure in something is like affirming it. Accordingly, pleasure is not merely a second-order psychic condition, but an affirmative attitude. Now, Aristotle is surely careful and right to say that the soul merely does something "like" (*hoion*) affirm, at least if we take affirmation to require a proposition as its object. In the case of sense-perception the object, which is a proper sensible quality, is non-propositional. Strictly speaking, then, one cannot affirm such a thing. One can, however, adopt some sort of pro-attitude toward it. For example, one can like or have an attraction to a flavor, scent, color, or sound.

I take this line of interpretation to be, as I said, intriguing and also attractive. But even if it is correct or broadly congenial to Aristotle's thought, it must be emphasized that Aristotle's treatment of this idea remains undeveloped and unclear.

ARISTOTLE ON KINDS OF PLEASURE

The preceding discussion has focused on Aristotle's answer to the identity question and attempted to show that in engaging this question Aristotle largely has Plato in mind – initially sympathetically, later critically. Moreover – if my reading of the distinction between the treatments in *Eudemian Ethics* 6 and *Nicomachean Ethics* 10 is correct – Aristotle ultimately becomes his own critic.

Like Plato, albeit to a lesser extent, Aristotle also takes an interest in the kinds question. Again like Plato, Aristotle's interest in this question is largely motivated and informed by concerns with value. That is, Aristotle is interested in distinctions among kinds of pleasure insofar as he is interested in determining which kinds of pleasure have more or less value. Aristotle's most focused and sustained discussion of the kinds question occurs in *Nicomachean Ethics* 10.5.[35] At the beginning of this section, he articulates the principle according to which he distinguishes kinds of pleasure:

This is also, it seems, why pleasures differ in kind. For we think that where things differ in kind, what completes them is different . . . and similarly with activations too: if they differ in kind, we think of what completes them as differing in kind. (1175a)

In short, kinds of pleasure are distinguished according to kinds of activation. I will first clarify Aristotle's hedonic distinctions, then return to consider the grounds of the principle he uses to distinguish these kinds.

Since pleasures complete kinds of psychic activation, kinds of pleasure are distinguished according to distinctions among kinds of psychic activation. Principally, kinds of psychic activation are distinguished according to psychic faculties, at least those psychic faculties that entail awareness. Thus, in *Nicomachean Ethics* 10.5 Aristotle distinguishes sense-perceptual and intellectual pleasures, and he distinguishes kinds of sense-perceptual and intellectual pleasures according to distinctions among sense-perceptual faculties and kinds of intellection. In drawing these distinctions, Aristotle characterizes them, reminiscently of Plato, in terms of degrees of purity:

Just as activations are distinct, so too are their pleasures. Sight differs from touch in purity, as do hearing and smelling from taste. So the pleasures too differ in a similar way, as do the intellectual pleasures from these sense-perceptual ones, and each of the two kinds [of intellectual pleasures] among themselves. (1176a)

Sarah Broadie explains Aristotle's appeal to degrees of purity here in terms of "degrees of independence from physical involvement with the object of cognition" and suggests that "such independence is assumed to carry greater cognitive refinement."[36] I agree. Indeed, in discussing the hierarchy of pure pleasures at the end of *Philebus*, we suggested that Plato operates with a similar view. Even so, Plato's conception of purity principally concerns

[35] Aristotle draws or implicitly draws numerous hedonic distinctions in *Rhetoric* 1.11, many of which follow Plato's contributions. But Aristotle does not draw these distinctions in a very principled way. Hence I am restricting my focus to the treatment in *Nicomachean Ethics* 10.5.

[36] Sarah Broadie and Christopher Rowe, *Aristotle: Nicomachean Ethics*, Oxford University Press, 2002, 438.

freedom from admixture with pain. Thus, Plato's conception of purity is primarily ontological. As such, Plato's and Aristotle's conceptions of the purity of pleasure fundamentally differ.

Let us speak of Aristotle's conception of purity here as "cognitive." A cognitive conception of purity of pleasure is in fact compatible with an ontological conception. Still, there are clear differences of interest and emphasis. Following Broadie, cognitive purity relates to modes of cognition that are to varying degrees free from contact or involvement with matter. Such freedom is necessary if one is to attain what Aristotle regards as the highest forms of cognition, namely, understanding of formal entities: universals, mathematical objects, the soul, and god. At the other end of the cognitive hierarchy, touch and taste provide the least pure sense-perceptual pleasures, for the hedonic objects of touch and taste come into most intimate contact with our bodies. The sensible objects of sight, hearing, and smell all operate at a greater distance from their objects. Objects of intellection, practical and theoretical, are formal, but the objects of theoretical intellect are further removed from matter than those of practical intellect. Aristotle views god, whose contemplation he regards as the supreme form of intellection, as a wholly formal being. Accordingly, in *Nicomachean Ethics* 10.7 Aristotle writes: "philosophy is thought to bring with it pleasures amazing in purity " (1177a). Likewise, in his exhortatory *Protrepticus* Aristotle argues, much as Plato does in *Republic* 9, that the philosophical life is also the most pleasant life: "Complete and unimpeded activation contains within itself delight, so that the activation of theoretical intellect must be the most pleasant of all" (fr. 87).

In *Nicomachean Ethics* 10.5 Aristotle additionally distinguishes kinds of pleasure according to species of animal. For instance, he writes: "a horse's pleasure, a dog's, and a human's are different [in kind]" (1176a). But these animal-specific hedonic distinctions can be viewed as continuous with the cognitive hedonic distinctions just described. This is because the psychic functions of animals vary, whether in extent of cognitive capacities or in variations within specific cognitive capacities, precisely, sense-perceptual ones. For example, the powerful olfactory capacities of dogs entail distinct olfactory pleasures within this species. This is my example. But consider what Aristotle says in his treatise *On the Parts of Animals* about the pleasure snakes derive from eating, given that they have forked tongues:

Among serpents and lizards . . . the tongue is long and forked so as to be suited to perceiving flavors. So long indeed is this part in snakes that although it is small while in the mouth, it can protrude a great distance. In these same animals it is forked and has a fine and hair-like extremity, because of their great liking for food. For by this arrangement they derive a two-fold pleasure from flavors, their gustatory perception being, as it were, doubled. (660b)

Again, in the same treatise Aristotle explains that the sense-perceptual organs by means of which animals take pleasure in food differ across species:

As all animals are sensitive to the pleasure derivable from food, they all feel a desire for it. For the object of desire is the pleasant. The part, however, by which food produces the sense-perception is not alike in all of them. (661a)

Likewise, of course, the kinds of food various species desire differ in accordance with their distinct constitutions, as Aristotle notes in his treatise *On the Generation of Animals*; and this distinction also explains the diversity of their appetitive pleasures:

The life of animals is divisible into two parts, procreation and feeding, for on these two acts all of their interests and life concentrate. Their food varies chiefly according to the matter of which they are severally constituted, for the source of their growth in all cases will be this substance. And whatsoever is in conformity with nature is pleasant, and all animals pursue pleasure in keeping with their nature. (589a)

In considering Aristotle's distinctions in hedonic kinds, let us turn now to the question of how the principle upon which the hedonic distinctions depend is justified, namely, the principle that as activations differ in kind so do the pleasures that complete them. Consideration of this point in fact illuminates how Aristotle understands the notion of a distinct hedonic kind. Aristotle supports his principle by appealing to several further claims.[37] Two of these, which are also complementary, are particularly instructive. One is that "what contributes to increasing something is congenial (*oikeion*) to it" and that "the activation's congenial (*oikeia*) pleasure fosters it" (1175a). Aristotle gives the following example: someone who takes pleasure in music will cultivate this practice. The second and complementary claim is that "activations are impeded by" alien (*allotriai*) pleasures, that is, pleasures congenial to other activations. Aristotle offers the following example: "lovers of pipe-music are incapable of paying attention to a discussion if they happen to hear someone playing the pipes" (1175b). These two supporting claims suggest that the relation between pleasure and the first-order psychic activation in which the

---

[37] The first is simply the more general principle that where things differ in kind, that which completes them differs in kind. Aristotle claims that this holds for natural and artificial entities: animals, trees, a picture, a statue, a house, a piece of furniture. The trouble is that it is difficult to make sense of two things here: what completes these kinds and how what completes them relates to them as kinds.

pleasure is taken has a certain sort of psychic depth and what may be called "organic intimacy." It is for this reason that I find the translation "congenial" of the Greek term "*oikeion*" particularly felicitous. For example, one cannot simply detach the pleasure taken in one kind of activation and apply it to an activation of a different kind.[38] In other words, what differentiates pleasures in kind, for Aristotle, is that distinct pleasures have psychic affinities to distinct activations. In the case of the appetitive pleasures of various animal species, it is clear that such psychic affinities are a function of their physiological constitution and thus run very deep indeed. For instance, carnivorous animals could not be habituated to take pleasure in eating a vegetarian diet. In contrast, ethical and intellectual pleasures in humans must be developed along with these capacities, through habituation and learning. While Aristotle hardly touches upon this in the context of his discussion of the distinction among hedonic kinds in *Nicomachean Ethics* 10.5, much of the remainder of *Nicomachean Ethics* can be viewed as supporting this idea. Recall the passage I cited from 2.3: "We should treat the pleasure or pain that is added to a person's actions as an indicator of his [ethical] dispositions" (1104b).

This conception of pleasure as having a psychic affinity with its activation is an interesting and plausible view, at least in the case of certain pleasures. Whether or not it covers all pleasures, there is a noteworthy problem in Aristotle's account. According to the definition of pleasure in *Nicomachean Ethics* 10.4, pleasure completes an activation. But, in defense of his differentiation of kinds of pleasure in 10.5, Aristotle claims that pleasure fosters its proper activation. However, if an activation can be developed, then it is not complete. This problem cannot, of course, be resolved by the suggestion that when he claims that pleasure completes an activation Aristotle means that pleasure conduces to the completion of an activation. The verb "to complete" (*teleioun*) can in fact be used to mean "conduce to the completion of" or the like. But the manner in which Aristotle describes "completion" when he advances this definition prohibits the interpretation that he is using "completion" in that way.

Finally, before we leave Aristotle's treatment of the kinds question, it should be noted that although within his discussion of hedonic kinds Aristotle does not address the question of true and false pleasures, he does, albeit to a limited extent, distinguish merely apparent pleasures from pleasures strictly or properly speaking. Indeed, this distinction also occurs in *Eudemian Ethics* 6. Recall the point that in contrast to the account in

---

[38] Aristotle does not examine how pleasures come to be congenial to their activations. Presumably the grounds vary, depending on the natures of the subjects, their habituation, and learning.

Magna Moralia, where both restorative and non-restorative pleasures are treated as genuine pleasures, in *Eudemian Ethics* Aristotle maintains that restorative pleasures are not genuine pleasures, but only so-called in a qualified way:

When [one's natural disposition] has been re-established, [one takes] pleasure in things that are pleasant without qualification; but while it is being restored, [one takes] pleasure even in things that are the contrary of these – even sharp and bitter things, neither of which is either naturally pleasant or pleasant without qualification. (1153a)

Likewise, earlier in *Eudemian Ethics* 6.12 he writes:

Other [changes] are not even pleasures, but only appear so, namely, those that are accompanied by pain and are for the sake of healing, such as the ones sick people undergo. (1152b)

Finally, compare the following passage from the end of *Nicomachean Ethics* 10.5:

[Assuming that] excellence and the good man ... are the measure [of what is the case] for each sort of thing, then so too with pleasures: the ones that appear so to him will be pleasures, and the things that he takes pleasure in will be pleasant. But if the things that disgust him appear pleasant to some other person, there is nothing surprising in that, since there are many forms of corruption and damage to which human beings are subject. (1176a)

Aristotle's commitment here and in *Eudemian Ethics* 6 to a distinction between apparent and genuine or what he calls "natural" pleasures or pleasures in an unqualified way is equivalent to a commitment to the concepts of ontologically true and false pleasures.

Accordingly, if, for example, a masochist takes pleasure in some sort of self-mutilation, his is merely an apparent pleasure. Furthermore, this example and the concept of apparent pleasure per se indicate that there is a normative condition on genuine pleasure. According to the account in *Nicomachean Ethics* 10, genuine pleasure must complete an activation, and a complete activation is necessarily good.

APPENDIX: ARISTOTLE AND THE PERIPATETIC 'PROBLEMS'
ON SEXUAL PLEASURE

Since our discussion of sexual pleasure in the Hippocratic treatise *On Generation* in Chapter 3, we have had little to say on the topic. By and large, Greek philosophers avoided the topic. The reason for this is that most hedonic theorizing occurred within an ethical context, more precisely in a normative ethical context, and sexual pleasure was generally regarded as particularly base. For example, in *Nicomachean Ethics* 10.3, where Aristotle is discussing self-control and self-indulgence and the "bestial and slavish" pleasures to which they are related, he underscores pleasures of touch, among which he includes sexual pleasure.[39] Aristotle criticizes tactile pleasures on the ground that they "belong to us not insofar as we are human beings, but insofar as we are animals. [Thus,] to take pleasure in such things . . . and to be attached to them more than anything else is bestial" (1118a). More precisely, Aristotle is careful to distinguish certain nobler tactile pleasures, which we experience in athletic activities such as wrestling, from other sorts:

For the tactile pleasures most appropriate to free men lie outside the sphere of self-indulgence, for example, the ones in gymnasia produced through rubbing and warming; for the touching that is characteristic of the self-indulgent person has to do not with the whole of the body but only with certain parts of it [namely, sexual and appetitive parts]. (1118a–b)

Given this, it is understandable that, should they occur at all, incisive explanations of sexual pleasure will be found outside of ethical theory.[40] As in the case of the Hippocratic *On Generation*, Aristotle discusses the topic in *On the Generation of Animals*, a biological treatise. There is also some discussion of sexual pleasure in a Peripatetic text called *Problems* that has been transmitted with the Aristotelian corpus. The treatments of sexual pleasure in these three texts can profitably be discussed together since Aristotle appears to be critically responding to the Hippocratic treatment or at least to a treatment in agreement with the Hippocratic treatment, and the treatment in the *Problems* diverges from Aristotle's treatment.

Early in Book 1 of *On the Generation of Animals* Aristotle expresses his aim to explain what he calls the "the moving [or efficient] explanatory factor" of generation or reproduction. (715a) By "moving explanatory factor" here Aristotle means sperm, that is, reproductive or generative seed (*sperma*). This is to be contrasted with what Aristotle calls the "material cause," by which he means the matter that nourishes the generative seed. According to Aristotle, all sanguineous animals that move and some non-sanguineous animals that move are generated through the

---

[39] This itself is noteworthy insofar as Plato never explicitly commits to this position. Recall the implicit distinction between brute and non-brute somatic pleasures in *Timaeus*.
[40] Plato treats sexual pleasures briefly and rather elusively in the context of the discussion of mixed bodily pleasures in *Philebus*.

reproduction of male and female members of their species. In my discussion of the Hippocratic treatise, I had mentioned that there was a long-standing debate among physical theorists over what males and females contribute to reproduction. Recall that according to the Hippocratic author, presumably Polybus, both sexes contribute seed. For example, "that is why [seminal fluid] flows when the boy reaches puberty and the girl reaches her menses" (1.3); and "If [the woman's] desire for intercourse is excited, she [emits] seed before the man" (4.2). On Aristotle's view, it is the male alone that contributes reproductive seed; the female contributes only the material explanatory factor, that is, nourishment for the seed. This is a point for which Aristotle argues in sections 17–18 of Book 1. The other topic Aristotle engages in 1.17–18 is whether sperm derives from the whole body or only from a part. He views the two questions as linked, for if sperm comes from the whole body, then this favors the view that it comes from both male and female:

> Now it is thought that all animals are generated out of sperm, and that the sperm comes from the parents. That is why it is part of the same inquiry to ask whether both male and female produce it or only one of them, and to ask whether it comes from the whole of the body or not from the whole. For if the latter is true, it is reasonable to suppose that it does not come from both parents either. (721b)

Indeed, Polybus holds that sperm derives from the whole body. For example: "[In the case of men,] veins extend from the whole body to the penis. When these are gently rubbed and heated and filled, a sort of friction occurs, and from this pleasure and heat arise in the whole body" (1.1). I will call this the "pansomatic" theory of sperm.

Given his view of the relation between the bodily source of sperm and the sexual identity of the contributor, Aristotle first takes up the question whether sperm comes from the whole body. He considers four arguments for the pansomatic theory. The first relates to the intensity of sexual pleasure:

> For the same affection (*pathos*) is more pleasant if multiplied, and that which affects all parts is multiplied as compared with that which affects only one or a few. (721b)

Later, Aristotle criticizes the pansomatic theory. Among his criticisms, two target the argument just presented:

> As to the intensity of pleasure in sexual intercourse, (1) it is not because the sperm comes from the whole body, but because there is a strong friction, wherefore if this intercourse is often repeated, the pleasure is diminished in the persons

concerned. (2) Moreover, the pleasure comes at the end of the act, but it ought, on the theory, to be in each of the parts, and not at the same time, but sooner in some and later in others. (723b–724a)

In short, Aristotle rejects the pansomatic theory on the grounds that the intensity of sexual pleasure can be explained as a function of the acute friction that ejaculation involves and because if sperm were derived from the whole body, the intensity of the pleasure would be experienced sequentially and not merely at the moment of ejaculation. It is noteworthy, however, that the Hippocratic author maintains that pleasure does occur throughout sexual intercourse. For example, "once intercourse has begun, [the woman] experiences pleasure through the whole time" (4.2). Moreover, this is compatible with the author's view that ejaculation is the most pleasant stage of sexual intercourse: "The reason that the man experiences more pleasure is that the [emission of the seminal fluid] in his case occurs suddenly and as the result of a more violent disturbance than in the woman's case" (4.2).

With Aristotle's view in mind, at any rate, let us now turn to the treatment of sexual pleasure in the Peripatetic *Problems*. The Peripatetic *Problems* was probably compiled sometime between the second and first centuries BCE. It consists of thirty-eight books whose subject matter ranges extremely broadly, although mainly within physical inquiry. For example, Book 1 concerns the causes of disease; Book 2 concerns questions relating to perspiration; Book 3 concerns questions relating to drinking and drunkenness. Book 4 concerns questions relating to sexual intercourse, and a couple of sections within it treat questions relating to sexual pleasure. These varied treatments appear to be edited assemblages of earlier Peripatetic treatments, including but not limited to Aristotelian and Theophrastean contributions.

The discussion of each topic in *Problems* is prompted by a set of questions, which is then followed by one or more answers. For example, Book 23 concerns questions relating to the sea and salt-water. The first question is why waves do not ripple in the deep ocean, but only where it is confined and shallow. The second is why waves sometimes begin to move before the wind reaches them. In some cases, the author endorses a particular answer. In other cases, he presents various answers without advocating one.

Section 15 of Book 4 is devoted to the following question:

Why is sexual intercourse the most pleasant of all things to animals, and is it so of necessity or with some purpose in view? (878b)

In presenting the question, the author suggests two possible kinds of answer: sexual intercourse is pleasant *by necessity* or *with some purpose in view*. In other words, the author entertains the possibilities of a causal-materialistic explanation and a teleological explanation of sexual pleasure respectively. In the ensuing discussion, the author proposes a dual causal-materialistic and teleological explanation.

Causal-materialistically, sexual intercourse is most pleasant because the sperm comes from the whole body or at least from all of the veins extended through the body. Furthermore, when the sperm is drawn through the body or the vascular system, its movement creates friction. Moreover, "the friction is pleasant because it involves the emission of vaporous moisture enclosed unnaturally in the body" (878b). This, then, explains the extreme pleasantness of sexual intercourse as a function of the scope of natural restoration: "the sensation extends to the whole body." In short, contra Aristotle, the author endorses the pansomatic theory.

Teleologically, sexual intercourse is explained as being most pleasant because "the act of generation is an emission of similar matter for its natural purpose" (878b). In other words, the function of sexual inter-course is reproduction, and the pleasantness of sexual intercourse serves to motivate animals to engage in sexual intercourse: "For it is the pleasure more than anything else that incites animals to sexual intercourse" (878b).

Thus, the author concludes that sexual intercourse is "pleasant both of necessity and for the sake of something – of necessity because the way to a natural result is pleasant if realized by the senses; and for the sake of something, namely, the reproduction of animal life" (878b).

A second question concerning sexual pleasure raised in Book 4 of the Peripatetic *Problems* is worth noting insofar as it overlaps with the topic of habit, which we briefly raised in our discussion of Aristotle's commitment to the restoration theory in *Rhetoric* I.II. Recall that Aristotle there speaks of pleasure as a restoration to the "prevailing" condition. I had explained that the prevailing condition may be a natural or a habitual condition, and moreover that a habitual condition may derive from natural or unnatural habituation. *Problems* 4.26 raises the question "why some men find pleasure in submitting to sexual intercourse [that is, receiving anal sex], and why some take pleasure in performing the active part" (879a). The author proposes that some men are unnaturally constituted so that sperm collects in the bowels rather than the penis and testicles:

In those whose [seminal] veins are in an unnatural condition, owing either to the blockage of the veins leading to the reproductive organs . . . or to some other cause, all such moisture collects in the bowels; for by this way it passes out of the body. (879b)

Consequently, sexual desire expresses itself as a desire for anal friction and thereby the release of the superfluity of the sperm in the bowels.

The author suggests that this unnatural condition may derive from various causes. One of these is an unnatural "effeminate" constitution. Another is a physical accident, for example, castration, as in eunuchs. A third derives from habituation, of which the author explains:

This condition is sometimes the result of habit, for men take pleasure in whatever they are accustomed to do and emit sperm accordingly. They therefore desire to do the acts by which pleasure and the emission of sperm are produced, and habit becomes more and more a second nature. For this reason, those who have been accustomed to submit to sexual intercourse about the age of puberty and not before, because recollection of the past presents itself to them during the act of copulation, with the recollection of the idea of pleasure, they desire to take a passive part owing to habit, as though it were natural to them to do so. (879b–880a)

CHAPTER 7

Epicurus and the Cyrenaics on katastematic and kinetic pleasures

This chapter discusses Epicurean and Cyrenaic conceptions of pleasure in relation to one another. The reason for juxtaposing their contributions will be clear shortly. For now, let it suffice to say that the Epicureans and Cyrenaics contend over the relation between and the very existence of what they call "katastematic" and "kinetic" pleasures. These terms will be explained in due course. To begin, let us introduce the antagonists.

Epicurus was born in 341 BCE and raised on the island of Samos. His father was an Athenian citizen, and at this time Samos was subject to Athenian control.[1] Epicurus left Samos for Athens for a brief stint of mandatory military service in 323. This service happened to coincide with the death of Alexander the Great, upon which the Athenians revolted from Macedonia. Among the ramifications of this revolt was that Alexander's general Perdiccas expelled the Athenian settlers on Samos. Epicurus' family emigrated across the water to Colophon on the Ionian coast. This is where Epicurus presumably joined them upon his return from Athens in 322/321. He remained in the east for the next fifteen odd years.

Epicurus' initial, significant philosophical education may have come under the tutelage of the Democritean philosopher Nausiphanes of Teos.[2] If so, Epicurus' association with Nausiphanes presumably began before his military service in Athens. However, it is not clear how long before his military service, nor whether the association continued afterward. Nausiphanes would most likely have introduced Epicurus to Democritus' atomistic physics as well as to Democritus' ethics. Subsequently, Epicurus briefly set up his own school in Mytilene. Later he taught in Lampsacus on the Hellespont.

---

[1] See Graham Shipley, *A History of Samos 800–188 BC*, Clarendon Press, 1987, 155–180.
[2] Teos was also an Ionian coastal city, near Colophon.

In 306, for what precise reasons we do not know, Epicurus moved to Athens and remained there for the rest of his life. He established a philosophical school and community outside the walls of the city not far from the site of Plato's Academy, on a plot of land subsequently referred to as "the Garden" (*kêpos*). Following his death in 270, Epicurus' Garden community persisted, becoming one of the most important philosophical schools of the Hellenistic period and enduring well into the Roman Imperial age.

Our knowledge of the history of the Cyrenaic school is sketchy. We encountered their founder or at least figurehead, Aristippus the Elder (*c.* 430–350), in our discussion of pleasure in the pre-Platonic ethical tradition in Chapter 2. As I mentioned, in the late fifth century Aristippus came to Athens from Cyrene and became an associate of Socrates. Aristippus educated his daughter Arete in philosophy, and she in turn educated her son and grandfather's namesake Aristippus. Aristippus the Younger, also known as the "mother-taught" (*mêtrodidaktos*), seems to have been a central figure in the school's history, perhaps because he consolidated, refined, or publicized their doctrines. We also know of a number of splinter groups, including the Annicerians, Hegesians, and Theodoreans, which formed in and persisted through the third and perhaps second centuries. By the late second century, so far as we know, these splinter groups and the Cyrenaic school itself had ceased to exist.

Our evidence for Epicurus' conception of pleasure is rather meager. We have four primary sources, all rather brief and none directly or strictly focusing on what pleasure is: Epicurus' *Letter to Menoeceus*, the *Principal Doctrines*, the so-called *Vatican Sayings*, and scattered and brief fragments from some of Epicurus' lost writings. In addition, we have various texts and fragments composed by Epicureans over the 600 years between the time of Epicurus and approximately the third century CE. The most important of these is the Roman philosopher Lucretius' *On the Nature of Things*, an epic poem in six books, mainly devoted to Epicurean physical theories. We also have various more and less fragmentary Epicurean papyri from a library in Herculaneum. These were preserved when this town and its more famous neighbor Pompeii were destroyed by the eruption of Vesuvius in 79 CE. Many of the papyri were composed by Philodemus (*c.* 110–40), originally of Gadara (modern day Umm Quais, Jordan), who led one of the most important Epicurean schools of the late Roman Republic. Finally, we have a fragmentary collection of stones that once constituted a wall on which principles of Epicurean philosophy were engraved. The author of this stone inscription is the third-century CE philosopher Diogenes of Oenoanda (in modern day Incealiler, south-western Turkey).[3]

Finally, we have various ancient sources that paraphrase or comment on Epicurus' views. The most important of these is Cicero's *On Goals*, the first two books of which critically examine Epicurus' ethical views, including Epicurus' views of pleasure. In my opinion, however, Cicero is often ultimately confused and misleading. Plutarch (46–120) is another important source – although also a hostile one, as the titles of his treatises *On the Impossibility of Life according to Epicurus* and *Against Colotes* indicate; Colotes (*c.* 320–250) was an important disciple of Epicurus, against whose lost treatise *On the Impossibility of Life according to the Philosophers* Plutarch's was composed.

In the case of the Cyrenaics, we are in much worse shape. Aside from several very brief testimonies from disparate ancient authors such as Sextus Empiricus, Clement of Alexandria, and Cicero, Diogenes Laertius' *Lives and Opinions of Eminent Philosophers* (hereafter simply *Lives*) is our principal source. Following his life of Aristippus the Elder in Book 2, Diogenes presents a doxography of Cyrenaic ethics, sections 85–96, followed by shorter doxographies of the Annicerians, Hegesians, and Theodoreans. This material, precious though it is, is still quite brief. Moreover, like many of our ancient doxographies, it is at least third-hand, probably worse. In particular, it is questionable to what extent the Cyrenaic doxography is coherent.

Diogenes Laertius is in fact our primary source for Epicurus' thought as well as the Cyrenaics'. His *Lives* is composed in ten books, beginning with the earliest Greek philosophy and ending with Epicurus. Epicurus does not come last for chronological reasons, but apparently because Diogenes views Epicurus' contribution as the crowning achievement of Greek philosophy. In other words, Diogenes seems to have been an Epicurean himself. It is in Book 10 that Diogenes preserves Epicurus' summary of his ethics in the *Letter to Menoeceus* as well as his *Principal Doctrines*. Diogenes' inclusion of the Cyrenaic ethical doxography in Book 2 may owe to his interest in Epicureanism. At several points in the doxography, the Cyrenaics' views are contrasted with Epicurus'. Likewise, among Diogenes' comments on Epicurus' ethics in Book 10, Epicurus' views are contrasted with the Cyrenaics'.

---

[3] Although we have various forms of evidence of Epicureanism across several centuries, our aim here is to clarify the conception of pleasure of Epicurus himself. In any case, we lack adequate evidence to chart any development in conceptions of pleasure held by Epicureans from Epicurus to Diogenes of Oenoanda.

Diogenes' engagement of Epicurus and the Cyrenaics is apt. Both Epicurus and the Cyrenaics are hedonists, but hedonists of different kinds. Simply put, the Cyrenaics are bodily or somatic hedonists. That is, they hold that the good is bodily pleasure. In contrast, Epicurus maintains that the good is absence of pain in the body (*aponia*) and absence of psychic or mental distress (*ataraxia*). But Epicurus identifies absence of pain or distress itself as pleasure. Consequently, it may be convenient to refer to Epicurus as an "analgesic hedonist."

Here are some ancient expressions of the preceding distinction between Epicurus' analgesic hedonism and the Cyrenaics' somatic hedonism. The first passage derives from Cicero's treatise on Academic skepticism, the second from the Roman orator Quintilian (35–100). Note that, in these two cases, Aristippus is being treated as a representative of the Cyrenaic school. The third passage is from Epicurus' *Letter to Menoeceus*. The fourth is from Clement of Alexandria:

Aristippus looks on as though we have no soul, just a body alone. (*Prior Academics* 2.139)

And Aristippus would not exhort us to this task [that is, to rhetoric,] since he places the highest good in the pleasure of the body. (*Institutes of Oratory* 12.2.24)

When we say that pleasure is the goal ... [we mean] not experiencing pain in the body and not experiencing disturbance in the soul. (*Letter to Menoeceus* 131)

These Cyrenaics reject Epicurus' definition of pleasure, namely, the removal of what causes pain, stigmatizing it as the condition of a corpse. (*Miscellanies* 2.21.130.8)

Although somatic and analgesic hedonism are ethical theories and ethics is not our focus, our discussion will to some extent engage the distinction between Cyrenaic and Epicurean hedonism in order to clarify and explain their respective conceptions of pleasure.[4]

INTRODUCTION TO KATASTEMATIC AND KINETIC PLEASURES

Ancient commentators and doxographers draw a distinction between the Epicureans' and the Cyrenaics' conceptions of pleasure. They claim that the Epicureans are committed to two types of pleasure: kinetic and

---

[4] As I have noted earlier in the book, the distinction between bodily and psychic or mental pleasure (or pain) can be confusing, since all pleasure (and pain) is experienced by the soul. But bodily pleasure is pleasure that originates in the body, whereas mental pleasure originates in the soul. There is, in fact, more to be said about this distinction, but I will return to the point later.

katastematic, whereas the Cyrenaics are committed only to one: the Cyrenaics admit kinetic pleasure, but reject katastematic pleasure. It may be questioned whether this account more accurately represents the doxographical or commentary tradition, that is, the reception of Epicurean and Cyrenaic thought, than the original figures themselves. At least, we should be alive to this possibility. I will argue that the terminology is sound; however, it is easy to misconstrue the distinction.

To begin, let's review the terms "kinetic" and "katastematic." We have encountered the term "*kinêsis*," meaning "change" or "motion" (where motion is a particular kind of change), at several points in previous chapters. Indeed, we have seen that Plato in *Republic* 9 characterizes pleasure as a kind of *kinêsis*. Kinetic pleasure is, then, pleasure that somehow involves change or motion – precisely how is crucial to understand, and we will examine this shortly.

The term "katastematic" relates to the Greek verb "*kathistanai*," which means "to station, establish, or put in place." Cognate is the Greek noun "*katastêma*," which means "condition or state," where this in turn may be understood as something that has been established, stationed, or put in place. For instance, in a fragment from his ethical treatise *On the Goal*, Epicurus refers to bodily health as the "well-established condition (*katastêma*) of the body" (fr. 68).

The contrast between kinetic and katastematic pleasure may then appear to be a contrast between pleasure that somehow involves motion or change and pleasure that does not. Indeed, this is how Cicero understands and represents the distinction. In Book 2 of *On Goals*, Cicero discusses Epicurus' distinction between kinetic and katastematic pleasures at length; he refers to these pleasures using the Latin terms "*movens*" and "*stans*," that is, "moving" or "changing" and "standing" or "static."

We also encounter the distinction between katastematic and kinetic pleasure in Diogenes Laertius. Following the *Letter to Menoeceus* and preceding the *Principal Doctrines*, Diogenes comments on Epicurus' ethical philosophy, beginning as follows:

Epicurus disagrees with the Cyrenaics on the question of pleasure, for they do not admit katastematic pleasure, but only kinetic pleasure. But he admits both kinds in both body and soul, as he says in his *On Choice and Avoidance*, in *On the Goal*, in Book 1 of *On Ways of Life*, and in the *Letter to Friends in Mytilene*. Similarly, Diogenes [the Epicurean] in Book 17 of his *Selections* and Metrodorus in *Timocrates* take the same position: both kinetic and katastematic pleasures are conceived as pleasure. And Epicurus, in his *On Choice* [*and Avoidance*], says this: "For freedom from [mental] disturbance (*ataraxia*) and freedom from [physical] suffering (*aponia*) are katastematic pleasures, whereas joy (*chara*) and delight (*euphrosynê*) are seen as involving change through activation." (10.136)

Let me reiterate the contents of this passage – although not in the order in which they occur. Diogenes attributes to Epicurus a fourfold distinction between pleasures. There are two principal kinds of pleasure: katastematic and kinetic; and each principal kind contains two sub-kinds: bodily and mental:

	katastematic	kinetic
bodily	*aponia* (freedom from bodily pain)	*euphrosynê* (delight)
mental	*ataraxia* (tranquillity, freedom from mental pain)	*chara* (joy)

A couple of points deserve notice here. First, my translations of "*euphrosynê*" as "delight" and "*chara*" as "joy" are largely a convenience. I do not mean to suggest that, for example, "delight" actually means "kinetic pleasure of the body." Second, Diogenes speaks of pleasures of the body and the soul. I have referred to pleasures of the body and the mind. The soul is responsible for all sentience, awareness, or perception; thus, bodily as well as mental pleasure involves psychic activity. However, bodily pleasure involves one part of the soul, namely, the sense-perceptual faculties, whereas mental pleasure involves another part of the soul, namely, the mind or intellect. These two parts of the soul are also referred to as "irrational" (*alogon*) and "rational" (*logikon*) respectively. We have explicit evidence for this distinction in the Epicurean tradition. Consider the following quotation from a scholiast, that is, ancient commentator, on Epicurus' *Letter to Herodotus*:

[Epicurus] says elsewhere that the soul is composed of the smoothest and roundest of atoms, far superior in both respects to those of fire; that part of it is irrational, this being scattered over the rest of the body, while the rational part resides in the chest, as is manifest from our fears and joy. (66)

Consider also the following long quotation from Book 3 of Lucretius' *On the Nature of Things*. Lucretius here distinguishes the two parts of the soul using the Latin terms "*animus*" and "*anima*":

Mind (*animus*) and soul (*anima*), I say, are held conjoined one with other, and form one single nature of themselves. But chief and regnant through the entire frame is still that seat of counsel that we call the mind (*animus*) and intellect (*mens*) and that cleaves seated in the midmost breast. Here leap dismay and terror; round these haunts are blandishments of joys; and therefore here the intellect and the mind. The rest of soul is scattered throughout the body, but obeys, moved by the nod and motion of the mind. This, for itself, alone through itself, has knowledge; this for itself rejoices (*gaudet*), even when the thing that moves it moves neither soul nor body at all. And as when head or eye in us is smitten by assailing pain, we are not tortured then through all the body, so the mind alone is sometimes smitten, or livens with a joy, while the soul's remainder through the limbs and through the frame is stirred by nothing new. But when the mind is moved by shock more fierce, we mark the whole soul suffering all at once; along man's members, sweats and pallors spread over the body, and the tongue is broken, the voice fails, and the ears ring; mists blind the eyeballs, and the joints collapse. Indeed, men drop dead from terror of the mind. Hence, whoever can will readily remark that soul is conjoined with mind, and, when it is struck by the influence of the mind, at once in turn it strikes and drives the body too. (3.136–148)

There is no direct evidence for the distinction between rational and irrational parts of the soul among the Cyrenaics. However, I believe they must have been committed to this distinction as well. There are several reasons for thinking so. The main reason is that there is explicit evidence that they distinguished mental or psychic and bodily pleasures. Diogenes Laertius here reports:

[The Cyrenaics held that] not all psychic pleasures and pains depend upon somatic pleasures and pains. For example, there is joy in the impersonal prosperity of our country just as in our own prosperity . . . However, they say that bodily pleasures are far better than psychic pleasures, and bodily pains far worse than psychic pains. This is the reason why offenders are punished with bodily pains. For they assumed pain to be more repellent, pleasure to be more congenial. (2.89–90)

Additionally – although this is a relatively weak piece of evidence – it may be noted that most Greek philosophers at this time, including, as we have seen, Plato and Aristotle, recognized some distinction between rational and irrational parts of the soul.

I will proceed, then, on the assumption that both Epicurus and the Cyrenaics were committed to a bipartition of the soul and a correlative distinction between bodily and mental pleasures. In addition, it is worth emphasizing that, for Epicurus, the entire soul, like the body, is composed of atoms. But the atomic constituents of the soul differ from those of the body. For example, as we saw in the scholiast's report above, "the soul is composed of the smoothest and roundest of atoms." Elsewhere there are ancient reports that the soul is composed of three or four kinds of atom:

fire-like, air-like, wind- or breath-like (*pneuma*), and a fourth unnamed, especially subtle and smooth, kind.[5] The scholiast is evidently only referring to this last kind, which probably predominates in the rational part of the soul. I say that the soul is composed of "three or four (atomic) kinds" because breath is either to be construed as a combination of fire-like and air-like atoms or a distinct form of air-like atoms. In his *Letter to Herodotus* Epicurus describes the atomic constitution of the soul in the following words:

The soul is a fine-structured body diffused through the whole [bodily] aggregate, most strongly resembling wind with a certain blend of heat, and resembling wind in some respects, but heat in others. Yet there is a part that differs greatly from wind and heat in its subtlety of structure. (63)

As we will see, although the Cyrenaics agree that the soul has rational and irrational parts, they are silent on the material constitution of the soul.

Let me return now to Diogenes' remarks on Epicurus' and the Cyrenaics' views of katastematic and kinetic pleasures. Diogenes says that Epicurus makes or expresses the fourfold distinction between katastematic and kinetic bodily and mental pleasures in several of his writings: *On Choice and Avoidance*, *On the Goal*, *On Ways of Life*, and *Letter to Friends in Mytilene*. To support his attribution of this distinction to Epicurus, Diogenes cites a line from Epicurus' *On Choice and Avoidance*. Diogenes also claims that two of Epicurus' followers, Diogenes the Epicurean and Metrodorus of Lampsacus, the latter being one of Epicurus' principal disciples, also held that there are katastematic and kinetic pleasures. Diogenes Laertius does not specify whether these two men held that these two principal kinds of pleasure are also divisible into bodily and mental sub-kinds. But if Epicurus held the view, it is reasonable to think that his followers did too. Finally, Diogenes begins his claims about Epicurus' fourfold distinction by contrasting Epicurus' position with that of the Cyrenaics. Once again, the Cyrenaics admit kinetic pleasure, but reject katastematic pleasure.

In light of this, we must examine several questions: What exactly is kinetic pleasure? What exactly is katastematic pleasure? Why do the Cyrenaics reject the latter? Why does Epicurus accept both? And how does Epicurus conceive of the relation between katastematic and kinetic pleasures? Let us begin with kinetic pleasure.

---

[5] Aëtius 4.3.11.

Kinetic pleasure is often characterized as "smooth" change or motion. For example, Diogenes here refers to the Cyrenaics' conception of pleasure:

Pleasure is a smooth (*leia*) change (*kinêsis*); pain is a rough change. (2.86)

Compare Plutarch's reference to the Epicureans' description of kinetic pleasures of the body:

All by themselves and without a teacher, these noble, smooth (*leia*), and agreeable motions (*kinêmata*) of the flesh beckon, as [the Epicureans say]. (*Against Colotes* 1122e)

As I have mentioned before, such descriptions should also be understood to entail that the smooth changes are perceived or apprehended. For example, this view is expressed in the testimony of Clement of Alexandria:

The Cyrenaics say that their conception of pleasure is smooth and gentle (*prosênê*) change with a certain perception. (*Miscellanies* 2.20.106.3)

But it should also be emphasized that in the cases of bodily and mental kinetic pleasures the forms of awareness must differ. In the case of kinetic bodily pleasure, the mode of awareness is sense-perceptual. In the case of kinetic mental pleasure, the mode of awareness is not. For lack of a better term, we may simply refer to it as "mental awareness." For example, consider Plutarch's reference to the Cyrenaics' point that certain so-called visual and auditory pleasures are actually mental:

[Consider certain] experiences at the theatre. We see people dying and sick with distress, Philoctetes and Jocasta, but seeing them we are pleased and full of admiration. This, I have said, Epicureans, is also a great piece of evidence from the Cyrenaics for us that pleasure in hearings and sights is not in sight or in hearing, but in the intellect (*dianoia*). (*Dinner Conversations* 674a)

Diogenes Laertius reports the same view:

[The Cyrenaics maintain that] pleasures are not derived from bare sight or hearing alone. At least, we listen with pleasure to the imitation of mourning, while we listen with pain to those who are truly mourning. (2.90)

Epicurus' position regarding the mode by which kinetic pleasure is apprehended is further complicated by the fact that he recognizes a sixth form of exteroception in addition to those of the five standard modalities, namely, mental exteroception. Epicurus appeals to mental exteroception to explain such conditions as dreams and hallucinations. Instead of explaining dreams and hallucinations as products of the mind and imagination, Epicurus holds that images formed in the external environment and composed of extremely fine atomic compounds undetectable by sight enter the mind and are perceived thereby. Consider Lucretius' account:

> Listen and learn while I explain briefly the nature and source of the objects that enter the mind and stir it to thought. My first point is that countless subtle images of things roam about in countless ways in all directions on every side. When these meet in the air, they easily become interlinked, like cobwebs or gold leaf. They are far finer in texture than the images that occupy our eyes and provoke sight, since they pass through the interstices of the body, stir the subtle substance of the mind within, and so provoke perception. (4.722–732)

Given this, it is, in Epicurus' case, necessary to distinguish two forms of mental kinetic pleasure: mental-perceptual kinetic pleasure of the kind just explained and mental kinetic pleasure proper. Unfortunately, there is in fact relatively little discussion of mental kinetic pleasures in the surviving Epicurean texts.[6]

Granting the distinction between kinetic bodily and mental pleasures, let me focus now on the concept of smoothness (*leiotês*). In the present context, this concept is difficult to understand. One possibility is that "smoothness" refers to a subjective quality or *quale*, that is, to what it is like to experience pleasure. For example, "smoothness" may refer to the way the surface of a window feels when one runs one's hand over it. Alternatively, "smoothness" may refer to an objective property of some entity or object, for example, the texture of the surface of the window.

Consider the following passage from Eusebius, bishop of Caesarea (*c.* 263–339), who here in his *Preparation for the Gospel* is quoting from Aristocles of Messene's lost historical work *On Philosophy* (composed in the first century CE). Aristocles informs us more precisely about Aristippus the Younger's conception of pleasure, pain, and the intermediate condition:

> Aristippus the Younger defined the goal of life clearly as living pleasantly, maintaining that pleasure is a kind of change. For he says that there are three conditions that pertain to our constitution. The one according to which we experience pain – it is like a storm at sea. The other according to which we experience pleasure – this resembles a smooth wave; for pleasure is smooth change comparable to a heavenly wind. The third is the intermediate condition, according to which we experience neither pleasure nor pain; this is like a calm sea. (14.18.32)

---

[6] Since mental-perception may be irrational, in the sense of not involving reasoning or deliberation, the dichotomy introduced above between rational and irrational parts of the soul correlating with the mind and body is too crude. I note this problem, but will not dwell on it.

Aristippus' similes of the conditions of the sea might encourage us to interpret "smoothness" in an objective sense: "[pleasure] resembles a smooth wave; for pleasure is smooth change comparable to a heavenly wind." However, it is hard to see how this can be construed. In the simile, a body of water undergoes change. Setting aside the key idea that the change here undergone is smooth, consider what undergoes change in the objective construal of pleasure. Presumably, in the case of kinetic pleasure of the body, it is the body or that part of the soul whose form of awareness or sentience is closely related to the body, namely, the sense-perceptual faculties. For example, consider Cicero's remarks:

[Epicurus should have restricted his conception of] pleasure [to that] which Aristippus[7] does, namely, where the sense-perceptual faculty is gently and joyfully moved, that which animals, if they could speak, would call pleasure. (*On Goals* 2.18)

In the case of kinetic pleasure of the mind, then, it would be the rational part of the soul, what Lucretius calls the "*animus*," that is moved. But what is a smooth change in the irrational or rational part of the soul? Smoothness as a property of change might be thought to entail uniformity. But a uniform change could be painful as well as pleasant. For example, in being tortured by being drawn and quartered, one's body parts may be gradually, steadily, and evenly pulled apart. The simile also suggests that the change is gentle rather than violent. "Smooth" does not seem to capture this idea. But recall the testimony of Clement of Alexandria:

The Cyrenaics say that their conception of pleasure is smooth and gentle (*prosênê*) change. . . (2.20.106.3)

Perhaps the use of "gentle" should be taken to indicate the objective sense of "small" or "limited." The condition that the change be gentle also answers the counter-example of being tortured by being drawn and quartered: although the changes involved are incrementally small and uniform, aggregatively they are not. Even so, this account is unsatisfactory, for there are mild pains that come on gradually. If we can presume that the bodily or psychic parts involved in such cases are gently and uniformly altered, then either Epicurus and the Cyrenaics are simply wrong or they do not hold this view.

This is not all there is to be said on behalf of the objective interpretation, as we will see. But presently, in light of these difficulties, let us

---

[7] Cicero is here referring to Aristippus the Elder, who is standing as a representative for the Cyrenaic school.

consider interpreting "smooth" in the subjective sense. In this case, "smooth" cannot merely refer to a phenomenal quality of tactile perception, for there are kinetic pleasures of other sense-perceptual modalities, not to mention kinetic pleasures of the mind. Consequently, "smooth" must be used in a broader way. Indeed, we speak of tastes, for example, of wine, as well as sounds, for example, of jazz music, as smooth. "Smooth" might be thought to refer to the uniformity of the qualitative experience. However, as in the objective interpretation, this is unsatisfactory because pains may be qualitatively uniform as well.

It seems more likely that "smooth," particularly in conjunction with "change," refers to experience that involves absence of psychic resistance. That is, one is subjectively qualitatively altered in a way that one welcomes rather than resists. Note, however, that if this is correct, then smoothness is in fact not an intrinsic property of the change, but a response or reaction to it. Perhaps this could be elaborated and remedied by the idea that "smooth" also has the sense of conforming to natural inclination. That is, smooth are those qualitative experiences that we naturally incline to accept rather than resist. Since the Cyrenaics and Epicureans tend to talk of desires rather than inclinations, it is likely that they would express such a view in the following way: smooth are those subjective qualitative changes that conform to our natural desires.

Speculative though this is, it seems to me the most plausible interpretation of the Cyrenaics' conception of kinetic pleasure as involving smooth change. I do not, however, think it is Epicurus' view. I will explain Epicurus' view and then explain why the Cyrenaics would not have held it momentarily. Before doing so, a further problem of this subjective interpretation must be noted. Recall my statement above that when the commentators or doxographers speak of kinetic pleasure as smooth change, this must be understood as abbreviated for smooth change that is perceived or apprehended. Indeed, we saw that Clement of Alexandria describes the pleasure that way. The problem now is this: If smoothness is understood subjectively, isn't mention of perception or apprehension at least otiose and perhaps confusing? I see two answers to this question. One is to grant that Clement is confusing or confused. The other is to note that smoothness is here understood in the specific subjective sense of conforming to natural desire. Physiological or psychological events may occur that conform to desire, but without being perceived. For example, a bruise on one's arm may imperceptibly heal while one desires that it heal. Of these two possibilities, the second is more interesting, but I suspect that the first is more likely to be true. That is, Clement conveys a misleading view of the

Cyrenaics' conception of the smoothness of the change when he adds that this must be perceived in order for pleasure to occur.

So much then for the Cyrenaics' conception of kinetic pleasure – let us turn to the Epicureans' view. In several passages of *On the Nature of Things*, Lucretius explains kinetic pleasures, particularly kinetic pleasures of the body, in terms of the motion of atoms. In some of these passages, he explicitly refers to the smoothness involved in such motion. The most significant and general statement occurs in Book 2:

> You may readily agree that such substances as titillate the senses agreeably are composed of smooth round atoms. Those that seem bitter and harsh are more tightly compacted of hooked particles and accordingly tear their way into our senses and rend our bodies by their inroads. The same conflict between two types of structure applies to everything that strikes the senses as good or bad. You cannot suppose that the rasping stridulation of a screeching saw is formed of elements as smooth as the notes a minstrel's nimble fingers wake from the lyre-strings and mold to melody. You cannot suppose that atoms of the same shape are entering our nostrils when stinking corpses are roasting as when the stage is freshly sprinkled with saffron of Cilicia and a nearby altar exhales the perfumes of the East. You cannot attribute the same composition to sights that feast the eye with color and those that make it smart and weep or that appear loathsome and repulsive through sheer ugliness. Nothing that gratifies the senses is ever without a certain smoothness of the constituent atoms. Whatever, on the other hand, is painful and harsh is characterized by a certain roughness of the matter. (2.400–423)

Lucretius is here explaining sense-perceptual pleasures (as well as pains), in other words, kinetic pleasures of the body. Smoothness is described as a physical property of the atomic constituents of the compounds that affect the sense-perceptual faculties. Because these atomic constituents of the bodies impacting the sense-perceptual faculties are smooth, their contact with the atomic constituents of the sense-perceptual faculties causes movement of a particular sort in the sense-perceptual faculties. In particular, this movement preserves the intrinsic order or structure of the sense-perceptual faculties. Compare small waves or pulses through a body. Consider also Lucretius' description of gustatory pleasure in Book 4:

> When the particles of trickling savor are smooth, they touch the palate pleasantly and pleasurably tickle all the moist regions of the tongue in their circuitous flow. Others, in proportion as their shape is rougher, tend more to prick and tear the organs of sense by their entry. (4.622–627)

Lucretius' explanation of sense-perception generally and sense-perceptual pleasure in particular can thus also be seen to reduce to an explanation of touch or physical contact between atoms. Indeed, he says as much:

For touch and nothing but touch . . . is the essence of all our bodily perceptions . . .
It is touch again that is felt when the atoms are jarred by a knock so that they are
disordered and upset the senses. (2.436–440)

It is also useful here to contrast Lucretius' account with Plato's in
Timaeus. In *Timaeus*, Plato adverts to the smoothness or roundness of
elements in order to explain sentience itself. Recall that round particles
have greater kinetic properties than otherwise shaped particles. Consequently, round particles move through bodies and impact the soul. In this
case, it is not smoothness and consequently mobility that explains pleasure, but restoration. While destruction of the sense-perceptual faculties
explains pain in Lucretius as in Plato, restoration plays no role in
Lucretius.

Taking Lucretius' account as representative, we can say that, in sum, for
the Epicureans the smoothness of the motion of kinetic pleasure primarily
refers to or derives from the smoothness of the atoms constitutive of the
bodies that impact the sense-perceptual (or, in the case of mental kinetic
pleasure, mental) faculties. The smoothness of these impacting atoms in
turn affects the atoms of the perceptual or mental faculties by moving them
in a way that preserves their intrinsic, natural order. Such movement may,
by transference, be called "smooth," although – it should be emphasized –
this description is not explicit in any of our sources.

In short, then, in the case of Epicurus "smoothness" pertains to the
property of atoms and their movements and thus must be understood in
an objective sense. Momentarily, I will explain why "smoothness" cannot
be so understood in the case of the Cyrenaics. Before I get to that point,
I want to register a difficulty with Epicurus' position. The account
apparently fails to explain the fact that usually when we experience
visual and auditory pleasures in particular, it is not isolated colors and
sounds in which we take pleasure, but their combinations. Consequently,
it does not make sense to think of the pleasure as deriving from the
smoothness or roughness of the constituent atoms, but rather from
the smoothness or roughness of the composites. I do not know how to
resolve this problem. But the following idea seems to be an appropriate
point of departure: the composites themselves are structured in a deriva-
tively smooth way, which is to say, in a way that titillates the senses while
preserving their intrinsic order.

Let me return now to the point that the Cyrenaics cannot understand
"smoothness" of pleasure in the way Epicurus does. The Cyrenaics were
not atomists. More generally, the Cyrenaics rejected the study of physical

theory. In this they followed Socrates. Recall my mention in Chapter 2 of Socrates' renunciation of physical inquiry in Plato's *Phaedo*. Aristippus the Elder followed Socrates here, and his followers in turn followed him:

Aristippus, following Socrates, only focused on philosophizing about ethical matters. (Eusebius, *Preparation for the Gospel* 15.62.7)

The Cyrenaics devote themselves to the ethical part of philosophy only; they dismiss the physical and logical part as useless for living well. (Sextus Empiricus, *Against the Mathematicians* 7.11)

Finally, granted the distinctions between their respective views, we can say that both Epicureans and Cyrenaics hold that the smoothness of change or motion involved in pleasure entails conformity to nature (and the roughness of change, non-conformity with nature). But this description correctly applies to both schools only because the phrase "conformity to nature" is vague. It must be variously interpreted with respect to each school.

KATASTEMATIC PLEASURE

Let us now turn to katastematic pleasure. Recall that in the fragment that Diogenes Laertius cites from Epicurus' *On Choice and Avoidance* where Epicurus distinguishes katastematic and kinetic pleasures of body and soul, Epicurus describes katastematic pleasure of the body as freedom from physical suffering (*aponia*) and katastematic pleasure of the soul as freedom from psychological disturbance (*ataraxia*). As such, katastematic pleasure of the body is a condition of health, and katastematic pleasure of the soul is a condition of psychological well-being. Recall that the Cyrenaics and Aristippus the Younger in particular refer to these conditions as intermediates; and since they maintain that all pleasure is kinetic, they criticize Epicurus for maintaining that there are katastematic pleasures:

The bodily pleasure, which is the goal of life, is not katastematic pleasure, the absence of discomfort that comes from the removal of pains, which Epicurus admits and claims is the goal of life. (Diogenes Laertius 2.87)

Contrary to Epicurus, [the Cyrenaics] think that the removal of pain is not pleasure. Nor do they think that the absence of pleasure is pain. For they think that pleasure and pain involve change, whereas absence of pain and absence of pleasure are not change. For absence of pain is like the condition of one who is asleep. (2.89)

[The Cyrenaics] named the intermediate conditions [between pleasure and pain] absence of pleasure (*ahêdonia*) and absence of pain (*aponia*). (2.90)

These passages indicate that Epicurus holds that katastematic pleasure is a state or condition of absence of pain or suffering, be it of the body or mind, that is, of the irrational or rational parts of the soul. This, in turn, explains Cicero's conception of katastematic pleasure as static (*stans*) as opposed to moving or changing (*movens*).

Indeed, I think this distinction is accurate. However, it is easy to misconstrue. Consider the following passage from Book 2 of Lucretius' *On the Nature of Things*:

Pain occurs when bodies of matter that have been unsettled by some force within the living flesh of the limbs stagger in their inmost stations. And when they move back into place (*inque locum remigrant*), soothing pleasure comes into being. (2.963–966)

Compare also the following account of the pain of hunger from Book 4:

Since animals are always on the move, they lose a great many atoms, some squeezed out from the innermost depths by the process of perspiration, some breathed out through the mouth when they gasp and pant. By these processes, the body's density is diminished and its substance is sapped. This results in pain. Hence food is taken so that, when duly distributed through limbs and veins, it may underpin the frame and rebuild its strength and sate its open-mouthed lust for eating. (4.861–869)

In this second passage only pain is described, not the pleasure that, presumably, should accompany the restoration of the nutritional deficit, the "rebuilding" of the depleted frame and reconstitution of the animal's strength. Nonetheless, in light of the previous passage from Book 2, it seems reasonable to infer a correlative pleasure.[8] This seems to indicate that Epicurus recognizes restorative pleasures.

Another body of evidence that suggests that Epicurus is committed to restorative pleasure comes from statements that removal of all pain is the highest or greatest pleasure:

The removal of all pain is the limit of the magnitude of pleasures. (*Principal Doctrines* 3)

As soon as the pain produced by want is removed, pleasure in the flesh will not increase (*epauxetai*). (*Principal Doctrines* 18)

---

[8] Note that in these cases, pain is not merely a function of the disarrangement of atomic structures, but also their depletion. Thus, the restorative process can be understood in both ways.

Compare also Plutarch's comment:

Epicurus has assigned a common limit to [the pleasures,] the removal of all pain –
as though nature increased pleasure up to the point where it eliminates what is
painful, but did not permit it to make any further increase. (*On the Impossibility of
Life according to Epicurus* 1088d)

Since these passages indicate that complete removal of pain is the limit
of pleasure, they also suggest that pleasure increases as pain diminishes.
According to Lucretius' account of hunger involving a certain diminution
of atoms in a living being, the restoration of those atoms entails increasing
pleasure.

Let us assume, at least tentatively and momentarily, that Epicurus
admits restorative pleasure. In fact, many Epicurus scholars maintain
that Epicurus does admit restorative pleasure. However, these scholars
hold that restorative pleasure is a kind of kinetic pleasure, the other kind
being the smooth motion of the sense-perceptual faculties that we previously discussed. Indeed, as we have seen, Plato himself refers to hedonic
restoration as *kinêsis* and generation or coming-to-be (*genesis*). I suggest,
however, that strictly speaking Epicurus does not admit restorative pleasure. Moreover, I suggest that he admits that restoration may involve
pleasure, but that the pleasure that restoration may involve does not entail
change. This should seem paradoxical or at least unclear.

First – to dismiss the view of those who think that kinetic pleasure includes
restorative pleasure – observe that there is no evidence that so-called restorative pleasure involves smooth motion in the sense of atomic smoothness that
we described above. Indeed, it is hard to see how restoration could be limited
in this way. This would require, one, that all compounds for which we have
physiological needs are predominantly composed of round and smooth
atoms and, two, that restoration of damaged or disarrayed bodily parts always
involves a predominance of smooth and round atoms.

Second – now onto the paradoxical point – restoration is indeed a
process and thus essentially involves change. Observe, moreover, that
restoration can occur in two ways. (These ways may overlap to varying
degrees, but I starkly distinguish them here for the sake of explication.)
Consider the derangement of an atomic complex, that is, the derangement of a collection of atoms constitutive of a single structure. The
restoration of this complex may occur in such a way that each atomic
constituent of the complex *sequentially* returns to its proper place. That is,
one part of the complex after another is restored. Compare the way a
fallen wall may be restored one brick at a time. Let us call this "partitive

restoration." Alternatively, the restoration of the complex may occur in such a way that all of the atomic constituents simultaneously, however gradually, return to their proper places. Let us call this "coordinated restoration." The fundamental difference between partitive and coordinated restoration is that in the case of coordinated restoration no proper part of the atomic complex will have been restored without the whole atomic complex having been restored. In the case of coordinated restoration, then, pain in principle exists until the process concludes, for at each point in the process until the terminus, the atoms constitutive of the complex are displaced, albeit to increasingly lesser extents. In the case of partitive restoration, pain in principle incrementally diminishes and pleasure, that is, absence of pain, incrementally increases as successive parts of the complex are restored.

Now, in his *Principal Doctrines* Epicurus explicitly says that pain and pleasure are exclusive:

As long as pleasure is present, so long as it is present, there is no pain, either of body or soul or both at once. (3)

I take this maxim to entail that during restoration pleasure can only increase insofar as absence of pain prevails over an increasingly large scope of the body or soul. Thus, prior to its conclusion coordinated restoration does not entail increase in pleasure. In other words, only partitive restoration involves increase in pleasure during restoration. In short, for Epicurus, restorative pleasure is a misleading concept. Indeed, Epicurus never uses the phrase.

The Neoplatonic philosopher Damascius (458–c. 538), in his commentary on Plato's *Philebus*, appears to interpret Epicurus' *Principal Doctrine* 3 as a point of contrast with Plato's conception of simultaneously mixed pleasure:

Epicurus thinks that pain cannot [simultaneously] mix with pleasure ... Plato, on the contrary, holds that this does occur, both in the soul and in the body and in combination. (197)

But it must be emphasized that there is a crucial difference between Plato's conception of mixed pleasure and Epicurus' apparent denial of it in *Principal Doctrine* 3. Plato does not hold the logically impossible view that restoration and depletion – the core constituents of pleasure and pain – concur in the same bodily or psychic part. Rather, he holds that contrary processes occurring in distinct, if adjacent, parts register psychically in some sort of phenomenally unified, but nonetheless complex, way.

Epicurus must and indeed does allow that derangement of some parts and arrangement of other parts concur. What is unclear is the subjective psychic significance of this. I note this problem here and will return to it at the conclusion of the chapter.

Presently, I am proposing that katastematic pleasure itself does not involve change. Rather, katastematic pleasure requires a stable, that is, natural, condition of the body or soul or part thereof.[9] In contrast, kinetic pleasure, which is limited to smooth motions of the sense-perceptual faculties, essentially involves change. Kinetic pleasure is precisely the movement of the sense-perceptual faculties in such a way as to preserve their natural structure.

The distinction between the view I am presenting here and the view of those who maintain that kinetic pleasure may be restorative as well as involve smooth motion of the sense-perceptual faculties may also be put as follows. According to the latter view, kinetic pleasure may be independent of katastematic pleasure. According to my view, kinetic pleasure depends upon katastematic pleasure. Kinetic pleasure depends upon katastematic pleasure precisely because kinetic pleasure is a variation on a state of absence of pain.

At least two further sets of evidence support the view that kinetic pleasure depends upon katastematic pleasure. One set of evidence relates to a point that Epicurus and his commentators emphasize on several occasions. For example, in Book 1 of *On Goals*, Cicero reports:

Epicurus thinks that the greatest pleasure terminates in complete absence of pain. Beyond this, pleasure can vary and be of different kinds, but it cannot be increased or augmented. (1.38)

Epicurus makes a similar claim in *Principal Doctrine* 18, specifically with respect to bodily pleasure:

Pleasure in the flesh will not increase once pain produced by want is removed; it is only varied.

Likewise, Plutarch comments:

Epicurus has assigned a common limit to [the pleasures], the removal of all that causes pain, as though nature increased pleasure up to the point where it eliminates the painful, but did not make any further increase in its size – although it admits of certain non-necessary variations once it gets free of distress. (*On the Impossibility of Life according to Epicurus* 1088c)

---

[9] The only qualification to be borne in mind here is that Epicurus holds that all atoms are in perpetual motion. Thus, in speaking of katastematic conditions as stable, it should be understood that the atomic complexes that constitute these conditions are structurally stable, even while the individual atoms that constitute the structures are continually vibrating.

In these cases the hedonic variations, which are kinetic pleasures, all depend upon absence of pain.

Another set of evidence in favor of the view that kinetic pleasure depends upon katastematic pleasure relates to the fact that on the few occasions where Epicurus specifies pleasures that appear to involve change, these pleasures do not appear to involve restorations. For example, consider the following fragment from Epicurus' *On the Goal* where he refers to pleasures that involve stimulations of the sense-organs:

I do not know how to conceive the good if I withdraw the pleasures of taste, sex, hearing, and the sweet changes from the sight of form. (Diogenes Laertius 10.6)

Compare the quotation and comment on this fragment by the rhetorician and grammarian Athenaeus of Naucrates (second to third century CE):

Not only Aristippus and his followers, but also Epicurus and his followers welcomed kinetic pleasure; and I will mention what follows to avoid speaking of the rushes and the delicacies, which Epicurus often cites, and the titillations and spurs, which he mentions in *On the Goal.* For he says, "I at least do not even know what I should conceive the good to be, if I eliminate the pleasures of sex, of listening, the pleasant changes in vision from a visible form." (*Sophists' Dinner* 546e–f)

Taken individually, the various sets of evidence that we have considered may be subject to objections. But taken collectively they provide compelling reasons to think that Epicurus held that so-called kinetic pleasure depends upon katastematic pleasure.

KINETIC PLEASURE AS ACTIVATION

I have argued, then, that kinetic pleasures depend upon states of the sense-perceptual or mental faculties when those faculties are intact, in other words, when they are in what Aristotle calls their "natural" state. In such cases, the changes, specifically smooth changes or motions, that the faculties undergo are, as Aristotle would put it, *energeiai*, that is, activations of the natural state. I suggest that this is in fact how Epicurus himself conceives of kinetic pleasure, at least in his ethical treatise *On Choice and Avoidance*. Recall that it is from this treatise that Diogenes Laertius cites evidence of Epicurus' commitment to the distinction between katastematic and kinetic pleasures. Diogenes cites the following line:

For freedom from [mental] disturbance and freedom from [physical] suffering are katastematic pleasures, whereas joy and delight are seen as involving change through activation (*energeiai*). (10.136)

It is intriguing to observe the use of the word "*energeia*" here. In our discussion of Aristotle's conception of pleasure in Chapter 6, we saw that "*energeia*" is a distinctly Aristotelian term. Indeed, scholars have been puzzled by the occurrence of this term in an Epicurean text. Some in fact have suggested that the text is corrupt and that "*energeiai*" should be emended to "*enargeiai*." "*Enargeia*" is an Epicurean epistemological term; it means "clear evidence." In fact, there are at least a couple of other passages among Epicurus' surviving writings where in the process of textual transmission "*enargeia*" has surely been corrupted to "*energeia*." Following this emendation, the quotation would read:

For freedom from disturbance and freedom from physical suffering are katastematic pleasures, whereas joy and delight as [pleasures] involving change are viewed through clear evidence (*enargeiai*).

The idea here would then be that kinetic pleasures are apprehended in a different way from katastematic pleasures. That is, there is clear and direct evidence for the occurrence of kinetic pleasure that katastematic pleasure lacks. This idea itself might be true. However, this reading, in addition to requiring a textual emendation – albeit one with precedents – does not make good sense of the quotation as a whole. As we discussed above, the whole quotation appears to be contrasting two sub-kinds of katastematic pleasure with two sub-kinds of kinetic pleasure. But on the emendation, the emphasis in the second clause on how kinetic pleasures are apprehended seems unwarranted by the content of the first clause. For example, the first clause does not state how katastematic pleasures are apprehended.

On the reading of the text as transmitted, that is, without the emendation, the phrase "through activation" indicates how joy and delight involve change. They involve change through activation. Insofar as the first and second clauses stand in contrast to one another, this information, more closely than the emended version, contrasts with the content of the first clause. The claim that joy and delight involve change through activation seems basically to mean this: following Aristotle, certain faculties or dispositions that stand ready for operation are, under the right circumstances, engaged and activated. Kinetic pleasures occur under some such conditions.

Consider also how Epicurus might have come to appropriate the Aristotelian term "*energeia*." Outside of Aristotle, among surviving Greek texts from the fourth through the first half of the third centuries BCE, the term "*energeia*" occurs exclusively among philosophers, mainly among members of Aristotle's school, for example, Theophrastus, Eudemus of Rhodes, and Strato of Lampsacus. However, the word also occurs in the non-Aristotelian philosophers Nausiphanes of Teos and the Epicurean Polystratus. This indicates that at this time, the late fourth and early third centuries, the word "*energeia*" remained a term of philosophical art. It is notable that the term occurs in one of Nausiphanes' fragments, for, as I mentioned above, Nausiphanes might have been a teacher of Epicurus in Ionia. Here is the Nausiphanes fragment:

> We are not claiming that it is only the man who is in a condition of activation (*energounta*) who has an architect's disposition (*hexis*), nor do we merely look at the activation (*energeia*) itself. Rather, we look at the ability that the man has, when taking up the wood and appropriate tools, to fashion a product on the basis of his architectural skill. (fr. 1)

Epicurus himself might have encountered the concept of *energeia* under Nausiphanes' tutelage. It is also notable that the term occurs in Polystratus, for Polystratus was an Epicurean philosopher; he became head of the Garden after Epicurus' successor Hermarchus, *c.* 250 BCE. This indicates that at least one other Epicurean had appropriated Aristotle's term.

As I mentioned above, Epicurus came to Athens in 323 BCE at the age of eighteen just at the time when Aristotle left Athens to return to his ancestral home in Calchis in Macedonia. This was the year before Aristotle's death, the year when the death of Alexander the Great encouraged the Athenians to liberate themselves from Macedonian control. Athenian hostility toward Macedonians is the salient reason given for Aristotle's departure at this date. Epicurus would not then have heard Aristotle lecture. Nor is there evidence that Epicurus had anything to do with the Lyceum so that he would have had access or desired to gain access to the school's esoteric materials, in which, as we have seen, Aristotle explains pleasure in terms of *energeia*. On the other hand, at some point in his early philosophical education, Epicurus would likely have come into contact with Aristotle's most popular exoteric text, *Protrepticus*. Epicurus himself wrote a work entitled *Protrepticus*, now lost. Possibly, Nausiphanes was the one who introduced Epicurus to Aristotle's *Protrepticus*, if someone in Athens did not. In his *Protrepticus*, Aristotle both explains the distinction between being on stand-by or ready-for-operation and being activated, and he speaks of pleasure as an activation (*energeia*) in terms very close to those he uses in *Eudemian Ethics* 6.12. First, consider the following two fragments, one of which I introduced in Chapter 6, that show Aristotle's clarification of the concept of *energeia*:

> Things are said to be alive in two senses, in virtue of ability (*dynamei*) and in virtue of activation (*energeiai*), for we describe as seeing both those animals that have sight

and are naturally capable of seeing, even if they happen to have their eyes shut, and those that are using this faculty and are looking at something. (fr. 79)

Thus, we say that a waking man is alive to a greater degree than a sleeping man, and that a man who is activating (*energounta*) his soul lives to a greater degree than a man who merely possesses a soul. (fr. 83)

Now consider the following passages, where Aristotle describes the relation between pleasure and *energeia*:

Again, perfect and unimpeded activation contains in itself delight; so that the activation of contemplation must be the most pleasant of all. (fr. 87)

If there is more than one activation of the soul, still the chief of all is that of understanding as well as possible. It is clear, then, that necessarily the pleasure arising from understanding and contemplation is, alone or most of all, the pleasure of living. Pleasant life and true enjoyment, therefore, belong only to philosophers, or to them most of all. (fr. 91)

In sum, there is good reason to believe that Epicurus appropriated Aristotle's term "*energeia*" in his own understanding of a certain kind of pleasure, namely, kinetic pleasure.

One further piece of supporting evidence for Epicurus' use of the phrase "involving change through activation" (*kata kinêsin energeiai*) can be derived from Epicurus' use of a similar phrase in the summary of his epistemological and basic physical theories, the *Letter to Herodotus*. In the following passage, Epicurus is explaining the function of the soul, in relation to the body, in the production of sense-perceiving (*aisthêsis*):

Hence on the departure of the soul, [the body] loses [the capacity for] sense-perception. For [the body] does not possess the power (*dynamis*) [of sense-perception] in itself, but another thing [the soul] congenital with (*syngegenêmenon*) the body provides it. And this other thing, when the power (*dynameôs*) it has (*peri auto*) has been realized (*syntelestheisês*) through change (*kata tên kinêsin*), at once produces (*apoteloun*) in itself a sense-perceptual quality (*symptôma aisthêtikon*) and through its joint affection and collaboration transmits (*apedidou*) it to the body. (64)

I am particularly interested in the phrase "power realized through change" (*dynameôs syntelestheisês kata tên kinêsin*). In this case, it is the soul's power or capacity for perception that is realized through change. The change here is an alteration of the sense-perceptual faculty of the soul, which involves the production of a sense-perceptual quality. In short, the sense-perceptual faculty of the soul undergoes a change from a condition of being capable of sense-perceiving to a condition of actively sense-perceiving, where the condition of actively sense-perceiving entails having a perceptual quality. This "realization" (*syntelesis*) of sense-perception by the sense-perceptual power of the soul is, I suggest, analogous to the activation of kinetic pleasure.

In short, then, the fragment from Epicurus' *On the Goal*, which Diogenes Laertius cites as evidence that Epicurus distinguished katastematic and kinetic pleasure, and which contains the Aristotelian term "*energeia*," can be interpreted in a way that is consistent with the view I am proposing that sense-perceptual pleasures, which are kinetic pleasures, depend upon katastematic pleasures. More precisely, sense-perceptual pleasures depend upon katastematic pleasure, which occurs when the body or soul or somatic or psychic part is in its natural condition.

<h2 style="text-align:center">TORQUATUS' ARGUMENT THAT ABSENCE
OF PAIN IS PLEASURE</h2>

A central problem of Epicurus' analgesic hedonism is his view that absence of pain itself is pleasure. We have seen that the Cyrenaics criticize Epicurus for this position; and we can see that in doing so, the Cyrenaics agree with Plato that calm or the neutral condition should not be confused with pleasure. We have yet to consider why Epicurus holds the view that absence of pain itself is pleasure.

The only text that explicitly purports to give Epicurus' reasons for thinking that absence of pain is pleasure occurs in Book 1 of Cicero's *On Goals*. In this text, Cicero has the Roman Epicurean philosopher Manlius Torquatus explain Epicurus' position. In my opinion, Torquatus' argument is confused and misleading in numerous ways. Nonetheless, it is a useful point of departure. In fact, I will structure my discussion around Torquatus' argument, specifically around problems it raises and proposals for resolving them.

It is convenient to divide Torquatus' argument into two successive parts. Here is the first part:

We [Epicureans] do not only pursue that pleasure that moves our very nature with a certain soothingness and that is perceived by our senses with a certain agreeableness. The pleasure we hold to be the greatest is that which is perceived when all pain has been removed. When we are released from pain, we take pleasure (*gaudemus*) in that very liberation from and absence of all that is disturbing. Just as everything by which we are distressed is pain, everything in which we take pleasure (*gaudemus*) is pleasure (*voluptas*). Thus, every release from pain is pleasure. For example, when hunger and thirst have been driven out by food and drink, that very removal of the disturbance yields pleasure. So in every other case, withdrawal of pain causes the succession of pleasure. And thus, Epicurus did not hold that there was some intermediate [state] between pain and pleasure. (1.37–38)

Torquatus begins here by distinguishing two kinds of pleasure: kinetic and katastematic, although without using corresponding Latin words. Kinetic pleasure is the pleasure that is said to move "our very nature with a certain soothingness and that is perceived by our senses with a certain agreeableness."[10] In contrast, katastematic pleasure is said to be "perceived when all pain has been removed." Torquatus appears to have in mind kinetic and katastematic pleasure of the body, both because he speaks of stimulation of the senses and because he subsequently uses an example of bodily pleasure, the pleasure of eating and drinking. Granted this, his reference to bodily pleasure in arguing for katastematic pleasure is compatible with the view that there are also mental kinetic and katastematic pleasures. Indeed, following his example of hunger and thirst, he claims: "So in every other case, withdrawal of pain causes the succession of pleasure." In other words, Torquatus generalizes from his specific example.[11]

The first part of Torquatus' argument raises several problems. Consider the following four.

Problem 1: Attitude or object?

The central claim in Torquatus' argument is the following:

Everything in which we take pleasure (*gaudemus*) is pleasure (*voluptas*).

There appears to be a distinction here between the psychic attitude of taking pleasure (*gaudium*) and the object of this attitude. The object of the attitude is identified as pleasure (*voluptas*). But why should the object of the attitude rather than the attitude itself be identified as pleasure? Additionally, this account of pleasure is either circular, for it defines pleasure in terms of taking pleasure, or it trades one problem for another because it leaves unexplained why pleasure should be explained in terms of taking pleasure. The fact that the Latin terms "*gaudium*" and "*voluptas*" are not cognate barely obscures these problems.

---

[10] This claim deserves some interpretation in its own right. I will return to it momentarily.

[11] Note that the same verb "to be perceived" (*percipi*) is used to refer to the apprehension of kinetic and katastematic pleasure. This may be significant in indicating that "perceived" should be construed more broadly than as perception by means of the stimulation of the sense-faculties, for katastematic pleasure by definition does not involve stimulation of the sense-perceptual faculties.

Problem 2: The masochist

The central claim of Torquatus' argument seems to entail the following difficulty. Suppose someone, for example, a masochist, takes pleasure in what others normally find distressing or painful. In that case, the extensions of "pleasure" and "pain" overlap. This seems to be absurd.

Problem 3: Pain and the neutral condition

Closely related to problem 2 is the following one. Absence of pain is the neutral or intermediate condition. This is the same as absence of pleasure, at least absence of kinetic pleasure – although the causes of absence of pain and absence of kinetic pleasure differ. But one might be distressed by the intermediate state. So once again, the intermediate state would be pain, not pleasure; and so pain and pleasure would overlap. Recall Plato's argument in *Republic* 9: it is mistaken to identify the neutral condition with pleasure; doing so compels one to identify the neutral condition with pain; for if pleasure follows removal of pain, by parity of reasoning pain would follow removal of pleasure. Plato's view is that, in both cases, the neutral condition may merely appear pleasant or painful. Compare also the Cyrenaics' position: they describe the one intermediate condition as *ahêdonia* (absence of pleasure) and the other as *aponia* (absence of pain).

Problem 4: Two different objects of the attitude?

Assume with Epicurus that one takes pleasure in the absence of pain. Even so, why think that absence of pain is pleasure? Why not instead maintain that the hedonic attitude may have distinct kinds of object, including pleasure (its proper object) and absence of pain?

So much for the four problems that the first part of Torquatus' argument presents. Immediately following the passage cited above, Torquatus' argument continues, constituting what I am calling its second part:

Indeed, with regard to the [state] that some think is intermediate (*medium*), since it is free from all pain, not only does [Epicurus] think it is pleasure, but in truth the greatest pleasure (*summam voluptatem*). Whoever is aware of how he is affected is necessarily either in a condition of pleasure or pain. But Epicurus thinks that the greatest pleasure terminates in complete absence of pain. Beyond this, pleasure can vary and be of different kinds, but it cannot be increased or augmented. (1.38)

The second part of Torquatus' argument raises a further problem.

Problem 5: Absence of pain is greatest pleasure

Epicurus not only claims that absence of pain is pleasure, but that it is the greatest pleasure (*summam voluptatem*). How is this to be understood? And what justification can be given for this position?

Finally, let me add a sixth problem, which pertains to the argument as a whole.

Problem 6: Pleasure itself

Grant Epicurus his conception of katastematic pleasure. Katastematic and kinetic pleasures seem to be two quite different conditions. What then is pleasure itself in virtue of which both kinetic and katastematic pleasures are pleasures?

In view of the conclusions of our previous discussion of Epicurus' view of the nature and relation between katastematic and kinetic pleasure, some of these problems can, at least partially, be resolved immediately. Working backward, with regard to problem 6 – what kinetic and katastematic pleasures have in common – we have seen that kinetic pleasure depends upon and entails katastematic pleasure. So both pleasures have katastematic pleasure in common. Moreover, kinetic pleasure does not increase katastematic pleasure; it merely varies it. Katastematic pleasure is absence of pain, more precisely, absence of pain that is perceived or of which one is aware. This, then, constitutes pleasure and is what katastematic and kinetic pleasure have in common in virtue of which they are pleasure. This, at least, is a significant step in resolving problem 6. It remains to explain why absence of pain is pleasure, in other words, to resolve the remaining problems.

Observe that the answer to problem 6 also resolves problem 4, again, at least to an extent. Problem 4 concerns the suggestion that pleasure and absence of pain may be distinct objects of the hedonic attitude of taking pleasure. But pleasure and absence of pain could only be distinct objects of the hedonic attitude if pleasure were both limited to kinetic pleasure and kinetic pleasure did not entail katastematic pleasure.

Problem 5 – how absence of all pain can be the greatest pleasure – is at least partially resolved by the view that absence of pain is pleasure. From this it follows that absence of all pain is the greatest pleasure. Once again, however, this solution is only partial because it remains to explain why absence of pain is pleasure to begin with as well as why it is reasonable to hold that kinetic pleasures, as variations of absence of pain, do not constitute greater pleasures.

Let us, then, address the question of why Epicurus thinks that absence of pain is pleasure. Recall that I referred to the following as the central claim in the argument:

Everything in which we take pleasure is pleasure.

I suggest that Cicero introduces this idea in a misleading way. As I mentioned above, it licenses the unacceptable view that the extensions of "pleasure" and "pain" overlap as well as the view that absence of pain or the intermediate state need not be pleasure since it is possible for one not to take pleasure in the absence of pain. But Epicurus does not in fact hold the view that anyone in a state of absence of pain will, as a matter of fact, react with pleasure. Rather, Epicurus holds that *someone with the right state of mind* will take pleasure in absence of pain. First, observe the pronoun "we" in the first part of Torquatus' argument (with my italics):

We do not only pursue that pleasure that moves our very nature with a certain soothingness . . . The pleasure *we* hold to be the greatest is that which is perceived when all pain has been removed . . .

"We" can be interpreted in two ways here: it may refer to the Epicureans, or it may refer to human beings (or even animals) in general. Above I glossed the first "we" as "we [Epicureans]." The second "we" supports this gloss. It is the Epicureans, not just anyone, who hold that the pleasure that is perceived when all pain has been removed is the greatest.

But this interpretation of the pronouns seems to introduce a difficulty. If Torquatus is trying to convince others of the Epicureans' position, it does not help simply to state that the Epicureans hold that absence of pain is pleasure. It is necessary to provide others with a reason to believe so. Again, consider the following lines from Torquatus' argument (with my italics):

When *we* are released from pain, *we* take pleasure in that very liberation from and absence of all that is disturbing. Just as everything by which *we* are distressed is pain, everything in which *we* take pleasure is pleasure.

Do the pronouns still refer to the Epicureans? In the first of these lines, it seems that "we" is being used to refer to people in general. But then in the second line, it is unclear. It seems that Torquatus is trying to justify why the Epicureans think that absence of pain is pleasure – not merely to report the conclusions that the Epicureans accept – by appealing to something that we all believe.

I will not attempt to sort out the problems of the pronoun here. I merely want to draw attention to them. As I said, I think Cicero's presentation of the argument is confused. Nonetheless, I continue to think that examination of the argument is useful. Consider now the following fragment that Plutarch cites from Epicurus' *On the Goal*:

For the stable condition of the flesh and the reliable expectation concerning this contain the highest and most secure joy *for those who are able to reason it out.* (*On the Impossibility of Living according to Epicurus* 1098d, with my italics)

In other words, certain bodily and mental conditions constitute the greatest pleasure *for someone with the proper understanding.* The person with the proper understanding is the wise man, in this case, the Epicurean sage. So, I suggest, the Epicurean sage takes pleasure in absence of pain because he is wise. Consequently, the Epicurean principle that lies behind Torquatus' central claim is closer to the following:

Genuine pleasure is that in which one takes pleasure when one possesses wisdom.

In fact, I will suggest below that this principle still doesn't get Epicurus' view quite right. But, for now, the principle provides at least partial solutions to problems 2 and 3. The Epicureans can maintain that someone such as a masochist who takes pleasure in what is in fact pain is psychologically defective. Likewise, the Epicureans can charge that someone who is pained by the intermediate state is psychologically defective.

EPICUREAN WISDOM

In light of the preceding conclusion, we need to know more about Epicurean wisdom. What does it consist of? And how does it enable its possessor to take pleasure in what I am calling "genuine pleasure"? In a nutshell, Epicurean wisdom consists of physical and epistemological knowledge that securely allays fear and, in conjunction with ethical-psychological knowledge, directs desire in a natural way (where "natural" is being used in a normative sense). In other words, Epicurean wisdom governs choice and avoidance in such a way as to constitute a good life. The Neoplatonist philosopher Porphyry of Tyre (234–305), remarking on Epicurus' views, encapsulates this point well in the following quotation:

For a man is unhappy either because of fear or because of unlimited and groundless desire. And by reining these in he can produce for himself the reasoning [that leads to] blessedness. (*Letter to Marcella* 29)

The genuine pleasure that is the goal of life for Epicurus – here and elsewhere also called "blessedness" (*makaria*) – is not simply absence of pain, but bodily health and freedom from mental distress. The sort of mental distress whose eradication Epicureanism seeks principally derives from being socialized within traditional Greek culture. More precisely, mental distress derives from certain misguided mythological and specifically theological and eschatological beliefs. Consider, for instance, the situation of the average Greek citizen. He is a farmer. His livelihood depends upon favorable meteorological conditions, but he believes that capricious gods, whom he may strive in vain to placate, control meteorological events. Compare Epicurus' following description from his *Letter to Herodotus*, in which he criticizes the common identification of celestial bodies as divinities:

The worst disturbance occurs in human souls because of the opinion that these [celestial bodies] are blessed and indestructible and that they have wishes and undertake actions and exert influence in a manner inconsistent with these attributes, and because of the constant expectation and suspicion that something bad might happen such as the myths relate, or even because they fear the very lack of consciousness that occurs in death … And freedom from disturbance is a release from all of this. (81–82)

Another of Epicurus' surviving letters, *To Pythocles*, is wholly devoted to de-mythological, that is, purely physical, explanations of celestial and meteorological entities and events. Epicurus states the purpose of this inquiry as follows:

There is no other goal to be achieved by knowledge of meteorological phenomena, whether discussed in conjunction with physical theory in general or on their own, than freedom from disturbance and a secure conviction (*bebaios pistis*), just as with the rest of physical theory. (85)

In short, the purpose of the study of all physical theory as well as Epicurus' empiricist epistemology on which it is based is peace of mind.

Observe further that the fears that Epicurean philosophy seeks to allay all ultimately concern bodily health, in other words, freedom from bodily pain. This is because the fears all ultimately concern bodily harms that humans may suffer at the hands of the gods in life and after death. As such, mental pleasure is explanatorily dependent upon bodily pleasure. This point holds as well for the aspect of Epicurean wisdom that concerns desire.

As I have noted, wisdom requires an understanding of desire as well as fear. Here in particular Epicurus seems indebted to Democritus. Recall from Chapter 2 Democritus' central point concerning desire:

Aim at measured acquisition and measure [your] labor according to what is necessary. (B285)

I had mentioned that "what is necessary" here refers to what conforms to our nature or natural constitution. According to our nature, we have modest physical or material needs. Consequently, these can be easily satisfied.

Epicurus himself distinguishes natural from what he calls "empty" desires. He further distinguishes necessary natural and unnecessary natural desires. Necessary natural desires are those whose satisfaction constitutes or contributes to the constitution of katastematic pleasures, that is, bodily health and peace of mind. Non-necessary natural desires are those whose satisfaction constitutes or contributes to the constitution of kinetic pleasures. It is because kinetic pleasures merely vary katastematic pleasures, without adding to the pleasure, that they are natural, but non-necessary. All other desires are empty and to be avoided. This is how Epicurus puts it in the *Letter to Menoeceus*:

One must reckon that of desires, some are natural, some empty; and of the natural desires, some are necessary and some merely natural; and of the necessary, some are necessary for happiness [= peace of mind] and some for the freeing of the body from troubles and some for life itself. The unwavering contemplation of these enables one to refer every choice and avoidance to the health of the body and the freedom of the soul from disturbance, since this is the goal of a blessed life. (127–128)

Epicurus also draws the trifold distinction between necessary natural, non-necessary natural, and empty desires in his *Principal Doctrine* 29. A scholiast on this *Doctrine* provides a helpful explanation of these distinctions as follows:

Epicurus thinks that those [desires] that liberate us from pains [when satisfied] are natural and necessary, for example, drinking in the case of thirst; natural and not necessary [desires] are those [whose satisfaction] merely provides variations of pleasure, but without removing pain, for example, luxurious foods; neither natural nor necessary [desires] are, for example, [for] crowns and the erection of statues [= political power].

Epicurus' theory of desire teaches that what we need for bodily health, in other words, the avoidance of bodily pain, is easy to acquire and thus within our control:

Natural wealth is both limited and easy to acquire. (*Principal Doctrine* 15)

Compare Democritus' views:

The things the body needs are easily available to everyone without labor and trouble. (B223)

A man is successful who is content with modest possessions; unsuccessful, who is discontent with many possessions. (B286)

If you do not desire many things, a little will seem much for you; for small desires make poverty as strong as wealth. (B284)

For Epicurus, as for Democritus, understanding our natural needs and the ease with which they can be satisfied also conduces to peace of mind. Thus, as I said above, freedom from mental distress is explanatorily dependent upon freedom from physical suffering.

Now, to hear these ideas expressed in a cursory way cannot provide the sort of "secure conviction" (*bebaios pistis*) of which Epicurus speaks and which he holds is required in order to attain genuine peace of mind. Rather, one must study in great detail the empiricist epistemological basis of Epicurean physical theory and the physical theory itself as well as the ethical and psychological views. The progress of such study, when earnestly and successfully undertaken, transforms the mind, increasingly yielding intellectual strength and with that stability, security, and confidence.

So much, then, for a brief account of the nature of Epicurean wisdom – how does this wisdom or the reasoning that constitutes it enable its possessor to experience genuine pleasure? It does so through the understanding it provides of how to live one's life as well as possible. Bodily health and freedom from disturbance are viewed as points about which the best human life is constantly oriented. Wisdom then informs an attitude taken toward these objects. This attitude is taking pleasure. Precisely, the pleasure taken in bodily health and freedom from disturbance entails an appreciation of these conditions as constituting the greatest human goods. This, finally, explains why Epicurus holds that absence of pain that is perceived or apprehended is pleasure.[12]

Epicurus' view that the wise man takes pleasure in genuine pleasure should be compared with similar views in both Plato and Aristotle. Recall that in *Republic* 9 Socrates claims that the truest pleasures are rational pleasures. Thus, the rational man takes pleasure in the truest pleasure. (Of course, it is ironic that Plato and Epicurus agree that the wise man knows what pleasure really is, but hold antithetical positions regarding the relation between absence of pain and pleasure.)

Recall also Aristotle's view from *Nicomachean Ethics* 10.5 that the good man is the measure of what pleasure is:

We consider to be so that which appears so to a good man. If this is correct, as it seems to be, and if excellence and a good man insofar as he is good are the measure of each thing, then what seem to him to be pleasures are pleasures and what he takes

---

[12] I emphasize once again the glaring problem – noted above in 'Problem 1: Attitude or object?' – insofar as pleasure is here being used both to identify the attitude of taking-pleasure-in and the object in which pleasure is taken. I return to this point shortly below.

pleasure in is pleasant. It is not surprising that something that is disagreeable to him is pleasant to someone else. For there are many ways in which men can become corrupted and perverted. Still, such things are not in fact pleasant. (1176a)

EPICURUS' CONCEPTION OF PLEASURE

Let us return now to problem 1 of Torquatus' argument, namely, why Torquatus identifies pleasure with the object of the attitude of taking pleasure rather than with the attitude itself. Moreover, as I said, the fact that the attitude is employed in accounting for the object seems circular or at least to trade one difficulty for another: If the attitude is not pleasure, then what justifies appeal to the attitude in defending the view that absence of pain is pleasure? Once again, I believe that these questions and problem 1 itself derive from the misleading way that Cicero casts Torquatus' argument. Recall once again what I originally described as the central premise of the argument:

Everything in which we take pleasure is pleasure.

And recall that I suggested that Epicurus' actual principle must have been closer to the following:

Genuine pleasure is that in which one takes pleasure when one possesses wisdom.

I suggest that this principle cannot be quite right either. Instead, I suggest that Epicurus' view is the following:

Pleasure consists of the conjunction of an attitude and an object of that attitude. The attitude is taking pleasure. The object is that in which pleasure is taken. Moreover, genuine pleasure consists of taking pleasure in the right sort of object. Such objects are bodily and mental states of health and tranquillity as well as bodily and mental states transitional to the former. Additionally, the set of the right sort of hedonic objects includes smooth variations of bodily and mental states of health and tranquillity.

In short, I am suggesting that Epicurus does not in fact identify genuine pleasure with the object of the attitude of taking pleasure; he identifies genuine pleasure with the conjunction of the attitude and the object.

This proposal raises at least three further questions, which I will pursue in the remainder of this section. First, how are we to understand the pleasures that irrational beings such as infants may experience, since they lack wisdom? Second, why are the objects of genuine pleasure limited to conditions of the subject who takes pleasure? For example, isn't another person's well-being or the flourishing of one's city-state a genuine good, in which one can and should take pleasure? Third, how is the attitude of taking pleasure to be understood? I will address these questions in the order presented.

Epicurus holds that all animals, human and non-human, are naturally motivated toward pleasure. In fact, he uses this view to support his position that pleasure is good. The psychological states of infants and animals are natural, that is, uncorrupted. Assuming that the object of natural desire is good, pleasure is. The Cyrenaics argue similarly, as does Aristotle, and before him the mathematician and astronomer Eudoxus of Cnidus (*c.* 400–350). The problem is that animals and infants lack wisdom. So if wisdom is required to take pleasure in the right sort of hedonic objects, then animals and infants do not experience genuine pleasure. Note, however, that in my final rendition of Epicurus' conception of pleasure I excluded mention of wisdom. I simply said that genuine pleasure is taking pleasure in the right sort of hedonic objects, and I specified those objects. Animals and infants take pleasure in the right sort of objects due to the uncorrupted condition of their souls. Adult humans, who typically become corrupted through mis-socialization or mis-education, require wisdom to take pleasure in the right sorts of object. Accordingly, different psychological explanations are needed to explain how adult humans and infants and animals experience genuine pleasure. The Peripatetic commentator Alexander of Aphrodisias (third century CE) appears to capture this idea well when he writes:

The Epicureans maintain that what is first congenial to us, unqualifiedly, is pleasure, but they say that as we get older this pleasure becomes more fully articulated (*diarthrousthai*). (*Supplement to On the Soul* 150.33–34)

At least one way to understand the claim that this pleasure becomes more fully developed as we age is that – assuming we are properly educated – we come to understand pleasure better and thus that our hedonic attitudes develop in the sense that they come to have reasons justifying them.[13]

Our second problem concerns the range of the objects of genuine pleasure. These are limited to bodily health and peace of mind as well as to the smooth changes of the sense-perceptual and mental faculties that depend upon the former. In sum, hedonic objects are limited to mental and bodily states of the subject. This suggests that Epicurus is an egoist hedonist; that is, he maintains that pleasure is the good, but more precisely, that

---

[13] I note, but will not pursue, the point that the Epicureans' views of animal minds is more complex than the stark dichotomy of rationality and irrationality suggests. The Epicureans admit that animals have minds, albeit less complex minds than humans, and can perform a range of mental functions analogous to mental functions in humans. Even so, animals lack the capacity for wisdom.

pleasure taken in one's own mental and bodily conditions is the good. On the other hand, it may be that Epicurus' restriction of the objects of genuine pleasure to mental and bodily states of the subject is compatible with the view that genuine pleasure may be taken in the well-being of others or of one's community. This could be if such other-regarding pleasure were construed in terms of one's own mental states, precisely, if such other-regarding pleasure were construed in terms of kinetic mental pleasure. For example, in order to take pleasure in the well-being of another, one must perceive that the other is faring well. Such perception is a kinetic mental state. But there is a problem with this solution, for on this construal we have shifted the object of pleasure in a way that seems at odds with the original condition. One does not take pleasure in the fact that one perceives that another is faring well. Rather, one takes pleasure in the fact that another is faring well. In short, Epicurus must either insist upon egoist (analgesic) hedonism or broaden his conception of the hedonic objects of genuine pleasure.

Our third question concerns the nature of the attitude of taking pleasure. What is this attitude? Torquatus' claims suggest that it is a kind of perception or awareness:

We [Epicureans] do not only pursue that pleasure that moves our very nature with a certain soothingness and that *is perceived by our senses* (*percipitur sensibus*) with a certain agreeableness. The pleasure we hold to be the greatest is that which *is perceived* (*percipitur*) when all pain has been removed. (Cicero, *On Goals* 1.37)

Whoever *is aware* (*sentit*) of how he is affected is necessarily either in a condition of pleasure or pain. (Cicero, *On Goals* 1.38)

Indeed, some scholars have suggested that Epicurus conceives of pleasure and pain as forms of proprioception. This view is also consistent with some of Lucretius' descriptions, for example, his description of gustatory pleasure cited above:

When the particles of trickling savor are smooth, they touch the palate pleasantly and pleasurably tickle all the moist regions of the tongue in their circuitous flow. Others, in proportion as their shape is rougher, tend more to prick and tear the organs of sense by their entry. (4.622–627)

On this interpretation, Epicurus' conception of the hedonic attitude resembles Plato's view of the appearance or phenomenal aspect of pleasure. And as in the discussion of Plato's view, it is questionable here whether Epicurus holds that the hedonic attitude always involves feeling. Scholars dispute this question, specifically with regard to katastematic conditions. The Cyrenaics and one of their splinter groups, the

Annicerians, apparently took Epicurus' view to be that katastematic pleasure does not involve feeling; and they ridiculed this position:

These Cyrenaics [namely, the Annicerians] reject Epicurus' definition of pleasure, the removal of what is painful, calling it the condition of a corpse. (Clement, *Miscellanies* 2.21.130.8)

[The Cyrenaics held that] painlessness is the state of someone asleep. (Diogenes Laertius 2.89)

I myself am unsure whether for Epicurus all pleasure involves feeling. The question is problematic both because our textual evidence is unsatisfactory and because the nature and scope of feeling, as we use this word today, is unclear. If awareness entails feeling then, since the hedonic attitude entails awareness, it entails feeling. But this conception of feeling is vacuously liberal.

At any rate, assuming the hedonic attitude entails awareness, is it merely a form of awareness or perception? In a recent contribution to Epicurus' psychology, Elizabeth Asmis emphasizes that pleasure and pain are not merely cognitive conditions. That is, they do not merely indicate our bodily and psychic conditions. Additionally, they have a "practical function." Precisely, they involve pro and con attitudes:

[Pleasure and pain] comprise an attitude, pro or con, concerning the object of awareness. To attend to something pleasant is to be attracted to it; to attend to something painful is to have an aversion to it.[14]

On Asmis's view, then, the hedonic attitude is complex. This is a plausible interpretation, for Epicurus speaks of pleasure and pain as both epistemological and practical standards.[15] But although the interpretation is plausible, it must be emphasized that, among the surviving evidence, Epicurus, like Aristotle, focuses more on the objects of pleasure than the attitude.

ATTENTION AND THE PROBLEM OF MIXED PLEASURE

There is a good deal more to say about Epicurus' and the Cyrenaics' conceptions of pleasure, but I will conclude my account here with a brief consideration of a question raised above in the context of the discussion of katastematic pleasure. The question concerns Epicurus' view of simultaneously mixed pleasure. I have already stated that Epicurus rejects the

---

[14] Note that I am citing here from a draft of Asmis's chapter "Epicurean Psychology," forthcoming in the *Oxford Handbook of Epicureanism.*

[15] Diogenes Laertius 10.34, 128–129 (as cited by Asmis).

concept of simultaneously mixed pleasure (hereafter simply mixed pleasure).[16] Atomic complexes in sentient or conscious beings are either naturally or properly arranged or they are not. In the former case, there is absence of pain; in the latter, there is pain. Admittedly, Epicurus could use a condition here like Plato's to the effect that only significant derangement of atomic complexes causes pain. But setting this point aside, assume that one part of an animal's body is significantly deranged, that is, damaged. Assuming the rest of the animal's body is in a state of absence of pain, it would seem to follow that the animal experiences a mixed pleasure. And yet this seems absurd.

Here it may be helpful to introduce the concept of attention (*epibolē*), which Epicurus was the first to introduce into psychological and epistemological theory. Attention may be voluntary or involuntary. For example, one may focus one's gaze on a particular part of a scene; or a particular object may, as we say, simply grab one's attention. In either case, attention is selective. That is, in attending, the mind or perception focuses on something to the exclusion of other things. Consequently, an animal that is partly wounded will not experience mixed pleasure insofar as it attends to its wound.

This resolves one simple problem posed by the concept of mixed pleasure. It remains questionable how an animal, say, a pet dog, that is suffering from some general bodily illness would experience the pain of his condition while simultaneously being comforted by having his belly stroked. Likewise, consider the case of seeing a beautiful object, while simultaneously hearing a cacophonous sound. I do not know how Epicurus would have explained such conditions. They evidently require an explanation of the scope of mental or perceptual attention. Insofar as Epicurus holds that mixed pleasure does not occur, he must hold that attention is, at any given moment, particularly limited in scope.

The preceding cases are of what Plato in *Philebus* calls mixed bodily pleasures. In the case of mixed psychic pleasure, again I do not know what sort of explanation Epicurus would have given. Epicurus does, however, speak of a case of what Plato would call mixed psychosomatic pleasure. This occurs in a passage from a letter Epicurus composed a few days before his death to one of his closest friends, Idomeneus:

---

[16] Epicurus clearly recognizes sequentially mixed pleasure, which poses no theoretical problem for him. For example, I presume he is referring to sequentially mixed pleasure in *Principal Doctrine* 12 when he says: "A man cannot dispel his fear about the most important matters if he does not know the nature of the cosmos, but suspects the truth of some mythological story. Consequently, without physical theory, it is not possible to achieve unmixed (*akeraious*) pleasures."

On this truly blessed day of my life, as I am at the point of death, I write this to you. The dysentery and strangury are pursuing their course, lacking nothing of their natural severity. But against all this is the joy in my mind at the recollection of my past conversations with you. (Diogenes Laertius 10.22)

If Epicurus' description of his psychic state here is to be understood as consistent with his psychology and hedonic theory, then it appears that he was able to focus his attention on pleasant intellectual memories, which is to say kinetic mental pleasures, while suppressing the pain or rather ignoring the atomic derangements of his body, which otherwise would have been painful. Presumably Epicurus' selective attention here should be understood to depend upon his estimation of these memories as being of considerably greater value than the disvalue of his physical condition.

If this interpretation is in principle correct, it must nonetheless be emphasized that Epicurus' theoretical position requires more substantive explanation and defense. I mentioned that attention may be voluntary or involuntary. Evidently, Epicurus' attention to his intellectual memories and ignoring of his physical illness entails voluntary attention. But according to his view of *epibolê*, Epicurus holds that the sense-perceptual faculties can, and typically do, attend to objects involuntarily. This accords with common sense. For example, when one accidentally puts one's hand on a stove, one's attention is involuntarily drawn to the heat. Given this, it is questionable how, in the case Epicurus reports to Idomeneus, it is possible for the mind to, so to speak, override the involuntary attention of bodily perception through its voluntary attention to memories.

In short, we would like to know more about Epicurus' conception of attention as it relates not only to mixed pleasure, but to Epicurus' conception of pleasure generally. For example, is the hedonic attitude of taking pleasure a kind of attention? Or does it follow upon attending? Do some kinds of pleasure require attention, while others do not? For example, the assumption that katastematic pleasure requires attention would explain why merely being in a katastematic condition, say, being physically healthy, would not be pleasant. Rather, one would have to attend to this condition and, as I have suggested, do so with the right state of the soul.

CHAPTER 8

The Old Stoics on pleasure as passion

Insofar as we are interested in the Stoic conception of pleasure, we are dealing with a school of thought – as we did in the case of the Cyrenaics – rather than with a single figure such as Plato, Aristotle, or Epicurus. Stoicism endured much longer than Cyrenaicism. In fact, it was the dominant philosophical outlook of the Greco-Roman world from about the third century BCE until about the third century CE.

Through these 600 odd years, there was a great deal of continuity among Stoic philosophers. In general, members of the school desired to adhere to the positions of their founders. Inevitably and understandably, however, there were also adjustments, disparities, and renunciations. This applies to the Stoic conception of pleasure as well as to other areas of their thought. Here we focus on the foundational position.

The foundations of Stoic philosophy, normally referred to as the philosophy of the "Old Stoa," are identified with the views of the first three successive heads of the school: Zeno of Citium (334–262), Cleanthes of Assos (331–232), and Chrysippus of Soli (279–206). Unless otherwise indicated, I will hereafter use "Stoic" to mean "Old Stoic." Generally, it is agreed that the philosophy of the old Stoa receives its most refined form in the work of Chrysippus. Thus, much of what passes for Stoic philosophy is the philosophy of Chrysippus. For reasons that will become clearer as we proceed, however, the Old Stoic conception of pleasure that we will be discussing cannot or should not straightforwardly be identified as Chrysippus'. Here we can note at least two reasons for this. First, there may be disparities between Zeno and Chrysippus. Second, since a significant portion of Chrysippus' conception of pleasure derives from Zeno and since we can to some extent specify Zeno's contribution, we should appreciate originality where it is due. For convenience, I will refer to the "Stoic conception of pleasure," but now we should understand that this conception itself might not have been unified.

The Stoic conception of pleasure that we will be discussing is typically said to be a technical philosophical conception. This point needs explanation for two reasons. First, the Stoics seem to have operated with two conceptions of pleasure, a commonsensical one and a technical philosophical one. This is actually a complex issue, and I will return to the idea below. But taking the point at face value, we can emphasize that we are focusing on the technical philosophical conception *to the exclusion of* the commonsensical conception.

Second, it might be thought that insofar as Plato, Aristotle, Epicurus, and the Cyrenaics theorized about the nature of pleasure in a philosophical way, they all developed technical philosophical conceptions of pleasure. As such, emphasis on the Stoics' conception as technical and philosophical appears otiose. But arguably there is a difference with the Stoics' position. Whereas Plato and his successors' theoretical point of departure and at least part of their *explanandum* was the common experience of pleasure, arguably this is not true of the Stoics. Arguably, the Stoics were interested in explaining a different entity than the common experience of pleasure; yet partly for convenience they applied the term "pleasure" or rather "*hêdonê*" to this entity. On this view, "pleasure" in the Stoics' technical philosophical sense is a term of art.

Now if this were the case and all there were to the story, it would make little sense to discuss the Stoics' conception of pleasure within a study of ancient Greek conceptions of pleasure. However, in my view, this is not all there is to the story. There are good grounds for discussing the Stoics' technical philosophical conception of pleasure within a study of ancient Greek conceptions of pleasure. The Stoics did not merely, for the sake of convenience, apply the term "*hêdonê*" to the entity they were examining. There is a closer and more substantive relation between the entity and the term. Thus, within the context of theorizing about pleasure, the Stoics' conception of pleasure is illuminating as a conception of pleasure.

If this view is correct, then it in turn raises a question about the Stoics' other use of "pleasure," that is, according to the commonsensical conception. The idea that the Stoics used both a commonsensical conception and a technical philosophical one makes sense on the view that the technical philosophical one is not simply a development of the commonsensical conception. But if the technical philosophical conception is substantively related to the experience of pleasure, then it is hard to understand the idea that they used both. This is a problem whose solution cannot be well formulated until we have worked through the technical philosophical conception. I defer the answer accordingly. Let us turn to the technical philosophical conception.

Our evidence for the philosophical views of the three foundational figures of the Stoa is fragmentary, in some respects extremely fragmentary.

Not one of the works of these three men survives intact. This applies, of course, to their views of pleasure. On the other hand, we are able to situate at least some of these fragments regarding pleasure within their original context. Here is how. The Stoics view pleasure as a species of psychological *pathos*. The Greek word "*pathos*" is cognate with the word "*pathêma*," which we encountered in the context of discussing Plato's conception of pleasure in Chapter 3. Recall that "*pathos*," like "*pathêma*," derives from the verb "*paschein*." The verb means "to undergo (something)" or "to be affected (by something)." The noun "*pathos*" is variously translated as "affection," "passion," and "emotion." There is some justification for each translation, and none is completely adequate. As we have seen, in Plato "*pathos*" or "*pathêma*" is used to refer to the way a body or soul is affected; hence "affection." This usage persists through antiquity. But in tandem with it, at least as early as Aristotle, "*pathos*" also develops the sense of "emotion." For example, in *Rhetoric* 2.1 Aristotle defines a *pathos* as follows:

The *pathê* are those things because of which people's judgments are altered and that are attended by pain or pleasure. Such are anger, pity, fear, and the like, with their opposites. (1378a)

A related, but distinctive, use of "*pathos*" occurs in Epicurus' ethics, where pleasure and pain are treated as the two basic kinds of *pathos*:

Pleasure is our first and congenital good. It is the starting point of every choice and avoidance, and we return to it since we make *pathos* the standard by which to judge every good. (*Letter to Menoeceus* 129)

Here "affective states" seems to be the right translation.

When the Stoics speak of pleasure as a *pathos*, they are clearly using the word in a more precise sense than "affection," but not exactly as "emotion." They identify pleasure as one of four fundamental kinds of *pathos*, along with pain, fear, and desire. To that extent, "emotion" may seem appropriate. But for Aristotle, the development of good character requires habituation to the right sort of emotional dispositions; and under the right circumstances, emotions, directed toward the right objects, to the right extent, and in the right way, are appropriate. In contrast, the Stoics hold that ethical development requires transcendence of *pathê* altogether. In other words, no *pathos* is ever good. In his treatise *Tusculan Disputations*, Cicero voices an instructive concern over how to render the Stoic term "*pathos*" into Latin:

These are the sorts of thing [that the Stoics] call *pathê*. I could call them diseases (*morbi*), and that would be a literal translation. But that would not conform to our [Latin] usage ... It would be best for us to call [pity, envy, exultation, and enjoyment] disturbances (*perturbationes*); but to call them diseases would be somewhat unusual. (3.23)[1]

"Passion" in the older sense of a "suffering," which we find most notably in the phrase "the passion of Christ," more adequately captures the Stoic view. This is the translation I will use, with the understanding that I specifically mean "psychic or mental suffering." In short, then, the Stoics' account of pleasure occurs within their discussions of passion.

Now, Zeno composed a work *On Passions* (*peri pathôn*) – apparently in one book. Chrysippus composed a work by the same title in four books. The first three of these and the first in particular dealt with the question of what a passion is; it was followed by a discussion of the various kinds of passion, including pleasure. I will begin with Zeno's conception of a passion.[2]

ZENO ON PASSION

Basically, two accounts of passion are attributed to Zeno. In book 7 of his *Lives*, which is devoted to the Stoics, Diogenes Laertius reports that:

According to Zeno [presumably in his *On Passions*], passion itself is an irrational (*alogos*) and unnatural (*para physin*) change (*kinêsis*) of the soul or (*ê*) an excessive impulse (*hormê pleonazousa*). (7.110)

Note that Diogenes reports that passion is an irrational and unnatural change of the soul "or" (*ê*) an excessive impulse. There are numerous ways this "or" can be taken: exclusively – affection is A or B, but not both; inclusively – affection is A or B or both; epexegetically – affection is A, alternatively describable as B. Whatever Diogenes meant, a correct understanding of the relation between irrational and unnatural change of the soul, on the one hand, and excessive impulse, on the other, is important. I believe that they are coextensive. That is, for Zeno, all affections are both irrational, unnatural changes of the soul *and* excessive impulses. On this view, and assuming Diogenes reports accurately, the "or" should be construed epexegetically.

---

[1] Brad Inwood, *Ethics and Human Action in Early Stoicism*, Clarendon Press, 1985, 128 notes that in considering the translation of "*pathos*" as "disease" (*morbus*), Cicero is actually confusing the disposition that gives rise to the *pathos* with the *pathos* itself. The *pathos* would be better likened to the symptoms of a disease.

[2] So far as we know, Cleanthes did not write a treatise entitled *On Passions*. Interestingly, he seems to have written a treatise *On Pleasure*, in at least two books.

In his *Epitome of Stoic Ethics*, partly preserved in Stobaeus' *Anthology*, Arius Didymus (*c.* first century BCE to first century CE) reports a nearly identical account of Zeno's conception of affection. Arius' report uses "and" instead of "or,"[3] and then proceeds to say:

Hence also every fluttering (*ptoia*) is a passion, and every passion is a fluttering [of the soul]. (*SVF* I.206.)

Like all our sources for Stoic thought, Arius' *Epitome* cannot simply be taken at face value. It is largely a synthesis of Stoic ethics that does little to indicate who contributed what and where there are disparities among the individual Stoics. Possibly, the claim that every passion is a fluttering is not Zeno's view, but, say, Chrysippus'. Fortunately, Arius is explicit on this point; elsewhere in the *Epitome* he reports:

[Zeno] defined [passion] in this way: "passion is a fluttering of the soul," likening the volatility of the passionate part of the soul to the movement of wings. (*SVF* I.206)

In short, then, Zeno conceives of a passion as:

an irrational and unnatural change of the soul,
an excessive impulse,
a fluttering [of the soul].

Let us examine each of these accounts in turn.

PASSION AS IRRATIONAL AND UNNATURAL CHANGE OF THE SOUL

The first conception refers to a change of the soul. So let me begin by saying something about the Stoics' conception of the soul. The Stoics are materialists. Hence they view the soul as bodily. More precisely, they view the soul as breath (*pneuma*), a term later translated into Latin as "*spiritus*" and subsequently spiritualized as "spirit." Precisely, *pneuma* as breath is a material compound constituted by proportions of fire and air.[4]

---

[3] "They [the Stoics] say that passion is an excessive impulse and (*kai*) a movement of the soul that is disobedient to choosing reason or contrary to nature" (*SVF* I.205). The abbreviation "*SVF*" stands for the Latin title *Stoicorum Veterum Fragmenta* (*Fragments of the Old Stoics*) compiled in four volumes in 1903–1905 by Hans von Arnim. There is no English translation of this work. However, many fragments are translated in the following works: A. A. Long and D. N. Sedley, *The Hellenistic Philosophers*, Cambridge University Press, vol. I, 1987; *Epitome of Stoic Ethics*, Arthur J. Pomeroy, translation, Society of Biblical Literature, 1999; Brad Inwood and L. P. Gerson, *The Stoics Reader*, Hackett, 2008.

[4] There is some question about whether all of the early Stoics viewed *pneuma* in the same way. See David Hahm, *The Origins of Stoic Cosmology*, Ohio State University Press, 1977, 156–163.

The ancient view that *pneuma* is instrumental in psychic activity emerges in Aristotle's thought and becomes central in the century after his death, saliently in the medical theory of Praxagoras of Cos (*floruit c.* 300 BCE).[5] The Stoics recognize different kinds of soul, fundamentally distinguished by different proportions of fire and air that constitute *pneuma*, and correspondingly different psychic capacities. The Stoics also recognize different proper parts of the soul. The soul of an adult human soul consists of eight spatially distinct parts, each associated with one or more distinct psychic functions: five sense-perceptual parts, a reproductive part, a vocal part (for generating linguistic sounds), and what they call "*dianoia*" (mind or intellect) or equivalently "*hêgemonikon*" (the ruling part).

The *hêgemonikon* is distinctive of the adult human soul. Thus, it is the part on which hereafter I focus. As I have mentioned in previous chapters, there was a long-standing debate in Greek philosophy and medicine over the principal bodily site of psychic activity, with the brain and heart as the main contenders. The Stoics sided with Aristotle and Epicurus, against Plato and Hippocrates, in plumping for the heart. Hence, the *hêgemonikon* and so the psychic *pneuma* constitutive of the *hêgemonikon* are thought to pervade the heart.

Most of the parts of the soul are capable of one distinct function each. For example, the visual faculty serves to see; the vocal faculty serves to make linguistically articulate sounds. In contrast, the *hêgemonikon* is capable of four distinct functions: appearance (*phantasia*), assent (*synkatathesis*), impulse (*hormê*), and reason (*logos*). I will say more about the first three of these functions of the *hêgemonikon*, in particular, in the ensuing discussion. Presently, since according to Zeno passions are a kind of impulse and impulse is a kind of change in the soul, the relevant change in the soul occurs in the *hêgemonikon*. For this reason as well this part of the soul will be the focus of our discussion. Indeed, passions are conditions restricted to an adult human soul, for impulses are. In short, the claim that a passion is a certain change of the soul should be understood more precisely as a certain change of the *hêgemonikon*.

Let us now turn to the way this change is characterized, namely, as irrational and unnatural. "Irrational" can be construed in at least two ways: as not involving reason(s) or as involving reason(s), but not good reason(s). For example, a plant, in contrast to a human, is an irrational life

---

[5] See Gad Freudenthal, *Aristotle's Theory of Material Substance: Heat and Pneuma*, Oxford University Press, 1995.

form; it lacks reason. A plan to walk across the Gobi desert with a single liter of water is irrational in the other sense; it is based on bad reasons. The use of "irrational" in the description of Stoic passion entails bad reason. Hereafter, this is the way I will use "irrational." (I will use "nonrational" to refer to the other sense.)

To clarify the idea that passions are irrational will require several steps. I'll take one further step now. This involves saying something about the Stoics' broad conception of the cosmos. The Stoics viewed the cosmos as wholly designed and governed by a supreme, omniscient god, immanent in the cosmos, and variously called "Zeus," "Nature," "Fate," among other things. Accordingly, the course of cosmic events is wholly determined by and proceeds wholly according to the mind or reason of Zeus. Indeed, worldly events are conceived as actions instigated by the intentions or will of Zeus.

The mind of Zeus, instigating worldly events, is also called "Right Reason" (*orthos logos*). The concept of irrationality in the phrase "irrational movement of the soul" must then be understood specifically in relation to that of Right Reason so conceived. Irrationality is adult human cognition inconsistent with that of Right Reason. A passion, as an irrational change of the *hêgemonikon*, is thus a change inconsistent with the will or intentions of Zeus. Below, I will take further steps in clarifying how a change of the *hêgemonikon* can be inconsistent with the will or intentions of Zeus.

Presently, let me turn to the concept of unnaturalness, which can now be easily explained in terms of the concept of irrationality. An unnatural change or impulse of the soul is one that is inconsistent with that of Nature, where Nature is identified with Zeus and the course of cosmic events governed and guided by Zeus. Now, given the Stoics' commitment to a deterministic world-order, the very notion of an unnatural change or impulse should appear inconsistent or at least paradoxical. Indeed, it is at least paradoxical. Perhaps the central philosophical problem of Stoic philosophy is the attempt to reconcile freedom or responsibility with determinism. This is too large and complicated a problem to pursue here. It must suffice to say that the Stoics allow that while our psychological attitudes can in some sense be inconsistent with the will of Zeus or Right Reason, these psychological attitudes cannot cause changes in the cosmic order that are inconsistent with the will of Zeus. Compare the psychological state of a man who has been pushed off a cliff: as he falls, he wants with all his might not to be falling; yet his wanting is completely in vain.

IMPULSE

Let us now turn to the account of affection as excessive impulse. I'll begin with impulse. First, "impulse" is a standard, but can be a misleading, English translation of the Greek "*hormê*." The English word "impulse" typically suggests suddenness. For example, Webster's Collegiate Dictionary gives the following sense: "a sudden spontaneous inclination or incitement to some usually unpremeditated action." Hence, also "impulsive." For the Stoics, or at least Zeno, "*hormê*" causes action or at least bodily movement (beyond the psycho-physical change of the impulse itself); but it needn't arise spontaneously or suddenly. Indeed, it may result from lengthy deliberation.

"Impulse" is thus a misleading translation of "*hormê*." At least one earlier translator renders "*hormê*" as "conation." "Conation" has the advantages of not having the misleading sense of "impulse" and of sounding rather peculiar and thus indicating that it is a rather technical term for the Stoics. However, "*hormê*" is not an unusual Greek term, and "impulse" is now a well-entrenched translation.

Impulse is described as a movement (*phora*) of the *hêgemonikon* toward or away from something.[6] More precisely, rational impulse – where "rational" is used in the first sense, that is, impulse in a rational being such as an adult human (versus a lobster) – is described this way:

And one would properly define rational impulse by saying that it is a movement (*phora*) of the mind (*dianoia*) toward something that is involved in action. Opposed to this is an impulse away from [something], a movement [of the mind away from something involved in action]. (*SVF* III.169)

This statement makes it appear as if impulses are necessarily practical: they yield action. The preceding passage derives from Arius Didymus but, in another passage from him, practical impulses seem to be but one kind of impulse:

All impulses are assents (*synkatatheseis*), and *practical ones* (*tas de praktikas*) also include that which is kinetic (*to kinêtikon*) [that is, stimulative of motion]. (*SVF* III.171, my italics)

A natural reading of the relation between the two clauses in this report is that "practical ones" refers to "practical impulses," in which case it is implied that there are also non-practical impulses. Scholars dispute this

---

[6] *SVF* III.169; III.377.

point. I favor the view that impulses are necessarily practical. In other words, there are no non-practical impulses. Rather than treating Arius' report or the transmitted text of it as corrupt, however, it may be read in a way that accommodates this interpretation:

All impulses are assents, and the practical ones [that is, the practical assents] also include that which is kinetic.

As we see here, impulse is also identified as a kind of assent. This is another tricky problem we need to address. To clarify this new problem, we need to introduce some other passages from Arius. First:

They [the Stoics] say that what stimulates impulse is nothing but an impulse-relevant (*hormetikê*) appearance (*phantasia*) of what is appropriate (*kathêkon*). (*SVF* iii.169)

Phantasiai are ways things appear to us to be, hence the translation of "*phantasia*" as "appearance."[7] Appearances may be sense-perceptual. For example, I look out my window and there appears to me to be an urban neighborhood with cars parked along the curb and people walking briskly over the pavement. Appearances may also be theoretical. For example, I am contemplating what an obligation is, and it appears to me that an obligation is a kind of rule. Appearances may also be evaluative. For example, I pass a homeless man on my way to work; he is lying on a street vent. This appearance is sense-perceptual; but it also appears to me that it is a bad thing that this man is lying here. Now, a type of evaluative appearance is that it is fitting or appropriate (*kathêkon*) that I help this homeless man. It is to this type of evaluative appearance that Arius is referring when he reports that "what stimulates impulse is nothing but an impulse-relevant (*hormetikê*) presentation (*phantasia*) of what is appropriate (*kathêkon*)." I will refer to this as a "practical" appearance.

   The concept of *kathêkon*, a term standardly translated as "appropriate" or "fitting," relates to what is proper to the nature of and consequently to what is of practical interest or relevance to a given animal. For example, food is obviously in some sense proper to the nature of animals and thus of practical interest to them. As Arius reports, the content of an impulse-relevant appearance must include something appropriate to the agent. For example, if a thirsty Bedouin sees an oasis, this will appear to him to be *kathêkon* precisely in the sense that it will appear to him as something from which to slake his thirst. We may say, in short, that what appears as

---

[7] "Impression" and "presentation" are other common translations.

kathêkon is what appears as having practical value, that is, as having value relevant to action. Consequently, an impulse-relevant appearance, which contains an appearance of something as *kathêkon*, stimulates impulse.

The Stoics think that impulse-relevant appearances stimulate the impulses of non-rational animals automatically. Such animals simply accede or yield to them. For example, a thirsty dog sees a bowl of water and automatically has an impulse to drink from it. In contrast, the impulses of rational beings require what the Stoics call "assent" (*synkatathesis*). Assent is rational response to an appearance. In the case of the thirsty Bedouin, before he drinks, he will assent to the appearance that it is *kathêkon* for him to drink from the oasis. Note that assent here and in general does not require deliberation. Indeed, it may seem to occur instantaneously and so automatically. But the Stoics maintain that in rational beings action is based on reason, to which the agent in principle has cognitive access. Thus, the Bedouin can in principle specify that he drinks because he believes he ought to, or some such thing. Accordingly, assume that instead of a Bedouin, it is some ascetic who is wandering through the desert. Assume that because the ascetic is thirsty, when he stumbles upon the oasis, drinking from it also at once appears *kathêkon* to him. Yet he need not commit himself to act according to the appearance. Rather, as he reflects on his ascetic principles, drinking from the oasis may cease to appear *kathêkon* to him. Thus, he does not assent to the initial appearance of what is *kathêkon*; and following reflection he assents to a different view of what is *kathêkon*, namely, walking past the oasis and enduring his thirst.

In rational beings, assent to a practical appearance is, then, required in order for action to ensue. The question now is how assent and impulse are related. In the passage we have been considering, Arius reports that "all impulses are assents." But the passage continues:

> But assents are of one thing (*allôn*), impulses are toward another (*ep' allo*). Assents are to certain assertions (*axiômata*), but impulses are toward (*epi*) the predicates (*katêgorêmata*) that are in some way contained in the assertions to which we assent. (*SVF* III.171)

In order to understand this point, contrast the following three sentences:

> The Bedouin assents to the assertion that it is fitting for him to drink.
> The Bedouin has an impulse to drink.
> The Bedouin assents to the assertion that this is water.

In the first sentence, the content to which the Bedouin assents is the assertion (*axiôma*) "it is fitting for me to drink." In the second sentence, the content of the impulse is the predicate (*katêgorêma*) "to drink," which evidently is contained in the assertion. In the third sentence, the content to which the Bedouin assents is the assertion "this is water." The difference between the assertions in the first and third sentences is that the former is practical, whereas the latter is not. Assent to the non-practical assertion does not, then, yield action. Assent to the practical assertion does. Precisely, assent to a practical assertion engenders or entails an impulse to the predicate contained in the assertion, as in the case of the second sentence. Thus, by assenting to the assertion that it is fitting to drink, one has or comes to have the impulse to drink. This at least in part clarifies the relation between (practical) assent and impulse. But it remains a question how impulse is a kind of assent.

Suzanne Bobzien notes: "The [ancient] sources vary between suggesting that rational impulse actually is assent . . . and that it [assent] accompanies it [rational impulse]."[8] Indeed, the sources are inconsistent. In particular, the following set of claims appears inconsistent:

Impulses are assents.
Assents are of/to assertions.
Impulses are toward predicates.

Perhaps compounding the confusion is the view, often attributed to Chrysippus, that affections *are* judgments (*kriseis*). For example, in his treatise *On the Opinions of Plato and Hippocrates*, which contains substantive quotations and critical commentary on Chrysippus' *On Passions*, the physician and philosopher Galen of Pergamum (129–199 or 129–217) comments:

Chrysippus in the first book of *On Passions* tries to prove that the passions are certain judgments (*kriseis*) (5.1.4)

Compare Diogenes Laertius' report:

[The Stoics] believe that passions are judgments (*kriseis*), as Chrysippus says in his book *On Passions.* (7.111)

We have, then, the following set of seemingly inconsistent claims to contend with:

Passions are impulses.
Impulses are assents.

---

[8] *Determinism and Freedom in Stoic Philosophy*, Oxford University Press, 1998, 241.

Assents are of/to assertions.
Impulses are toward predicates.
Passions are judgments.

One solution might be to parcel out some of these views to Zeno and others to Chrysippus and thereby to maintain that Zeno and Chrysippus held incompatible views about passions. At one point Galen explicitly says as much:

[In contrast to Chrysippus, who held that passions are judgments,] Zeno did not believe that the passions are the judgments themselves. [He held] that they are the contractions and expansions, the swellings and deflations of the soul that follow upon the judgments. (5.1.5)

But Galen is more reliable as a quoter of Chrysippus than as a commentator on him. Even here his distinction of Chrysippus' and Zeno's positions cannot be correct because Zeno identifies passions with impulses, not with contractions and expansions, swellings and deflations. We will in fact have something to say below about the relation between passions and contractions and expansions, swellings and deflations.

Still, Galen may be right that Zeno and Chrysippus held different views: Zeno evidently held that passions are impulses; and there is no uncontroversial evidence that he held that passions are judgments. Chrysippus evidently held that passions are judgments. Let us consider Chrysippus' view that passions are judgments and return to Zeno after that.

What is the relation between an assent and a judgment? I believe that assents entail judgments. For example, I look out the window and have the sense-perceptual appearance that it is snowing. I might hesitate to assent to the appearance, for perhaps I might wonder whether what appear to be snowflakes are actually bits of paper blowing by. But assume I assent to the appearance; that is, I assent to the appearance that it is snowing. Consequently, I judge that it is snowing. All assents, therefore, entail judgments. Accordingly, if I assent to a practical appearance, I make a practical judgment. For example, if I assent to the appearance that I ought to put on my winter coat, then I judge that I ought to put on my winter coat. But, I suggest, assents to practical appearances, that is, practical assents – in contrast to assents to non-practical appearances or non-practical assents – also entail impulses. In other words, an assent to a practical appearance entails not merely a judgment but also an impulse. Practical assent or practical judgment and impulse are therefore parallel, but not identical, mental events. Accordingly, Chrysippus can consistently maintain all five claims.

It is possible that Zeno held this view as well. But it is simply unclear whether he held that practical judgment and impulse are parallel processes entailed by practical assent. Possibly, he held that practical assent entails practical judgment, but that practical assent and judgment cause impulse. This would at least explain why commentators report the view that Zeno identified passion with impulse and are silent about whether Zeno identified passion with judgment. If Zeno and Chrysippus held these slightly different views, it is a further question why Chrysippus maintained against Zeno that impulse and practical judgment are parallel events. I do not have an answer for this.

So much for impulse – let us turn to the concept of excess.

EXCESS

A natural way to understand the concept of excess (*pleonasmos*) is in opposition to deficiency. Aristotle, for his part, understands virtue or excellence as a relation to an intermediate condition (often translated as "the mean"), precisely an intermediate condition between excess and deficiency. There are, accordingly, vices of excess as well as deficiency. For example, we say that the punishment should fit the crime; consequently, we can overreact as well as underreact to offenses. But this construal of excess doesn't fit the commitments of Stoic thought. Passions are conceived merely as excessive; we hear nothing of deficient impulses or judgments.

In conceiving of passion as excessive (*pleonazousa*), Zeno does not seem to have had Aristotle in mind. Instead, we should understand the Greek concept here in the sense of "going out of or beyond bounds," in other words, in the sense of "transgressive." Accordingly, the opposite concept is that of being in bounds, and thus the notion of deficiency has no place.

This, at least, is a first step toward understanding the concept of excess in the present context. Next, we need to clarify what bounds excessive impulse transgresses. We can make some headway by returning to Zeno's concept of *kathêkon*. Diogenes Laertius describes this as follows:

Zeno was the first to use the term *kathêkon*. The term is derived from the phrase *kata tinas hêkein* [literally, to reach, arrive at, or come to a certain point]. A *kathêkon* action itself is one that is fitting according to the arrangements of nature. For of the things done according to impulse, some are appropriate (*kathêkonta*); some go beyond (*para*) what is appropriate; and some are neither appropriate nor inappropriate. (7.108)

My suggestion, accordingly, is that affections are *excessive* impulses insofar as they are transgressive, that is, insofar as they go beyond the boundaries –

in Diogenes' expression, "the arrangements" (*kataskeuai*) – of nature. To this extent, there is little difference between the sense of "excessive" in the phrase "excessive impulse" and the senses of "unnatural" and "irrational" in the phrase "unnatural and irrational movement of the soul."[9] Granted this, it remains to explain how passions transgress nature.

The view that passions are excessive in failing to conform to the bounds of nature was first advocated by Zeno and subsequently upheld by Chrysippus. Consider the following passage, in which Galen is quoting from Chrysippus' *On Passions*:

> We have also spoken of the excess (*pleonasmos*) of the impulse, because they [that is, excessive impulses] exceed the . . . natural symmetry (*symmetria*) of impulses . . . For the symmetry of natural impulse conforms to reason and extends only as far as reason deems right. (4.2.14–18)

When Chrysippus speaks here of the "natural symmetry of impulses," he is referring to the impulses of Nature, that is, to the impulses of Zeus, which govern the course of cosmic events. Likewise, when he speaks of natural impulse conforming to reason, he is referring to Right Reason – in disobedience to which passions are irrational. Compare also the following reports from Clement of Alexandria, Plutarch, and Cicero respectively:

> A passion is an excessive impulse or one that extends beyond (*hyperteinousa*) the measures set by reason (*ta kata ton logon metra*). (*SVF* III.377)

> [The soul] is called irrational (*alogon*) whenever, through the excessive (*pleona-zousa*) and powerful force of impulse, it is driven toward something unnatural (*atopon*) beyond (*para*) what reason (that is, Right Reason) chooses. (*On Ethical Excellence* 441c)

> [Zeno] defines passion as a movement of the mind turned away from reason and contrary to nature, or more briefly as a too-vigorous impulse (*vehementior*). By "too vigorous" he means an impulse that widely departs from the consistency of nature. (*Tusculan Disputations* 4.47)

But how do passions transgress Nature by extending beyond the measures set by Right Reason? This is a difficult question that does not admit an uncontroversial answer. Possibly, the Stoics' views were not consistent on this point. I will consider two interpretations.

---

[9] Cf. Brad Inwood's comments: "Chrysippus discussed the meaning of this standard definition of [affection as irrational and unnatural change of the soul or excessive impulse] in a long text preserved for us by Galen. This explanation makes it plain that 'irrational,' 'unnatural,' 'disobedient to reason' and 'excessive' (which are all specifications of the kind of impulse which constitutes an [affection]) must be elucidated in terms of one another" (1985, 155).

All the Stoics drew a trifold distinction between values: good, bad, and indifferent (*adiaphoron*). They held that only virtue or that which depends on virtue (for example, a virtuous person) is good, and that only vice or that which depends on vice is bad. Everything else is indifferent. But most Stoics, including all three founders, also distinguished between two kinds of indifferent: preferred (*proêgmena*) and dispreferred (*apoproêgmena*). For example, bodily health is an indifferent, for it is not virtue. However, it is a preferred indifferent. In contrast, bodily sickness is a dispreferred indifferent. Accordingly, under normal circumstances, it is preferable to pursue health and avoid sickness. However, there may be exceptional circumstances under which it is preferable to pursue sickness. This scheme of values raises many questions of its own, but these are best treated within the context of Stoic ethics. The basic trifold distinction of values into good, bad, and indifferent is all we need here to articulate the first interpretation.

Above we said that all rational action depends upon assent to what is *kathêkon*. Actually, this statement needs qualification. Although all rational action follows assent to an appearance of something as *kathêkon*, the appearance of something as *kathêkon* does not entail its actually being *kathêkon*. Consequently, we should state more precisely that all rational action – that is, all action involving some reason(s) – proceeds according to what is *apparently kathêkon*. In short, all rational action depends upon assent to what appears *kathêkon*.

Granted this, assent to what appears *kathêkon* in turn depends upon a conception of something as good, bad, or indifferent. For example, being physically healthy and exercising are indifferent, albeit preferred indifferents. So a Stoic sage or sage in training will think that it is a preferred indifferent to be physically healthy and to exercise. Accordingly, under appropriate circumstances that person will assent to the assertion that it is fitting (*kathêkon*) to exercise and consequently will have the impulse to exercise, and indeed exercise. Similarly, a non-philosopher may think that it is good to be physically healthy and so to exercise. Accordingly, under appropriate circumstances, that person will assent to the assertion that it is fitting to exercise and consequently will have the impulse to exercise, and indeed exercise. In this case, however, since the impulse depends upon an assent or judgment that something is good, the impulse will be irrational and so constitutive of a passion.

It is a condition on passions that they depend upon judgments or assents that something is good or bad. Let us call this the "evaluative condition" on passions. The evaluative condition seems explicable on the ground that passions are stirring or rousing mental events, and evaluating a situation as either good or bad, as opposed to indifferent, is stirring or rousing. Consequently, passions, which entail excessive impulses, may be excessive in that they *over*-value situations. Precisely, they value as good or bad situations that are in fact indifferent. This interpretation, then, both explains how such impulses transgress Nature or Right Reason and offers an intuitively plausible account of the excess of the impulse. Note also that this interpretation entails that all passions depend upon *false* judgments or assents. The judgments or assents are false precisely because they misconstrue the value of indifferents as good or bad.

There is some reason to think that this was Cleanthes' view of passions. If so, most likely he expressed the view in his *Hymn to Zeus*. Books 3 and 4 of Cicero's *Tusculan Disputations* are wholly devoted to Hellenistic philosophical theories concerning the management of passions. In one passage of Book 3, Cicero focuses on theories and therapies of consolation. Cicero reports that Cleanthes' view of the responsibility of the consoler is to "teach the sufferer that what has happened is not bad at all" (76). In other words, events such as death of kin, poverty, and sickness, which are conventionally held to be bad, are for the Stoics indifferent, albeit dispreferred. But Cicero is critical of this therapeutic method:

It seems to me that Cleanthes does not take sufficiently into account the possibility that a person might be distressed over the very thing that Cleanthes himself counts as the worst thing [namely, vice]. For we are told that Socrates once persuaded Alcibiades that he was unworthy to be called human and was no better than a manual laborer despite his noble birth. Alcibiades became very upset, begging Socrates with tears to rid him of his shameful character and give him a virtuous one. What are we to say about this, Cleanthes? Surely you would not deny that the circumstance that occasioned Alcibiades' distress was really a bad thing? (77)

This passage suggests that Cleanthes held that passions dependent on the judgment that something is bad must be cured by teaching the sufferer that his situation is actually indifferent. This in turn suggests that Cleanthes thought that passions depend upon false (value) judgments. If Cleanthes did hold this view, it is probable that Zeno held it as well – although we have no explicit evidence about Zeno's view here. At any rate, as I have suggested, on this interpretation impulses are excessive and so transgressive of nature and reason, because they are false and precisely because they overvalue indifferents as good or bad.

Chrysippus seems to have held a different view of the irrationality of passions; and this brings us to our second interpretation. It is true that most passions will in fact be based on overvaluations of indifferents as good or bad. After all, most people are not Stoic sages; therefore, they think that many things are good or bad aside from virtue or vice. However, there are cases where non-sages act according to their view that something genuinely virtuous is good or that something genuinely vicious is bad. In such cases, their assents are both true and involve evaluations of things as good or bad. And in such cases, Cleanthes and perhaps Zeno would maintain that the impulses dependent on such assents are not passions. But there is evidence that Chrysippus held a different view. In the passage from Book 3 of *Tusculan Disputations* in which he criticizes Cleanthes on precisely these grounds, Cicero explicitly advocates Chrysippus' therapy for the passions against Cleanthes':

> Chrysippus ... holds that the key to consolation is to rid the person of the belief that mourning is something he ought to do, something just and fitting ... The most dependable method ... is that of Chrysippus, but it is a hard method to apply in time of distress. It's a big task to persuade a person that he is grieving by his own judgment and because he thinks he ought to do so. (76, 79)

This passage is complex. Cicero is actually conflating two ideas. One relates to a situation where someone is mistakenly pained at an indifferent because he falsely believes it is a bad thing. The other relates to a situation where someone is pained at vice, judging correctly that it is a bad thing. I am interested in this latter situation – although Chrysippus' therapeutic recommendation in the face of both situations is the same. Chrysippus holds that one ought not to convince the sufferer that the situation is indifferent. In the latter case, this would involve deliberately convincing someone of a falsehood. Again, the presence of vice is genuinely bad. Instead, Chrysippus maintains, one ought to convince the sufferer that grief or pain is not the appropriate reaction. In other words, the sufferer ought not to be pained or aggrieved.

Why then should Chrysippus maintain that one *ought not* or that *it is not fitting* to be deflated by this situation? The reason is this. Circumstances such as when and how we die or anyone else does, whether we become ill or impoverished, are not circumstances over which we genuinely have control; they are not, as the Stoics would say, within our power (*eph' hêmin*). In contrast, it is a central doctrine of Stoicism that the attitude we adopt toward such situations is *within our power*. In other words, situations over which we have no genuine control are valued as indifferent. But although discovering, for instance, that we are vicious is discovering something genuinely bad about ourselves, this is precisely something that we have the power to change.[10] Thus, as Chrysippus suggests, we *ought not* to be deflated.

If this interpretation of Chrysippus' position is correct, then it suggests the following. Chrysippus was critical of Cleanthes' (and perhaps Zeno's) view that passions are excessive because they depend upon false judgments that something is good or bad. Passions may depend upon *true* judgments that something is bad or good. In addition, it suggests that Chrysippus held that the evaluative condition on passions – which is to say, the view that assent is to the goodness or badness of something – is necessary, but not sufficient, for a passion. In addition, one must assent that one *ought to* or that *it is fitting for one to* pursue or avoid, be elated or deflated by, that good or bad thing. Let us call this the "practical condition." Zeno and Cleanthes no doubt held that passions require the satisfaction of the practical condition as well as the evaluative condition. But Chrysippus appears to have observed the flaw in Cleanthes' view that passions depend upon *false* assents to the goodness or badness of something.

Remedying the flaw, however, presents a problem, particularly in a case such as Alcibiades' where one recognizes that one is vicious. What here is the appropriate response? Evidently, Chrysippus held that the appropriate response is that one ought *not* to be pained, deflated, aggrieved. Presumably, the appropriate response is simply to pursue virtue. Thus, passion would occur, as it appears to in the case of Alcibiades, when one both recognizes that it is bad that one is vicious and believes that one ought to be aggrieved. In that case, passion as excessive impulse will depend upon a false judgment, not the false judgment that something is good or bad, but the false judgment that one ought to be aggrieved at something. Consequently, the irrationality of passions can still be explained in terms of their dependence on falsity.

Another problem, however, immediately arises. Assume that, upon recognizing one's vice and that vice is bad, one correctly judges that one ought to pursue virtue on the grounds that virtue is good. In this case, both the evaluative assent and the practical assent or judgment will be true. Yet, surely, Chrysippus would maintain that the corresponding impulse to pursue virtue is excessive and so that the motivation is a passion. To see why, consider the following. First, the claim that one correctly judges that one ought to pursue virtue is ambiguous and in fact cannot, on one interpretation of it, yield any impulse. The judgment that one ought to pursue virtue is of a general character; it does not specify any particular course of action. In order

[10] There is a deep problem here about how, in a deterministic cosmos, we have power to make change. Once again, I note the problem, but cannot pursue it here.

for an impulse to occur, one must specify a course of action, for example, that such-and-such particular action is instrumental to the achievement of virtue. Granted this, a vicious person will simply be incapable of determining precisely how to achieve virtue. This is because the Stoics hold that virtue is a kind of knowledge and correlatively that vice is a kind of ignorance. Being vicious, one will therefore not know what virtue is and therefore not know precisely how to achieve it. Moreover, even if one hit upon the right course of action, one would fail to understand precisely why it was the right course of action. For the Stoics, the standards for virtue as knowledge are very high. In particular, the standards of justificatory or explanatory reasoning (*apologismos*) on which knowledge depends are very high. By definition, no vicious person can satisfy them. Hence, the grounds upon which a vicious person acts will inevitably be infected with falsehoods. Thus, whether falsity lies in the judgments associated with the evaluative condition, the practical condition, or elsewhere, in the case of a person who undergoes passions it will always lie somewhere.

What this shows is that all assents are actually beliefs (*doxai*), in a special Stoic epistemological sense of "belief." In order to clarify this point, it is necessary to say a word about Stoic epistemology. We have seen that judgments are propositional; they are assents to (assertoric) propositions (*axiômata*). Judgments may be true or false. But the Stoics also distinguish between what may be called doxastic and epistemic judgments, that is, judgments that are symptomatic of belief (*doxa*) and judgments that are symptomatic of knowledge (*epistêmê*). We have said that knowledge entails justificatory or explanatory reasons of an elaborate nature. Let us say simply that knowledge requires fully cogent reasoning. In contrast, belief falls short, be it to a greater or lesser extent, of fully cogent reasoning. Accordingly, a judgment supported by fully cogent reasoning is an instance of epistemic judgment, whereas a judgment not supported by fully cogent reasoning is an instance of doxastic judgment, in other words, belief. On this view, the Stoics draw a technical distinction between judgment (*krisis* or *hypolêpsis*), which is the mental act of assent to an assertoric proposition, and belief (*doxa*), which is a kind of judgment, namely judgment unsupported by fully cogent reasoning. Thus, the judgment on which a passion depends is a belief. Note that the Stoics used the term "belief" (*doxa*) in this technical sense interchangeably with "weak judgment" (*asthenês hypolêpsis*). For example, Arius reports:

In the case of all the soul's passions, when [the Stoics] call them beliefs (*doxai*), "belief" is used instead of "weak judgment." (*SVF* III.378)

This, finally, is the sense in which Chrysippus views passions as excessive: given Right Reason as the fully cogent set of reasons upon which judgment ought to be based, the judgment upon which a given passion is based transgresses, goes beyond, or simply does not conform to Right Reason. Thus, even when the judgment is true, it is excessive. For example, if a Stoic sage tested Alcibiades by pressing him to explain or justify his judgment that virtue ought to be pursued, Alcibiades would be unable to provide an adequate defense of his motivation. His reasons would ultimately emerge as inconsistent. Because of this inconsistency, his reasons would be exposed as unstable and thus weak. Compare Arius' report on the wise man, who is equivalent to a Stoic sage:

[The Stoics] say that the wise man never makes a false judgment . . . owing to his not having belief and his being ignorant of nothing. For ignorance is changeable and weak assent. But the wise man judges nothing weakly, but rather securely and firmly; and so he does not have beliefs either. (*SVF* III.548)

Support for this interpretation of excessive impulse as impulse based on inadequately justified judgment can be derived from the following further consideration. Above we glossed the concept of *kathêkon* as "that which is proper or fitting (to do)." Diogenes Laertius offers the following further characterization:

Moreover, [the Stoics] say that *kathêkon* is that which, when done, has a well-reasoned justification (*eulogon apologismon*). (7.107)

Compare also Arius:

The *kathêkon* is defined as that which is consistent in life, that which, when done, has a well-reasoned defense (*eulogon apologian*). (*SVF* I.230)

FLUTTERING

This brings us to Zeno's third description of passion as a fluttering (*ptoia*). As we saw above, the concept of fluttering is intended to liken passions to the fluttering of bird wings. This comparison is in turn supposed to indicate in a graphic way the instability and volatility of passions. The question is: In what sense are passions volatile? We can see now that passions are volatile insofar as the cognitive conditions on which they depend are unstable. This is because those cognitive conditions do not, either explicitly or implicitly, wholly conform to those of Nature, Right Reason, or equivalently Zeus. Inevitably, then, such a man's attitude toward events will be at odds with the cosmos. Accordingly, a motto of Stoic ethics is that one must live in accordance with Nature, thereby ensuring, as the Stoics often put it, a "smooth flow of life."[11]

But there is more to such a man's instability. For not only will his mind be out of conformity with that of the cosmos, it will be unstable because internally inconsistent. In the passage I cited above where Galen is quoting from Book 1 of Chrysippus' *On Passions*, there was an ellipsis, which I now fill in (in italics):

We have also spoken of the excess of the impulse, because they exceed *their own* (*kath' hautous*) symmetry and the natural symmetry (*symmetria*) of impulses.

The capacity for Right Reason and thus for living in accordance with Nature is innate in humans. In other words, there is a natural tendency in human development – never or almost never in practice realized – toward the realization of complete rationality. Passions are thus symptomatic of internal psychological conflict. And so a man whose attitudes are inconsistent is inherently unstable.

THE FOUR PRINCIPAL KINDS OF PASSION

Let us turn now from what passions themselves are to the principal kinds of passion, pleasure being one. Beginning with Zeno himself, the Stoics distinguish four principal kinds of passion, as well as numerous sub-kinds of each. Here is Diogenes Laertius' report, which also mentions the Stoic philosopher Hecato of Rhodes (*floruit c.* 100 BCE), himself a disciple of the Stoic philosopher Panaetius of Rhodes (185–110/109):

There are four principal kinds of passion, as Hecato says in the second book of his *On Passions* and Zeno in his *On Passions*: pain (*lypê*), fear (*phobos*), desire (*epithymia*), and pleasure (*hêdonê*). (7.110)

Among these four principal types, two are conceived as primary and two as secondary. Arius elaborates:

Desire and fear go first. The former is toward the apparent good; the latter is toward the apparent bad. Pleasure and pain follow upon these. Pleasure occurs whenever we obtain what we were desiring or escape from what we were fearing. Pain occurs whenever we do not attain what we were desiring or come upon what we were fearing. (*SVF* 1.211)

Desire and fear are, then, future-oriented. They are motivations to attain or avoid things. Pleasure and pain are present-oriented. They are

---

[11] I note in passing the correlation between this conception of smoothness as conformity to nature with the conception of smoothness in the Cyrenaics' conception of kinetic pleasure.

responses to the presence of what has been sought or avoided. Hence, as Arius says, they follow upon desire and fear and thus are subordinate.

Observe that Arius speaks of desire and fear as directed toward the *apparent* good and bad respectively. Accordingly, pleasure and pain are also directed toward the apparent good and bad respectively. Consequently, scholars often illustrate the four principal passions using the following diagram:

	apparent good	apparent bad
future-oriented	DESIRE	FEAR
present-oriented	PLEASURE	PAIN

The evaluative condition on passions explains Arius' reference here to the apparent good and bad. As we have also seen, the evaluative judgments of things as good or bad will usually be false and thereby mistake what is indifferent for a good or bad thing. This, at least, seems to be the position of Zeno and Cleanthes. However, as we discussed, according to Chrysippus the evaluative judgments need not be false. They may be true, but based on beliefs or weak judgments. In either case, of course, the subject takes something to be good or bad; thus, passions are directed toward the "apparent" good and bad. Yet insofar as Arius' description intends the apparent good or bad to stand in contrast to what is actually good or bad, it is likely that he is reporting Zeno's position rather than Chrysippus'. Chrysippus' position would be better expressed by replacing "apparent" with "doxastic" as follows:

	doxastic good	doxastic bad
future-oriented	DESIRE	FEAR
present-oriented	PLEASURE	PAIN

PLEASURE, PAIN, AND FRESH BELIEF

A work *On Passions*, falsely attributed to Andronicus of Rhodes (*floruit c.* 60 BCE), who was actually a Peripatetic philosopher, reports the following Stoic accounts of pleasure and pain:

Pain is an irrational contraction (*systolē*), or (*ē*) a fresh (*prosphatos*) belief that a bad thing is present, at which they think one ought to contract. ... Pleasure is an irrational swelling (*eparsis*), or (*ē*) a fresh belief that a good thing is present, at which they think one ought to swell. (*SVF* III.391)

Note the disjunctions in pseudo-Andronicus' accounts. Pleasure and pain are either irrational swelling and contraction *or* fresh beliefs that a good or bad thing is present at which one ought to swell or contract. Here too we are confronted with the question how we should interpret the disjunction. I suggest that the disjunction is epexegetic. In other words, we have descriptions of two aspects of the same event. I will discuss the psycho-physical alterations, the swellings and contractions, below. Presently, let us focus on the beliefs. As pseudo-Andronicus indicates – and here I will focus on pleasure – pleasure is not merely a belief that a good thing is present, but also a belief that one ought to respond to the presence of the (apparent) good thing by swelling. There are a couple of things to emphasize in this description. One is that it involves two evaluative appearances or at least one complex evaluative appearance. The first appearance or aspect is that a good thing is present. Above I referred to this as the evaluative condition. The second is that one ought to swell at the presence of this good thing. Above I referred to this as the practical condition. This is the impulse-relevant condition. In this case, the action encouraged is a psycho-physical one: the swelling of the soul. By "psycho-physical," I mean to indicate that a bodily change occurs, but that since the Stoics view the soul as corporeal, the change is psycho-physical.

Another thing to note about the description is that the belief is characterized as "fresh" (*prosphatos*). Compare Arius' report:

When [the Stoics] say that [passions] are [fresh] beliefs ... "fresh" [is used to mean] that which stimulates an irrational contraction or swelling. (*SVF* III.378)

We should like to know how freshness is so stimulative. On this topic, Brad Inwood comments:

The most important fact about this fresh opinion is that, for both Zeno and Chrysippus, it does not refer primarily to a temporal recentness of the object about which the opinion is made, but rather to the fact that a fresh opinion is one which still has a certain kind of force for the agent.[12]

Inwood then proceeds to cite a helpful account of freshness by Cicero from Book 3 of *Tusculan Disputations*:

Pain is an opinion about a present bad thing, and in this opinion there is this element, that it is appropriate to feel pain. Zeno properly makes the addition to this definition, to the effect that this opinion about a present bad thing is "fresh" (*recens*). This word they interpreted thus: by "fresh" they do not mean only that

---

[12] (1985) 147.

which occurred a little while before, but as long as there is a certain force in that supposed bad thing so that it is strong and has a certain vitality (*viriditas*), for just so long it is called fresh. (74–75)

Cicero exemplifies his idea by referring to Artemisia, the sister and wife of Mausolus the Persian satrap of Caria. After the death of Mausolus (*c.* 352 BCE), Artemisia succeeded him as satrap of Caria. According to the account on which Cicero depends, Artemisia continued to grieve for her dead husband as long as she lived. Ultimately, then, Mausolus' death was not temporally recent. But Artemisia's belief that her soul ought to contract in grief at this apparent bad thing remained fresh, vital, or forceful, and thus stimulative of contraction. In short, Inwood concludes: "'freshness' is not determined by the clock or the calendar. The attitude of the agent is far more important."[13]

The preceding provides at least some clarification of the concept of fresh belief and its role in passion. I would like to address four further points. The first pertains to the terms in which the practical condition is expressed. Again, in the case of pain, this is the judgment that one's soul ought to contract; in the case of pleasure, this is the judgment that one's soul ought to swell. But clearly the descriptions of psychic contraction and swelling reflect Stoic, rather than lay, conceptions of the psycho-physical changes that follow pain and pleasure. Consequently, we should not think that people in general undergo pleasure or pain when they themselves judge that their souls ought to swell or contract at the presence of something good or bad. Rather, we would expect them to judge that they ought to be pleased or pained at the presence of something good or bad. In short, Andronicus' description is in Stoic terms, not in the lay terms that are more likely to accompany passions.

The second point concerns how fresh belief is supposed to operate in the case of pleasure. Logically, the answer is clear: the belief that one's soul ought to swell at the present good or rather that one ought to be pleased at the present good is robust, regardless of the time span between this judgment and the event or state of affairs evaluated. In contrast to the case of pain, however, it may be less easy to envision plausible, correlative psychic conditions for pleasure. Here is one sort of case. Long after the glory days of his youth have passed, a man whose psychological development has been arrested remains buoyed by some past youthful achievement. For instance, he often harks back to the day he scored the

[13] (1985) 148.

winning goal at his high-school team's championship game, and he takes this achievement, the fact that he scored the winning goal, to illustrate and to continue to illustrate his worth as a person.

Third, there is some confusion over whether fresh belief applies only to the passions of pleasure and pain or whether it also accompanies desire and fear. Andronicus only speaks of fresh belief in relation to pleasure and pain, but Arius also describes fresh belief in relation to desire and fear:

> [The Stoics] say that desire is a conative [that is, motivational] condition disobedient to reason, which is explained as a belief that a good lies ahead, and if that good were present we would fare well. Moreover, the belief contains the unruly, fresh stimulant that the [good thing really is desirable]. Fear is a disinclination disobedient to reason, which is explained as a belief that something bad lies ahead [, and if that bad thing were present we would fare badly]. Moreover, the belief [contains] the [unruly] fresh stimulant that this bad thing really is to be avoided. (*SVF* III.394)

In considering whether Andronicus justifiably or merely negligently omits desire and fear and whether Arius justifiably or rather by thoughtless extension includes desire and fear, let us return to the role of fresh belief in the cases of pleasure and pain. All passions require the satisfaction of the evaluative condition. But these evaluative judgments alone, so the Stoics think, do not cause action, in these cases, the psycho-physical changes of swelling or contraction. Additionally, one must believe that one ought to be pleased or pained. Given this, I see no reason to exclude correlative fresh opinions from desire and fear. Surely both passions motivate action, of pursuit and avoidance respectively.

Granted this, one may also wonder whether certain psycho-physical changes akin to, if not identical to, those attendant upon pleasure and pain would follow desire and fear. At least, it seems plausible that a contraction of the soul would follow fear, while a swelling of the soul might follow desire. If so, then how would the Stoics explain this? This is a difficult question. Consider that the fresh practical judgment that accompanies desire and fear cannot be directed toward the swelling or contraction of the soul or, in lay terms, toward being pleased or pained. This would conflate desire with pleasure and fear with pain, whereas the Stoics clearly distinguish these passions. It is important to bear in mind that desire and fear are directed toward pursuit and avoidance behavior. Unlike the Stoics, we tend to think of desire and fear themselves as psycho-physical changes and antecedent to pursuit and avoidance. The problem is compounded when we consider the difference between conditions such as anticipatory pleasure and appetite and intending to acquire some apparent good. For example, it is one thing to want a good meal; it is another to anticipate with pleasure a good meal; it is yet another thing to intend to acquire a good meal. Wanting a good meal does not entail the expectation that one will get a good meal or a meal at all. Anticipating with pleasure a good meal and intending to acquire a good meal do entail this expectation. But anticipation of a good meal does not entail intending to acquire a good meal, for it may be understood that a good meal is going to be coming one's way; for example, one has ordered the meal at a good restaurant. Hedonic anticipation entails an act of the imagination. Intending to acquire a good meal is the impetus for action. It is this that the Stoics seem to have in mind when they speak of desire. But put this way, any psycho-physical change that followed the desire would be incidental to it. It would not be the object of the passion as it is in the cases of pleasure and pain. The same holds for fear. In short, it is crucial to bear in mind that the various passions are distinguished by their objects.[14]

Our fourth and final point concerns the psycho-physical changes to which pleasure and pain are directed, namely, pneumatic swelling (*eparsis*) or dilation (*diachysis*) and contraction (*systolê*) or constriction (*tapeinôsis*) respectively. It is clear that these changes correlate with physical and psychic conditions that normally accompany pains and pleasures and their kin. English also embeds them; for example, we speak of being elated or deflated.

It is worth noting here a correlation, if merely a formal one, between the Stoics' conception and that of Diogenes of Apollonia. Recall that in Chapter 3 we considered the view, attributed to Diogenes in Theophrastus' *On Perceptions*, that pleasure derives from air mixing with the blood and expanding it. I am not aware of any direct link between the Old Stoics and Diogenes of Apollonia. So the correlation may be merely coincidental.

It is also worth comparing the relation between the psycho-physical conditions as the Stoics describe them and the conditions of replenishment or restoration and depletion or destruction in terms of which Plato characterizes pleasure and pain. In contrast to Plato's treatment of these conditions in *Timaeus* above all, the Stoics – at least among the surviving

---

[14] I note, but cannot further discuss, that anticipatory pleasure would, consequently, seem to be a kind of pleasure – although in a complex way. One takes pleasure in imagining, but the content of the imagination is future-oriented. There is, however, no evidence concerning Stoic discussion of anticipatory pleasure, although I have no doubt that they did discuss it.

fragments – offer no detailed accounts of the psycho-physical changes. This is explicable on the grounds that the Stoics' interest in passions or in pleasure and pain specifically is by and large not physical-theoretical – regardless of their corporeal conception of the mind – but psychological and ethical.

THE STOICS' CONCEPTION OF PLEASURE
AND COMMON SENSE

We have now clarified the Stoics' conception of pleasure. For the Stoics, pleasure – along with pain, fear, and desire – is one of the four principal kinds of passion. Passions are excessive impulses. These impulses are excessive in that they transgress the boundaries of nature and reason. They are transgressive and so irrational in that they are not based on good reasons. Not only are passions based on bad reasons, they are themselves judgments, at least according to Chrysippus. More precisely, passions are doxastic judgments, that is, beliefs, in the particular Stoic sense of "belief." Pleasure specifically entails two beliefs: the evaluative belief that some present thing is good and the practical belief that one ought to be elated by the presence of this good thing. The freshness of the fresh belief does not refer to the temporal recentness of the event conceived as good, but to the attitude that this event presently justifies a hedonic reaction or rather a particular sort of mental act. This reaction or act is elation, a swelling of the soul. And this swelling is a psycho-physical change.

At the beginning of this chapter, I noted that the Stoics appear to operate with two conceptions of pleasure, a theoretical and a conventional one. We are now in a position to comment on this point. Insofar as the Stoics refer to pleasure in a conventional sense, it seems to me that they are referring to the psycho-physical swelling described in the technical conception. This or rather the subjective psychic correlate of this psycho-physical change is what people commonsensically and naively take themselves to be referring to when they speak of pleasure. Evidently, this conception is not entirely divorced from the technical conception; it merely entails a part of that conception, the terminal part. Compare the following Stoic criticism of psychological hedonism (maintained by Epicurus and the Cyrenaics, among others), which is reported by Diogenes:

Regarding the claim some make that pleasure is object of an animal's primary impulse, the Stoics show that this is false. For they say that if pleasure does occur, it is an after-effect (*epigennêma*), which the soul itself takes (*apolabê*) only after it has attained that which suits its constitution. (7.85–86)

Given this, it seems to me doubtful that the Stoics use two radically different conceptions of pleasure.

In addition, there is reason to doubt whether the Stoics' so-called technical conception of pleasure is a technical conception that bears little relation to pleasure itself.

The Stoics' technical conception of pleasure – hereafter simply "the Stoics' conception" – seems related to the conception of pleasure as being-pleased-that as, for example, in the sentence: "I am pleased that you are here." We first encountered this conception or type of pleasure or something akin to it in the context of the discussion of anticipatory pleasure in Plato's *Philebus* in Chapter 5. Being-pleased-that entails belief. Precisely, being-pleased-that-p entails belief-that-p, where p is a proposition.[15] Furthermore, being-pleased-that-p entails the belief that p is (in some sense) good. For example, if I am pleased that you are here, I believe that you are here and that it is (in some sense) good that you are here.

In addition, the Stoics seem to be correct in maintaining that belief that p is good is not sufficient for being-pleased-that-p. Consider, for example, someone's grudging admission that his enemy is good at something, an admission that entails no pleasure. The Stoics hold that pleasure requires not only an evaluative judgment but also what I have called a practical belief. The practical belief is stimulative of action, in this case a psychic act of pneumatic swelling. This practical belief is clearly absent in the example of the grudging admission. That is, one does not think one ought to be elated by the given fact about one's enemy.

One significant point at which the Stoics' conception of pleasure diverges from the concept of being-pleased-that is that the Stoics hold that pleasure entails irrationality. Nonetheless, the Stoics' conception of pleasure as irrational can be seen to be well motivated at least in the following way. Other Greek philosophers maintain that pleasure is or at least can be irrational in the sense of non-rational. For example, such a view is expressed by Epicurus and the Cyrenaics as well as Aristotle when they argue that pleasure is or may be good insofar as humans and animals naturally seek it. But given the Stoics' view of the adult human mind as pervasively rational, no such mental condition could be admitted. Hence,

---

[15] Note that the concept of belief I am employing here is not the idiosyncratic Stoic epistemological concept.

the Stoics apply the term "*hêdonê*" to what is an irrational condition, in their sense of "irrational." This also explains the negativity that the Stoics associate with pleasure.

GOOD PASSIONS ('EUPATHEIAI')

Granted that pleasure entails irrationality and negativity for the Stoics, we might wonder how they would respond to the idea that there might be, if only in a sage, a condition analogous to pleasure, but based on good reasons: in short, a rational swelling of the soul or sound judgment that something good is present accompanied by a fresh sound judgment that one ought to be elated at its presence. Indeed, the Stoics, at least some of them, did countenance and admit such a psychic condition. Instead of calling it "pleasure" or a "passion," they called it "joy" and a "*eupatheia*," literally, a good (*eu-*) passion.

Diogenes Laertius describes good passions (*eupatheiai*) as follows:

[The Stoics] say that there are three *eupatheiai*: joy (*chara*), caution (*eulabeia*), and rational desire (*boulêsis*). Joy is the counterpart to pleasure, it being a well-reasoned (*eulogos*) swelling. Caution is the counterpart to fear, it being a well-reasoned disinclination. For although the wise man will never experience fear, he will be cautious. And they say that rational desire is the counterpart to appetite (*epithymia*), it being well-reasoned desire. (7.116)

Focusing on joy (*chara*), then, we should expect joy to be a rational impulse that conforms to the bounds of nature and that is stable. It entails the epistemic, rather than doxastic, judgment that something good is present and that one ought to be elated by this presence. For example, Inwood writes that "a *eupatheia* is . . . the impulse of a fully rational man."[16]

The concept of *eupatheia* does not figure among Zeno's fragments. Possibly, it was Chrysippus who introduced the idea. This would at least be consistent with Diogenes Laertius' description of these conditions as "well reasoned" (*eulogos*) as opposed to, say, merely true or merely genuine versus apparent.

Compare, then, the following diagram of *eupatheia* with the fourfold diagram of the passions presented above:

	genuine, epistemic good	genuine, epistemic bad
future-oriented	VOLITION (*boulêsis*)	CAUTION (*eulabeia*)
present-oriented	JOY (*chara*)	–

---

[16] (1985) 173.

Observe the absence of a fourth term correlative with pain (*lypê*). This is due to the fact that nothing bad can be present to a sage. The only bad thing is vice, and a sage is virtuous. Granted this, it may also be wondered how a sage could have a rational wariness or caution (*eulabeia*) of some future bad, for insofar as he is a sage, his virtue is stable and thus nothing bad can come to him. But *eulabeia* should not be thought to entail the judgment that one is in fact going to be subject to something bad. Rather, it is the recognition that such-and-such must be avoided in order to avoid the presence of something bad. It must be appreciated, then, that sage-hood is not a state of cognitive idleness, but a continuous exercise of the knowledge that constitutes virtue. Compare an expert mountain climber who has climbed the same mountain umpteen times and is certain to make the ascent this time. The climber must continually deploy his expertise, including his wariness of steps he must avoid.

It is worth taking note of the terms the Stoics use to identify the *eupatheiai*. Recall that "*chara*" was used as early as Prodicus to distinguish one of his three kinds of refined pleasure. Prodicus' choice of "*chara*" was, in turn, probably influenced by the common Greek use of "*chara*" for mental as opposed to bodily pleasure. We also saw that Epicurus uses "*chara*" in reference to mental pleasure, specifically mental kinetic pleasure.

A similar story can be told about "*boulêsis*," which Plato uses to refer to the motivational state of the rational part of the soul, in other words, to rational desire. Aristotle follows Plato in this usage.

"*Eulabeia*" is more difficult to explain in these terms. At least, I know of no pre-Stoic philosophical use. On the other hand, the prefix "*eu-*" provides some semantic justification for the Stoics' appropriation of this term as a species of *eupatheia*.

Similar things can be said about the Stoics' distinctions of sub-kinds of the principal kinds of *eupatheiai*. We do not have an exhaustive taxonomy of sub-kinds for any of the kinds. However, we learn from Andronicus that the Stoics distinguished at least the following three kinds of joy (*chara*):

Terpsis is joy (*chara*) appropriate to the benefits one has. *Euphrosynê* is joy at the deeds of a sound-minded person. *Euthymia* is joy at the process and wisdom of the cosmos. (*SVF* III.432)

Recall that Prodicus uses both "*terpsis*" and "*euphrosynê*" to distinguish kinds of refined pleasure. Plato also contrasts "*euphrosynê*" as a rational pleasure with "*hêdonê*" as a bodily pleasure. Finally, recall that Democritus had used "*euthymia*" to refer to the contentment of the wise man. Both in this case and in the case of "*euphrosynê*" the Stoics were surely also encouraged by the "*eu-*" prefix.

KINDS OF PLEASURE

Turning from kinds of joy, I will conclude my discussion of the Stoics' conception of pleasure by briefly noting their distinctions among kinds of pleasure. We are slightly better informed about this topic than about the kinds of joy. At least, four different authors – three Greek, one Latin – report on these distinctions. Unfortunately, their reports are not identical. Consider the following diagram, which organizes the testimonies of the three Greek authors:

	Andronicus (§5)	Arius (*SVF* III.402)	Diogenes Laertius (7.114)
asmenismos	at unexpected goods	at unexpected things	–
kêlêsis	evoked through hearing either from speech and music or through deception	–	evoked through the ears
epichairekakia	at the misfortunes of one's neighbors	at bad things that befall others	at another's misfortunes
goêteia	because of deception or magic	through the eyes because of deception	–

Clearly some of these reports are corrupt. I offer a few comments on some of them, starting from the last. "*Goêteia*" is the word that Socrates uses in *Republic* to describe hedonic as well as visual illusions. The Stoics obviously appropriated the term to describe (irrational) pleasure taken in visual appearances.

We introduced the word "*epichairekakia*," the Greek equivalent of *Schadenfreude*, in our discussion of Socrates' account of mixed psychic pleasure in *Philebus*, specifically in the context of Socrates' account of what we called "diminishing-desire" (*phthonos*). Andronicus' description of pleasure "at the misfortunes of one's neighbors" is particularly apt. The Stoics are surely influenced by Plato's treatment here too.

The Stoics also seem to be influenced by Plato in their use of "*kêlêsis*." The word "*kêlêsis*" occurs three times in Plato. Two of these are found in a passage of the dialogue *Euthydemus*. There Socrates refers to one part of the art of the enchantment (*kêlêsis*) as involving charming and persuading juries, assemblies, and other crowds.[17] The other instance occurs in book 10 of *Republic* where Socrates speaks of the poet who employs an imitative and thus deceptive art involving enchantment (*kêlêsis*) by words.[18] *Republic* was an important text for many post-Platonic philosophers. But we know that *Euthydemus* was especially important to the Stoics because it contains an argument they appropriated for the view that virtue is the only good and that such things as health and wealth only have value insofar as they are accompanied by virtue.

The source of "*asmenismos*" is unclear to me. In fact, the word is first attested in the present Stoic context. The cognate adjective "*asmenos*" (pleased, glad) is common enough. But I am unaware of its use in a philosophical context that sheds light on the Stoics' appropriation of it.

Finally, in Book 4 of his *Tusculan Disputations* Cicero refers to three kinds of pleasure (*voluptas*, the Latin term equivalent to the Greek *hêdonê*). Two of these fit the kinds we have considered. "*Malivolentia*" refers to pleasure at "another's misfortune, without oneself benefiting." This clearly corresponds to "*epichairekakia*." "*Delectatio*" refers to pleasure of "hearing that soothes the soul through its gentleness" (4.20). This seems to correspond to "*kêlêsis*." Cicero's third kind "*iactatio*" is said to refer to pleasure "accompanying insolent conduct." This does not correspond to anything on the list above. There is nothing surprising in this, since the Greek authors' lists individually and collectively must be incomplete.

The incompleteness of the distinctions and the absence of an original context or contexts for them also contribute to our difficulty in making sense of why the distinctions were made. In other words, the sub-kinds of both pleasure (*hêdonê*) and joy (*chara*) do not appear principled – even if individually they correspond to familiar conditions. In short, beyond the generic distinction between pleasure and joy itself, it is difficult to understand why the Stoics subdivided pleasure and joy as they did.

---

[17] 290a.   [18] 601b.

CHAPTER 9

Contemporary conceptions of pleasure

I will conclude this study with an examination of the ancient contributions in relation to contemporary conceptions of pleasure. To that end, this penultimate chapter presents an overview of contemporary treatments of pleasure. As with my discussions of the Greek material, my treatment of the contemporary material is, among other things, intended to underscore the historical nature of the contributions – and this is so, even while some of the history here is very recent. In the course of the chapter, the reader will also notice many points of comparison with the ancient material. To facilitate the exposition, I note some of these points, but relegate them to footnotes. Once again, I return to the points of comparison, which will be the focus of the discussion, in the final chapter.

INTRODUCTION TO PHILOSOPHICAL EXAMINATION
OF PLEASURE IN THE CONTEMPORARY PERIOD

In the first half of the twentieth century, philosophical discussion of the identity question was sparse. Contrast the work of psychologists who had been examining the nature of pleasure extensively since the end of the nineteenth century, that is, since the work of Wilhelm Wundt (1832–1920) and Edward Titchener (1867–1920).[1] It was only in the second half of the twentieth century that philosophers began a concerted examination of the identity and the related kinds question. Accordingly, I will refer to this period of philosophical investigation of pleasure as the "contemporary" period.[2]

---

[1] Due to space constraints and disciplinary interests, I will not examine this early psychological work here. Those interested should consult J. G. Beebe-Center, *The Psychology of Pleasantness and Unpleasantness*, Van Nostrand, 1932, which summarizes much of this work up to 1932, in addition to developing the discussion; and Magda Arnold, *Emotion and Personality*, Columbia University, 1960, vol. 1, Chapters 1–3, which summarizes the work up to 1960.

[2] In the contemporary period I focus on Anglophone literature. I am not aware of any substantial debate over the identity question in so-called Continental or European philosophy at this time.

I suggest that an account of the discussion of the identity question and the related kinds question in the contemporary period can to a large extent be divided into an early and a recent period, with the early period running from about World War II until the mid to late seventies and the recent period running from 2000 to the present. This entails a lacuna in the contemporary period of about a quarter century. Compare the remarks of Murat Aydede at the beginning of his 2000 paper "An Analysis of Pleasure vis-à-vis Pain":

In 1949, Gilbert Ryle launched an attack on the then popular conception of pleasure as a *feeling episode* or as a kind of *sensation*, and argued in its stead for a purely *dispositional* account of pleasure. This was in accordance with his behaviorist program. Subsequently, the following two decades witnessed a very lively discussion of whether pleasure was a disposition or a sensation. My aim in this paper is to revive this unresolved discussion that seems to have withered away after around 1975.[3]

Aydede's comments also point to some other signposts along the path we will follow. Presently, the question arises why the lacuna exists. One reason relates to Aydede's remark about behaviorism. Assuming that Aydede is correct that the early period was characterized by a debate over whether pleasure is a disposition and assuming that this debate was influenced by views stemming from behaviorism, the lacuna can be explained on the grounds that by the seventies behaviorism was moribund.

But this explanation is not wholly satisfactory. The debate over whether pleasure is a disposition did not exhaust the discussion of the identity question in the early period. For instance, assume that pleasure is a disposition. It remains to clarify what sort of disposition it is. Again, assume that pleasure is not a disposition, but an episode or occurrence. It remains to clarify what sort of episode or occurrence; sensation is one possibility, but there are others. In addition, discussion of pleasure in the early period was influenced by other questions. One was the kinds question. For example, in his 1963 paper "Pleasure," C. C. W. Taylor insists that the study of pleasure had to that point been "haunted by the *unum nomen unum nominatum* fallacy":

In order to lay this spectre once and for all we should consider the following idioms, which by no means exhaust the riches of the concept: I take great pleasure in humiliating him. I fish purely for pleasure. I fish for fun. I fish because I enjoy it (because I like it). I enjoy fishing. Fishing is pleasant. I shall be

---

[3] *Philosophy and Phenomenological Research* 61 (2000) 537–70, at 537.

very pleased (glad, happy) to come fishing. I was very pleased at the result. We are far from pleased with your progress. Your success gives me the greatest possible pleasure (satisfaction). Reading is his only pleasure. He was much given to the pleasures of the table (the flesh).[4]

As if in reply,[5] central to the contributions of Terence Penelhum and David Barton Perry is the view that there are two fundamental kinds of pleasure: enjoyment and being-pleased-that.[6] Aydede's explanation of the lacuna of the late seventies to nineties does not relate to this issue. In fact, following Perry's contribution, there was – at least among philosophers concerned with contemporary philosophy, in contrast to scholars of ancient philosophy – almost no discussion of being-pleased-that until Fred Feldman's 1988 article, "Two Questions about Pleasure."[7] I don't have any explanation for this.

There was, incidentally, a significant exchange of views between Richard Warner and Wayne A. Davis over the nature of enjoyment (1980–1987).[8] But this, like Feldman's piece, is a curiously isolated event within the lacuna-period. Warner and Davis's exchange is not informed by the disposition-episode debate of the early period. Indeed, one remarkable fact about Warner's article is that he approaches the subject in near-complete ignorance of his predecessors' contributions.

Other prominent topics in the early period discussion of pleasure concern the intentionality and truth-aptness of pleasure.[9] The former topic had been raised, albeit without use of the term "intentionality," at

---

[4] *Analysis*, suppl. vol. 23 (1963) 2–19, at 2–3.

[5] I say "as if" because neither Penelhum nor Perry cites Taylor's contribution, and I assume neither was aware of it.

[6] Terence Penelhum, "Pleasure and Falsity," *American Philosophical Quarterly* 1 (1964) 81–91; David Barton Perry, *The Concept of Pleasure*, Mouton, 1967.

[7] This paper was originally published in *Philosophical Analysis: A Defense by Example*, D. Austin, ed., Reidel, 59–81; it is reprinted in *Utilitarianism, Hedonism, and Desert*, Cambridge University Press, 1997, 82–105.

[8] Wayne A. Davis, "A Causal Theory of Enjoyment," *Mind* 91 (1982) 240–256; Richard Warner, "Davis on Enjoyment: A Reply," *Mind* 92 (1983) 568–572; Wayne A. Davis, "Warner on Enjoyment: A Rejoinder," *Philosophy Research Archives* 12 (1986–1987) 553–555.

[9] "Intentionality" is being used here in its philosophical sense (not in the commonsensical sense of "deliberateness") to refer to the fact that certain mental states are *directed toward* or are *about* objects, propositions, or states of affairs. For example, belief that the price of gold is soaring is an intentional mental state in that it is directed toward gold and its current rising value. Likewise, insofar as pleasure can be taken in something, for example, one may be pleased that the price of gold is soaring, pleasure appears to be an intentional mental state. It is a hallmark of intentionality that its objects may not exist presently (for example, one may recall the hike one took in Zion National Park) or ever (for example, one may hope the tooth-fairy puts a quarter under one's pillow). By the "truth-aptness" of pleasure I mean the property of being or being able to be true or false. For example, belief is truth-apt, but it is questionable whether pleasure is.

the beginning of the period, that is, by Ryle himself in the early fifties when he argued that pleasure relates to objects in a distinctive way from that of moods. The question, then, is what that relation is. The topic of pleasure's truth-aptness arose in part in the context of considering the nature of pleasure's objects. In his 1959 article Bernard Williams suggests that pleasure can take facts or propositions as its objects.[10] Indeed, this is central to the concept of being-pleased-that in contrast to the concept of enjoyment. Accordingly, in his 1962 article "False Pleasures" Irving Thalberg argues that since propositions can be false, so too can pleasures whose contents or objects are false propositions.[11] Indeed, Williams explores a range of ways in which pleasure relates to falsity. This is also the central subject of Terence Penelhum's 1964 paper, and Perry, in his 1967 book, devotes some space to the topic as well.

The decline of behaviorism does not explain why scholars stopped discussing pleasure in relation to intentionality and truth-aptness. Indeed, a number of discussions in the recent contemporary period engage these and related topics. One other question has also been prominent in the recent period. It too can be construed in terms of intentionality. The question is whether pleasure is a feeling or an attitude, where "attitude" may be glossed as "intentional state." Moreover, whether pleasure is a feeling or an attitude, it is questionable what sort of feeling or attitude it is.

In the following sections, I discuss these aspects of the early and recent contemporary period discussions of pleasure in somewhat greater detail. It must be emphasized, however, that this chapter is merely a sketch, a sketch of the principal contours of the historical discussion, including salient arguments for some of the salient positions advanced. Considerably more contemporary than ancient literature on the identity question exists; so in terms of sheer quantity of material, it would be easy to compose a book-length study in which the first chapter was devoted to ancient conceptions of pleasure, while the remainder was devoted to contemporary conceptions.

GILBERT RYLE'S ACCOUNT OF PLEASURE

As the foregoing intimated, Gilbert Ryle (1900–1976) was responsible for sparking discussion of pleasure in the contemporary period. He discusses the identity question in several places: briefly in his influential 1949 book

[10] Bernard Williams, "Pleasure and Belief," *Proceedings of the Aristotelian Society,* supplementary volume, 33 (1959) 57–72.
[11] *Journal of Philosophy* 59 (1962) 65–74.

The Concept of Mind and more elaborately in two pieces both published in 1954, both entitled "Pleasure": a symposium article from *Proceedings of the Aristotelian Society* and a chapter from his Tarner Lectures *Dilemmas.*[12]

In *The Concept of Mind*, Ryle claims that there are two different uses of "pleasure": one to denote certain moods such as elation, joy, and amusement; the other to refer to a mode of engagement in activity.[13] "Mode of engagement in activity" is my phrase, not Ryle's. I will return to it below. For now, consider Ryle's own words: "there is another sense in which we say that a person who is so absorbed in some activity . . . that he is reluctant to stop . . . is 'taking pleasure in' or 'enjoying' doing what he is doing."[14]

In the 1954 article and chapter, Ryle treats pleasure as a mode of engagement in activity and argues that it is not a mood. Indeed, in the article Ryle's central thesis is that pleasure is not a feeling, in various senses of "feeling," one of which is a mood. Consequently, Ryle appears to have changed his mind and ultimately to have maintained that "pleasure" should be treated univocally. I will therefore focus on Ryle's view that pleasure is enjoyment or liking.

The dominant conception of pleasure against which Ryle argues can be viewed either as a commonsensical one or as one that was first formulated in late nineteenth-century experimental introspective psychology. According to the academic psychological view, pleasure is a kind of psychological element or atom, precisely, a certain kind of feeling.[15] Such a view of pleasure is to be understood as analogous to pain, specifically, bodily pain, for example the bodily pain of a headache. Ryle also refers to tingles and twinges as examples.[16] Such feelings are called "sensations," meaning "bodily sensations." It must be emphasized, however, that in the use of "sensation" in this context, no implication of sensing or information-gathering or representing is intended. The present use of "sensation" would in fact be synonymous with "feeling" or "*quale*," were it not for the view that there are other kinds of feeling, such as non-bodily or purely mental hedonic feelings.[17]

---

[12] *The Concept of Mind*, 1949, 107–109; "Symposium: Pleasure," *Proceedings of the Aristotelian Society*, suppl. vol. 28 (1954) 135–146; "Pleasure," in *Dilemmas*, Cambridge University Press, 1954, 54–67.

[13] (1949) 108. Ryle's view here is comparable with Aristotle's. Indeed, Ryle was influenced by his reading of Aristotle.

[14] (1949) 107–108.   [15] On this view, see Arnold (1960) Chapter 1.

[16] It is worth noting that the assumption that bodily pains, twinges, and tingles constitute a unified class is controversial. For instance, bodily pains either necessarily or at least normally have an affective property; precisely, they are painful. But tingles do not.

[17] This view of pleasure as a sensation is also commonsensical. Cf. W. B. Gallie, whose response piece to Ryle was published in the same volume of *Proceedings of the Aristotelian Society*. "Ryle's thesis rests on his rejection of the natural if naïve view that at least some parts of our 'pleasure/displeasure' vocabulary can be used to stand for describable experiences or episodes, or for intrinsic qualities of

In the 1954 article, Ryle argues that pleasure is not a "feeling" in any of three senses of "feeling." To start with, pleasure is not a feeling in the sense of "(bodily) sensation" for three reasons. First, one can ask whether one likes or dislikes a certain sensation, but not whether one likes – let alone dislikes – a pleasure. In other words, the sensation view leads to a regress: "Enjoying or disliking a tingle would be . . . having one bodily feeling plus one non-bodily feeling. Either, then, this non-bodily feeling is, in its turn, something that can be pleasant or unpleasant, which would require yet another, non-bodily feeling . . ."[18]

Second, Ryle maintains that sensations are amenable to certain sorts of description inappropriate to pleasure. Ryle does not generalize about the sorts of description that are inappropriate to pleasure. Rather, he cites several examples. It is intelligible to ask of a tingle whether it is "like an electric shock" or whether "it mounts and subsides like waves"; however, it is not intelligible to ask such things of enjoyment.

Third, Ryle maintains that whereas sensations can be objects of critical attention, enjoyment cannot. That is, one cannot focus one's attention on one's enjoyment of something without the enjoyment ceasing.

Pleasure is not a feeling in a second sense of "feeling" as "emotion or passion," such as wrath, amusement, alarm, and disappointment are.[19] Ryle offers three reasons why pleasure cannot be so construed. First, one can be "assailed" or "overcome" by emotions or passions, but not by enjoyment. Second, emotions or passions, but not enjoyment, can distract one from thinking straight. Third, emotions or passions, but not enjoyment, can be resisted.

Pleasure is not a feeling in a third sense of "feeling" as "mood." Once again, Ryle offers three reasons for this position. First, moods have duration independently of activities, whereas pleasure cannot be "clocked" independently of the activity that one enjoys. Second, moods lack objects, whereas one enjoys or takes pleasure in something. Third, enjoyment is what one in a certain mood, say, cheerfulness, is disposed to.

---

such episodes" ("Symposium: Pleasure," *Proceedings of the Aristotelian Society,* suppl. vol. 28 (1954) 147–164, at 147). I discuss Gallie's piece further below. Contrast William Lyons's remarks: "The nineteenth-century psychologists felt that they had to construe psychological items as entities or occurrences if they were to make psychology into a dynamic Newtonian science with proper mechanistic causal laws. It was this imposition of a Newtonian mechanistic strait-jacket which led psychologists into the category mistake of thinking of pleasure as an isolatable sensation when it is not" (*Gilbert Ryle: An Introduction to His Philosophy,* Harvester Press, 1980, 159).

[18] (1954) 136.   [19] These examples of emotions or passions are Ryle's.

Beyond this critical aspect of his discussion, Ryle offers a few constructive, albeit inconclusive, points. He maintains that pleasure is a species of
the "polymorphous" genus of attention. More precisely, the kind of
attention that pleasure entails is a kind of interest, more precisely still, a
kind of spontaneous interest. Either it is like absorption or like occupation
without resistance. In conveying these last two ideas, Ryle uses the similes
of blotting paper and fraternal military occupation. He concludes by
admitting that the discussion ought to advance beyond such "picturesque"
descriptions, but that he is unable to. In short, Ryle maintains that
pleasure is not a sensation, emotion, or mood, but a kind of attention
like absorption or being occupied by something without resistance.

Ryle's general treatment of mind and of mental concepts is often
construed as conforming to the program of philosophical or analytical
behaviorism, dominant at the time of his contributions. In fact, this is a
controversial interpretation of Ryle.[20] Certainly nothing in the preceding
account of Ryle's discussion of pleasure smacks of behaviorism. But this is
because the behavioristic or at least behavioristic-seeming character of
Ryle's treatment of pleasure is insulated from the 1954 pieces. The behavioristic character does emerge when one considers Ryle's conception of
attention, of which, as we have just seen, pleasure is conceived as a species.

In *The Concept of Mind*, Ryle subsumes "attending," "being conscious
of," "noticing," "recognizing," and other such terms as well as their
correlative species under the rubric of heed terms. These, Ryle argues,
do not refer to inner mental processes, but rather to dispositions. For
instance, attending (to a discussion) may be analyzable as being able to
say something (about the content of the discussion). Accordingly, enjoyment as a kind of attending must be analyzed dispositionally. More
precisely, Ryle maintains that enjoyment is a "mongrel-categorical" term.
That is to say, the concept of enjoyment is a mixture of dispositional
and categorical concepts. The term "categorical" here stands as a correlate of "dispositional" and means "occurrent or activated." Enjoyment is
said to entail a categorical concept because enjoying requires an activity.[21] That is, one who is enjoying is not simply enjoying, but enjoying
something, where that something is an activity. For example – to take
one of Ryle's favorite pastimes – one is enjoying gardening. The activity,

---

[20] Cf. Ryle's own comments at the end of *The Concept of Mind*, 327–30. See also Lyons (1980)
196–201; Julia Tanney, "Gilbert Ryle," in *Stanford Encyclopedia of Philosophy*, §§2, 8.

[21] There is a notable contrast here between Aristotle's and Ryle's views. For Aristotle, pleasure either is
or accompanies an activation. But in the case where pleasure accompanies an activation and does so
as an attitude toward that activation, pleasure is *not* a disposition.

in this case, gardening, is not a disposition, but an occurrence or, as philosophers of Ryle's day often refer to it, an episode. Enjoyment is, then, a mongrel-categorical term in that it must be analyzed by giving a categorical account, in this case an activity, precisely, gardening, and a dispositional account. The dispositional account would be given in terms such as "*s* would express annoyance or reluctance if compelled to stop φ-ing (where "φ" stands for some action-verb)." As we have seen, however, Ryle does not get very far in articulating the kind of attention enjoyment entails. A fortiori, he does not get very far in articulating the kind of attention in dispositional terms.

DISPOSITION, EPISODE, SENSATION

The conjunction of Ryle's intellectual stature, the influence of *The Concept of Mind*, and the novelty of his particular thesis about pleasure galvanized critical responses and thereby philosophical discussions of the identity question. Over the next two decades or so, one dominant debate around the identity question was whether pleasure is a disposition or episode (= an occurrence), and if an episode, what kind. Contributors to this debate include, but are not limited to: W. B. Gallie (1954), U. T. Place (1954), Terence Penelhum (1957), Gerald E. Myers (1957), Anthony Kenny (1963), C. C. W. Taylor (1963), R. J. O'Shaughnessy (1966), William P. Alston (1967), David Barton Perry (1967), Warren S. Quinn (1968), Roland Puccetti (1969), Mary A. McClosky (1971), Richard M. Momeyer (1975), and William Lyons (1980).[22] It is not desirable, possible, or necessary to discuss all of these contributions here, let alone all of them in detail. I will limit myself to noting salient points from some of the most important ones.

In his 1954 article "The Concept of Heed," U. T. Place argues forcefully against Ryle's general thesis that heed concepts, of which attending is central, should be analyzed dispositionally. Place defends what he calls the

---

[22] Gallie (1954) 147–164; U. T. Place, "The Concept of Heed," *British Journal of Psychology* 45 (1954) 243–255; Terence Penelhum, "The Logic of Pleasure," *Philosophy and Phenomenological Research* 17 (1957) 488–503; Gerald E. Myers, "Ryle on Pleasure," *Journal of Philosophy* 54 (1957) 181–188; Anthony Kenny, "Pleasure," in *Action, Emotion, and Will*, Routledge and Kegan Paul, 1963, 127–150; Taylor (1963) 2–19; R. J. O'Shaughnessy, "Enjoying and Suffering," *Analysis* 26 (1966) 153–160; Perry (1967); William P. Alston, "Pleasure," *The Encyclopedia of Philosophy*, Macmillan, 1967, 341–347; Warren S. Quinn, "Pleasure – Disposition or Episode?" *Philosophy and Phenomenological Research* 28 (1968) 578–586; Roland Puccetti, "The Sensation of Pleasure," *British Journal of Psychology* 20 (1969) 239–245; Mary A. McClosky, "Pleasure," *Mind* 80 (1971) 542–551; Richard M. Momeyer, "Is Pleasure a Sensation?" *Philosophy and Phenomenological Research* 36 (1975) 113–121; Lyons (1980) 156–169.

traditional "contemplative" view, according to which heed terms refer to "private internal occurrences within the individual."[23]

At the heart of Place's criticism is his argument that Ryle's dispositional view of attending or heeding founders in the face of the experience of sensations and states of observing objects in one's environment. In *The Concept of Mind* Ryle himself admits that having a sensation is one mental event that cannot be given a dispositional analysis. Granted this, as we have noted above, Ryle treats attending as a mode of engagement in some activity. But, as Place argues, there are cases where attending itself is the only activity occurring.[24] One such case is observing an object in one's environment; another is the experience of sensations. Observing an object in one's environment is not an activity that one may or may not attend to; likewise, having a sensation is not an activity that one may or may not attend to: "to have a sensation itself entails paying at least some heed to the sensation."[25] Since observing objects and having sensations are basic forms of attending, Place infers that Ryle's account of heed fails.

Place charitably offers Ryle the following dispositional alternative:

To observe or pay attention to something is to bring about a change in oneself such that the impingement of the object or phenomenon in question on one's receptor organs prepares one to respond both verbally and otherwise in a manner appropriate to the presence of something.[26]

In other words – and simplifying – on this revised dispositional account, to attend to something is to be prepared to respond verbally and otherwise in a manner appropriate to the presence of something, namely, the object of attention.

But this revised dispositional account is unsatisfactory for several reasons. (Note that the following two are my reasons, not Place's.) One is that animals and infants evidently can attend to objects in their environments; yet they lack verbal capacities. Thus, they cannot be prepared to respond verbally to the presence of something. The account should therefore be emended to: "be prepared to respond verbally *or* otherwise in a manner

---

[23] (1954) 243. Cf. also "The expression 'paying attention' refers to an internal activity of the individual presumably of a non-muscular variety whereby he exercises a measure of control over the vividness or acuteness of his consciousness of (a) the sensations to which he is susceptible at that moment, or (b) such features of the environment as are impinging on his receptors" (244).

[24] "If Ryle's theory were correct, it should be nonsensical to talk of someone paying attention to anything other than an activity which he himself is performing. In fact, of course, we speak with perfect propriety of paying attention to any kind of object, phenomenon, or sensation" ([1954] 249).

[25] (1954) 250.   [26] (1954) 251.

appropriate to the presence of something." Even here, it is unclear what an infant's response to the presence of, say, a mobile dangling over its crib *should appropriately* be. Another problem has to do with the notion, in Place's formulation, of "bringing about a change in oneself" so that one is prepared to respond to objects of attention. This bringing about of internal change appears to be a mental act. This mental act must be given a dispositional account; otherwise, the revised dispositional account of attending founders.

Place himself is generally sympathetic to the revised dispositional account he gives[27] – with one important qualification: he maintains that the revised account is incomplete. Precisely, "it is incomplete because it makes no reference to the internal state of the individual which enables him to describe and respond appropriately to the presence of objects in his vicinity [or to the sensations that he experiences]."[28] Generally speaking, Place maintains, "it always makes sense to ask the individual to describe what it is like to watch, listen, observe, or be conscious of something."[29] Once again, insofar as we assume that animals and infants are conscious and can attend to things, the description condition here must be abandoned and the point must be reformulated as follows: there is something it is like to watch, listen, observe, or be conscious of something, and what it is like to attend to something or to be conscious of something is not simply to be disposed in a certain way.

In the wake of Place's criticism of Ryle's dispositional account of attending, it is worth noting two points. One is that although, following Place, Ryle's dispositional account of attending fails, this failure in no way affects the idea that pleasure, as enjoyment, is a kind of attending. The other, related, point is that Place's criticism entails that if enjoyment is a kind of attending, then there is something it is like to enjoy something. Place does not discuss enjoyment specifically; thus, he does not discuss what it is like to enjoy something.

In his 1957 article "The Logic of Pleasure," Terence Penelhum approvingly cites Place's criticism of Ryle's dispositional account of heed concepts.[30] Once again, this is compatible with enjoyment entailing attending or heeding. Indeed, Penelhum maintains that enjoyment is a kind of heeding. But he is careful to distinguish attending as a species of heeding and to maintain that enjoyment is not a species of attending.

---

[27] "Stated in this way, my quarrel with the dispositional theory is less substantial than my agreement with it" ([1954] 251).
[28] (1954) 251.   [29] (1954) 252.   [30] (1957) 497 n. 6.

Whereas certain kinds of heeding such as attending, concentrating, and applying one's mind to can be done at will, being attracted to, absorbed by, and interested in cannot – even though it may require attending, concentrating, and applying one's mind to something to then come to be attracted to, absorbed by, or interested in it. Enjoyment belongs to this latter type of unwillable heeding. Penelhum, thus, agrees with Ryle that enjoyment is closely related to absorption and being interested in, but implicitly criticizes Ryle's view that absorption and being interested in are species of attending. As he says, enjoyment is "effortless."[31]

Insofar as Penelhum accepts Place's criticism of Ryle's dispositional account of heed concepts, he maintains that enjoyment is "episodic," that is, occurrent or operative rather than dispositional. Moreover, he maintains that it is a private rather than a public episode.[32] He offers four points in support of this view. First, one is directly aware of whether one is enjoying something. In other words, one does not need to infer from evidence that one is enjoying something. Second, and related, one cannot be mistaken about whether one is enjoying something.[33] Contrast mental concepts that Penelhum admits, with Ryle, are dispositional such as laziness. One might be mistaken about whether one is lazy; one needs evidence to confirm such an attribution. Penelhum's third point is weaker, but nonetheless worth noting: enjoyment is gradable; in other words, enjoyment comes in degrees. A dispositional account cannot easily or well explain this. Penelhum grants that it is possible to construe such gradability in terms of the degree of difficulty that would be encountered in interrupting and compelling the subject to cease his activity. However, he insists that this is "surely less plausible than holding that these factors are merely *effects* of the different degrees of his enjoyment."[34] Fourth, insofar as Ryle maintains that what we enjoy are our activities, it is impossible to enjoy what someone else is doing. Penelhum suggests that this problem might be met by the claim that when we enjoy, for example, our children playing, we are enjoying the activity, our activity, of watching our children playing. The problem with this response, he notes, is that

---

[31] (1957) 502. I do not see much correlation of this point (and the larger discussion to which it belongs) with ancient treatments. However, it may be notable that Plato regards pleasure as a *pathos*, which is to say, a passive condition or condition of being affected, whereas Aristotle regards it as an activation or, if my interpretation of *Nicomachean Ethics* 10 is correct, something like an affirmation of an activation.

[32] Contrast laughing aloud, which is a public episode.

[33] These two points are to be contrasted with Plato's views in *Republic* and *Philebus* that one can be mistaken about whether one is experiencing pleasure.

[34] (1957) 500.

it entails the view, contrary to Ryle, that watching is an activity, an occurrence or episode. Once again, Ryle endeavors to construe such heed concepts in dispositional terms.[35]

Granted, then, that enjoyment is a kind of private episode, what kind of private episode is it? Penelhum agrees that enjoyment is not a sensation and accepts most of Ryle's arguments against the sensation view. As we have seen, Penelhum holds that enjoyment is a kind of effortless heeding that admits degrees. He speaks of it as a passive condition (not something that can be willed) rather than as an activity (something that can be willed), in which one's awareness is drawn *by* something rather than directed *to* it. He also maintains that it is a reaction or response to a stimulus. Note that this claim is not equivalent to the claim that enjoyment is an effect of some cause – assuming effects can outlast their causes. Enjoyment, he maintains, cannot outlast its stimulus. This is explained by the fact that enjoyment entails awareness of the stimulus to which enjoyment is a reaction.

Both William P. Alston (1967) and Warren S. Quinn (1968) offer defenses of dispositional theories. Quinn explicitly engages Penelhum's treatment and offers a somewhat tentative defense of the view that pleasure, understood as enjoyment, is a short-term disposition to have or maintain an experience for its own sake.[36] Alston offers a more putatively conclusive dispositional account of "getting pleasure," a phrase he uses as a catch-all expression for enjoyment as well as distinct, but related, hedonic experiences such as feeling contented, feeling good, getting satisfaction from. Alston suggests that getting pleasure may be defined as follows:

To get pleasure is to have an experience [that], as of the moment, one would rather have, on the basis of its felt quality, apart from any further considerations regarding consequences.[37]

Alston specifically classifies this account as a "motivational theory of pleasure." The motivational aspect is expressed in the description given by the phrase "one would rather have [the experience] ...": in other

---

[35] Penelhum does not make the point, but one may also wonder whether this gets the intentionality of the pleasure right. When one enjoys watching one's children playing, one need not be and usually is not taking pleasure in *the fact that one is watching one's children playing*. Rather one normally takes pleasure in *one's children's well-being or enjoyment of themselves*.

[36] More precisely, Quinn maintains that enjoyment is a complex, rather than simple, short-term disposition. This distinction, which Quinn introduces, is in fact poorly formulated; hence my discarding of it. Nonetheless, it is introduced to serve an argumentative purpose, which is significant, and to which I will return below.

[37] (1967) 345.

words, by this reference to preference. Indeed, Alston comments: "This account makes pleasure a function not of a pre-existing desire but a preference one has at the moment of experience."[38]

Alston also explicitly maintains that this is a dispositional theory:

> [To say this is to] say something dispositional – for example, that one would choose to have an experience just like this rather than not if one were faced with such a choice at this moment and if no considerations other than the quality of the experience were relevant.[39]

It strikes me as odd and problematic that Alston restricts pleasant experiences to those that have *felt* qualities. Consider, by way of counter-example, the enjoyment of reading through a mathematical proof. Setting this difficulty aside, let us consider both why Alston rejects what he calls a "felt-quality theory" in favor of his motivational-dispositional account and why Quinn favors his dispositional account over Penelhum's episodic view.

Alston's central criticism of a felt-quality theory is that it gets the phenomenology of pleasure wrong: there is no feeling or *quale* that the various kinds or cases of getting pleasure share, he holds. For example, contrast getting satisfaction from avenging oneself on one's enemy with enjoying a performance of Sibelius's *Finlandia*. On Alston's motivational-dispositional view, pleasure is the preference to have or maintain these experiences, each of which has its particular phenomenology.[40] Observe, however, that this criticism misses Penelhum's position, which makes no claims about the phenomenology of the unwilled response to stimulus that constitutes enjoyment. Indeed, Penelhum could accept that the various phenomenal characters are aspects of the stimuli to which enjoyment is a response.

Similarly, Quinn rejects Penelhum's episodic account on the ground that there is no "pleasure phenomenon" common to the various forms that enjoyment may take, for example, enjoying eating ice cream and enjoying reading a book. In speaking of a "pleasure phenomenon" Quinn commits himself to interpreting Penelhum as holding that all hedonic responses to stimuli share a phenomenal character. But, once again, nothing in Penelhum's discussion compels this thesis.

---

[38] (1967) 345.

[39] (1967) 345.

[40] Although we discussed the role of the appearance aspect (= *phainomenon*) of pleasure in the case of Plato's treatments in *Republic* and *Philebus*, it is worth emphasizing that "phenomenology" and equivalently "phenomenal character" here are being treated much more narrowly, precisely, as limited to the *quale* or *qualia* of pleasure.

Recall that among Penelhum's central criticisms of Ryle are the views that one has direct or privileged access to one's pleasure and, relatedly, that one cannot be mistaken about whether one is getting pleasure. Again, contrast such dispositional mental conditions as laziness or generosity. Alston and Quinn interestingly differ in their responses to this consideration. Alston maintains that an individual has privileged access to mental conditions such as intentions, attitudes, and beliefs, none of which are felt qualities. Likewise, one has privileged access to the motivational disposition that constitutes one's pleasure. In contrast, Quinn admits that according to his dispositional account we do not have direct access to our enjoyment – even if we normally have better access than others – and thus that we can be mistaken about whether we are enjoying something. In other words, Quinn rejects Penelhum's thesis.

Finally, Alston suggests that his motivational theory has the following advantage over felt-quality theories. Consider the following sentence: "I get a lot of satisfaction out of teaching, but I see absolutely no reason to do it." Alston claims that this is self-contradictory. Indeed, it appears so. But "if pleasure is an unanalyzable quality of experience," then it is merely a contingent truth that it is desirable. In contrast, the motivational-dispositional theory explains why pleasure is, of necessity, desirable.[41] Since Penelhum does not hold a felt-quality theory, this criticism may not apply to his view. If enjoyment is a pro-reaction to stimuli and if pro-reactions are desirable, then enjoyment is desirable.

The real heart of the debate between Alston–Quinn and Penelhum is the question whether enjoyment or getting pleasure is dispositional or episodic, not whether it is dispositional or a felt quality. Here some remarks by Place regarding the logic of heed concepts may be applied in favor of an episodic view. Place notes that some heed concepts have the logical form of activity concepts. For example, attending, in contrast to knowing, seems to entail activity of a kind. Admittedly, attending differs from some other activity concepts in that it is not describable as occurring slowly or quickly. But Place suggests that in this respect attending is akin to holding. Now, we have seen that Penelhum rejects the view that enjoyment is an activity insofar as it cannot be willed. Instead, we might say, enjoyment is a passion – in the etymological and grammatical sense of something that is undergone. Passions, like actions, are episodic.

---

[41] Alston is careful to note that this view does not entail psychological hedonism, since (1) other things may be, indeed, are intrinsically desirable, and (2) in some cases there may be stronger reasons to attain those other intrinsic desirables rather than pleasure.

ENJOYMENT, BEING-PLEASED-THAT,
AND OTHER HEDONIC KINDS

Roland Puccetti's 1969 article "The Sensation of Pleasure" targets Ryle and defends the view that pleasure is a sensation. Puccetti's discussion draws on the results of the early experimental psychological work of James Olds (1922–1976).[42] In the context of exploring the reticular activating system of the rat brain by implanting an electrode through its skull and sending an electrical stimulus through the instrument, Olds and his colleagues allegedly accidentally hit upon "pleasure centers."[43] Subsequent experimental work suggested that the firing of neural circuits in these areas – which are situated in the upper brainstem and associated midline region of the brain, and which also control sexual, digestive, excretory, and similar basic organic processes – relates to the satisfaction of primary drives.[44] Puccetti argues from such conclusions, as well as extensions in experimental work on certain primates,[45] that pleasure is indeed a sensation, separable from its source. He suggests, moreover, that refined pleasures such as those taken in "playing tennis or gardening or listening to classical music" entail hedonic sensations caused by these activities. Insofar as such mental entities are sensations, not only are they separable from their sources, but, contra Ryle, clockable.

Admittedly, given the inarticulate subjects of the experiments, questions about the localizability and describability of these sensations cannot be answered, at least not easily. But insofar as Ryle grants that sensations may be non-local as well as local – and he does – the former question presents no problem. The latter is trickier. But the problem here is as much Ryle's as his critic's. Recall that Ryle does not specify what *sorts* of descriptive property sensations entail. He merely gives examples: "Is it like having an electric shock? Does it mount and subside in waves?"[46] Presumably, it is safe to say that the neural firings in the rat brain are not like those the rat experiences when it receives an electric shock. Puccetti notes:

[42] This work was conducted in 1954–1960.

[43] See James Olds, "Pleasure Centers in the Brain," *Scientific American*, Oct. (1956) 105–116; "Differentiation of Reward Systems in the Brain by Self-Stimulation Technics," *Electrical Studies on the Unanaesthetized Brain*, E. R. Ramey and D. S. O'Doherty, eds., Paul B. Hoebner, 1960, Chapter 2.

[44] Puccetti (1969) 243.

[45] Puccetti here cites the work of John C. Lilly, "Learning Motivated by Subcortical Stimulation," in *Electrical Studies on the Unanaesthetized Brain*, E. R. Ramey and D. S. O'Doherty, eds., Paul B. Hoebner, 1960, Chapter 4.

[46] (1954) 136.

[The rat subjects] would cross wire grids that gave them painful shocks to the feet to get to the [bar they needed to depress to have the electrode implanted into the pleasure center in their brain fire], something they could not be induced to do for food even in a semi-starved state.[47]

Regarding the property of mounting and subsiding in waves, alleged hedonic sensation either does or does not possess this property. Assume that it does not. Neither does the sensation of a pin-prick. But it is a sensation nonetheless. To this extent, Ryle's criticism fails.

At this point, it is convenient to draw a distinction between two views of the relation between pleasure and sensation. One is Puccetti's: all pleasures are sensations. The other is that some proper subset of pleasures are sensations. The latter view is advanced by Ryle's earliest critic, Gallie (1954), who suggests that "pleasure" is equivocal and that in one of its uses "pleasure" refers to a local sensation. Consider, for example, certain sexual pleasures. Penelhum admits as much, and Alston agrees: "Indeed there are uses of the term 'pleasure' in which it seems to stand for a kind of bodily sensation. Thus we speak of 'pleasures of the stomach' and 'thrills of pleasure.'"[48] At the same time, Gallie, Penelhum, Alston, McCloskey, and others maintain that the use of "pleasure" to refer to a sensation is a minor one. As McCloskey puts it and argues, the use of "pleasure" as "enjoyment" is paradigmatic. Penelhum, O'Shaughnessy, Quinn, among others, agree. Alston is exceptional in taking the broader category of getting pleasure – of which enjoyment is but one kind – as the paradigm of pleasure.

In his 1964 article "Pleasure and Falsity," Penelhum changed his mind and suggested that there are two rather than one basic use of "pleasure." One use refers to enjoyment. The other occurs in the phrase "pleased that p," where p stands for a fact or proposition. For example, one may be pleased that one has arrived in Kauai.[49] Penelhum distinguishes enjoyment and being-pleased-that in three respects:

(1) Nature of objects: being-pleased-that typically has facts (or propositions) as objects; enjoyment typically has actions or events.
(2) Nature of awareness: being-pleased-that requires knowing or thinking one knows about the fact; enjoyment requires active engagement or

---

[47] (1969) 241.

[48] (1967) 341. Cf. also McCloskey (1971) 543–544.

[49] In a 1959 article Bernard Williams ("Pleasure and Belief," *Proceedings of the Aristotelian Society*, suppl. vol. 33, 57–72) had focused on this use of "pleasure," although without entering the discussion of its centrality or relation to enjoyment. I will return to Williams's treatment below. The Stoics' conception of pleasure appears to be a conception of being-pleased-that.

"paying fairly close attention to it, or rather [having] my attention drawn by it or [being] absorbed in it"[50]

(3) Temporal relation to object: being-pleased can perdure for a considerable period of time following the thing that pleased one; "it is a (mild) emotion that can affect one's actions over a considerable period of time";[51] but enjoyment ceases when its object ceases.

To concretize and illustrate the distinction, compare enjoying an ice cream with being pleased that one has made the winning move in a chess game. When one enjoys an ice cream, one enjoys eating the ice cream; such enjoyment needn't entail any knowledge or belief. For example, an infant or animal might enjoy eating something. But clearly one must be aware of the object of enjoyment in a certain way. Finally, the activity of eating the ice cream and the enjoyment of that activity must be contemporaneous. One might get pleasure from anticipating eating the ice cream or from recollecting eating the ice cream, but in such cases the anticipation and the recollection are the activities, mental activities, contemporaneous with the enjoyment. In the case of being pleased that one has made the winning move in chess, the object is the fact or proposition that one has made the winning move; and given that the object is a fact (or proposition), one's awareness of it must be cognitive. At least according to Penelhum's suggestion, the pleasure can outlast the fact; for example, one may still be glowing from the win, although one has now moved on to another activity. I say "at least according to Penelhum," since the temporal relation between being-pleased and the fact or proposition is a tricky issue.[52]

Finally, with respect to the relation between being-pleased-that and enjoyment, Penelhum has little to say. This inconclusiveness, which we will also find in David Barton Perry's work, is noteworthy. It is puzzling to be told that enjoyment and being-pleased-that are two fundamental kinds of pleasure or two fundamental ways in which "pleasure" is used or two fundamental pleasure concepts, but without an explanation of what pleasure itself is so that we can understand their relation to one another and pleasure itself.

In his 1967 book *The Concept of Pleasure*, Perry does not cite, and I assume was not aware of, Penelhum's article. But Perry defines and distinguishes enjoyment and being-pleased-that as the two fundamental pleasure concepts. His definitions are as follows:

---

[50] Penelhum (1964) 82.   [51] Penelhum (1964) 82.

[52] I discuss the Stoics' view of this matter in Chapter 10.

Enjoyment: a non-evaluative, non-conative pro-attitude toward some actual object, where the object is an activity or experience of the subject.[53]

Being-pleased-that: a positively evaluative, non-conative pro-attitude toward something of recent knowledge or belief and of personal interest.[54]

For Perry, then, enjoyment and being-pleased-that are kinds of pro-attitude. Perry does not attempt a definition of pro-attitude, but, drawing on Nowell-Smith's popularization of the term in his 1954 book *Ethics*,[55] elucidates the concept by a range of kinds, including liking, approval, love, fondness, wanting, and desire, among others. Perry does argue that pleasure is not a conative attitude, that is, not a form of desire or wanting. Being-pleased-that-p is evaluative in that it entails the belief that p is good,[56] whereas enjoyment does not entail any such evaluation of its object. An infant or non-human animal need not have any evaluative concepts, yet may still enjoy things.

Perry, like Penelhum, recognizes that enjoyment and being-pleased-that require different kinds of object; moreover, they agree on the kinds of object required. Perry also maintains that the fact or proposition that is the object of being-pleased-that must be of personal interest. For example, one can learn that the maintenance department has just fixed a leaky water pipe in some building on campus and hence believe that it is a good thing, but not be pleased by the fact since one has little personal interest in the matter.

Like Penelhum, Perry also holds that enjoyment and its object must be contemporaneous (note the word "actual" in Perry's definition); but in contrast to Penelhum, Perry maintains that when one is pleased-that-p, one must have recently come to know or believe that p. Consider that one may be pleased to learn that one's favorite team has won the World Series. But six months later, one (allegedly) cannot be pleased by knowing or believing that one's favorite team won the World Series. The idea seems to be that the novelty of the information causes or produces pleasure, but that the hedonic impact of the information wears off rather quickly. I find this suggestion dubious. At least, it is certainly psychologically possible, even if not very common, to be pleased repeatedly over a long stretch of time upon calling to mind a certain fact.[57]

---

[53] Perry (1967) 214.   [54] Perry (1967) 216.

[55] P. H. Nowell-Smith, *Ethics*, Penguin Books, 1954, 112–113.

[56] I emphasize in passing that Perry's view entails cognitivism about evaluative sentences and mental states. See p. 245, n. 103.

[57] I return to this point in Chapter 10.

(Note also that this is different from enjoying recollecting something, since the latter is an imaginative act.)[58]

Finally, as I mentioned above, Perry, like Penelhum, finds himself unable to explain the relation between enjoyment and being-pleased-that and the relation of each to pleasure. Of course, both come out as kinds of non-conative pro-attitude. But Perry admits to being unable to explain the relations further.[59]

ENJOYMENT IN THE EIGHTIES: THE WARNER–DAVIS DEBATE

As I mentioned in the introductory section to this chapter, it is worth noting that in the early period, after Perry, almost no one seriously pursued the concept or condition of being-pleased-that.[60] Rather, the focus remained on enjoyment. This is also the case for what I referred to as the curiously isolated exchange between Richard Warner and Wayne A. Davis in 1980–1987.

The exchange was prompted by Warner's 1980 article "Enjoyment."[61] As I mentioned in the introductory section, Warner approaches his subject as though in a vacuum, that is, apparently without recognition of the work done in the early contemporary period.[62] At any rate, Warner argues for the following definition of enjoyment:

A subject x enjoys an experience or activity φ at time t iff there is an array of concepts C such that the following three conditions are satisfied:

(1) x φs at t' (where t' is a moment slightly prior to t);
(2) x's φ-ing causes x at t:
    (i) to believe, of x's φ-ing, that the concepts in C apply to x's φ-ing;[63]
    (ii) to desire, of x's φ-ing, under the concepts in C, that x's φ-ing occurs;
(3) x desires for its own sake what (2ii) describes x as desiring.

---

[58] In Chapter 10, I discuss the relation between the various ancients' conceptions of pleasure and the distinction between enjoyment and being-pleased-that.

[59] Note also that while Alston (1967) focuses on the broad genus of getting pleasure, he makes no attempt to clarify distinction among the species of this genus. Perry is the only scholar I know who broaches the subject in any significant way.

[60] No one, that is, working in contemporary philosophy. Some scholars working in ancient philosophy, specifically on Plato's *Philebus*, employed the concept of being-pleased-that in attempts to explain or justify some of Plato's views that pleasure can be false. Davis (1982, 243–244) does in fact contrast being-pleased-that with enjoyment as a distinct way of getting pleasure, but he does not conduct a sustained examination of being-pleased-that.

[61] Richard Warner, "Enjoyment," *Philosophical Review* 89 (1980) 507–526.

[62] He begins his article as follows: "Enjoyment has received less attention than it deserves in contemporary philosophy ..." ([1980] 507).

[63] Note that Warner discusses this condition in a way that makes clear that he does not mean to exclude lower animals from enjoyment ([1980] 518–519).

Warner's position agrees with those of Penelhum and Perry in taking the object of enjoyment to be an experience or activity. But beyond that, Warner's view diverges. First, Warner views the temporal relation between the enjoyment and its object not as contemporaneous, but as sequential or overlapping. In particular, the activity or experience must slightly precede the enjoyment. This is apparently because the activity or experience *causes* a complex mental state, which constitutes the enjoyment, and because causation is assumed to require the non-contemporaneity of cause and effect. The mental state is a complex of belief and desire. In particular, the subject desires that an experience or activity, construed according to a concept-array C, occur; and the subject believes that the experience or activity so construed is occurring. Put simply, enjoyment requires subjective desire-satisfaction: "your activity [or experience] causes a desire which it simultaneously satisfies."[64]

Note also that Warner adds that the subject desires the occurrence of the experience or activity "for its own sake." For example, the subject does not desire the experience or activity instrumentally, as, say, one might desire to take bitter medicine for the sake of restoring one's health. I will refer to this as "intrinsic desire."[65] Compare this condition with Alston's: "To get pleasure is to have an experience that, as of the moment, one would rather have, *on the basis of its felt quality, apart from any further considerations regarding consequences.*" Likewise, in the case of enjoyment, Perry clarifies that the pro-attitude must be for the actual object "for what it is in itself."[66] And Gallie characterizes enjoyment as "directed onto an object or activity regarded as a unit per se and not in virtue of its consequences."[67]

What is the role of the concept-array C in Warner's definition? A given activity or experience may be conceived in various ways, not all of which may be intrinsically desired. Warner's point then is that one comes to conceive, of the experience or activity, that it is a certain way, and one intrinsically desires the experience or activity as such. For example (Warner's example), one may come to enjoy the experience of deep-sea fishing because one comes to conceive of it as exhilarating, as involving

---

[64] (1980) 517. (Contrast this complex mental state with Penelhum's and Perry's vague awareness.)
[65] It is noteworthy that although Perry is careful to distinguish the pro-attitude of enjoyment from desire, he maintains that the pro-attitude is toward the object "for what it is in itself."
[66] (1967) 214.   [67] (1954) 160–161.

distinctive physical challenges and aesthetic and social attractions, as opposed to tedious or repulsive or unethical.[68]

In his 1982 article "A Causal Theory of Enjoyment," Wayne A. Davis argues for a definition of enjoyment that in several respects is closely related to Warner's:

An experience causes a subject to have a number of occurrent beliefs concerning the experience, which collectively add significantly to the pleasure the subject takes.[69]

Observe that the concept of pleasure figures in the definition. This is not problematic for Davis because he – idiosyncratically relative to his predecessors – views pleasure as a constituent of enjoyment. In order to understand Davis's definition of enjoyment, then, we need his conception of pleasure. This he offers in his 1981 paper "Pleasure and Happiness."[70] There he identifies pleasure with happiness and describes this as "an occurrent and non-relational state," which may be glossed as "feeling good" or being "in high-spirits." More precisely, Davis defines pleasure as follows. At any given moment one has a number of thoughts, some of which are desired. For example, one may think that one is in the presence of one's beloved, which is desired, or that one is in the presence of one's enemy, which is not. Granted this, take the sum of the product of the thoughts one has and the thoughts one desires. If this product is greater than zero, then one is in a state of pleasure or happiness. In short, Davis views pleasure as a function of one's global psychological state of subjective thought-desire-satisfaction.

Recall now that Davis views enjoying an experience as that experience's causing occurrent thoughts, which one believes, about the experience that collectively *add significantly* to the pleasure the subject is experiencing. The condition that the believed thoughts caused by the experience must add significantly to one's pleasure is an important condition for Davis and further distinguishes his view from Warner's. In 1983 Warner published a criticism of Davis's view,[71] and in 1987 Davis published a rejoinder.[72] Central to the exchange is Davis's objection that subjective

---

[68] Note that the concept-condition in Warner's definition invites the objection that it precludes animals from enjoying experiences or activities insofar as they lack the ability to conceive of experiences or activities as falling under concepts. Warner addresses this objection and maintains that animals can have concepts.

[69] (1982) 249.   [70] *Philosophical Studies* 39 (1981) 305–317.

[71] Richard Warner, "Davis on Enjoyment," *Mind* 92 (1983) 568–572.

[72] Wayne A. Davis, "Warner on Enjoyment: A Rejoinder," *Philosophy Research Archives* 12 (1986–87) 553–555.

desire-satisfaction need not yield enjoyment. For example, assume a terminally ill cancer patient is in excruciating pain; his daughter kisses him; and he wanted her to. However, he may be in too much pain to enjoy the kiss. Warner responds that the patient *could* enjoy the kiss, for enjoyment can be impure, that is, mixed with aversion. For example, one may enjoy gossiping about one's colleagues, but hate oneself for doing so. Davis concedes that of course the patient could enjoy the kiss; but, again, all that the objection requires is that it be possible that the patient could not enjoy the kiss. The point is that Davis is conceiving of a situation where the patient's suffering is too great: the subjective satisfaction of desire, therefore, does not add *significantly* to his pleasure and thus does not constitute enjoyment.

Finally, it should be noted that Warner is silent on the phenomenology of pleasure. Davis claims that pleasure "feels good." However, he does not work to justify his claim. Warner's silence and Davis's undefended claim are significant. Contrast the position of those committed to dispositional theories such as Ryle, Quinn, and Alston who must in virtue of their dispositionalism maintain that pleasure has no phenomenal quality. Warner and Davis are not dispositionalists, but desire-satisfaction theorists. The question now arises: Is pleasure identical to some form of desire-satisfaction, or does desire-satisfaction rather cause pleasure? Warner and Davis maintain the former view.

PLEASURE AND INTENTIONALITY IN THE EARLY CONTEMPORARY PERIOD

Discussion of the relation between pleasure and intentionality might be characterized as implicit from the beginning of the early period.[73] For example, as I mentioned above, one of Ryle's arguments against identifying pleasure as a mood is that pleasure takes an object, whereas moods do not. For example, contrast enjoying the symphony with being cheerful. Again, as we have also discussed, both Penelhum and Perry distinguish kinds of pleasure partly in virtue of distinct kinds of object. Moreover, these authors' other commitments about pleasure strongly suggest that they view the relation between pleasure and its objects as intentional. Contrast the position of Davis who characterizes the experience or activity in enjoyment as causing pleasure, but the pleasure itself as "non-relational." Likewise,

---

[73] We have seen that an intentional conception of pleasure is central to much ancient hedonic theorizing.

Puccetti's view of pleasure as a sensation entails that pleasure is non-relational (in Davis's sense).

In the case of authors whose positions suggest or commit them to the intentionality of pleasure, we may distinguish their views about the nature of the intentional objects from their views about the nature of intentional modes. For example, we have now repeatedly distinguished the views of Penelhum and Perry that enjoyment's object is an experience or activity and that the object of being-pleased-that is a fact or proposition. Likewise, we have seen that Ryle views enjoyment's intentional mode as a kind of heed or attending, namely, absorption or benign occupation. Gallie also distinguishes different kinds of attention, and he argues that enjoyment is a kind of appraisive attention: positive and non-comparative.[74] We have mentioned that Penelhum in his 1957 piece rejects the view that enjoyment is a kind of attention, since attention is voluntary. Instead, he maintains that pleasure is a passion or passivity. He also maintains that enjoyment requires heed – distinguishing attention as a species of heed – but an effortless form of heed, whereby one's awareness is drawn *by* something and not directed *to* it.[75] Perry also maintains that enjoyment requires awareness, whereas being-pleased-that requires doxastic evaluation (that is, belief that *p* is good).[76] But as consideration of Perry's position indicates, one cannot simply infer that, because he thinks that pleasure requires awareness or belief, he takes the intentional mode of enjoyment or being-pleased-that to be awareness or belief. Recall that for Perry enjoyment is a pro-attitude. I presume that the pro-character of the attitude is the intentional mode that is directed toward enjoyment's object, the experience or activity. Awareness, however, is not a pro-attitude. Similarly, I take the pro-attitude to be the intentional mode of being-pleased-that, not the doxastic evaluation.[77]

It is in Williams's 1959 paper "Pleasure and Belief" that the suggestion is first explicitly advanced (in the contemporary period) that the relation between pleasure and its objects is "intentional."[78] Without the benefits of Penelhum's and Perry's distinctions and without recognizing a distinction between enjoyment and being-pleased-that himself, Williams in fact

---

[74] (1954) 160–161.

[75] Cf. A. R. Manser, "Pleasure," *Proceedings of the Aristotelian Society* 61 (1960–1961) 223–238, who also maintains that pleasure requires awareness, but not attention.

[76] In this respect, among others, Perry's and the Stoics' views are akin.

[77] Likewise, the Stoics do not take what I called the evaluative condition to be sufficient for pleasure. It is questionable to what extent their practical condition is akin to Perry's pro-attitude.

[78] *Proceedings of the Aristotelian Society*, suppl. vol. 33 (1959) 57–72.

principally focuses on being-pleased-that.[79] He motivates his discussion by noting that we can be pleased by what we merely believe to be the case. Since belief can be false, we can be pleased that, say, we have inherited a fortune, when in fact we have not. Williams concludes that since the alleged object, the inherited fortune, does not exist, the relation between pleasure and its objects cannot be "object-causal."

Williams pursues the idea that instead the relation is belief-causal, that is, that belief-that-p causes being-pleased-that-p. He presents several arguments against this belief-causal hypothesis. Only one of these seems plausible to me, although another contains an idea that may fruitfully be brought to bear on the proposal. The plausible argument Williams makes is that a causal hypothesis is corrigible, whereas it is nonsense to claim that one is mistaken in thinking that a certain occurrent belief caused one's pleasure, at least, one's being-pleased-that. For example, "I cannot be mistaken in saying 'I am pleased because I have inherited a fortune' in the same way as I can in saying, for instance, 'I have a stomach ache because I ate some bad fruit.'"[80]

Consider also the following point. The case of false belief in the inherited fortune indicates that such a subject does not take himself to be pleased merely because he believes that p, but rather because of p. That is to say, the subject would not allow that he is pleased merely because he believes he has inherited a fortune, regardless of whether the belief is true. So even if the belief that p plays a causal role in the subject's being-pleased-that-p – and it surely does – its causal role does not satisfactorily explain the subject's being-pleased-that-p. Again, however, although this seems to me an important corroborative point, it is not exactly a point Williams makes.

At any rate, Williams concludes that the belief-causal hypothesis cannot be sustained. Consequently, he first pursues the idea that the relation between pleasure and its objects is analogous to that of action and its grounds. That is, being pleased because of p is analogous to performing some action because of or for some reason. But he rejects this idea, for three reasons. First, pleasure is not an action, but a passion or "something that happens to us."[81] Second, if activity is the object of pleasure – as some who discuss pleasure as enjoyment hold – the activity does not constitute pleasure's grounds. Third, in many cases – in fact, all cases of being-pleased-that – pleasure does not entail activity. For example, being

---

[79] Some of the discussion in Williams's paper is in fact vitiated by his failure to appreciate the distinction.
[80] (1959) 59. [81] (1959) 59; compare Penelhum (1957).

pleased because one has inherited a fortune entails believing that one has inherited a fortune; but believing is not a mental activity.

Finally, Williams pursues the idea that the relation between pleasure and its objects is analogous to the relation between drawing someone else's attention to something or having one's attention drawn by something and the objects of such attention. Given the erroneous case of being pleased because one has inherited a fortune, Williams focuses on analogies between hedonic mistakes, on the one hand, and errors in pointing and attention, on the other. Consider the following six cases:

(1) misremembering what pleased one in the past and misremembering what one pointed to in the past;

(2) pointing to the red of the "hibiscus" flowers, when they're not hibiscus flowers, and being pleased by what one takes to be a Picasso painting, when it is a Braque painting;

(3) pointing to the thing one thinks is the Queen, when it is not the Queen, and being pleased, at least in part, by what one takes to be a Picasso because one takes it to be a Picasso, although it is a Braque;

(4) pointing to a hallucinated dagger and being pleased because one falsely believes one has inherited a fortune;

(5) having one's attention drawn to an illusory feature of a thing, when one knows that an illusion is occurring, and being pleased by a feature one knows to be illusory;

(6) something's drawing one's attention without one's knowing exactly what it is about that thing that draws one's attention and being pleased by something without knowing what it is about that thing that pleases one.

In the wake of discussing these analogies, Williams suggests that they are in fact not merely analogies: the relation between pleasure and its objects *is* the relation between attention and its objects. Further, as Ryle and others suggest, Williams maintains that "pleasure is one mode or species of attention."[82] Whatever this result achieves, it leaves open the question of the relation between attention and its objects. Williams concludes by stating that the relation is "one of those that some philosophers have investigated under the title of 'intentionality'; and though I have deliberately avoided the word, I hope the present remarks may suggest a line for clarifying this obscure notion."[83]

---

[82] (1959) 71. [83] (1959) 72.

In his response to Williams's paper in the same 1959 *Proceedings of the Aristotelian Society*,[84] Errol Bedford argues that the relation between pleasure and its objects is not that of attention and its objects. Attending, Bedford suggests, is confined to looking and listening. This is because attending "involves following and understanding, or at least trying" to do so.[85] In contrast, "smells and tastes, together with temperature sensations and most sensations of touch, do not have a structure that [one] can follow or fail to follow, although they are qualities that can draw [one's] attention to themselves."[86] Bedford's point about smells, tastes, and touches strikes me as wrong. Surely oenophiles and gourmets regularly attend to the flavors; perfumers attend to fragrances; and bodily sensations may have a complex phenomenology, as the doctor's question "Can you describe the pain?" suggests. All such objects, I think, have a complex and temporally extended structure. Nonetheless, Bedford has a point: one may be pleased by a simple property, and such pleasure need not involve attention to that entity.

Bedford contrasts attending with noticing. Thus, one may notice and be pleased by something, without attention or attending to it. To this extent, Bedford suggests that the relation between pleasure and its objects would be better analogized in terms of awareness and its objects. Awareness is a broader mental state than attention, and attention is but one kind of awareness. But Bedford rejects the view that pleasure and its objects are related as awareness and its objects. Most damagingly, Bedford argues, Williams's primary motivating case, being pleased because one has inherited a fortune (when one has in fact not inherited a fortune), cannot be understood in terms of awareness because one cannot be aware of something that does not exist.[87]

Instead, Bedford defends the view, which Williams considers but rejects, that pleasure (and, more generally, emotion) and its objects are related as action and its grounds or reasons are. Actions too can have non-existent objects. For example, one may guard against the bogey-man. I will not here examine Bedford's reasons for maintaining that pleasure and its objects are related as actions and their grounds. Nor does Bedford describe this relation as intentional. However, since non-existent objects are a hallmark of the contents of intentional states, we can affirm that Bedford's position also characterizes the relation between pleasure and its objects as intentional.

---

[84] "Pleasure and Belief," suppl. vol. 33 (1959) 73–92.
[85] (1959) 80.   [86] (1959) 80.   [87] (1959) 83.

PLEASURE AND TRUTH-APTNESS IN THE EARLY
CONTEMPORARY PERIOD

As we saw, Williams's discussion of the analogies between pleasure and its objects and attention and its objects involves discussion of various hedonic mistakes.[88] But Williams never suggests that pleasure itself can be false. Likewise, in his response to Williams, Bedford does not entertain the idea of false pleasure, although he also considers the relation between hedonic mistakes and mistakes in attending and action. In the contemporary period, the first student of contemporary philosophy to address the concept of false pleasure is Irving Thalberg, in his 1962 piece "False Pleasures."[89]

Like Ryle, Thalberg maintains that "pleasure" primarily refers to an attitude, not a sensation. Yet he criticizes Ryle for failing to consider cases of what he calls "propositional pleasure." Propositional pleasures are conditions of being-pleased-that-p, where "p" stands for a proposition. Thus, Thalberg suggests that in cases where the proposition p is false, the pleasure is false. Thalberg does not seem to be aware of Williams's paper, but – to take Williams's key example – one may be pleased that one has inherited a fortune, although one has not inherited a fortune. On Thalberg's view, this would be a false propositional pleasure.[90]

Thalberg considers several objections to this proposal. One derives from Socrates' interlocutor Protarchus in Plato's *Philebus*: false pleasure entails not really being pleased. But surely one is pleased despite one's false belief that one has inherited a fortune. This objection, Thalberg notes, is misguided because it confuses falsity with unreality (in my terminology from Chapter 5, it confuses the ontological sense of "false" as "unreal" with the representational sense).

A second objection, also derived from Protarchus, is that the relation between pleasure and belief is causal; and whereas the belief is false, the pleasure is not. Thalberg's response to this objection is weak. He rejects the view that the relation between the belief and pleasure is causal. This rejection might be correct. But Thalberg's grounds are poor. He suggests that the causal interpretation is wrong because in cases of causation it is sensible to ask how soon the effect occurred after the cause, whereas it is not sensible to ask how soon the pleasure occurred after the belief.

---

[88] In this, Williams was at least influenced by Plato's discussion in *Philebus*.

[89] *The Journal of Philosophy* 59 (1962) 65–74.

[90] Thalberg explicitly expresses his dependence on Plato's *Philebus*, as the next two paragraphs indicate.

Somewhat more persuasively, he suggests that being-pleased-that-*p* entails believing that *p*; and he takes this to indicate that the relation between the pleasure and belief is a "most intimate one" and one of "inseparability."[91] This is unsatisfactorily vague. Does Thalberg mean that the belief is a constituent of the pleasure or that the pleasure entails the belief? Without further clarification, one can only say that if Thalberg's thesis is true, he has not given adequate grounds for thinking so.

One further objection Thalberg considers, which is worth noting here, is that one might be pleased by an unasserted proposition. In other words, one might be pleased by the mere thought of something. Thalberg takes appeal to this sort of case to be a non sequitur, for his position does not claim that all pleasures must have truth-value: "mere thoughts or unasserted propositions are neither true nor false."[92] What is noteworthy about this response is its commitment to the view that propositions themselves are not bearers of truth-value, but rather that the possession of truth-value is a function of a certain attitude taken toward a proposition. This position has a certain prima facie appeal. After all, we comfortably speak of true and false beliefs, but not, say, true and false desires. Upon scrutiny, however, the position becomes vulnerable. When we speak of true and false beliefs, we are referring to what is believed, that is, to the content (or what I also described in Chapter 5 as the object) of the belief – not to the attitude of believing. For example, Pastor George's belief that the end is near is false, but it is nonsensical to say that Pastor George's believing that the end is near is false. Rather, we may say that his believing this is unfounded or unwarranted. The problem is, however, not so simply dispatched. First, if when we speak of true and false beliefs we thereby only refer to the propositional contents of the beliefs, why do we not comfortably speak of true and false desires in cases where the desires have propositional contents? Moreover, we do in fact speak of false hopes and fears. What this indicates or at least suggests is that our talk of truth-value in relation to propositional attitudes is untidy. Consequently, we need deeper reasons to affirm or deny that propositions per se are truth-bearers. I have no intention of resolving this question here. I raise it only to indicate the problem and its significance.[93]

---

[91] (1962) 67–68.   [92] (1962) 70.

[93] Recall the related discussion regarding Plato's false pleasure kind 1 in Chapter 5. The *crucial* difference between the position Socrates there advances and the position under consideration here is this. In Socrates' case, pleasure and belief are construed as complexes with attitudes and objects as constituents. The question was whether the complex could be false if its object component was.

Two other students of contemporary philosophy from the early contemporary period engage the question of the truth-aptness of pleasure:
Perry and Penelhum. Note that, in accordance with their distinctions
between being-pleased-that and enjoyment, Penelhum and Perry discuss
the relation between falsity and each kind of pleasure separately.

Penelhum's treatment occurs in his 1964 article "Pleasure and Falsity."
There, after distinguishing being-pleased-that and enjoyment, he examines various ways that these pleasures relate to falsity. He distinguishes two
"spheres where error would seem to be possible with regard to pleasure."
The first sphere is error with respect to pleasure's object.[94] Here Penelhum considers three kinds of error: factual error about the object,
appraisive (that is, evaluative) error about the object, and error about
what object the pleasure actually has. The second sphere is error with
respect to pleasure itself, that is, with respect to what above I called
pleasure's "intentional mode." Penelhum examines the possibility of these
errors in the cases of being-pleased-that and enjoyment sequentially.

In the case of being-pleased-that, factual error about the object is the
sort of case that Thalberg discusses: one believes that p and is pleased that
p, but one's belief that p is false. Penelhum concludes: "The pleasure can
appropriately be called mistaken if the revelation of the falsity of this
judgment concludes it, leaving the subject not pleased at all, or pleased at
something else."[95] Penelhum draws the same conclusion for appraisive
error about the object. For example, the pleasure can be called mistaken if
when one is pleased that p and falsely believes it is good that p, one's
pleasure ceases upon disclosure of the falsity of the belief. In the putative
cases of error about what object being-pleased-that has and about whether
one is in fact pleased, Penelhum suggests that we do not have cases of
error so much as self-deception. I will return to this point below.

Penelhum broadly draws the same conclusions with respect to the
relation between error and enjoyment. That is, if one enjoys something
under a false description or according to a false appraisal, insofar as the
enjoyment depends upon the error, the enjoyment should cease upon
disclosure of the error.[96] Likewise, in the putative cases of error about
what object enjoyment has and about whether one is enjoying oneself,
Penelhum thinks that self-deception rather than error is occurring.

In the present case relating to Thalberg's discussion, the question is whether the attitude is truth-
apt and specifically whether it can inherit the truth-value of its object.

[94] (1964) 83.   [95] (1964) 85.   [96] (1964) 87.

There are several problems with Penelhum's claims to this point. First, he does not specify whether those cases of mistaken pleasure could properly be characterized as "false pleasure." Second, assuming that they can, Penelhum does not satisfactorily defend this position. One entity x may ontologically or metaphysically depend upon another entity y, and y may have a property P, but from this it does not follow that P can be ascribed to x as well as to y. Other problems specifically relate to mistaken enjoyment. I follow Perry in maintaining that being-pleased-that-p requires two beliefs: belief that p and belief that p is good. These doxastic requirements explain the possibility of factual and evaluative errors. But it is questionable whether enjoyment entails any beliefs at all. Once again, animals and infants can enjoy themselves. Thus, even if enjoyment can, in some sense, depend upon false factual and evaluative beliefs, the nature of this dependence relation is not the same as that for being-pleased-that.

I return now to the cases of self-deception about pleasure. In cases of self-deception not pertaining to one's inner states, Penelhum takes satisfaction of the following conditions to be required: belief in the face of strong evidence, the subject's knowledge of the evidence, and the subject's recognition of the import of the evidence. These conditions collectively constitute a "conflict-state in which there is partial satisfaction of the opposed criteria for belief and for disbelief."[97] Moreover, self-deception usually, although not necessarily, also involves the following motive: "the supposed fact which [the self-deceiver] asserts in the face of evidence is one which he has reason to wish (or even to try to make) to be so."[98] Granted this, Penelhum maintains that these conditions cannot apply to cases of self-deception about one's own inner states, since one does not "find out from evidence that one is pleased by, or enjoys, something."[99] This might suggest that it is impossible to be self-deceived about whether pleasure is occurring or about what an occurrent pleasure's object is. But Penelhum insists that "we do wish to speak at times of people falsely claiming to have, or not to have, a pleasure, yet not being wholly hypocritical. [And] calling this self-deception, when the people do exhibit behavioral ambivalence characteristic of self-deception, does allow this sort of description to have application."[100]

In considering Penelhum's position here, an example will be helpful. Penelhum himself offers the following one: a man deceives himself in thinking that he is horrified by something when in fact he is pleased and where this self-deception occurs because he views the pleasure as morally

---

[97] (1964) 88.   [98] (1964) 88.   [99] (1964) 90.   [100] (1964) 90.

unjustifiable and wishes not to have it. A related, but somewhat more picturesque example, which I develop from Perry, is this: a censorious abbess reads literature containing pornographic scenes in order to expurgate these scenes for her nuns' reading. The abbess is exhilarated by and takes pleasure in the scenes, but she believes her exhilaration and pleasure come from locating and expurgating them. For the sake of argument, I grant the possibility of such self-deception. The question is whether such a case constitutes or exemplifies false pleasure. I will assume, as I did in the earlier cases, that Penelhum maintains that it does. But once again, we have inadequate defense of the concept of false pleasure. Allowing that one may have false beliefs about whether one is experiencing pleasure or about what the object of one's pleasure is does not straightforwardly imply that the pleasure itself is false.

In *The Concept of Pleasure* Perry, like Penelhum, discusses falsity in relation to being-pleased-that and enjoyment sequentially. Perry maintains that enjoyment logically entails only one belief: that the object of enjoyment, under some conception, exists. Moreover, this belief is infallible since enjoyment requires an object. Consequently, Perry concludes: "there is nothing in the notions of enjoyment or belief nor in their logical relationship which dictates that enjoyment arising out of false belief must be considered false."[101] There is at least one problem with this position. Why should we think that enjoyment logically requires any beliefs whatsoever? Once again, animals and infants can enjoy activities and experiences. So if belief entails lexical concepts, then animals and infants can enjoy things without beliefs. Perry does not adequately clarify conditions for belief. Less controversially, enjoyment of *x* requires awareness of *x*. But awareness needn't be propositional or (lexically) conceptual.

The preceding, then, constitutes a better reason for thinking that enjoyment cannot be false. But the question remains whether enjoyment can have truth-value. Grant Perry his view that enjoyment entails one existential belief and that this belief is infallible, does this entail that enjoyment is necessarily true? I am confident that Perry would answer this question negatively.[102] However, he does not address the question.

Perry also denies that, properly speaking, being-pleased-that can be false. The reason here differs. As I've mentioned, Perry holds that being-pleased-that-*p* entails two beliefs: the belief that *p* and the belief that it is good that *p*. Let us call these "factual" and "evaluative" beliefs respectively. The belief that

---

[101] (1967) 132–133, and see 112–133 more broadly.
[102] The reason for my confidence will emerge in the following discussion of being-pleased-that.

p can be false. At least, the proposition *p* can be false. Perry assumes that the truth-value of the doxastic attitude derives from that of the propositional content. Assume cognitivism about evaluations, as Perry does.[103] In that case, the evaluative belief or rather its content can be false. Granted this, Perry maintains that the falsity of either does not imply that being-pleased-that is false – although it permits that being-pleased-that is false. He reasons as follows. Recall that, in addition to the two belief-conditions, Perry holds that being-pleased-that requires that the supposed fact (*p*) be "fairly recent news" and "of some measure of personal interest." Perry, assuming an Aristotelian conception of definition according to genus and differentia, insists that any one of these conditions might be "chosen" as generic, with the remainders as differentiae. For example, being-pleased-that might belong to the genus of propositions whose contents are in some measure of personal interest, differentiated by belief in the given proposition, belief in the goodness of the proposition, and the fact that the proposition is fairly recent news. It could only be, Perry continues, if being-pleased-that were construed as a species of belief that it would be justified to speak of the cases involving false beliefs as false pleasures. But, again, there is no logical requirement to construe being-pleased-that as a species of belief.[104] I will not evaluate this strange argument and conclusion, save to say the following. I doubt that we should remain committed to an Aristotelian conception of definition. But even if we do accept Aristotelian definitions, I am surprised by the suggestion that the choice between any of the necessary conditions of being-pleased-that for the genus of this psychological kind is arbitrary.

PLEASURE, INTENTIONALITY, AND REPRESENTATION IN THE RECENT CONTEMPORARY PERIOD

In the recent contemporary period, among philosophers interested in contemporary philosophy (again, as opposed to scholars of ancient philosophy), there has been little discussion of pleasure and truth-aptness per se.[105] There has, however, been some discussion of the relation between pleasure and intentionality as well as pleasure and representation.

---

[103] Cognitivism about evaluative sentences and mental states is the view that these sentences and states express or stand in relation to truth-apt contents. Non-cognitivism, in contrast, holds that such entities do not express or stand in relation to truth-apt contents. For example, on one construal the sentence "*x* is good" expresses a preference or liking or favoring of *x*.

[104] (1967) 133–153, especially at 150–153.

[105] But cf. the somewhat earlier piece by Sabina Lovibond, "True and False Pleasures," *Proceedings of the Aristotelian Society* 90 (1989–1990) 213–230.

In the case of the relation between pleasure and representation, it is useful to distinguish two conceptual possibilities: one is that pleasure's intentional object is representational;[106] the other is that pleasure's intentional mode is representational.[107] Assume that pleasure's intentional object or at least some of pleasure's intentional objects are representational. It remains questionable whether this fact implies that pleasure itself or pleasure's intentional mode is or may be representational. In fact, parties to the discussion have not engaged this latter question.

In their discussions of the intentionality or representationality of pleasure, it is a remarkable feature of recent contemporary period discussions that contributors have not taken enjoyment or being-pleased-that as theoretical points of departure. Instead, several focus on so-called sensory pleasure, where sensory pleasure is conceived as pleasure taken in a sensation.[108] Curiously, there has been little explicit justification for this theoretical move. But two considerations are worth noting. One is that sensory pleasure may be thought to be the most theoretically simple form of pleasure and thus the most theoretically tractable. Another consideration, explicit at least in one recent author, is that other putative forms of pleasure are reducible to sensory pleasure; thus, sensory pleasure is metaphysically basic.[109]

Sensory pleasure is the theoretical point of departure of Murat Aydede's 2000 paper "An Analysis of Pleasure vis-à-vis Pain."[110] As I noted in the introductory section of this chapter, Aydede frames his paper by reviving the early contemporary period debate over whether pleasure is a disposition. He maintains that the terms of the earlier debate were unjustifiably limited: it was thought that if pleasure is not a disposition, but an episodic or occurrent feeling, then it must be a sensation. For reasons that I will not rehearse here, Aydede maintains that pleasure is not a disposition. Thus, he maintains that pleasure is an occurrent feeling. However, he denies that pleasure is a sensation. The conception of

---

[106] This, for example, is the case with being-pleased-that-*p*. Cf. Plato's treatment of false pleasure kind 1 in *Philebus*.

[107] In other words, the pleasure itself, in contrast to what it is taken in, is representational. This, for example, is Plato's view of the appearance aspect of pleasure in *Republic* 9.

[108] Such pleasure may also be called "bodily or physical pleasure." In Chapter 10, I discuss the extent to which the ancients recognize sensory pleasures and distinguish these from other kinds of pleasure.

[109] This is the view of William S. Robinson, "What Is it Like to Like?" *Philosophical Psychology* 19 (2006) 743–765. But contrast this position with that of Fred Feldman (1988), who holds that sensory pleasure reduces to propositional pleasure.

[110] (2000) 537–570.

sensation that Aydede here uses is distinct from that of the early period discussion, which is that of a sense-datum. The perceptual theory of sense-data is now largely rejected, and certainly Aydede rejects the theory. But Aydede's rejection of the identification of pleasure with a sensation is not limited to his rejection of the sense-data theory.

Drawing on neuroscientific evidence, Aydede argues for a distinction between sensory (sensational or informational) and motivational-affective experiences, each of which depends upon a distinct neurological system. The sensory-discriminative system, which is to say the sense-perceptual system, is responsible for sensing or perceiving peripheral stimuli and is subserved by dedicated neural mechanisms. In contrast, the motivational-affective system, subserved by distinct neutral mechanisms, is responsible "for our aversive reaction or drive in response to ... stimuli."[111] Aydede argues that pleasure is purely a function of the motivational-affective system. As such, pleasure differs not only from the classic sense-perceptual faculties but also, and crucially, from pain. Pain, Aydede argues, normally involves a complex of sensory, precisely, nociceptive, and affective-motivational, precisely, aversive processes.

The evidence of a neurological disorder supports this conception of the complexity of pain. The disorder, which Daniel Dennett first introduced from psychological literature into the philosophical discussion in the late seventies and labeled "reactive disassociation,"[112] particularly affects patients who have undergone prefrontal lobotomies. They report pain experiences but without aversive reactions. In normal cases, Aydede then argues, the phenomenology of pain is a "fusion" of sensory and affective-motivational elements. In contrast, pleasure lacks a dedicated sensory neural mechanism. Hence, pleasure, vis-à-vis pain, is neurologically and phenomenologically simple. In short, Aydede maintains that:

[physical or bodily] pleasure is not itself a sensation but a ... reaction to sensations proper ... But pleasure is still a feeling, episodic in character. When we experience pleasure, we experience some non-sensory qualitative feel.[113]

---

[111] (2000) 548.
[112] Daniel Dennett, "Why You Can't Make a Computer that Feels Pain," in *Brainstorms*, MIT Press, 1978, 190–229, which draws on R. Melzack and K. L. Casey, "Sensory, Motivational, and Central Control Determinants of Pain: A New Conceptual Model," in *The Skin Senses*, D. Kenshalo, ed., Thomas, 1968, 223–43. Cf. also G. Pitcher, "Pain Perception," *Philosophical Review* 79 (1970) 368–93, which is another early philosophical appropriation of the psychological discussion.
[113] (2000) 557.

According to this account, bodily or sensory pleasure appears to be intentional, a pro-attitude directed toward sensations. Indeed, at one point Aydede writes: "Pleasure is an affective 'pro-reaction' that reveals itself in consciousness as a qualitative component of a total experience."[114] It is questionable, however, whether Aydede thinks that all pleasure is a pro-reaction or intentional. The neural mechanisms (in other words, the affective-motivational system) responsible for pleasure are principally located in the limbic system. But Aydede also discusses experiments on patients involving electrical self-stimulation of certain areas of the limbic system that produce hedonic experiences (for example, elation or euphoria), but which lack objects: "Whatever kind of pleasure [these] subjects are experiencing, in most of the cases, the pleasure is clearly 'objectless': it is not directed to … certain thoughts or sensations proper."[115] Consequently, Aydede appears to hold that pleasure is normally, but not necessarily, intentional. Consequently, bodily or sensory pleasure (again, pleasure directed toward a sensation) emerges as a psychological state with a certain complexity of its own, with pleasure itself as an element.

Timothy Schroeder's 2001 paper "Pleasure, Displeasure, and Representation" evinces no awareness of Aydede's contribution,[116] and I assume that Schroeder had not consulted and had not been able to consult Aydede's paper. At any rate, Schroeder defends a representational account of pleasure at odds with Aydede's affective-motivational conception.

Schroeder also rejects Ryle's dispositional conception of pleasure and maintains that pleasure is an occurrence or episode. He explicitly maintains that pleasure is an experience. Unfortunately, he does not clarify what he means by "experience." This obscurity is significant. Schroeder argues that since all other experiential states – under which he identifies the five classic senses, proprioception, stretch receptors in the stomach, sense of balance, sense of warmth and coldness – are representational, "the isolation of pleasure and displeasure is reason for suspicion."[117] This suggests that by "experience" Schroeder cannot mean "perception," let alone "psychological representation"; for otherwise his point would be question-begging. Possibly, by "experience" he means "an occurrent psychological condition that has a certain phenomenal character." In that case, Schroeder is claiming that, bracketing pleasure and

---

[114] (2000) 565. Aydede also refers to Nowell-Smith's terms "pro-" and "con-attitude" at (2000) n.30.
[115] (2000) 555.   [116] *Canadian Journal of Philosophy* 31 (2001) 507–530.
[117] (2001) 511. Note that Schroeder does not conflate pain with displeasure: "Displeasure is a strict counterpart of pleasure, pain is not." (513) Schroeder is also familiar with the literature on reactive disassociation.

displeasure, all occurrent psychological conditions with a certain phenomenal character are representational – and thus pleasure and displeasure must be. This strikes me as a weak inference or at least inadequately supported since there may be other occurrent psychological conditions that have phenomenal characters, but without being representational.

Schroeder argues, more precisely, that pleasure is a perceptual representation of a certain quantity of positive change in one's net state of intrinsic desire satisfaction.[118] Moreover, change in net desire satisfaction is a "function of satisfaction . . . of individual desires, with stronger desires being weighted more heavily than weaker desires in the global evaluation."[119] In the centrality of the role it accords to desire-satisfaction, Schroeder's position resembles Warner's and especially Davis's views of enjoyment, the latter of which also construed pleasure in terms of one's global psychological state. Recall:

WARNER: Enjoyment is of an experience or activity that causes or causally sustains a desire that it also simultaneously subjectively satisfies, where the desire is "intrinsic" or for-its-own-sake desire, of an experience or activity, that it be an experience or activity of such-and-such a sort.

DAVIS: Enjoyment is of an experience that causes occurrent beliefs that collectively add significantly to one's pleasure (where degree of pleasure is understood as *the positive sum of the product of each occurrent thought believed and desired*).

Note, however, that Schroeder's position differs from Warner's and Davis's in that it does not specify a doxastic element. More significantly, Warner and Davis do not take enjoyment or pleasure to represent, but to be constituted by, desire-satisfaction in distinct forms.

Assuming that pleasure is representational in the way Schroeder proposes, the question arises whether there are forms of hedonic *mis*-representation. Schroeder maintains that there are. In particular, he maintains that there are hedonic illusions and hallucinations. His consideration of this point arises within the context of the question of the extent to which hedonic representations are modular, that is, whether they may occur to some degree independently of other mental and specifically cognitive processes such as belief. Compare the optical Müller-Lyer illusion where parallel lines of equal length appear to be shorter and longer than one another when appended with arrowheads and inverted arrowheads respectively, despite the subject's belief

---

[118] Note that Schroeder raises, but remains neutral on, the question whether hedonic or affective representation is conceptual or non-conceptual.
[119] (2001) 514.

that the lines are of equal length. This illusion corroborates the view that the visual representational system is substantially modular, in particular, substantially autonomous from belief.[120]

Schroeder proposes that hedonic representational systems are "moderately" modular. For example, he takes the euphoria induced by heroin or cocaine to exemplify a hedonic hallucination insofar as it "hijacks" the midbrain's reward-signaling system and "induces a net increase in desire satisfaction, when in fact no such increase exists."[121] Hedonic illusions will then be cases where experience represents a greater or lesser net increase in desire-satisfaction than the quantity of desire-satisfaction that actually occurs. The case Schroeder offers is of a depressed person whose mood is unaffected by a promotion at work, despite the fact that the person believes the promotion to be a significant good.

Schroeder takes hedonic hallucinations and illusions to be "familiar sorts of experience."[122] Thus, one of the alleged virtues of his representational account is that it explains these familiar experiences in accordance with a unified representational account of experience. One further hedonic illusion Schroeder discusses, here explicitly within the context of discussing a virtue of his representational account, is the phenomenon of the simultaneous experience of pleasure and displeasure. That is, Schroeder takes it as given that we have simultaneously mixed or "bittersweet" affective experiences. On Schroeder's theory, such experiences are illusory because they involve simultaneous representation of "mutually exclusive properties,"[123] namely net increase in desire-satisfaction and net increase in desire-frustration (displeasure). Schroeder compares this hedonic illusion with another optical illusion, the waterfall illusion. In this case, when after staring at a waterfall for some time, one looks at a stationary rock, the rock appears to move. Since one believes the rock is stationary, motion and rest of the same object are simultaneously represented. Schroeder maintains that the hedonic illusion requires pleasure and displeasure to "depend for their existence upon distinct representational structures in order to accommodate the simultaneous representation of our desires as both satisfied and frustrated."[124]

---

[120] (2001) 516.   [121] (2001) 518.   [122] (2001) 516.   [123] (2001) 520.

[124] (2001) 520. (I note that Schroeder cites no neuroscientific evidence to support this claim.) Setting aside the discrepancy between Schroeder's view that pleasure represents desire-satisfaction and Plato's view that pleasure represents restoration to the natural state, Schroeder's account of hedonic illusion and hallucination in certain ways resembles Plato's accounts of false pleasures kind 2 and 3 in *Philebus*.

In his 2006 paper "What Is it Like to Like?"[125] William S. Robinson proceeds on the assumption that pleasure is equivalent to liking, and in pursuing the question "What is it like to like?" he engages and offers an alternative to Aydede's and Schroeder's accounts of pleasure. Like Aydede and Schroeder, Robinson begins with the point, contra Ryle, that pleasure is a conscious occurrent. Crucially, however, he argues that pleasure does not belong to any of the familiar three categories of conscious occurrent: sensation, thought, and emotion.[126] In other words, Robinson suggests that the list of categories of conscious occurrent must be expanded. Drawing on the work of Bruce Mangan, in particular Mangan's 2001 paper "Sensation's Ghost: The Non-Sensory 'Fringe' of Consciousness,"[127] Robinson argues that pleasure is a non-sensory conscious experience. Other examples of non-sensory conscious experience that Mangan cites include: the feeling of immanence (that is, the feeling that more detailed information is available for retrieval on the periphery of consciousness),[128] the feeling of familiarity, the feeling of knowing or certainty, the feeling of awe or of the sublime, among many others.

Mangan suggests that the following four basic features distinguish non-sensory phenomenology from sensory phenomenology: translucence (non-sensory experiences allow sensations to "pass through" them);[129] low resolution ("they are fuzzy, slurred, cloud-like in character in contrast to the fine grained detail and texture of typical focal sensory experience"); elusiveness ("they elude direct introspective access"); and the tendency of phenomenological location to lie at the periphery of consciousness.[130] It may be questioned whether we in fact have a unified class here. But, more pressingly, it is questionable whether pleasure or liking – especially on Robinson's construal counts as a member.

I will not rehearse Robinson's arguments that pleasure or liking is not a sensation or thought. I take this view to be very plausible. But it is more dubious that it is not an emotion. Robinson assumes that emotion is some complex of sensation, thought, and bodily reaction.[131] On this construal,

---

[125] *Philosophical Psychology* 19 (2006) 743–765.
[126] Note that Robinson operates with Aydede's conception of sensation.
[127] *Psyche* 7 (2001), available at: theassc.org/files/assc/2509.pdf.
[128] For example, sensing that a word is "on the tip of one's tongue" exemplifies this feeling.
[129] I interpret this to mean that non-sensory experiences admit compresence with sensory-experience and, perhaps, more precisely that non-sensory experiences take sensory-experiences as objects. For example, one may experience a certain scent as familiar.
[130] Mangan includes variability in intensity as a basic property of non-sensory experiences, but I exclude it insofar as it does not distinguish non-sensory experiences from sensory experiences.
[131] "I am simply going to assume that emotions can be adequately analyzed as sensations, thoughts, and bodily reactions standing in some suitable set of relations" ([2006] 752).

I grant that pleasure is not an emotion. But it is noteworthy that Mangan's list of non-sensory experiences actually includes what would normally be characterized as emotions: "the sorrow of the willow or the joy of sunshine are non-sensory experiences."[132]

More precisely, Robinson maintains that pleasure is a positively evaluative conscious occurrent. In contrast to, say, Perry, he maintains that evaluations, which may be expressed in terms such as "*x* is good," are not themselves judgments or thoughts.[133] In other words, Robinson is a non-cognitivist about at least hedonic or affective evaluations. Finally, evaluation and so pleasure is intentional; one evaluates or in this case likes something, for example, a sensation.

In the penultimate section of his paper, Robinson examines eight consequences of this conception of pleasure. Four are noteworthy here. First, Robinson maintains that although pleasure is intentional, it is not representational. That is, pleasure is directed toward entities, for example, sensations; however, pleasure does not represent its intentional objects as "about" anything. Compare visual perception, which represents colors as properties of objects. Pleasure does not represent pleasantness as a property of its objects. In the context of this discussion, Robinson also specifically criticizes Schroeder's representational conception of pleasure. He argues that if pleasure were representational, then it would make knowledge of what one likes or takes pleasure in inferential.[134] Indeed, Schroeder argues that our pleasures can reveal our non-apparent desires to us.

Note further that although he rejects Schroeder's conception of pleasure's representationality, when he himself denies that pleasure is representational, Robinson appears to be operating with a different conception of representation. For Robinson, once again, pleasure's being representational amounts to the mind's attribution of pleasantness to objects. For example, if one took pleasure in the taste of a beer shandy, then if pleasure were representational, the beer shandy would appear to have the property of pleasantness. But Schroeder does not suggest that, in the experience of pleasure, one takes one's net desire-satisfaction to appear to have the property of pleasantness. In light of this, it may be useful to distinguish kinds of representation. When, for instance, one visually perceives the moon as luminous, the moon is represented as having the property of luminosity. In this case, let us say that the representation is

---

[132] In the final subsection of the penultimate section of his paper (5.8), Robinson takes up the question whether non-sensory experience may be a component of emotion and thus whether liking or taking pleasure in a sensation would constitute an emotion. He maintains, however, that it would be misleading to claim so.

[133] (2006) 754.   [134] (2006) 756–758.

"attributive." Robinson clearly treats representation attributively when he denies that pleasure is representational. Again, pleasantness is not attributed to the beer shandy. For Schroeder, pleasantness represents net desire-satisfaction in that the occurrence of pleasure indicates the occurrence of net desire-satisfaction. We might call this kind of representation "indicative."

The second consequence of Robinson's conception of pleasure is, he argues, that the intentional objects of pleasure are limited to sensations and emotions. In other words, Robinson excludes thoughts as pleasure's possible intentional objects. This raises the question of how Robinson interprets cases of being-pleased-that. Although Robinson does not address the point in precisely these terms, he argues that it is actually feelings associated with thoughts that are liked. For example, taking pleasure in one's children's good health is not a matter of taking pleasure in the thought that one's children are healthy, but in the feeling, say, of satisfaction that accompanies this thought.

Third, contra Aydede, Robinson maintains that, although affective experience depends upon a different neural basis from sensation, this distinct neural basis need not contribute to the phenomenology of experience by "adding a feeling."[135] In short, Robinson maintains that pleasure is not a feeling of any kind. (Note also that here again Robinson's position seems to diverge from Mangan's.)

Finally, Robinson also criticizes Aydede's position that pleasure may be objectless. Recall Aydede's reference to the electrical self-stimulation experiments that induced euphoria and elation. Here Robinson suggests that pleasure's object is everything; in other words, euphoria is a state in which the subject likes all of his sensations and emotions.

PLEASURE, INTENTIONALITY, AND FEELING IN THE RECENT
CONTEMPORARY PERIOD

Aydede's position, for example, shows that pleasure may have both an intentional and a feeling or qualitative aspect. But another strain of the recent contemporary period discussion pits these two possibilities against one another. A useful point of entry into this debate in fact is Alston's 1967 article on pleasure in *The Encyclopedia of Philosophy*.

In discussing his contribution above, I touched upon the fact that, in reviewing his predecessors' contributions, Alston draws a basic division

[135] "The limbic system need not be supposed to make its contribution to phenomenology by contributing a feeling episode. It can be supposed to make its contribution by bringing about a non-sensory experience that is directed upon sensation" ([2006] 761).

between "conscious-quality" theories and "motivational" theories. According to the former, pleasure is an ultimate or unanalyzable, immediate or directly apprehended quality of consciousness.[136] For example, the view that pleasure is a sensation is treated as one variant of the conscious-quality theory.[137] The ultimate reason why Alston rejects any form of the conscious-quality theory is that it is phenomenologically implausible. Precisely, the various cases of getting pleasure do not share a common felt quality or some common qualitatively identical respect.[138]

In contrast, Alston characterizes the motivational theory in the following way: pleasure occurs when some entity is present to a subject, which the subject apprehends as good or desirable and which the subject has had some motivation toward, such as appetite, inclination, or striving.[139] More precisely, Alston countenances (without accepting) the following motivational definition of pleasure:

To get pleasure is to be in a state of consciousness that includes awareness that one has obtained something one wants.

One central objection to this definition is that some simple sensory pleasures occur without prior wants. For example, one may taste mango for the first time and enjoy it. A general line of response to this objection, which some motivationalists maintain, is to "generously posit instincts and other nonconscious 'tendencies' and 'strivings.'"[140] An alternative, however, is to emend the definition in the following way:

To get pleasure is to have an experience that, as of the moment, one would rather have than not have, on the basis of its felt quality, apart from any further considerations regarding consequences.[141]

As we have seen, this is in fact the conception of pleasure that Alston himself endorses.[142] According to this definition, pleasure is a function "not of a pre-existing desire, but of a preference one has at the moment of experience."[143] Moreover, as we have also seen, Alston explicitly characterizes this preference as dispositional:

---

[136] "Quality" is here glossed as "intrinsic distinguisher of a state" ([1967] 342).

[137] Note that, according to Aydede's account, sensation is not unanalyzable. But that is another matter.

[138] (1967) 344.   [139] (1967) 344.   [140] (1967) 345.   [141] (1967) 345.

[142] He also attributes the view to Sidgwick. Cf. "I propose to define pleasure ... as a feeling which, when experienced by intelligent beings, is at least implicitly apprehended as desirable or – in cases of comparison – preferable" (Henry Sidgwick, *The Methods of Ethics*, Hackett, 1981, 127, cited from Feldman [1988]).

[143] Alston (1967) 345.

To say that one has the preference at the moment is not to say that one expresses the preference even to oneself; it is not to say anything about what is before one's consciousness at the moment. It is, rather, to say something dispositional – for example, that one would choose to have an experience just like this rather than not if one were faced with such a choice at this moment and if no considerations other than the quality of the experience were relevant.[144]

This statement is important and valuable in indicating that dispositional theories of pleasure, including those of Ryle and Quinn, are in fact forms of the motivational theory. Compare Quinn's concluding statement:

The short-term complex disposition which we call pleasure or enjoyment will be such that all the action or impulse episodes will *aim at having the experience for its own sake*. And, I should add, it seems plausible to me that *desires and impulses, such as to prolong and intensify the experience*, are part of the enjoyment of that experience [that is, are part of the short-term disposition].[145]

However, motivational theories of pleasure do not have to be dispositional. For example, on Aydede's view pleasure is an occurrent state. Indeed, Aydede identifies the affective-motivational attitude of pleasure with "desiring*" or "reacting*" (note the asterisks). Desiring* and reacting* are here distinguished from desiring and reacting, where the latter are treated as cognitive attitudes toward propositional contents. Desiring* and reacting* are more primitive attitudes, directed toward non-conceptual sensory/informational content.[146] Consider also that Robinson's position might be viewed as a variant of the motivational theory, according to which pleasure (or liking) is episodic or ocurrent rather than dispositional. Indeed, the earliest contemporary proponent of an occurrent motivational theory is Penelhum, who in his 1957 piece maintains that pleasure is an episodic pro-reaction to some stimulus.

If we are to include positions such as Robinson's among motivational theories, however, then we should be more precise in our use of terms. In particular, we need a term to cover both desires/wants and likings. I think, and the tradition has shown, that we may do no better than "pro-attitude." Accordingly, I suggest that we redescribe Alston's division as between conscious-quality and pro-attitude theories – while also recognizing that mixed positions of some sort, such as Aydede's, are possible. In other words, pro-attitudes may themselves have feelings.

In considering the recent contemporary period debate over conscious-quality versus pro-attitude theories, I will discuss four papers,

[144] (1967) 345.   [145] (1968) 86, with my italics.   [146] (2000) 559–560.

by Fred Feldman, Stuart Rachels, Christopher Heathwood, and Aaron Smuts, respectively.

Fred Feldman's 1988 paper "Two Questions about Pleasure," reprinted in his 1997 book *Utilitarianism, Hedonism, and Desert,* may be said to begin an influential strain in recent contemporary treatments of the conscious-quality versus pro-attitude question.[147] Feldman's paper pursues two principal questions: Is there some feature common to all sensory pleasures in virtue of which they are pleasures? And what is the relation between sensory pleasure and propositional pleasure? Feldman refers to the former as the "heterogeneity question." (Recall that a negative answer to this question led Alston to endorse a form of the pro-attitude theory. Feldman responds in a similar way.) Feldman refers to the latter question as the "linkage question." Both questions may be viewed as attempts to determine the unity of pleasure.

Following criticisms of some of his predecessors' answers to the heterogeneity and linkage questions, Feldman offers the following answers. To the heterogeneity question: all sensory pleasures are alike in virtue of the fact that individuals who have them take a certain sort of propositional pleasure in the fact that they have them when they have them. To the linkage question: when we say that a person experiences sensory pleasure, we mean that there is some sensation he is having that he is intrinsically pleased to be having. In short, for Feldman, propositional pleasure is the fundamental concept; sensory pleasure can be reduced to propositional pleasure. Feldman describes propositional pleasure as a pro-attitude, belonging to the same family as wanting and favorably evaluating (where favorably evaluating is assumed to be a belief-state, for example, believing *x* to be good). He argues, however, that propositional pleasure is not identical to wanting/desiring or to favorably evaluating.

Two conspicuous problems arise for Feldman's position. One is that, by his own admissions, the role of propositional pleasure in his account need not in fact be played by propositional pleasure. Contrast the following two claims: Saul is intrinsically pleased to be feeling a certain sensation; Saul is intrinsically pleased that he is feeling a certain sensation. The latter is propositional; the former is ambiguous and on one interpretation is non-propositional. Precisely, the kind of sensory pleasure with which Feldman is concerned is so-called *de se* sensory pleasure, that is, pleasure taken in a sensation that one takes to be one's own (*de se*). (Contrast a sadist who takes pleasure in another's pain sensation.) Feldman maintains that a person can

---

[147] Hereafter I will refer to the pagination of the 1997 version.

have a *de se* attitude even though he is not explicitly aware of himself. For example, while lying on the beach one can take pleasure in the warmth of the sun. Observe the difference between taking pleasure in the warmth and being pleased that one is being warmed. Indeed, Feldman grants: "It might be that there is no such proposition as the proposition that I myself am feeling warmth. Perhaps it would be better to say that the object of a *de se* attitude is a property."[148] But since Feldman grants this, it is not propositional pleasure per se to which sensory pleasure is being reduced. Rather, it is a pro-attitude, not identical to wanting/desiring or favorably evaluating, which may take a sensation as its intentional object. The second conspicuous problem with Feldman's position now emerges: it fails to clarify the pro-attitude of pleasure, except by negative contrast with desire or want and favorable evaluation.[149]

In short, Feldman's position amounts to the view that pleasure is some sort of pro-attitude. This view is similar to Perry's. Arguably, however, Feldman fudges the distinction between enjoyment and being-pleased-that since the latter does seem to require a favorable evaluation. Note also Feldman's position relative to Robinson's. Robinson clarifies what the pro-attitude of liking is: an intentional, but non-representational and non-doxastic state of evaluation.

In his 2000 paper "Is Unpleasantness Intrinsic to Unpleasant Experiences?"[150] Stuart Rachels defends a version of what Alston calls the conscious-quality theory and which Rachels himself calls "Intrinsic Nature." Rachels's leading question is: What does the unpleasantness of unpleasant experience consist in? In principle Rachels treats unpleasantness and pleasantness simultaneously and analogously: "Each of these theories [about unpleasantness] stands or falls with its corresponding view of pleasure."[151] In fact, as we will see, most of Rachels's arguments are directed toward unpleasantness; and it is sometimes not easy to find compelling reasons or examples pertaining to pleasantness. It is also worth emphasizing that Rachels is concerned with the relation between un/pleasantness and experience. Thus, he does not examine the condition of being-pleased-that.

---

[148] (1997) 102–103.
[149] Cf. the criticism of Feldman in Elinor Mason, "The Nature of Pleasure: A Critique of Feldman," *Utilitas* 19 (2007) 279–287.
[150] *Philosophical Studies* 99 (2000) 187–210. Cf. also his "Six Theses about Pleasure," *Philosophical Perspectives* 18 (2004) 247–267.
[151] (2000) 187.

Prior to defending Intrinsic Nature, Rachels criticizes several alternatives, two of which are variants of the pro-attitude theory:[152] Pro-motivation and Like.[153] According to the version of Pro-motivation on which Rachels focuses, for an experience to be pleasant is for the experience to make the person want its continuation. According to Like, for an experience to be pleasant is for the person to like the experience. One of the attractions of Pro-motivation and Like is that they offer straightforward explanations of pleasure's variable intensity: the stronger the pro-motivation or liking, the greater the intensity.

Rachels offers the following general criticism of Pro- and Con-motivation: degree of motivation is inconsistent with degree of un/pleasantness. He offers five types of case to exemplify this point. Only one of these, however, relates to pleasantness. In this case, degree of pro-motivation supposedly falls short of pleasantness: "the soothing pleasure of a massage can be highly intense, yet relaxing; so the subject is not strongly moved to prolong it."[154] The example strikes me as weak. Being relaxing seems consequential upon the high intensity of the massage, not simultaneous with it. Likewise, the soothing pleasure seems consequential, not simultaneous with the high intensity. Indeed, soothing pleasure and high intensity seem to me contradictory properties.

A more attractive objection to Pro-motivation is this: people want their pleasure to continue because it is pleasant. But on Pro-motivation, this amounts to saying: people want their pleasure to continue because they want it to continue, which is nonsense. This objection is also voiced by Aaron Smuts, another recent defender of a conscious-quality theory of pleasure, and discussed by Christopher Heathwood, a recent defender of a pro-attitude theory. I will return to this below.

According to Like, one must have a favorable emotional attitude toward the experience considered merely as a feeling. Moreover, "such an attitude needn't be cognitively sophisticated, given that kittens feel [pleasure]."[155] (Compare Aydede's reacting* versus reacting.) Rachels offers several criticisms of Like. All turn on the idea that there can be an inconsistency between the pleasantness of an experience and the amount one likes it; hence pleasantness and liking cannot be identical.

---

[152] Rachels also discusses a third, Damage, which is a representational theory. He focuses here on pain, and does not substantively entertain a hedonic correlate. I will therefore ignore this section of his paper.

[153] Rachels in fact calls the former "Motivation" and the latter "Dislike," given his focus on unpleasantness.

[154] (2000) 192.   [155] (2000) 193.

For example, Rachels suggests, the amount that one likes an experience might be influenced "unduly" by the way it contrasts with a prior state. For example, following an ecstatic experience, one's pleasure might plummet. In that case, Rachels proposes, one might dislike the mildly pleasant state that follows precisely because it is so mild.[156]

Having disposed of Pro-Motivation and Like, Rachels defends Intrinsic Nature, which, again, is a conscious-quality theory. According to Intrinsic Nature, it is an intrinsic, non-relational fact about certain experiences that they are un/pleasant, where un/pleasantness supervenes on *qualia*. Rachels offers the following reason in support of Intrinsic Nature vis-à-vis unpleasantness: when you twist your ankle or jam your finger, the experience itself seems to hurt. So introspection, though fallible, provides evidence for Intrinsic Nature.[157] In support of Intrinsic Nature vis-à-vis pleasure, we need to construe a correlate: when you have a pleasant experience, for example, drinking a glass of Coke or ice water on a sweltering summer day, the experience itself seems to be pleasant.

Rachels considers and takes himself to allay several objections to Intrinsic Nature.[158] I will not discuss these here, save for one that can in fact be treated as a point of clarification. According to Intrinsic Nature, some intrinsic property of experience should integrate the category of all pleasant experience. In other words, all pleasant experiences have something in common, an intrinsic property. Rachels offers three distinct versions of Intrinsic Nature. Pleasures are just those experiences:

(A) that are intrinsically good due to how they feel;
(B) that are good for the people who have them due to how they feel;
(C) that one ought to like merely as a feeling.

Although Rachels remains agnostic about which version of Intrinsic Nature to endorse, Aaron Smuts[159] defends version (A), which he calls the "feels good" theory of pleasure. I will discuss Smuts's view shortly.

---

[156] In the face of this proposal, Rachels entertains the following counter-objection: liking and pleasantness fail to correspond here due to causes foreign to the experience, namely, the prior ecstatic state; but the pleasantness of an experience consists in *its* causing liking. Rachels responds by claiming that external causes almost always influence liking; so pleasure's intensity will almost never be supposed to correspond to *actual* degree of liking. Given this, Like is hard to test. But in that case, there are no good grounds for Like.

[157] (2000) 196.

[158] Again, some of these target unpleasantness and are difficult to exemplify in a compelling way for pleasantness. This is particularly true of objection 3 (pp. 198–200).

[159] "The Feels Good Theory of Pleasure," *Philosophical Studies* 155 (2010) 241–256.

First, I consider Christopher Heathwood's 2007 paper "The Reduction of Sensory Pleasure to Desire."[160]

Heathwood defends a version of the pro-attitude theory. He begins by admitting a distinction between three types of pleasure: sensory pleasure, being-pleased-that (or propositional pleasure), and enjoyment. Heathwood admits that while he would like to argue for a reduction of all three to desire, thereby unifying pleasure, he will restrict himself to an argument for the reduction of sensory pleasure to desire.

Like Feldman as well as recent proponents of the conscious-quality theory, Heathwood recognizes the heterogeneity problem (once again, that there are many pleasures, and it is unclear what they qualitatively have in common). He notes that whereas conscious-quality theorists attempt to unify pleasures by appeal to some intrinsic feature of the pleasing sensation, "the desire-based solution appeals to an extrinsic feature of the sensation: that its subject has some attitude (some pro-attitude) toward it."[161]

After considering several inadequate reductions of sensory pleasure to desire, Heathwood defends the following analysis:

A sensation S, occurring at time t, is a sensory pleasure iff the subject of S desires, intrinsically and *de re*, at t, of S, that S be occurring at t.

In other words: "the sensation occurs. Its subject becomes acquainted with it. Its subject forms an intrinsic *de re* desire for it while it is still occurring. Then, and only then, I say, does sensory pleasure occur."[162]

In the concluding sections of his paper, Heathwood considers several objections to his analysis. I will consider two. The first is that desire is prospective and cannot be for what the subject takes himself to have or to be the case. As we have seen, most who endorse a pro-attitude theory of pleasure construe the pro-attitude as "intrinsic." Thus, they would not agree with Rachels's construal of Pro-Motivation, that the motivation is for the experience to continue. Rather, it is simply for the experience

---

[160] *Philosophical Studies* 133 (2007) 23–44.   [161] (2007) 29.

[162] (2007) 32. In order to understand the phrase "*de re* desire," that is, desire concerning the thing itself, consider the following two sentences: "Oedipus desires to sleep with Jocasta" and "Oedipus desires to sleep with his mother." Jocasta is, unbeknownst to Oedipus, Oedipus' mother. The entity that "Oedipus' mother" refers to, that woman, is the entity that Oedipus desires to sleep with. So concerning the thing itself (*de re*) Oedipus desires to sleep with his mother. But with respect to the way he conceives of that object, Oedipus does not desire to sleep with that object. In this last case, we contrast *de re* desire with *de dicto* desire, where "*de dicto*" is Latin for "concerning the thing as spoken (or in this case conceived) of." So, according to Heathwood's analysis, one's desire is for the sensation itself.

itself. This raises a question whether one can desire an experience for itself, which one takes to be present. Smuts objects: "If not logically or even psychologically impossible to desire what one already has, it is, no doubt, exceedingly rare. Of course one might 'want' something to stay the same . . . in such cases ['want'] is just shorthand for 'wanting to keep,' which is essentially a desire for a future state, something we don't have."[163]

Heathwood offers "one simple example" to demonstrate that one can desire what one takes to be the case.[164] A car owner has parked his car outside. It begins to rain. Someone says to the car owner, "I bet you prefer that your car be in the garage right now."[165] But the car is dirty, and the owner thinks the rain will clean the car, which he desires. He replies, "No, I want my car to be right where it is." I think this example is not uncontroversial. Arguably, the owner wants the car *to remain* where it is *over the course of the rain spell.* Thus, this can be construed as a prospective, that is, future-directed, attitude.

Heathwood considers another objection, which he refers to as the "Euthyphro problem." Recall Rachels's criticism of Pro-Motivation: people want their pleasure to continue because it's pleasant. But on Promotivation, this amounts to saying: people want their pleasure to continue because they want it to continue, which, as we said, is nonsense. Since Heathwood's pro-attitude theory does not entail that the subject want the sensation to continue, Heathwood puts the concern this way. We commonly say of things that we desire them because they're pleasant. But if pleasure reduces to desire, then this reduces to our desiring sensations because we desire them. Heathwood's response is to claim that "I desire x because it is pleasant" should be interpreted to mean "I prospectively desire x because x will produce a non-prospective, intrinsic desire." For example, when a person says "I desire to taste that beer because I will find the taste pleasant," he means "I desire to taste that beer because when I taste that beer I will be intrinsically desiring the taste I get."[166]

In my opinion, the central problem of Heathwood's account is his reduction of sensory pleasure to *desire.* Heathwood claims that the notion of desire is primitive. But he does say of it the following: desire is "the paradigmatic pro-attitude . . . to desire something is simply to favor it, to be

---

[163] Smuts (2010) n. 10. Smuts derives support for this point from Kenny (1963) 115–116.

[164] (2007) 34.

[165] (2007) 34. Incidentally, the phrase "I bet you prefer" does not strike me as grammatical or idiomatic. Heathwood is evidently using the verb "prefer" in the present indicative because he needs the pro-conative attitude to be present tense. His example can survive this error, however.

[166] (2007) 38. Note that Heathwood himself refers to Rachels's objection at n. 24.

for it, to be 'into' it. Metaphorically speaking, it is to give the thing a mental 'thumbs up.'"[167] This construal seems to me fundamentally mistaken. In particular, it conflates desiring and liking. Moreover, as we have seen in the context of Robinson's and Rachels's discussions, it is a substantive question whether pleasure is explicable in terms of liking rather than desiring.[168]

Finally, I turn to Aaron Smuts's 2010 paper "The Feels Good Theory of Pleasure."[169] As I have mentioned, Smuts defends a version of the conscious-quality theory, specifically, the distinctive-feeling version of this theory. In advancing his position, Smuts raises two objections against Heathwood's position.

Smuts's first criticism of Heathwood is that we often intrinsically, contemporaneously (that is, non-prospectively) desire non-pleasures. Smuts here focuses on the paradox of painful art: "audiences seek out artworks that they know will arouse negative emotions, [although] people generally avoid situations that elicit such reactions in their normal lives."[170] Two different sorts of point need to be made with respect to this objection. One is that the objection is *ad hominem.* This is because Smuts is not committed to the view that there are contemporaneous desires; Smuts allows the idea merely for the sake of argument.[171] That is, he suggests that, even if there are contemporaneous intrinsic desires, sensory pleasure cannot be reduced to them. The other point regarding Smuts's first objection is that the idea that we sometimes seek negative aesthetic experiences for their own sake is controversial. I am not persuaded by Smuts's argument. I incline to think that such aesthetic experiences are pursued extrinsically, for various reasons. Indeed, Smuts himself concludes the discussion of the objection: "I will not rest my argument on a contentious solution to the paradox of painful art."[172]

Smuts's second objection to Heathwood relates to the Euthyphro problem. Smuts develops this objection in two steps. Initially he raises the Euthyphro problem, but only to concede that the pro-attitude theorist

---

[167] (2007) 25.
[168] There is, moreover, neuroscientific evidence for the distinction between wanting and liking. Cf. Kent Berridge, "Pleasure, Pain, Desire, and Dread: Hidden Core Processes of Emotion," in D. Kahneman *et al.*, eds., *Well-Being: The Foundations of Hedonic Psychology*, Russell Sage, 1999, 525–557; Kent Berridge and T. Robinson, "What is the Role of Dopamine in Reward: Hedonic Impact, Reward Learning, or Incentive Salience?" *Brain Research Reviews* 28 (1998) 309–369.
[169] *Philosophical Studies* 155 (2010) 241–256.
[170] (2010) 249.
[171] See Smuts (2010) n. 1: "For the sake of argument, I will assume that it makes sense to desire what we already have."
[172] (2010) 248.

has a response available: "She simply needs to deny that the aspects that explain the desire for any given experience are common to all pleasurable experience. She can describe the various aspects of a particular experience as a way of explaining [her] desire; she just cannot [have] recourse to pleasure."[173] For example, the pro-attitude theorist could explain why she intrinsically desires the cool mist of the sprinkler on a hot summer's day by referring to certain tactile sensations. Indeed, this seems to me to be the right way to respond to the Euthyphro problem.

Provisionally granting this response to the Euthyphro problem, Smuts argues that the pro-attitude theorist *cannot* explain the fact that pleasure comes in degrees. This Smuts call the "intense Euthyphro problem." Recall Rachels's admission that Pro-motivation elegantly explains the variable intensity of pleasure as a function of the variable intensity of desire. Here Smuts objects:

Desires are thought to be painful, or at least unpleasant. Further, on our ordinary understanding of the phenomenology of desire, the more intense a desire, the more unpleasant it is ... Desires do not seem to be the right kind of thing to explain the intensity of pleasure.[174]

This seems to me a reasonable criticism of pro-attitude theories like Heathwood's that reduce pleasure to desire. Note, however, that this objection falters in the face of a pro-attitude theory like Robinson's that treats pleasure as liking. Surely the more one likes something, the more pleasure rather than displeasure one takes in it.

Having rejected Heathwood's position and (allegedly) pro-attitude theories of pleasure in general, Smuts turns to his so-called feels good theory of pleasure. Recall the first of Rachels's construals of Intrinsic Nature (A): pleasures are just those experiences that are intrinsically good due to how they feel.[175] This is Smuts's position: what is common to all pleasant experiences is that they feel good. Smuts appears to accept, with Rachels, that the good feeling of pleasure supervenes on sensory experience. But in clarifying this feeling, he focuses on its phenomenology. Smuts admits that "to 'feel good' is about as close to an experiential primitive as we get."[176] Consequently, not unlike Heathwood's account of desire, his description resorts to metaphors: "we might say that the locus

---

[173] (2010) 250.   [174] (2010) 252.
[175] Recall that this view was intended to avoid the hedonic-tone theory, according to which all pleasant experiences have some invariant quality of pleasantness.
[176] (2010) 254.

of the pleasurable sensation *glows*; we feel a *warm* feeling; the good feeling *hums* like the vibration of a tuning fork."[177]

Furthermore, Smuts takes feeling good to be qualitatively identical across pleasant experiences. Thus, he rejects the heterogeneity problem. It is noteworthy, however, that this rejection involves an idiosyncratic pruning of the alleged range of hedonic cases. In particular, Smuts denies that so-called propositional pleasures and intellectual pleasures are necessarily pleasant. In other words, being-pleased-that does not entail pleasure. Likewise, Smuts maintains that "flow" or "being in the zone" are not the same thing as getting pleasure. Smuts states, but does not argue for, this view; and it may be wondered whether the restricted range of pleasures that he admits is question-begging.

Finally, it is worth noting that Smuts classifies his feels-good theory as belonging to one of two types of conscious-quality theory, namely, a hedonic-tone theory as opposed to a distinctive-feeling theory. The distinction between hedonic-tone and distinctive-feeling versions of the conscious-quality theory derives from Fred Feldman's 2001 article "Hedonism."[178] According to the distinctive-feeling theory, pleasure is a distinctive feeling "analogous to such feelings as the sensations of hot and cold."[179] In other words, hedonic feeling is a distinctive quality of consciousness. Thus, a cold lemonade may be experienced as a phenomenal complex constituting of a gustatory character (the flavor), a tactile quality (the coldness), and pleasantness.[180] In contrast, the hedonic-tone theory holds that a range of experiences or qualities of different kinds may all share a "certain phenomenally given dimension," called a hedonic or positive tone.[181] For example, the taste of lemonade, the smell of sandalwood, and the sound of rain falling might all share a hedonic tone. Thus, the hedonic-tone theory overcomes the central difficulty of the distinctive-feeling view, which is that there does not appear to be any phenomenally distinct quality isolatable among various pleasant experiences or conditions. Nonetheless, if the hedonic-tone theory is not to lapse into a

---

[177] (2010) 255.

[178] *Encyclopedia of Ethics*, L. and C. Becker, eds., 2nd edn., Routledge, 2001, 662–669.

[179] Feldman (2001) 662.

[180] For a recent defense of the distinctive-feeling theory, see Ben Bramble, "The Distinctive Feeling Theory of Pleasure," *Philosophical Studies* 156 (2011), available at present only online.

[181] Earlier advocates include C. D. Broad, *Five Types of Ethical Theory*, Kegan Paul, Trench, Trubner & Co., 1930, 229 (cited by Rachels); and K. Dunker, "On Pleasure, Emotion, and Striving," *Philosophy and Phenomenological Research* 1 (1941) 391–430 (cited by Smuts). Another more recent advocate is J. S. Feibleman, "A Philosophical Analysis of Pleasure," in *The Role of Pleasure in Behavior*, R. G. Heath, ed., Littlefield Adams, 1995, 250–278.

pro-attitude theory, it must be maintained that various qualitatively distinct experiences can share some quality in virtue of which they are pleasures. Again, this quality is not distinct from the various qualities. For instance, compare intensity, which may be a property of qualities across a range of sense-perceptual modalities. Pleasure or pleasantness is some such thing.

SOME CONCLUSIONS AND SUGGESTIONS FOR FUTURE INVESTIGATION

In the wake of this long and relatively detailed overview, it will be helpful to conclude with some summarizing remarks. In addition, I will make some suggestions regarding the direction for future inquiry, which are also intended to clarify the state of the discussion.

The distinction between conscious-quality and pro-attitude theories of pleasure is, to a large extent, a useful way of organizing the various contributions of the last fifty odd years. As I mentioned above, dispositional theories can be subsumed under pro-attitude theories, which might then be distinguished as dispositional and occurrent. At this stage in the history of the discussion, however, it is not reasonable to place too much weight on dispositional accounts. No substantial dispositional account has been offered since the mid seventies. Pro-attitude theories have certainly been more numerous than conscious-quality theories. But as Rachels's and Smuts's papers indicate, there are substantive recent defenses of conscious-quality theories. And, as I mentioned in a footnote, most recently Ben Bramble has defended the distinctive-feeling theory.

But although the dichotomy of pro-attitude and conscious-quality theories well suits an account of the history of contemporary discussions, it is doubtful whether it should constitute the framework for future consideration. In particular, as I mentioned in the case of Aydede's discussion, pro-attitude and conscious-quality theories are not logically exclusive, even if they have tended to be historically exclusive. In other words, pleasure might be a pro-attitude with a certain tone or distinctive feeling. Given this, it might be more reasonable to frame the inquiry in terms of the dichotomy of feeling and non-feeling theories. Following this division, feeling theories may be subdivided according to pro-attitude and non-intentional theories.[182]

---

[182] I believe that, as a matter of fact, although perhaps not as a matter of logic, all non-feeling theories are pro-attitude theories.

If this is a profitable way of further pursuing the identity question, relating the structure of this pursuit to the pursuit of the kinds question is another matter. Indeed, at this stage, it is unclear to me how pursuit of the kinds question should relate to or how it may converge with the identity question. In terms of the history of the contemporary discussion, the state of the kinds question is oddly disordered. As we saw, in the early period the identity question was largely pursued as the question "What is enjoyment?" And although some scholars argued for a basic distinction between enjoyment and being-pleased-that, there has been little discussion of being-pleased-that. With the exception of Feldman's 1988 paper, the last serious examination of being-pleased-that was Perry's 1967 treatment. Furthermore, it is very strange that recent period discussions have tended to focus on sensory pleasure, while ignoring or bracketing enjoyment. In other words, scholars have failed to notice or comment on this significant discontinuity between the early and recent period discussions. Moreover, in light of the early period discussion, recent contributors have an obligation to defend the view either that sensory pleasure is indeed a distinct kind of pleasure or simply that all pleasure is sensory pleasure.

I incline to think that sensory pleasure is in fact distinct from enjoyment. Enjoyment seems to require an object that is temporally extended to a greater degree than that of sensory pleasure – although, of course, every object of sensory pleasure must be temporally extended to some extent. To appreciate this point, imagine that you are at a perfume shop and are being presented with a series of fragrances sprayed onto tabs of paper. After smelling each successive tab, you are asked whether you liked the fragrance, which is to say, whether the fragrance pleased you. It seems to me that it would be unnatural to be asked whether you *enjoyed* the fragrance. If this is correct, it supports the suggestion that the objects of enjoyment must be temporally extended to a greater degree than the objects of sensory pleasure. At any rate, some argument needs to be generated in defense of the discussion of sensory pleasure to the exclusion of enjoyment.

Let me return now to the identity question. I'll conclude with some general comments, one specifically on feeling theories, one specifically on pro-attitude theories, and a couple that apply to both, in that order. Lest the debate over whether pleasure entails feeling reduce *merely* to conflicting brute intuitions, it would be helpful to get more clarity on the range and diversity of kinds of conscious quality, feeling, and phenomenal character, including whether these are equivalent categories. There has been almost no discussion of this matter within discussions of the identity question. Robinson's exceptional appeal to Mangan's category of non-sensory experience is a good starting point, whether or not pleasure belongs to this category.

Mention of Robinson also brings me to a general point about pro-attitude theories. Future proponents of pro-attitude theories must be careful to distinguish desire and liking. Recall my criticism of Heathwood for conflating the two. Heathwood's conflation is particularly puzzling, given that Rachels clearly distinguishes these conditions and given that Heathwood cites Rachels's paper in his bibliography. Likewise, Smuts's refutation of pro-attitude theories is vitiated by the fact that he takes Heathwood's position as the most compelling pro-attitude formulation and thereby fails to appreciate the distinctions between desire and liking. Like Rachels, Robinson clearly distinguishes the two. Unfortunately, the most recent contributions to the discussion have ignored Robinson's paper.

Assuming the distinction between desire and liking, and assuming that liking is the better candidate of the two for the pro-attitude of pleasure, it would be helpful to clarify the relation between liking and desire-satisfaction – especially since a number of contributors have identified pleasure or enjoyment with desire-satisfaction in some form. Likewise, it would be helpful to clarify the relation between liking and pro-evaluation. Is liking a form, perhaps a primitive form, of pro-evaluation? Or is liking a psychological precursor to pro-evaluation?

Now for a couple of remarks that apply to both feeling and pro-attitude theories. First, the question of whether pleasure or pleasure in some form is representational, at least in some way, remains open. I say this, even though I do not find Schroeder's argument persuasive. As I mentioned above, in pursuing the issue of pleasure's representationality, it is important to distinguish the question whether pleasure's intentional mode itself is representational, that is, whether the pro-attitude itself is representational, from the question whether pleasure's object is or may be representational. It is, then, a further question whether pleasure's object's being representational entails that the pro-attitude of pleasure is representational. Two points may be noted here. One is that it is common to treat sensations as representational. Accordingly, sensory pleasure will be representational, again, at least insofar as its object is. The other is that recent proponents of the conscious-quality theory have ignored the question whether pleasure qua feeling is representational. These are, of course, two distinct questions. Nonetheless, I encourage consideration of their relation, and I underscore the relevance of this question to the important, lively question within current philosophy of mind, namely, whether there are *qualia*, where "*qualia*" is here understood in a narrow sense as *non-representational* conscious qualities.

Finally, I want to close this chapter by encouraging consideration of an intriguing point that Penelhum emphasizes in his 1957 paper, but which has since largely been ignored: pleasure is a passion or condition of passivity in that it cannot be willed. That is, one cannot make oneself take pleasure in something, even if one can to varying extents manipulate conditions conducive to getting pleasure. This property distinguishes pleasure (as well as pain or displeasure) from sense-perception, since one can look, listen, smell, tactilely feel, and taste at will. That is, one can bring heightened focus of one's sense-perceptual faculties on a given sensible object.[183] I do not know what reflection upon this point will yield, but, again, it strikes me as a remarkable point worthy of attention.

---

[183] The passivity of pleasure (as well as pain or displeasure) must also be distinguished from the point, made by several contemporary scholars since Ryle, that, in contrast to one's pain, one cannot focus on one's pleasure without the pleasure terminating or diminishing.

CHAPTER 10

Ancient and contemporary conceptions of pleasure

Having completed a sketch of the history of contemporary treatments of the identity and kinds questions, my aim in this conclusion is to offer some comments on the ancient treatments in light of contemporary treatments.

We have seen that Plato, under the influence of Socrates' "What is *F*?" question, is the original source of the identity question. The identity question arises for Plato within the context of ethical inquiry. The question that provokes him is what the value of pleasure is and what place pleasure has within the good life. In the contemporary period, it is Ryle, at least within the context of philosophical discussion, who resurrects the identity question. For Ryle, the identity question arises within the philosophy of mind. The problem that provokes him is what the right sort of analysis of this mental state is insofar as it is a mental state. The distinct theoretical contexts of Plato's and Ryle's seminal contributions are representative of ancient and contemporary discussions generally.

While there is some treatment of pleasure within the ancient physical tradition, most accounts fall within the sphere of ethics. This is true even though the Greeks, for the most part, view ethics and physical inquiry as continuous.[1] Aristotle's treatments are a striking testimony to this point. Most of Aristotle's surviving writing lies in biology, but his central hedonic theorizing occurs within his ethical treatises. In the case of contemporary treatments, there are certainly scholars whose pursuit of the identity question is intended to serve the interests of ethics. Recall William Alston's statement, cited in Chapter 1, p. 5:

One can make an intelligent judgment on these doctrines [of ethical and psychological hedonism] only to the extent that he has a well-worked-out view as to the nature of pleasure. Otherwise, he will be unable to settle such questions

---

[1] This is true of Plato, Aristotle, Epicurus, and the Stoics. It is not true of the Cyrenaics, who reject physical inquiry.

as whether a putative counterexample, for instance, a desire for the welfare of one's children, is or is not a genuine example of desiring something other than pleasure for its own sake.[2]

Likewise, Stuart Rachels emphasizes the importance of the identity question for ethics: "Why does this issue matter? ... A correct account of [pleasantness] should cast light on why [pleasantness] is [good] ... [Promotivation] and [Like], if true, yield a powerful new argument for the role of desire in ethics."[3] Nonetheless, concerns within the philosophy of mind are the principal drivers of contemporary contributions to the identity question.

What does this distinction between the ancient and contemporary theoretical contexts of the identity question indicate? In the case of antiquity, it indicates the paramount importance of ethics or at least the good for ancient philosophy. In the case of the contemporary period, the theoretical context of the identity question indicates the centrality of the problem of explaining the mind.[4] Recall that Ryle conceives of pleasure as a kind of attention, which in turns belongs to the category of heed. Heed is equivalent to awareness, which I take to be equivalent to consciousness. Since pleasure is clearly a mental state (and since there is no consideration of whether pleasure is an unconscious episode), the question whether pleasure is a disposition or episode amounts to whether pleasure is a state of consciousness. Recent contemporary contributions, having settled in favor of the latter alternative, are concerned with what sort of conscious state pleasure is: intentional, representational, propositional, conative, feeling?

The distinction between the contexts of ancient and contemporary hedonic theorizing also explains one of the key distinctions between ancient and contemporary responses to the identity question: ancient treatments focus rather heavily on the objects of pleasure, certainly as much as or more so than on the hedonic attitude or intentional mode. Epicurus' treatment is a signal example: we derive from the texts, fragments, and testimonies a view of the katastematic conditions of bodily and psychic health and well-being and the kinetic conditions of smooth motion dependent on the former, but we learn nearly nothing about the hedonic attitude of the wise toward these katastematic and kinetic conditions. For a philosopher who claims that pleasure is the beginning

---

[2] "Pleasure," *The Encyclopedia of Philosophy* 6 (1967) 341.
[3] *Philosophical Studies* 99 (2000) 187.
[4] I am not claiming that every contemporary contribution is explicitly so oriented. Some, perhaps most, are only implicitly so oriented. And a few are not so oriented.

and end of the blessed life, this is surely remarkable. Plato is another good example. In my discussion of his treatment in *Republic* 9, I distinguished appearance or phenomenal and core aspects of pleasure. Between these, it is clearly the core aspect, namely, restoration, that Plato views as the distinctive feature of pleasure. For example, at the end of the cathartic taxonomy in *Philebus*, in reviewing the preceding kinds of true and false, pure and impure pleasure, Socrates concludes that pleasure is a coming-to-be (*genesis*) or restorative process. He does not conclude that it is a perception (of coming-to-be) or some other attitude toward that restoration. Aristotle's case, at least in *Eudemian Ethics* 6, slightly differs since there he identifies pleasure and activation. But even there, and despite himself, what Aristotle is doing is focusing on what we would call the objects of pleasure, that is, activities (or activations), rather than on the hedonic attitude taken toward them. Similarly, in *Nicomachean Ethics* 10, although he emphasizes that pleasure completes rather than is an activation, Aristotle more clearly distinguishes the objects of pleasure than the attitude itself.

Why do the Greeks' explanations or analyses of pleasure focus on hedonic objects? One possibility derives from consideration of the physical tradition. In this context, the sort of object in question is not necessarily an intentional object. Rather, the object's relation to the phenomenal aspect may be causal or materially constitutive. Granted this, within the physical tradition, the appearance of things (*phainomenon*) is taken as a starting point for explanation and is to be explained in physical terms. Thus, the hedonic appearance (or attitude) is explained in terms of physical causes, correlates, or constituents. Plato's whole philosophical agenda is in some respects continuous with this program – despite the fact that for Plato getting beyond appearances further requires getting beyond physical explanations. But both cases evince a common tendency, which might be explained as follows. Appearances are available and obvious to all. That is, everyone experiences pleasure and intuitively and non-inferentially grasps what pleasure is. Hence there can be no *sophia* (specialized knowledge or wisdom) about appearances as such. The philosopher's task is to explain appearances by grasping what is not apparent; and what is non-apparent, in this case, are the physical entities reference to which explains the appearance. In the case of Plato specifically, this is the core aspect.

This view, that it is the physical constituents, correlates, and causes that are the non-apparent *explanantia*, is, however, theoretically limited. As Aristotle in particular emphasizes, entities can be explained formally and teleologically as well as materially and causally. Indeed, teleological explanation consistently enters into the Greeks' accounts of pleasure: for Plato, pleasure is a restoration and so a return *to the natural state*; for Aristotle, pleasure is an *unimpeded* activation of the *natural* psychic disposition or a *completion* of such an activation; for the Stoics, pleasure is an impulse following or paralleling an *unjustified* assent to *the presence of the good* and *the propriety of psycho-physical swelling* in view of that presence. Each of the italicized expressions has normative content. Additionally, each expression has formal content: pleasure is a restoration that is perceived, a psychic activation or the completion of a psychic activation, a certain sort of passion. These formal and teleological explanations variously relate to hedonic attitudes as well as to hedonic objects. The Greeks' emphasis on hedonic objects, therefore, clearly cannot be wholly explained in terms of narrow interest in physical explanation.

For a more satisfactory explanation of the Greeks' focus on hedonic objects, we must advert to their ethical interests. Hedonic objects have varying values; the hedonic attitudes taken in them derive their values accordingly. Compare Plato's rational, true, and pure pleasures; Aristotle's most pure pleasures of contemplation; and Epicurus' katastematic pleasures. Moreover, the Stoics are only partially exceptional here. They stipulate that pleasure's object is either not good or that it is good but not justifiably so judged; still, they recognize joy (*chara*) as a hedonic attitude directed toward a good object with rational justification.

In addition, I suggest that the Greeks' dominant ethical concerns to a large extent explain their responses to the kinds question. Precisely, kinds of pleasure tend to be distinguished according to their value. This is certainly true for a number of figures discussed within the pre-Platonic ethical tradition in Chapter 2. Recall Prodicus' refined and base pleasures, Xenophon's interpretation of Prodicus' hedonic distinctions as civically oriented and depraved, Democritus' measured and unmeasured pleasures, and Antisthenes' wise and foolish pleasures. Consider also Plato's tripartition of pleasures in *Republic* 9. This tripartition of course follows Plato's tripartition of the soul, and as such it depends upon his psychological theory. But Plato's psychological theory correlates with an ethical agenda: the rational part of the soul must govern; rational pleasures are truer and more pleasant than those of the other parts of the soul. Again, Aristotle's organization of kinds largely corresponds to a psychological hierarchy, but one that is likewise ethically laden.

Contrast this with contemporary responses to the kinds question. Among scholars who think that enjoyment, being-pleased-that (or propositional pleasure), and sensory pleasure are distinct hedonic kinds, none claims that one of these kinds has more or less value than another.[5] Indeed, as we have seen, there has been little headway in understanding the relation between hedonic kinds, let alone articulating a broad theoretical framework of any sort for distinguishing hedonic kinds.[6]

When the Greeks do focus on pleasure qua hedonic attitude, or on what in the case of Plato I call the appearance aspect, their concerns are variously epistemological and ethical. Plato's concern is, ostensibly, principally epistemological. He takes the hedonic attitude to be representational. Thus, he is interested in the appearance aspect representing or rather misrepresenting the core aspect. Why does Plato construe hedonic appearance as representational? One answer is that he takes cognition to be the distinctive function of the soul. This is consistent, for instance, with his treatment of pleasure and pain among forms of sense-perception in *Timaeus*. But this answer is inadequate since Plato takes motivation to be as salient a function of the soul as cognition. Examination and explanation of desire, in its various forms, is fundamental to Plato's philosophical project. The question might then be recast as follows: Why does Plato not take pleasure to be a form of motivation, but instead *an object* of desire? I do not have an answer to this question, except to say that, on the view of pleasure I favor, Plato errs here.

The Stoics are exceptional in the extraordinary degree of attention they pay to the hedonic attitude of pleasure. Their interests are also epistemological, but more precisely, epistemological-cum-ethical, since they view passions as practical judgments or assents. I incline to say the same for Epicurus, with the caveat that it is difficult to say very much about Epicurus' view of the hedonic attitude of pleasure. However, we have seen that Epicurus emphasizes the importance of wisdom for living well and specifically for taking pleasure in the right sorts of thing. For adult humans, at least, taking pleasure *ought* to depend upon wise judgment about the value of hedonic objects. That said, we do not know whether Epicurus conceives of the hedonic attitude (in adult humans) simply cognitively, as a judgment, or non-cognitively.

For Aristotle, attention to the hedonic attitude of pleasure is largely driven by ethical concerns. Beyond his emphasis on pleasure's being an

---

[5] Contrast J. S. Mill's distinction between higher and lower pleasures, which conforms to his ethical interest in pleasure.

[6] If there is some such framework to be found, I suspect it lies in an evolutionary psychological direction. For example, in contrast to enjoyment and sensory pleasure, propositional pleasure requires particular neocortical functions.

activation or the completion of an activation, rather than a restoration or process, Aristotle has very little directly to say about the hedonic attitude. What can be derived from his discussion of the hedonic attitude's kinship or congeniality (*oikeiotês*) with its object suggests that Aristotle's interest lies in the cultivation of the attitude and its correlative disposition, by habituation or learning, in conjunction with its object. At least, this is true for ethical and intellectual pleasures. Sense-perceptual pleasures have their proper or congenial objects fixed by the natural constitution of the animal. But granted that the hedonic attitude of ethical and intellectual pleasures requires the cultivation of ethical and intellectual capacities and dispositions, it remains unclear in these cases just what sort of attitude the hedonic attitude is.

In considering the persistent contemporary concern over whether pleasure is or involves feeling, it is a startling fact that ancient philosophical treatments of the identity question consistently ignore the idea of pleasure as a feeling. Although, under the influence of the concept *sphodrotês* (intensity) in particular, I include feeling among the elements of the appearance aspect in Plato's discussion in *Republic* 9, it must be emphasized that there simply is no Greek word for feeling, in contrast to awareness or perception.[7] Since I myself am not compelled by a conscious- or felt-quality theory of pleasure, I do not regard the Greeks' silence here as a confusion. Still, from Plato on, there is a tendency to view pleasure and pain as contraries, and pain does entail feeling.[8] Accordingly,

---

[7] It has been suggested that in Epicurus "*pathos*" is first used to mean "feeling." But I am skeptical of this claim, given my understanding of "feeling." I can accept that "*pathos*" is used to mean "affective condition," where "affective condition" is simply the genus of which pleasure and pain or pleasure and displeasure are species. But what pleasure and displeasure or pain share in virtue of which they constitute primary species of a common genus is questionable. Moreover, there are certainly feelings that are not, per se, hedonic or algesic; for example, tactile feelings, general bodily feelings such as feeling vertiginous or buoyant; and mental or cognitive feelings such as the feelings of familiarity, certainty, awe, and sublimity.

[8] There is a noteworthy exception here. The most important Peripatetic philosopher after Theophrastus was Alexander of Aphrodisias (*floruit* third century CE). Several of Alexander's commentaries on Aristotle's works survive as well as several original works. One of the works that has come down to us under his name is referred to as the *Ethical Problems*. This work divides into thirty relatively brief sections, each of which discusses some ethical problem. For example, section 2 concerns the claim that pleasures are not the same in kind, and section 13 concerns the claim, from *Nicomachean Ethics* 10.5, that pleasure is congenial (*oikeia*) to the activation that it completes. As these examples indicate, some of the discussions amount to commentary on certain Aristotelian positions. However, this is not exclusively so. In section six, Alexander articulates a position that, so far as I know, is first advanced here: it is distress (*lypê*) and not pain (*ponos*) that is the opposite of pleasure (*hêdonê*). Although I have not made much of the point, it has been an implicit assumption of almost all hedonic theorizing from Plato to the Old Stoics that pleasure and pain are opposites. Thus, Alexander's criticism of this point is or at least appears to be highly original. He argues as

we could just as well be wondering why the Greeks do not conceive of pain as a feeling. Related to this question, we might also ask why the conscious-quality theory of pleasure is a contender on the contemporary field. I do not have an answer to the ancient or the contemporary question. What is clear, I think, is that the concept of feeling and its history should be subject to serious inquiry.

Returning now to ancient and contemporary treatments of the kinds question, I would like to comment on the extent to which the contemporary distinctions between enjoyment, propositional pleasure, and sensory pleasure are applicable to the various ancient conceptions.

In his various treatments of pleasure, Plato arguably variously refers to sensory pleasures, enjoyment, and being-pleased-that. For example, sense-perceptual pleasures in *Timaeus* are, if anything is, equivalent to sensory pleasures. The same may be said for pure olfactory, visual, and auditory pleasures in *Philebus*. But in the cases of appetitive pleasures in *Republic* 9 and sequentially mixed bodily pleasures in *Philebus* it is difficult to distinguish sensory pleasures from enjoyment, for one can enjoy eating, drinking, and indeed sense-perceiving generally. In the case of spirited and rational pleasures in *Republic* 9, I take it that enjoyment and propositional pleasure are conflated. For example, one can enjoy political victories and power as well as intellectual pursuits; but one can also be pleased upon learning particular facts or alleged facts such as the spirited fact that one is honored by one's peers or the intellectual fact that the area of a square *S* whose side is equal to the hypotenuse of a square *T* is double the area of *T*. The same point applies to the mixed psychic pleasure involving diminishing-desire in *Philebus* – although the pleasure one takes in attending a comic drama presumably consists more of enjoyment than propositional pleasure.

In the context of Plato's treatments, perhaps the most interesting comparison case is that of false anticipatory pleasure in *Philebus*. We appear to have here a case of propositional pleasure or at least something like it, say, pleasure requiring the capacity for lexical conceptualization:[9] the content or object of the pleasure derives from that of a belief, which is or at least is typically taken to be propositional. Yet, the content of the

---

follows. Pain (*ponos*) is an affliction of the body. Distress (*lypē*) is a contraction of the soul. Accordingly: "If all pleasure consisted in bodily relaxation, pain would be opposite to it; but since pleasure is a certain relaxation of the soul which does not occur through the body or in respect of the body alone, it will not be pain that is the opposite to this sort of pleasure, but distress." Note also the influence here of the Stoics' notions of psychic swelling and contraction.

[9] For the qualification, see n. 16 of Chapter 5.

hedonic object is explicitly characterized as pictorial. Consequently, it appears that one is taking pleasure in imagining a scenario in which one is indulging oneself using the fortune one has gained. But taking pleasure in imagining something is a form of enjoyment whose objects are activities or experiences, not a form of propositional pleasure. Thus, if the hedonic attitude is to have truth-value, it must immediately derive from the hedonic object of the activity of imagining. In that case, a defense of Plato requires a defense of the truth-aptness of enjoyment, not propositional pleasure.

In discussing Plato's treatment of false anticipatory pleasure in relation to contemporary distinctions among hedonic kinds, it should also be emphasized that engagement with Plato has inspired the contemporary discussion. As we saw, Irving Thalberg, who in 1962 first explicitly identifies propositional pleasure and defends the view that propositional pleasure can be false, does so by engagement with Plato's *Philebus*. Similarly, in their discussions of the relation between pleasure and falsity, Bernard Williams and Terence Penelhum cite or discuss *Philebus*. More generally, the contemporary interest in pleasure that Ryle sparked in turn influenced scrutiny of certain ancient treatments, in particular those of Plato and Aristotle. One reason for this is that certain contemporary philosophers, particularly those trained in the United Kingdom, had substantial Classical training. This is true of Gilbert Ryle, Bernard Williams, Justin Gosling, Christopher Taylor, and Anthony Kenny.

Turning now to Aristotle, most commentators have taken Aristotle to be discussing enjoyment. Indeed, early discussions of enjoyment such as Ryle's explicitly advert to Aristotle's treatment and, occasionally, employ Aristotelian arguments.[10] In the face of passages such as the following, it is hard to deny that Aristotle is discussing enjoyment: "For the activation's congenial pleasure contributes to increasing the activation ... For example, those who take pleasure in geometry are the ones that become expert in it ... and similarly the lover of music and building."[11] This holds even while propositional pleasures to varying degrees figure within and

---

[10] For example, one of Ryle's arguments that pleasure is not a sensation is that sensations are clockable, whereas pleasure is not. The argument is dubious. But Ryle approvingly cites a related claim by Aristotle that one cannot take pleasure quickly or slowly. (Contemporary treatments of pleasure have been less influenced by engagement with Epicurus and the Stoics. The main reason for this is that the study of Hellenistic philosophy by scholars of ancient philosophy has itself enjoyed a renaissance only in the last thirty or so years. Epicurus does, however, play an important role in Fred Feldman's recent work, in particular in his book *Pleasure and the Good Life*, Oxford University Press, 2004.)

[11] *Nicomachean Ethics* 1175a.

contribute to what is enjoyed. Likewise, in the case of sense-perceptual pleasures, which, as we have seen, Aristotle also discusses, arguably there is also some conflation of enjoyment and sensory pleasure.

Epicurus is, once again, a difficult case. The role that wisdom plays in the genuine pleasure of the sage suggests that Epicurus is there referring to being-pleased-that. But since animals and infants take pleasure, Epicurus cannot be referring to being-pleased-that generally. Recall Alexander of Aphrodisias' comment on the Epicureans: "The Epicureans maintain that what is first congenial to us, unqualifiedly, is pleasure, but they say that as we get older this pleasure becomes more fully articulated."

As I suggested in Chapter 8, the Stoics' conception of pleasure is a conception of being-pleased-that. Indeed, the Stoics' conception is quite close to the account that David Barton Perry develops in his 1967 book *The Concept of Pleasure*. Both the Stoics and Perry hold that pleasure or being-pleased-that requires the belief that *p* is good. I called this the evaluative belief or judgment. In addition, the Stoics hold that a practical judgment is necessary, namely, that one ought to be elated that *p*. The Stoics' practical judgment and Perry's pro-attitude perhaps stand in some analogous relation. But the Stoics view their practical judgment as stimulative of action, albeit in this case a psychological act of pneumatic swelling, whereas Perry makes no such claim about the pro-attitude.

Another point of contact between the Stoics and Perry concerns the Stoic view that pleasure requires a *fresh* belief. In his analysis of being-pleased-that-*p*, Perry maintains that the subject of being-pleased-that-*p* must *recently* have come to believe (or know) that *p*: "The pleasure of one who is pleased about a thing is a non-conative, positively evaluative pro-attitude toward something which is *a matter of recent knowledge or belief*."[12] Perry suggests that it would be very odd for someone living now to come to be pleased that, for instance, Napoleon was defeated at Waterloo or that Caesar crossed the Rubicon.[13] In contrast, for the Stoics freshness does not require the recentness of the fact or alleged fact that pleases one. As we saw in Cicero's discussion of the freshness condition and in his example of Artemisia, the long-grieving wife of Mausolus, the subject need not have recently come to the belief that *p* and that *p* has a certain value. Rather, the subject must believe that *p* is or continues to be worthy of a certain reaction, regardless of when *p* occurred. In this respect, I think the Stoics' position is superior to Perry's.

---

[12] (1967) 216. Cf. p. 146.
[13] In any case, psychological oddness is one thing, logical or conceptual impossibility is another.

In concluding this historical study of philosophical conceptions of pleasure, I also want to emphasize the historicality of the conceptions of pleasure we have been examining. This is rather easy to see in the case of the ancients. Certainly, it is easy to see locally. For example, Plato's restorative theory derives from the Pythagoreans or from Greek medical theory. Aristotle's activation theory develops in criticism of Plato's restorative theory. And Epicurus' conception of pleasure seems influenced by Aristotle, especially if the word "*energeia*" in the fragment from *On Choice and Avoidance* has been correctly transmitted. More generally, although less conspicuously – as I have suggested – the dominant ethical orientation of ancient philosophy informs the way the ancients answer the identity and kinds questions.

As is commonly noted, it is more difficult to observe the historicality of one's own times. However, insofar as they do occur in time, contemporary contributions are obviously explicable historically as well. The early period debate between episodic and dispositional conceptions of pleasure well conforms to the behavioristic milieu in which the participants were writing and thinking. Discussions in the recent contemporary period evince current preoccupations with the intentionality and representationality of mental states. For example, in rejecting a representational account of pleasure as liking, William S. Robinson writes: "In this age of the hegemony of representation, it would not be surprising if pleasure too were held to be a representation; and, indeed, Timothy Schroeder . . . has held that it is."[14]

In emphasizing the historicality of philosophical conceptions of pleasure, however, I do not intend the facile point that all of the conceptions on offer are merely historical. I assume that some are true or closer to the truth than others. So, although one task of the historian of philosophy is to review the past in order to clarify the historicality of its ideas, this is not all there is to past ideas – and in fact this is not all there is to the task of the history of philosophy. History of philosophy can provide historical perspective on the present as well as the past, but it can also provide conceptual perspective on the present by offering an array of theoretical options within a broader field of conceptual or logical possibility. In doing so history of philosophy can also serve to disabuse those in the present from too narrow a focus on their subjects. As we have seen, this does not require reaching all the way back to antiquity. The memory of the living can be very short, or their research can be very spotty. For

---

[14] *Philosophical Psychology* 19 (2006) 756.

example, we have seen that the distinction between enjoyment and being-pleased-that has to a large extent been forgotten or obscured. And we have seen that the recent focus on sensory pleasure occurs without justification.

Some of these comments exemplify general ideas about the study of the history of philosophy. But there is, it must also be emphasized, a special significance to the study of hedonic theorizing in antiquity, namely, the importance of this topic for the ancients. I am unaware of any period in the history of philosophy in which pleasure has been so central to philosophers' concerns. A historical-philosophical investigation of pleasure in Greco-Roman antiquity is, therefore, especially apt.

Finally, returning to the distinction between the broad contexts of ancient and contemporary hedonic theorizing – it is worth noting that the relation between their dominant concerns, over pleasure and the good, on the one hand, and over pleasure and mind or pleasure and consciousness, on the other, is a contingent one: pleasure is a conscious occurrent, be it a feeling or pro-attitude or both, that also happens to be fundamental to human motivation. Hence the distinct foci of the ancients and contemporaries are theoretically justified. However, it is precisely this dual aspect of pleasure, its location at a deep nexus of ethics and philosophy of mind, that makes the identity question and its kin such compelling ones.

Suggestions for further reading

I'll begin here by referring the reader to primary texts pertaining to the ancient figures and schools. For Prodicus (and the other so-called sophists), John Dillon and Tania Gergel, *The Greek Sophists*, Penguin, 2003, is highly recommended. Note that Robert Mayhew, *Prodicus the Sophist*, Oxford University Press, 2011, is a recent edition of the fragments and testimonies, translated and with commentary, but one that appeared too late for me to consult. For Democritus, I suggest C. C. W. Taylor, *The Atomists: Leucippus and Democritus*, University of Toronto Press, 1999; and Jonathan Barnes, *Early Greek Philosophy*, revised edition, Penguin, 2002, which provides the fragments with bits of commentary and testimonies. The fragments and testimonies of Antisthenes and Aristippus are not available in translation. For other so-called Presocratics, including Empedocles and Diogenes of Apollonia, I recommend, in addition to Barnes (2002), G. S. Kirk, J. E. Raven, and M. Schofield, *The Presocratic Philosophers*, 2nd edn., Cambridge University Press, 1984. For Theophrastus' *On Perceptions*, see George Malcolm Stratton, *Theophrastus and the Greek Physiological Psychology before Aristotle*, George Allen & Unwin, 1917. For the Hippocratic *On Generation* and *Diseases IV*, Iain M. Lonie, *The Hippocratic Treatises "On Generation," "On the Nature of the Child," "Diseases IV,"* De Gruyter, 1981, is excellent. Plato's works are readily available in many places. *Plato: The Complete Works*, John Cooper, ed., Hackett, 1997, is recommended. This includes what is probably the most widely read translation of *Republic* (by G. M. A. Grube, revised by C. D. C. Reeve) and *Philebus* (by Dorothea Frede). Frede's translation is also available separately from Hackett, 1993. This contains a very good introduction. F. M. Cornford, *Plato's Cosmology*, Hackett, 1997 (originally published by Routledge in 1935) is still the best primary text on *Timaeus*. It contains elaborate and extremely helpful commentary. For Aristotle's complete works, see *The Complete Works of Aristotle*, Jonathan Barnes, ed., Princeton University Press, 1984, 2 vols. A very good translation and commentary on *Nicomachean Ethics* is Sarah Broadie and Christopher Rowe, *Aristotle: Nicomachean Ethics*, Oxford University Press, 2002. For Epicurus and the Stoics, I recommend A. A. Long and D. N. Sedley, *The Hellenistic Philosophers*,

Cambridge University Press, vol. 1, 1987. In addition, for Epicurus I recommend Brad Inwood, L. P. Gerson, and D. S. Hutchinson, *The Epicurus Reader*, Hackett, 1994. Cyril Bailey, *Epicurus: The Extant Remains*, Clarendon Press, 1926, also contains most of Epicurus' fragments in translation, with elaborate commentary, including a seminal appendix on Epicurus' conception of attention. For the Stoics, see Brad Inwood and L. P. Gerson, *The Stoics Reader*, Hackett, 2008. There is a translation of Arius Didymus' *Epitome of Stoic Ethics* by Arthur J. Pomeroy, Society of Biblical Literature, 1999. A good translation of Cicero's *On Goals* is Raphael Woolf, *Cicero: On Moral Ends*, Cambridge University Press, 2008. A good translation of Lucretius' *On the Nature of Things* is Martin Ferguson Smith, *Lucretius: On the Nature of Things*, Hackett, 2001. There is no translation of the Cyrenaics' fragments and testimonies. The reader should consult R. D. Hicks, *Diogenes Laertius: Lives and Opinions of Eminent Philosophers*, Harvard University Press, 1925, vol. 1, Book 2. There is no comprehensive or even partial work on contemporary philosophical conceptions of pleasure. I do not recommend the *Stanford Encyclopedia of Philosophy* article on the subject. Those interested in psychological accounts prior to Gilbert Ryle should consult J. G. Beebe-Center, *The Psychology of Pleasantness and Unpleasantness*, Van Nostrand, 1932; K. Dunker, "On Pleasure, Emotion, and Striving," *Philosophy and Phenomenological Research* 1 (1941) 391–430; Magda Arnold, *Emotion and Personality*, Columbia University, 1960, vol. 1, Chapters 1–3. For recent neuroscientific accounts, I recommend *Pleasures of the Brain*, Morten L. Kringelbach and Kent C. Berridge, eds., Oxford University Press, 2010.

INTRODUCTION

Those interested in learning more about the nature of our evidence for ancient philosophy should read Jaap Mansfeld's article "Doxography in Ancient Philosophy," available through the *Stanford Encyclopedia of Philosophy*, at: plato.stanford.edu/entries/doxography-ancient. If, following that, more is desired, I recommend Jaap Mansfeld and D. T. Runia's *Aëtiana: The Method and Intellectual Context of a Doxographer*, Brill, 1997–2008, 3 vols.

Those interested in alternative treatments of pleasure throughout the history of ancient philosophy have two options: J. C. B. Gosling and C. C. W. Taylor, *The Greeks on Pleasure*, Clarendon Press, 1982 and Gerd Van Riel, *Pleasure and the Good Life*, Brill, 2000. Gosling and Taylor's book is ground-breaking. It runs from the pre-Platonic tradition through Epicurus. It is not an easy book to read. Van Riel's book focuses on the influence of Plato and Aristotle on the Neoplatonists Plotinus, Proclus, and Damascius. However, it also has some discussion of Epicurus and the Stoics. This book is a good deal more accessible.

PLEASURE IN EARLY GREEK ETHICS

There is very little available here. My views on Prodicus are original and are based on my article "Prodicus on the Correctness of Names: The Case of *Terpsis, Chara,* and *Euphrosynê*," *Journal of Hellenic Studies* 131 (2011) 131–145. Gosling and Taylor have some discussion of Democritus ([1982] 27–37). There are several pieces available on Democritus' ethics and psychology, for instance: Charles Kahn, "Democritus and the Origins of Moral Psychology," *American Journal of Philology* 106 (1985) 1–31; Michael Nill, *Morality and Self-Interest in Protagoras, Antiphon, and Democritus*, Brill, 1985; John Procopé, "Democritus on Politics and the Care of the Soul," *Classical Quarterly* 39 (1989) 307–331; Julia Annas, "Democritus and Eudaimonism," in *Presocratic Philosophy*, V. Caston and D. Graham, eds., Ashgate Press, 2002, 169–181. The reader might also be interested in a debate concerning the relation between Democritus' ethics and physics: Gregory Vlastos, "Ethics and Physics in Democritus," *Philosophical Review* 54 and 55 (1945, 1946) 578–592, 53–64; C. C. W. Taylor, "Pleasure, Knowledge, and Sensation in Democritus," *Phronesis* 12 (1967) 6–27. On Antisthenes, there is next to no secondary literature on his ethics, let alone his views of pleasure. But see Fernanda Decleva Caizzi, "Minor Socratics," in *A Companion to Ancient Philosophy*, M. L. Gill and P. Pellegrin, eds., Blackwell, 2006, 119–135. On Aristippus, see the preceding and, again, Gosling and Taylor (1982, 40–43). My discussion of Aristippus in relation to Hesiod and Prodicus is original and based on my article "Hesiod, Prodicus, and the Socratics on Work and Pleasure," *Oxford Studies in Ancient Philosophy* 35 (2008) 1–18.

PLEASURE IN THE EARLY PHYSICAL TRADITION

Gosling and Taylor have a little bit to say on this subject ([1982] 16–25). Otherwise, I know of nothing. I would recommend that the reader turn to Stratton's translation of Theophrastus' *On Perceptions* and then to the primary texts on the so-called Presocratics.

PLATO ON PLEASURE AND RESTORATION

Another overview of Plato's conception of pleasure as restoration can be found in Dorothea Frede, "Disintegration and Restoration: Pleasure and Pain in Plato's *Philebus*," in *Cambridge Companion to Plato*, R. Kraut, ed., Cambridge University Press, 1992, 425–463. For an account of Plato's physical theory in *Timaeus*, I recommend Thomas Kjeller Johansen, *Plato's Natural Philosophy*, Cambridge University Press, 2004.

PLATO ON TRUE, UNTRUE, AND FALSE PLEASURES

Aside from numerous articles on false anticipatory pleasure in *Philebus*, little has been written on this subject. Not much of value has been written on pleasure in *Republic* 9. But see Jessica Moss, "Pleasure and Illusion in Plato," *Philosophy and*

Phenomenological Research 72 (2006) 503–35 and most recently James Warren, "Socrates and the Patients: *Republic* 583a–585b," *Phronesis* 56 (2010) 113–157. My own thoughts on the subject are more fully developed in "Pleasure and Truth in *Republic* 9," *Classical Quarterly* (2013) forthcoming. The most comprehensive accounts on *Philebus* are not in English: Dorothea Frede, *Platon: Philebos*, Göttingen, 1997; Antoine de La Taille, *Platon: Philèbe* (31b–44a), Paris, 1999; Sylvain Delcomminette, *Le Philèbe de Platon*, Brill, 2006. But see Sylvain Delcomminette, "False Pleasures, Appearance and Imagination in the *Philebus*," *Phronesis* 48 (2003) 215–237, and Matthew Evans, "Plato on the Possibility of Hedonic Mistakes," *Oxford Studies in Ancient Philosophy* 35 (2008) 89–124, for bibliography as well as for themselves. My distinctions between ontological and representational truth-conceptions and of gradable and absolute ontological truth-conceptions were aided by Jan Szaif, *Platons Begriff der Wahrheit*, Alber, 1998, and are discussed in my *Classical Quarterly* (2013) piece.

ARISTOTLE ON PLEASURE AND ACTIVATION

Another introductory piece is Dorothea Frede, "Pleasure and Pain in Aristotle's Ethics," in *The Blackwell Guide to Aristotle's Nicomachean Ethics*, R. Kraut, ed., 2006, 255–275. A more incisive, albeit more difficult, piece is Chapter 6 "Pleasure" of Sarah Broadie, *Ethics with Aristotle*, Oxford University Press, 1993, 313–365. Some important articles include: J. Urmson, "Aristotle on Pleasure," in *Aristotle: A Collection of Critical Essays*, J. Moravcsik, ed., Anchor Books, 1967, 323–333; G. E. L. Owen, "Aristotelian Pleasures," *Proceedings of the Aristotelian Society* 72 (1971) 135–152; Amelie Oksenberg Rorty, "The Place of Pleasure in Aristotle's Ethics," *Mind* 83 (1974) 481–497; David Bostock, "Pleasure and Activity in Aristotle's Ethics," *Phronesis* 33 (1998) 251–272; Francisco J. Gonzalez, "Aristotle on Pleasure and Perfection," *Phronesis* 36 (1991) 141–159; Gerd Van Riel, "Aristotle's Definition of Pleasure: A Refutation of the Platonic Account," *Ancient Philosophy* 20 (2000) 119–138; David Bostock, "Pleasure," in *Aristotle's Ethics*, Oxford University Press, 2000, 143–166. My account of Aristotle's conception of *energeia* is influenced by Jonathan Beere, *Doing and Being*, Oxford University Press, 2009; but this is difficult reading. Another recent, more accessible, account of Aristotle's conception of *energeia* is Christopher Shields, "An Approach to Aristotelian Actuality," in *Mind, Method, Morality*, J. Cottingham and P. Hacker, eds., Oxford University Press, 2010, 68–93. For an excellent overview of Aristotle's psychology, see Victor Caston, "Aristotle's Psychology," in *A Companion to Ancient Philosophy*, M. L. Gill and P. Pellegrin, eds., Blackwell, 2006, 316–346; and Christopher Shield's article on Aristotle's psychology in the *Stanford Encyclopedia of Philosophy*, available at: plato.stanford.edu/entries/aristotle-psychology. There is a recent edition of Aristotle's *Protrepticus* in German: Gerhart Schneeweiß, *Aristoteles: Protreptikos Hinführung zur Philosophie*, Wissenschaftliche Buchgesellschaft, 2005. Readers interested in this work should also be aware of D. S. Hutchinson and Monte Ransome Johnson, "Authenticating Aristotle's *Protrepticus*," *Oxford Studies in Ancient Philosophy* 29 (2005) 193–294.

EPICURUS AND THE CYRENAICS ON KATASTEMATIC AND KINETIC PLEASURES

An introductory piece that argues for a different view of Epicurus' conception of pleasure is Raphael Woolf, "Pleasure and Desire," in *Cambridge Companion to Epicureanism*, J. Warren, ed., 2009, 158–178. An earlier discussion of the relation between Aristotle's and Epicurus' conceptions of pleasure can be found in Philip Merlan, "*Hêdonê* in Epicurus and Aristotle," in *Studies in Epicurus and Aristotle*, Harrassowitz, 1960, 1–37. An important article on Epicurus' conception of pleasure, whose conclusions are closer to mine, is Jeffrey Purinton, "Epicurus on the Telos," *Phronesis* 38 (1993) 281–320. A recent discussion of Torquatus' argument and Cicero's treatment of Epicurus' conception of pleasure – albeit one that reaches different conclusions from mine – is James Warren, "Epicurean Pleasure in Cicero's *De Finibus*," *Symposium Hellenisticum*, forthcoming. Although I have altered some of my views, my discussion of Epicurus' conception of kinetic and katastematic pleasure is influenced by my article "Epicurus on *Euphrosynê* and *Energeia*," *Apeiron* 42 (2009) 221–257. On pages 240–253 of this article, I review the contributions of a number of my predecessors. David Konstan's revised book *A Life Worthy of the Gods: The Materialist Psychology of Epicurus*, Parmenides, 2008, is a helpful recent discussion of Epicurus' psychology, with comprehensive bibliography. Also highly recommended is Elizabeth Asmis's forthcoming chapter "Epicurean Psychology" in the *Oxford Handbook of Epicureanism*. James Warren, *Epicurus and Democritean Ethics*, Cambridge University Press, 2002, traces the concept of freedom from disturbance (*ataraxia*) from Democritus to Epicurus. There is little on the Cyrenaics' conception of pleasure, but see Tim O'Keefe, "The Cyrenaics on Pleasure, Happiness, and Future-Concern," *Phronesis* 47 (2002) 395–416. Voula Tsouna, *The Epistemology of the Cyrenaic School*, Cambridge University Press, 1998, mainly focuses on Cyrenaic epistemology, but contains discussion of the Cyrenaics' conception of pleasure, pain, and the intermediate condition as well. Tim O'Keefe also has an accessible overview article on the Cyrenaics online in the *Internet Encyclopedia of Philosophy*, available at: iep.utm.edu/cyren.

THE OLD STOICS ON PLEASURE AS PASSION

The seminal work on the Stoic conception of the passions is Brad Inwood, *Ethics and Human Action in Early Stoicism*, Oxford University Press, 1985. More recent and accessible discussions can be found in Tad Brennan, "The Old Stoic Theory of Emotions," in *Emotions in Hellenistic Philosophy*, J. Sihvola and T. Engberg-Pedersen, eds., Springer, 1998, 21–70; and Tad Brennan, "Stoic Moral Psychology," in *Cambridge Companion to the Stoics*, Brad Inwood, ed., Cambridge University Press, 2003, 257–294. Brennan's *The Stoic Life*, Oxford University Press, 2007, is also recommended as a very accessible overview of Stoic philosophy. A more demanding treatment of Chrysippus' work *On Passions* (here translated as *On Affections*) is Teun Tieleman, *Chrysippus' On Affections*, Brill,

2003. Finally, although I avoided the topic in my chapter, the seminal discussion of the Stoics' conception of causation, agency, and determinism is Suzanne Bobzien, *Determinism and Freedom in Stoic Philosophy*, Oxford University Press, 1999. This is a difficult, but rewarding, book.

SUGGESTIONS FOR READING ON ANCIENT POST-OLD-STOIC CONCEPTIONS OF PLEASURE

On April 7, 529 CE, the Roman emperor Justinian (483–565) issued the *Codex Justinianus*, a compilation of imperial decrees from the preceding three centuries. One of the decrees, which was formulated under Justinian's own authority, aimed at eliminating the teaching of non-orthodox Christian doctrine. But the restriction was intended to apply beyond so-called heretical Christian sects and to include non-Christian doctrines such as those of the Jews and pagan philosophers. The decree thus required, among other things, the closure of the ancient philosophical schools in Athens. Justinian's closure of the pagan schools is usually treated as the terminal point in the history of ancient Greek or Greco-Roman philosophy. Naturally, such a thing as (pagan) Greek philosophy cannot have an abrupt end. But the date of Justinian's decree is convenient for demarcating the vague boundary between periods in which pagan and subsequently Christian philosophy and theology prevailed. Between the death of Chrysippus (207 BCE) and Justinian's decree, Greek and Roman philosophers continued to examine and debate the nature of pleasure. In other words, over the next 700 odd years hedonic theorizing continued amid broader philosophical investigations. In this book I have not attempted an overview of the discussions that fall within this long period. There are several reasons for this. One is that our evidence of many treatments of pleasure in this period is extremely sketchy. I say this, disregarding those treatments we have discussed already, which cast light on the earlier conceptions, for example, Cicero's discussion and criticism of Epicurus' conception of pleasure. Second, very little research has been done on conceptions of pleasure during these centuries. This book is certainly not the place to break such ground. Consequently, it would not have been possible to offer a summary or outlines of views from the period on the basis of any foundational work. Finally, as noted in the Introduction, my aim in composing the book was not ineluctably historical, but historical-cum-philosophical.

For those interested in later ancient treatments of pleasure, there are several places to begin poking around. Those interested in the later Platonic tradition, known as the Neoplatonic tradition, should turn to Van Riel (2000), which will direct the reader to passages in Plotinus, Proclus, and Damascius. Damascius' lectures on Plato's *Philebus* deserve special mention, as it is the only surviving ancient commentary on this dialogue. An edition with translation can be found here: L. G. Westerink, *Damascius: Lectures on the Philebus*, North-Holland Publishing Company, 1959. The seminal work on Plotinus' psychology is H. J. Blumenthal, *Plotinus' Psychology*, Martinus Nijhoff, 1971. See also Blumenthal's article "On Soul and Intellect" in *Cambridge Companion to Plotinus*, L. Gerson, ed., 1996, 82–104; and Eyjolfur Emilsson, *Plotinus on Sense-Perception*, Cambridge University Press, 1988. Those interested in the later Peripatetic tradition should consult R. W. Sharples, trans. and ed., *Alexander of Aphrodisias Ethical Problems*, Duckworth, 1990; *Aspasius: On Aristotle Nicomachean Ethics 1–4, 7–8*, David Konstan, trans. and ed., Duckworth, 2007; Antonia Alberti and R. W. Sharples, *Aspasius: The Earliest Extant Commentary on Aristotle's Ethics*, De Gruyter, 1999. Additionally, those interested in the commentary tradition of Late Antiquity in general should read Andrea Falcon's article "Commentators on Aristotle" in the *Stanford Encyclopedia of Philosophy*. Those interested in later Stoic treatments should consult the following three works: John Cooper, "Posidonius on Emotions," in J. Sihvola and T. Engberg-Pedersen, eds. (1998) 71–111; Richard Sorabji, "Chrysippus–Posidonius–Seneca: A High-Level Debate on Emotion," in Sihvola and Engberg-Pedersen (1998) 149–169; and, for the Roman Imperial period, Margaret Graver, *Stoicism and Emotion*, University of Chicago, 2009. I am, unfortunately, not well acquainted with philosophical conceptions of pleasure within the early Christian tradition. However, one place to start is Nemesius' account, which can be found in R. W. Sharples and P. J. van der Eijk, *Nemesius On the Nature of Man*, Liverpool University Press, 2008, section 18 (pp. 134–139). A more general study of emotion and will from Stoicism to early Christianity is Richard Sorabji's remarkable book *Emotion and Peace of Mind*, Oxford University Press, 2003.

CONTEMPORARY CONCEPTIONS OF PLEASURE

As I mentioned above, there are no comprehensive or even partially comprehensive works on contemporary conceptions of pleasure. Here I list the works I discussed or mentioned, in chronological order: Gilbert Ryle, *The Concept of Mind*, Hutchinson, 1949; Gilbert Ryle, "Symposium: 'Pleasure'," *Proceedings of the Aristotelian Society*, suppl. vol. 28 (1954) 135–146; W. B. Gallie, "Symposium: 'Pleasure'," *Proceedings of the Aristotelian Society*, suppl. vol. 28 (1954) 147–164; Gilbert Ryle, "Pleasure," in *Dilemmas*, Oxford University Press, 1954, 54–67; U. T. Place, "The Concept of Heed," *British Journal of Psychology* 45 (1954) 243–255; Terence Penelhum, "The Logic of Pleasure," *Philosophy and Phenomenological Research* 17 (1957) 488–503; Gerald E. Myers, "Ryle on Pleasure," *Journal of Philosophy* 54 (1957) 181–188; Bernard Williams, "Pleasure and Belief," *Proceedings of the Aristotelian Society*, suppl. vol. 33 (1959) 57–72; Errol Bedford, "Pleasure and Belief," *Proceedings of the Aristotelian Society*, suppl. vol. 33 (1959) 73–92; A. R. Manser, "Pleasure," *Proceedings of the Aristotelian Society* 61 (1960–1961) 223–238; Irvine Thalberg, "False Pleasures," *Journal of Philosophy* 59 (1962) 65–74; C. C. W. Taylor, "Pleasure," *Analysis*, suppl. vol. 23 (1963) 2–19; Anthony Kenny, *Action, Emotion, and Will*, Routledge & Kegan Paul, 1963; Terence Penelhum, "Pleasure and Falsity," *American Philosophical Quarterly* 1 (1964) 81–91; R. J. O'Shaughnessy, "Enjoying and Suffering," *Analysis* 26 (1966) 153–160; W. P. Alston, "Pleasure," *The Encyclopedia of Philosophy*, Macmillan, 1967,

341–347; David Barton Perry, *The Concept of Pleasure*, Mouton, 1967; Joseph Lloyd Cowan, *Pleasure and Pain*, St. Martin's Press, 1968; Warren S. Quinn, "Pleasure – Disposition or Episode?" *Philosophy and Phenomenological Research* 28 (1968) 578–586; Roland Puccetti, "The Sensation of Pleasure," *British Journal for the Philosophy of Science* 20 (1969) 239–145; J. C. B. Gosling, *Pleasure and Desire*, Clarendon Press, 1969; Mary A. McClosky, "Pleasure," *Mind* 80 (1971) 542–551; Rem B. Edwards, "Do Pleasures and Pains Differ Qualitatively?" *Journal of Value Inquiry* 9 (1975) 270–281; Richard Momeyer, "Is Pleasure a Sensation?" *Philosophy and Phenomenological Research* 36 (1975) 113–121; Daniel Dennett, "Why You Can't Make a Computer that Feels Pain," *Synthese* 38 (1978) 415–456; I. Goldstein, "Why People Prefer Pleasure to Pain," *Philosophy* 55 (1980) 349–362; Richard Warner, "Enjoyment," *Philosophical Review* 89 (1980) 507–526; William Lyons, *Gilbert Ryle: An Introduction to His Philosophy*, Harvester Press, 1980; Wayne A. Davis, "Pleasure and Happiness," *Philosophical Studies* 39 (1981) 305–317; Wayne A. Davis, "A Causal Theory of Enjoyment," *Mind* 91 (1982) 240–256; Richard Warner, "Davis on Enjoyment: A Reply," *Mind* 92 (1983) 568–572; Wayne A. Davis, "Warner on Enjoyment: A Rejoinder," *Philosophy Research Archives* 12 (1986–1987) 553–555; Fred Feldman, "Two Questions about Pleasure," in *Philosophical Analysis*, D. F. Austin, ed., Kluwer, 1988, 59–81 (reprinted in Fred Feldman, *Utilitarianism, Hedonism, and Desert*, Cambridge University Press, 1997, 79–105); R. J. Hall, "Are Pains Necessarily Unpleasant?" *Philosophy and Phenomenological Research* 49 (1989) 643–659; D. Sobel, "Pleasure as a Mental State," *Utilitas* 11 (1999) 230–234; Stuart Rachels, "Is Unpleasantness Intrinsic to Unpleasant Experiences?" *Philosophical Studies* 99 (2000) 187–210; Murat Aydede, "An Analysis of Pleasure vis-à-vis Pain," *Philosophy and Phenomenological Research* 61 (2000) 537–561; Bruce Mangan, "Sensation's Ghost: The Non-Sensory 'Fringe' of Consciousness," *Psyche* (2001), available at: psyche.cs. monash.edu.au/v7/psyche-7-18-mangan.html; Fred Feldman, "Hedonism," *Encyclopedia of Ethics*, L. C. Becker and C. B. Becker, eds., 2001, 662–669; Timothy Schroeder, "Pleasure, Displeasure, and Representation," *Canadian Journal of Philosophy* 31 (2001) 507–530; Bennett W. Helm, "Felt Evaluations: A Theory of Pleasure and Pain," *American Philosophical Quarterly* 39 (2002) 13–30; Stuart Rachels, "Six Theses about Pleasure," *Philosophical Perspectives* 18 (2004) 247–267; Fred Feldman, *Pleasure and the Good Life*, Oxford University Press, 2004; Timothy Schroeder, "Pleasure and Displeasure," in *Three Faces of Desire*, Oxford University Press, 2004, 71–106; Timothy Schroeder, "An Unexpected Pleasure," *Canadian Journal of Philosophy* 36 (2006) 255–272; William S. Robinson, "What Is it Like to Like?" *Philosophical Psychology* 19 (2006) 743–765; Christopher Heathwood, "The Reduction of Sensory Pleasure to Desire," *Philosophical Studies* 133 (2007) 23–44; Julia Tanney, "Gilbert Ryle," *Stanford Encyclopedia of Philosophy* 2009, available at: plato.stanford.edu/entries/ryle; Aaron Smuts, "The Feels Good Theory of Pleasure," *Philosophical Studies* 155 (2010) 241–256; Ben Bramble, "The Distinctive Feeling Theory of Pleasure," *Philosophical Studies* 156 (2011), available at present only online.

General Index

Note that the entries for ancient and contemporary authors and their texts in this index refer to instances where the author or text is mentioned or discussed, but not quoted. For quotations from authors and texts, see the Index of Quotations from Ancient Authors and the Index of Quotations from Contemporary Authors.

activation (*energeia*) 106, 114–138, 163–167, 272
actuality 114, 115
Aelian (Claudius Aelianus) 21
Aëtius 37
affect, affective 67, 85
affection 50, 51, 67
Alcmaeon of Croton 31
Alexander of Aphrodisias 36, 177, 274
    Ethical Problems 36, 274
Alston, William 221, 225–227, 229, 232, 233,
    253–255, 256, 269
Anaxagoras of Clazomenae 31
Andronicus of Rhodes 203, 205
Anscombe, G. E. M. 1–3
Antisthenes of Athens 18–20, 21, 25, 272
    On Pleasure 18
Aphrodite 9, 18, 19, 38
appearance aspect (of pleasure) 64, 65–68, 70,
    74, 89, 96, 100, 101, 178, 226, 246, 271,
    273
Aristippus the Elder 20–23, 25, 28, 145, 154
Aristippus the Younger 145, 153, 158
Aristotle 8, 12, 26, 34, 35, 43, 103–139, 150,
    163–166, 175, 179, 182, 183, 184, 187, 194,
    209, 211, 218, 220, 224, 245, 269, 271, 272,
    273, 276–277, 278
    Categories 103, 120
    Eudemian Ethics 103, 105, 106, 114, 119–123,
    127–129, 131, 133, 137, 138, 165, 271
    Magna Moralia 103, 105, 124–130, 138
    Nicomachean Ethics 2, 18, 103, 105, 114, 121,
    130–138, 175, 224, 271, 274
    On Plants 43
    On Sense-Perception and Sensibles 50, 103,
    116, 119

    On the Generation of Animals 103, 136, 139
    On the Parts of Animals 127, 135
    On the Soul 50, 103, 116
    Physics 103
    Posterior Analytics 103, 109–114
    Problems 139, 141–143
    Protrepticus 104, 114, 165–166
    Rhetoric 103, 108–109, 111–114, 124
    Topics 103, 109–114, 120, 123, 124, 129
Arius Didymus 186
Arnold, Magda 214, 218
Artemisia, wife of Mausolus 205, 277
Aspasius 18, 20
attending *see* attention
attention 179–181, 220, 222, 223, 224, 227, 236,
    238, 239, 270
attitude, hedonic *compare* intentional,
    intentionality 9, 82, 132–133, 168, 170,
    175, 176, 178–179, 217, 220, 270, 271,
    272, 273
awareness *compare* attention; heed 58, 65, 68,
    152, 229, 233, 236, 239, 270, 274, 44
Aydede, Murat 215, 246–248, 251, 253, 254, 255,
    258, 265

Bedford, Errol 239
Beebe-Center, J. G. 214
behaviorism 215, 217, 220, 278
Berridge, Kent 262
Bramble, Ben 264, 265
Broad, C. D. 264

calm *compare* intermediate condition; stillness;
    and also Index of Greek and Latin
    Words and Expressions: *aponia*,
    ahêdonia 48, 64, 67, 89

cathartic taxonomy 76
character 121
Chrysippus of Soli 182, 186, 192–194, 197–201,
    203, 204, 208, 210
    On Passions 185, 192, 195, 202
Cicero 20, 146, 159, 171, 185, 277
    Tusculan Disputations 197
Cleanthes of Assos 182, 185, 197, 198, 199, 203
    Hymn to Zeus 197
    On Pleasure 185
Clement of Alexandria 26, 146, 155
cognitivism 231, 245
coincidental, coincidentally 19, 20, 117
conscious-quality (theory of pleasure) 226, 227,
    254–268, 274
core aspect (of pleasure) 65, 69, 74, 90, 100, 101,
    271, 273
Cynicism, Cynics 19, 23
Cyrenaics 8, 26, 144–158, 178, 182, 183, 207, 208,
    209, 269

Davis, Wayne 216, 232, 234–235, 249
definition 24, 25, 26, 245
Democritus 13–17, 20, 21, 24, 29, 31, 144, 173, 212,
    272
    On Contentment 13–17, 18, 29
Dennett, Daniel 247
de re 260
de se 256–257
desire-satisfaction 233, 234, 249–250, 252, 267
Diels, Hermann 35
diminishing-desire (*phthonos*) 93–94, 275
Diogenes Laertius 18, 151, 147
    Lives and Opinions of Eminent Philosophers 146
Diogenes of Apollonia 31, 34–35, 38 n. 6, 207
Diogenes of Oenoanda 146
dispositional (theory of pleasure) 220–221, 225,
    246, 248, 254, 255, 265, 270, 278
distinctive-feeling (theory of pleasure) 264
doxographer, doxographical, doxography 35, 37,
    146
Dunker, K. 264

Empedocles 30, 31–33, 34, 59, 60, 37
Epicurus 8, 25, 144–181, 182, 183, 184, 208, 209,
    211, 269, 270, 273, 274, 276, 277, 278
    Letter to Herodotus 149
    Letter to Menoeceus 146, 148
    Letter to Pythocles 173
    On Choice and Avoidance 148, 163
    On the Goal 148, 152, 167, 171
    Principal Doctrines 145, 148
    Protrepticus 165
    Vatican Sayings 145
episode, episodic 215, 221, 224, 246, 247, 248,
    270, 278

esoteric 104
Eudemus of Rhodes 164
Eudoxus of Cnidus 177
Eusebius of Caesarea 153
Euthyphro problem 261, 262, 263
evaluation, evaluative *compare* evaluative
    condition 190, 203, 204, 206, 208, 209,
    231, 236, 242, 243, 244, 252, 256, 257, 267,
    277
evaluative condition 196, 203, 236
excess, excessive 194–201
exoteric 104
explanation question 6

feeling 65–66, 67–68, 178, 217, 218–219, 226, 233,
    246, 247, 251, 253–265, 266, 270, 274, 279
Feibleman, J. S. 264
Feldman, Fred 216, 246, 256–257, 260, 264, 266,
    276
felt quality *see* feeling, compare *quale*
felt-quality (theory of pleasure) *see* conscious-
    quality (theory of pleasure)
filling *see also* replenishment, restoration
fluttering 202
fragments 6–8
fresh (*prosphatos*) 204–205,
    206, 277

Galen of Pergamum 192
Gallie, W. B. 218, 221, 229, 236
good passion (*euphatheia*) 210–213
Gosling, J. C. B. 276

habit, habituation 108–109, 142, 274
Heathwood, Christopher 256, 258, 260–262, 263,
    267
Hecato of Rhodes 202
hedonic-tone (theory of pleasure)
    263, 264
hedonism
    analgesic 147, 167–179
    ethical 4
    presentist 22–23
    psychological 4, 208, 227
heed, heeding 220, 221, 224, 227, 270
Hermarchus of Mytilene 165
Hermias of Alexandria 12
Hesiod 27
    Works and Days 27–28, 75
heterogeneity problem 256, 260
hierarchy, metaphysical or psychological 55, 98,
    102, 135
Hippias of Elis 35, 94
homonymous, homonymy 112–113, 116, 129
Horace 23
hylomorphic, hylomorphism 108, 118

identity question 3, 35
Illusion Argument (in *Republic* 9), 64–70, 86, 89, 96, 101
impulse 189–194
indifferents 196
in itself *see* coincidental, coincidentally
intentional, intentionality 216, 225, 235, 245, 248, 253–265, 270, 278, 239
intentional mode 236, 246, 270
intermediate condition *compare* calm; stillness; and also Index of Greek and Latin Words and Expressions: *aponia*, *ahêdonia* 153
"irrational" 187

Kenny, Anthony 221, 261, 276
kinds question 4

literalism 118, 119
Lovibond, Sabina 245
Lucretius 145, 154
    On the Nature of Things 145
Lyons, William 221

Mangan, Bruce 251, 251, 253, 266
Manser, A. R. 236
marrow (*myelos*) 58–59
Mason, Elinor 257
Mausolus, Persian satrap 205, 277
McCloskey, Mary 221, 229
Metrodorus of Lampsacus 148
Mill, J. S. 273
mixture
    sequential 79
    simultaneous 79
Momeyer, Richard 221
mood 218, 219, 235
motivational (theory of pleasure) 225, 227, 254–268
Myers, Gerald E. 221

natural, nature 41–42, 56–57, 64, 99, 108–109, 120, 155, 158, 163, 172, 272
Nausiphanes 144, 165
neutral condition *compare* calm; intermediate condition; stillness; and also Index of Greek and Latin Words and Expressions: *ahêdonia*, *aponia* 169
non-cognitivism *compare* cognitivism 252
"non-rational" 188
non-sensory (conscious) experience 251, 253
Nowell-Smith, P. H. 231

object, hedonic 9, 53, 81, 82, 94, 133, 135, 168, 170, 175, 176, 177–178, 179, 229, 231, 233, 235, 237, 270, 271–272

occurrence, occurrent *compare* episodic 215, 221, 224, 225, 234, 243, 246, 248, 251, 252, 255, 265, 279
Old Academy 115
Olds, James 228
Old Stoics *see* Stoics
O'Shaughnessy, R. J. 221, 229

Panaetius of Rhodes 202
Parmenides of Elea 31
passion, passivity 219, 225, 227, 236, 237, 268
Penelhum, Terence 216, 217, 221, 223–225, 226–227, 229–230, 231–232, 233, 235, 236, 237, 242–244, 255, 268, 276
perception (*aisthêsis*) 51
Peripatetic *Problems see* Aristotle, *Problems*
Perry, David Barton 216, 221, 230–232, 233, 235, 236, 244–245, 252, 257, 266, 277
"physical" 30
physical tradition 3, 39, 269, 271
Place, U. T. , 221–223, 227
Plato 3, 8, 11–12, 26, 37, 40–62, 63–102, 111, 125, 132, 133, 139, 150, 160, 175, 180, 182, 183, 211, 212, 224, 250, 269, 271, 272, 273, 274, 275–276, 278
    Gorgias 41, 44–47, 50, 77, 91, 106, 130
    Hippias Major 40, 41, 53–56, 73
    Phaedo 30, 91, 158
    Philebus 9, 40, 44, 55, 63, 64, 70, 74–100, 106, 134, 139, 161, 180, 209, 212, 224, 226, 232, 240, 271, 275, 276
    Protagoras 61
    Republic 40, 41, 44, 47–50, 55, 63, 68, 77, 78, 79, 85, 89, 91, 106, 124, 135, 148, 169, 175, 212, 213, 224, 226, 246, 271, 272, 274, 275
    Sophist 70
    Theaetetus 70
    Timaeus 34, 40, 41, 44, 50–62, 64, 72, 73, 77, 80, 98, 99, 106, 139, 157, 207, 273, 275
pleasure
    anticipatory false pleasure kind 1 77–80, 99, 210, 275
    apparent 4, 89, 137–138
    appetitive 52, 65, 102, 106, 127, 136, 137, 275, 50, 72
    auditory 54, 61, 78, 97, 98, 100, 152, 157, 163, 275
    base 13, 24, 53–56, 73, 272
    being-pleased-that 216, 229–232, 236, 237–238, 240–241, 242, 243, 244–245, 246, 253, 257, 260, 264, 266, 272, 275, 277, 279
    bodily 12, 20, 21, 61, 65, 76–77, 80, 90, 91–92, 99, 106, 139, 147, 149, 150, 156, 168, 246, 247, 248, 80
    brute 21, 52–53, 54, 61, 77, 80, 139

civic 11, 13, 17, 272
contemplative *see* rational
depraved 10, 13, 272
enjoyment 204, 216, 229–235, 236, 242,
    244, 249, 257, 260, 266, 272, 275–277,
    279
ethical 137, 274
false 137–138, 271, 102
false pleasure kind 1
    (in *Philebus*) 80–84
false pleasure kind 2
    (in *Philebus*) 84–88
false pleasure kind 3
    (in *Philebus*) 88,
false pleasure kind 4 in *Philebus see*
    mixed pleasure
fine 53–56, 73
foolish 20, 272
genuine *compare* true 67, 69, 73, 138, 172, 175,
    176–178, 277
gustatory *compare* appetitive 156, 163, 178
impure *see* mixed
intellectual *see* rational
katastematic 147, 158, 168, 170, 272
kinetic 147, 160, 162–167, 168, 170, 181, 207,
    211
measured 16–17
mental 84–88 *see* psychic
mixed 55, 74, 80, 90–97, 99, 100, 102, 139, 161,
    179–181, 271
natural 138
non-restorative 127, 128, 137, 124
nutritional 35–37, 52
of the belly 14–15, 16, 20, 24
of the soul *see* psychic
olfactory 54, 55–56, 67, 73–74, 79, 97, 98, 100,
    124, 135, 275
propositional *compare* being-pleased-that 240,
    246, 256–257, 260, 264, 272, 275
pseudo- *see* false
psychic 12, 54, 61, 77, 90, 92–96, 101, 147, 149,
    150, 152, 153, 211
psychosomatic 90, 91–92
pure 55, 74, 79, 97–99, 100, 124, 125, 134, 271,
    272, 275
rational 48–50, 52, 56, 61, 65, 70–72, 78, 97,
    100, 101, 102, 106, 134, 166, 175, 264, 272,
    274
refined 12, 13, 24, 54, 272
restorative 124–130, 138, 159, 160–161
sense-perceptual 50–62, 68, 73, 77, 80, 102,
    134, 135, 156, 274
sensory 246–248, 256, 260–262, 266, 273,
    275–277, 279
sexual 37–39, 52, 138–143, 163

somatic *see* bodily
spirited 48–50, 52, 56, 61, 65, 70, 78, 102, 106
true 4, 63, 100, 137–138, 175, 271, 272
untrue *see* false
visual 54, 78, 97, 98, 152, 157, 163, 275
wise 20, 272
Plutarch 28, 146
    Against Colotes 146
    Commentary on Hesiod's Works and Days 28
    On the Impossibility of Life according to
        Epicurus 146
Polybus of Cos 35, 37, 140
Polystratus the Epicurean 164, 165
"practical condition" 199, 236
Praxagoras of Cos 187
private 224–225
pro-attitude 133, 179, 220, 231, 232, 233, 236, 248,
    255, 256, 260, 261, 277, 279
pro-attitude (theory of pleasure) *compare*
    motivational (theory of pleasure) 255,
    263, 265, 267
Prodicus of Ceos 10–13, 21, 24, 48, 54–55, 61, 211,
    272
    The Choice of Heracles 10–11, 12, 13, 16, 17,
        27–28, 75
proposition, propositional *compare* pleasure,
    propositional 83, 133, 229, 241, 255, 270
"psychic" 4
Puccetti, Roland 221, 228–229, 236
purity 87–88
Pythagorean, Pythagoreanism 45–46, 56, 278
quale, qualia 65, 153, 218, 226, 259

Quinn, Warren 221, 225, 226–227, 229, 255

Rachels, Stuart 256, 258, 259, 262, 263, 265, 267,
    270, 260
replenishment (theory of pleasure) 36, 41–50, 101,
    278 *see also*
    filling, restoration
  source of 45–46
representation 70, 245, 278
representational (theory of pleasure) 248–250,
    252, 253, 258, 267, 270, 273
restoration *compare* filling; replenishment 42–43,
    44, 72, 101, 106, 107, 123–130, 157, 250,
    272, 274, 114
  coordinated 161
  partitive 161
Right Reason *compare* Zeus 188, 195, 197, 201,
    202
Robinson, William 246, 251–253, 255, 257, 261,
    262, 266, 267, 278
Ryle, Gilbert 2, 215, 217–225, 227, 228–229, 235,
    236, 238, 240, 248, 251, 255, 268, 270,
    276

Schadenfreude 94, 212
Schroeder, Timothy 248–250, 251, 252–253, 267, 278
sensation 65, 66, 218–219, 222–223, 228–229, 246, 251, 252, 254, 260, 267
"sense-perceiving" 116
Sextus Empiricus 146
Sidgwick, Henry 254
smooth, smoothness 153–158, 202, 270
Smuts, Aaron 256, 259, 261, 262–265, 267
Socrates 18, 24
soul and its parts, conceptions of 30, 46, 47–48, 58–61, 68, 72, 107–108, 149–151, 186–187
spiritualism 118
stillness *see* calm, intermediate condition, and also Index of Greek and Latin Words and Expressions, *aponia, ahêdonia*
Stobaeus, Johannes 8, 36, 186
Stoics 9, 182–213, 229, 230, 236, 269, 272, 273, 275, 276, 277
Strato of Lampsacus 164
sudden (as a characteristic of pleasure) 57–58, 106

Tanney, Julia 232 n. 20
Taylor, C. C. W. 221, 276
testimonies 6–8
Thalberg, Irving 217, 240–241, 242, 276
Theophrastus of Eresus 31, 33, 34, 164, 274
On Perceptions 31, 36, 50, 207
Timaeus of Locri, 41
Titchener, Edward 214

titles 18
True Filling Argument (in *Republic* 9), 70–74, 98
truth-apt, truth-aptness 216, 231, 240–245, 276
truth-conceptions
ontological 63, 69, 70, 71, 85, 89–90, 100, 102, 240
absolute ontological truth-conception 73
gradable ontological truth-conception 73, 97
representational 63, 69, 82, 90, 100, 102, 240
truth-value 69

unimpeded 128, 131, 166, 272, 123
unnaturalness 188
"untrue" 63, 69

variation, hedonic 162–163
violent (as a characteristic of pleasure) 57–58
vision, theories of 32, 57, 117, 166

Warner, Richard 216, 232–235, 249
"What is *F*?" question 24, 25
Williams, Bernard 217, 229, 236–238, 240, 276
wisdom, wise *see* pleasure, wise
Wundt, Wilhelm 214

Xenophon 10, 13, 17, 27–28

Zeno of Citium 182, 185–186, 187, 189, 193, 194, 195, 197, 198, 199, 201, 202, 203, 204, 210
On Passions 185, 202
Zeus 188, 201

Index of Greek and Latin Words and Expressions

The entries are given in the form in which they occur in the text and, in cases where there are cognate forms in a single entry, in the order in which they occur in the text. They are not given in standard lexical form, say, adjectives in masculine and feminine gender and nominative case followed by neuter gender and nominative case. I have opted for this unconventional style for the sake of the reader unfamiliar with Greek and Latin. Note that Greek and Latin are highly inflected languages, and not all inflected forms are listed here. Latin terms are indicated by (L).

adiaphoron (indifferent) 196

aisthêsis, aisthêseis (n.), *aisthêtika, aisthêtê* (adj.) (perception, sense-perception, perceptual, perceived) 50, 51, 54, 106, 116, 123, 166

ahêdonia (lack of pleasure) 158, 169

alêthes, alêtheis (true) 69, 97

allotriai, allotrion (foreign, alien) 136

alogos, alogon (irrational, without reason) 149, 185, 195

anempodistos, anempodiston (unimpeded) 119, 123

anima (L) (irrational part of the soul) 149

animus (L) (rational part of the soul) 149, 154

aphrodisia (sexual activity, intercourse) 38

aphros (foam) 38

apologismos (reasoning) 200, 201

aponia (lack of bodily pain) 147, 149, 158, 169

apoproêgmena (dispreferred) 196

aretê (excellence, virtue) 19, 55

asmenismos (gladness, a pleasure term) 212, 213

ataraxia (lack of disturbance, lack of psychological distress, tranquillity) 147, 148, 158

ateles, ateleis (incomplete) 129

athroa (sudden) 106

axiôma, axiômata (assertoric proposition, assertion) 191, 200

bebaios pistis (secure, firm conviction, persuasion) 173, 175

boulêsis (desire, rational desire) 210, 211

chara (joy, a pleasure term) 12, 13, 24, 149, 210, 211, 213, 272

dianoia (mind, intellect) 152, 187, 189

diaphora (difference), *differentia* (L) 113

doxa, doxai (belief) 68, 200

dynamis (power, ability, capability, "potentiality") 13, 114, 165, 166

ê (or) 185, 203

eidos (kind, type) 77, 78

enargeia (clarity, clear evidence) 164

energeia (activation, "actuality") 106, 110, 111, 114–138, 163–167, 278

eparsis (swelling) 203, 207

eph' hêmin (within our power) 198

epibolê (attention) 180, 181

epichairekakia (*Schadenfreude*, a pleasure term) 94, 212

epigenomenon, epigenomenê (adj.), *epigennêma* (n.) (added on, something added on) 130, 132, 209

epistêmê (knowledge) 200

epithymia, epithymiai (desire, appetite) 125, 202, 210

eulabeia (caution) 210, 211

eupatheia, eupatheiai (good passion) 210, 211

euphrosynê (delight, a pleasure term) 12, 13, 24, 61, 149, 211

euthymia (n.), *euthymos* (adj.) (contentment, content) 13, 17, 211

gaudium (n.), *gaudet, gaudemus, gaudere* (v.) (L) (pleasure, enjoyment, rejoicing, to rejoice) 150, 167, 168

geloion (ridiculous) 94

genesis (coming-to-be, process of coming into existence) 110, 123, 125, 129, 131, 160, 271

goêteia (bewitchment, a pleasure term) 212

hêdonê (pleasure) 9, 12, 61, 98, 183, 202, 210, 211, 213, 274

hêgemonikon (ruling part of the soul in Stoic psychology) 187

hexis, hexeis (disposition) 119–120

hormê (impulse, conation) 185, 187, 189

horos (definition) 25

hylê (matter, timber) 107

hyparchousa (prevailing) 106, 108

hypolêpsis (judgment) 200

idion (proper) 116

kallos (beauty) *see kalon*

kalon, kala (beautiful, fine, noble) 53, 54, 98

kata physin (natural, according to nature), 119

katastêma (condition, state) 148

katêgorêma, katêgorêmata (predicate, predicate expression) 191

kathara, katharon (pure) 74, 76

kathêkon (fitting, appropriate, obligatory) 190–191, 194

kêlêsis (enchantment, delight, a pleasure term) 212

kinêsis, kinêseis (n.), *kinêtikon* (adj.) (change, motion, kinetic) 48, 64, 65, 106, 109–110, 129, 148, 152, 160, 166, 185, 189

korê (eye-jelly) 118

krisis, kriseis (judgment) 192, 200

leia (adj.), *leiotês* (n.) (smooth, smoothness) 26–28, 152, 153

logikon (rational, with reason) 149

logos (study, reason, speech) 29, 187

makaria (blessedness, happiness, bliss) 172

megalôs (robustly) 96

megethos (largeness, robustness) 67

mens (L) (mind, intellect) compare *nous* 150

to metaxy (the medium of sense-perception) 117

metriês (measured) 16

morbus, morbi (L) (disease) 184, 185

morphê (shape, form) 108

movens (L) (moving, changing, kinetic) 148, 159

myelos (marrow) 58

nous (mind, intellect) 107, 120

oikeia, oikeion (adj.) *oikeiotês* (n.) (congenial, akin, belonging to one, congeniality, kinship, belonging) 136, 274

orthos logos (Right Reason) 188

orthotês onomatôn (correctness of names) 11

ousia (essence, being) 112

pathêma, pathêmata (affection) 50, 67, 184

pathos (affection, emotion, affective condition, passion) 50, 140, 184–185, 274

percipitur, percipi (L) (to perceive, sense) 168, 178

perturbatio, perturbationes (L) (disturbance) 185

phainomenon (appearance, appearance aspect) 65, 271

phantasia (imagination, appearance) 126, 190

phora (movement) 189

phronimon (rational part of the soul) 60

phthonos (diminishing-desire) 92, 93–94, 96, 212

physiologia (study of nature) 3, 29–30, 50

physis (nature) 13, 29

pithanon (persuadable) 45

pithos (urn) 45

pleonasmos (n.), *pleonazousa* (adj.) (excess, excessive) 185, 194, 195

pneuma (breath-like substance) 151

poiêma (action) 50

ponos (toil, labor, suffering) 19, 274

proêgmena (preferred) 196

prosênê (gentle, mild) 152, 154

prosphatos (fresh, stimulating) 203, 204

pseudes, pseudeis (false) 69, 88

psychê (soul) 4, 30

ptoia (fluttering) 186, 201

recens (L) (recent, fresh) 204

sêma (tomb) 46

sentio, sentit (L) (to sense, perceive, feel) 178

skiagraphia (shadow-painting) 64

sôma (body) 12, 46

sophia (wisdom, specialized knowledge) 271

sperma (seed) 37, 139

sphodron, sphodros (adj.), *sphodrotês* (n.) (intense, intensity) 67, 96, 274

stans (L) (standing, still) 148, 159

symbebêkos (coincidental) 117, 125, 126

symmetria (symmetry) 195, 202

synkatathesis (assent) 189, 191

syntelesis (realization, completion, fulfillment) 167

teleia (adj.), *teleioi, teleioun* (v.) (complete, to complete) 130, 137

telos (goal, end-point, completion) 25, 26, 110, 114, 120, 129, 130

terpsis (joy, delight, a pleasure term) 12, 13, 24, 211

tracheia (rough) 26–28

vehementior (L) (excessive, too vigorous) 195

viriditas (L) (vitality) 205

voluptas, voluptatem (L) (pleasure) 167, 168, 169, 213

Index of Quotations from Ancient Authors

Aelian (Claudius Aelianus) 21
Alexander of Aphrodisias
  Ethical Problems
    13 275
  Supplement to On the Soul
    150.33–34 177, 277
Andronicus of Rhodes
  On the Passions
    5 212
Antisthenes of Athens
  SSR 114 20
  SSR 120 19
  SSR 122 18
  SSR 123 18
  SSR 126 19
  SSR 127 19
  SSR 134 19
Aristotle
  Categories
    12a 120
  Eudemian Ethics
    1220b 120
  Magna Moralia
    1204b 125
    1205b 124
  Metaphysics
    987a 24
    1043b 25
  Nicomachean Ethics
    1102b 121
    1104b 132
    1105b 120
    1118a 139
    1152b 120, 138
    1152b–1153a 125
    1153a 123
    1154b 128, 129
    1173b 130
    1174b 130
    1175a 130, 134, 136, 276
    1175b 131, 136

    1176a 135, 138, 176
    1177a 135
  On Plants
    815a11–16 43
  On Sense-Perception and Sensibles
    436b–437a 122
    445a 56
  On Sleep
    454b 126
  On the Generation of Animals
    598a 136
    715a 139
    721b 140
    723b–274a 141
  On the Parts of Animals
    647a 108
    660b 136
    661a 136
    690b–691a 127
  On the Soul
    403a 118
    412b 107
    414b 126
    417a 129
    421a 98
    424a 119
    431a 133
  Physics
    195b 116
    201b 129
    247a 121
  Posterior Analytics
    87b 109
  Problems
    878b 141, 142
    879a 142
    879b 142
    879b–880a 143
  Protrepticus
    79 115
    83 166

Aristotle (cont.)
  87 135, 166
  91 166
  Rhetoric
    1361a 116
    1369b–1370a 106
    1370a 108
    1370b 93
    1378a 184
  Topics
    106a–b 112, 124
    112b 12
    114a 120
    121a 110
    124a 116
    135b 120
    146b 110, 114, 129
    147b 120
Athenaeus of Naucratis
  546e–f 163

Cicero
  On Goals
    1.37–38 168, 171, 178
    1.38 2.18 21, 26, 154, 162
  Prior Academics
    2.139 20, 147
  Tusculan Disputations
    3.23 185
    3.74–75 205
    3.76–79 198
    3.77 197
    4.20 213
    4.47 195
Clement of Alexandria
  Miscellanies
    2.20.106.3 26, 152
    2.21.130.8 147, 179

Damascius
  Commentary on Plato's Philebus
    197 161
Democritus
  B3 14
  B88 17
  B146 16
  B159 15
  B174 17
  B178 20
  B189 14
  B191 14, 17
  B194 16
  B211 16
  B215 17

B223 174
B224 16
B235 14
B245 17
B246 16
B284 15, 174
B285 15, 16, 173
B286 15, 174
Diogenes Laertius
  2.66 22
  2.85 25
  2.86 26, 152
  2.87 158
  2.89 158
  2.89–90 150
  2.90 152, 158
  7.85–86 209
  7.107 201
  7.108 194
  7.110 185, 202
  7.111 192
  7.114 212
  7.116 210
  10.6 163
  10.22 181
  10.34 179
  10.66 149
  10.136 149,
    163, 164

Epicurus
  Letter to Herodotus
    63 151
    64 166
    81–82 173
  Letter to Menoeceus
    127–128 174
    128–129 179
    129 184
    131 147
  Letter to Pythocles
    85 173
  On the Goal
    68 148
  Principal Doctrines
    3 159, 161
    12 180
    15 174
    18 159, 162
    29 174
Eusebius of Caesarea
  Preparation for the Gospel
    14.18.32 153
    15.62.7 158

Galen of Pergamum
  *On the Doctrines of Plato
    and Hippocrates*
    4.2.14 202
    4.2.14–18 195
    5.1.4 192
    5.1.5 193

Hermias of Alexandria
  Commentary on Plato's Phaedrus
    238.22–239.2 12
Hesiod
  Works and Days
    287–292 27
    311 27
Hippocratic texts
  Diseases IV
    39.5 35
  On Generation
    1.1 38, 140
    1.2–3 37
    1.3 140
    2.1 37
    4.1 38
    4.2 38, 140, 141
  On the Sacred Disease
    17.1–2 Littré 30
    17.2–4 Littré 31
Homer
  Iliad
    18.108–109 92
Horace
  Epistles 1
    17.17–29 23

Lucretius
    2.400–423 156
    2.436–440 157
    2.963–966 159
    3.136–148 150
    4.622–627 156, 178
    4.722–735 153
    4.861–869 159

Nausiphanes of Teos
    1 165

Plato
  Euthydemus
    290a 213
  Gorgias
    493a 45, 46
    493d 45
    493d–494a 44
    494a 45

    494b–c 45
    495e–497a 91
  Hippias Major
    298a 54
    298b 54
    298d 55
    298d–e 54
    299a 54
  Laws
    653a–c 132
  Meno
    71b 5
  Phaedo
    60b–c 91
    96a–b 29
  Philebus
    12b–c 9
    31d 76
    31e–32b 77
    32b–c 78
    32c 78
    33c 78
    34c 77
    37e–38a 80
    39c 85
    40e 83, 87
    41e–42a 85
    42b 86
    42b–c 86
    42c 88
    42a–b 85
    42d 106
    44a 89
    45a–b 97
    46b–c 90
    46d 90
    46d–e 91
    47c 91
    47c–d 92
    48a 93
    49b 95
    50e 97
    51a 88
    51b 98
    51b–d 98
    51e 55
    55c 76
  Protagoras
    337a–b 11
    337c 11
  Republic
    401e–402a 132
    583a 48
    583e 64

Plato (cont.)
    584a 64
    584b 67, 74, 91
    584b–c 55
    584c 49
    585b 48
    586b–c 64
    601b 213
  Timaeus
    29d–30a 96
    34a 51
    43c 51
    64a 52
    64b 60
    64c–d 56, 106
    65a–b 55, 57, 91
    67a 82
    77b 43
    77d–e 59
    80b 61
Plutarch
  Against Colotes
    1122e 152
  Commentary on Hesiod's Works and Days
    293–297 28
  Dinner Conversations
    674a 152
  On Ethical Excellence
    441c 195
  On the Impossibility of Life according to Epicurus
    1088c 162
    1088d 160
    1098d 172
Porphyry
  Letter to Marcella
    29 172

Quintilian
  Institutes of Oratory
    295.20 147

Sextus Empiricus
  Against the Mathematicians
    7.11 158
Stobaeus, Johannes
    1.50.31 36
    3.38.32 94
SVF
    1.205 186
    1.206 186
    1.211 202
    1.230 201
    3.169 189, 190
    3.171 189, 191
    3.377 190, 195
    3.378 200
    3.391 203
    3.394 206
    3.402 212
    3.548 201

Theophrastus of Eresus
  On Perceptions
    9 31
    16–17 33
    43 34

Xenophon
  Memorabilia
    1.2.56 27
    2.1.21 27
    2.1.23 11
    2.1.24 10

Index of Quotations from Contemporary Authors

Alston, William, "Pleasure" 5, 225, 226, 229, 254, 255, 270
Anscombe, G. E. M., *Intention* 2
Asmis, Elizabeth, "Epicurean Psychology" 179
Aydede, Murat, "An Analysis of Pleasure vis-à-vis Pain" 215, 247, 248

Bedford, Errol, "Pleasure and Belief" 239
Bobzien, Suzanne, *Determinism and Freedom in Stoic Philosophy* 192
Broadie, Sarah, and Rowe, Christopher, *Aristotle: Nicomachean Ethics* 134

Crane, Tim, *The Mechanical Mind* 82

Davis, Wayne A., "A Casual Theory of Enjoyment" 234

Feldman, Fred, "Two Questions about Pleasure" 257
"Hedonism" 264

Gallie, W. B., "Pleasure" 233
Gosling, Justin, and Taylor, C. C. W., *The Greeks on Pleasure* 111

Heathwood, Christopher, "The Reduction of Sensory Pleasure to Desire" 260, 261

Inwood, Brad, *Ethics and Human Action in Early Stoicism* 199, 204, 205, 210

Lyons, William, *Gilbert Ryle: An Introduction to his Philosophy* 219

Mangan, Bruce, "Sensation's Ghost: The Non-Sensory 'Fringe' of Consciousness" 252

Penelhum, Terence, "The Logic of Pleasure" 224
"Pleasure and Falsity" 242, 243
Perry, David Barton, *The Concept of Pleasure* 233, 244, 254, 277
Place, U. T., "The Concept of Heed" 222, 223
Puccetti, Roland, "The Sensation of Pleasure" 229

Quinn, Warren, "Pleasure – Disposition or Episode?" 255

Rachels, Stuart, "Is Unpleasantness Intrinsic to Unpleasant Experiences?" 257, 258, 270
Rapp, Christoph, "Aristotle's Rhetoric" 111
Robinson, William, "What Is it Like to Like?" 251, 253, 278
Ryle, Gilbert, *The Concept of Mind* 218
"Pleasure" 228

Schroeder, Timothy, "Pleasure, Displeasure, and Representation" 248, 249, 250
Sidgwick, Henry, *Methods of Ethics* 254
Smuts, Aaron, "The Feels Good Theory of Pleasure" 261, 262, 263

Taylor, C. C. W., "Pleasure" 216
Thalberg, Irving, "False Pleasures" 241

Warner, Richard, "Enjoyment" 232, 233
Williams, Bernard, "Pleasure and Belief" 237, 238

arrived in Lisbon from Coimbra with his "ill-read Proudhon under my arm." In Évora he quickly transfigures himself into a socialist radical of the day, a bona fide political journalist. This will be a short-lived interlude, however. He is able to bear the boredom of Évora for approximately seven months, between January and July 1867. But the Évora experience is more than likely a major source for Eça's gradually evolving abandonment of his youthful Romanticism. The political journalist who writes for the *Distrito de Évora* seems to be another Eça de Queirós, armed with an intense, spare lexicon. The vocabulary radiates a newly found impulse toward clarity and definition of objects. In one of the columns, for instance, he gives us a bracing antidote to the wild phantasmagoria that had so dominated his earlier "imaginative" essays; here the trivial catalogue begins to impose itself upon the imagination with a concretion of fact and perception that may well indicate a novelist in the making: "But today the air is so clear, the blue sky so serene, that it seems that the day itself is intelligent, and that seasons like this—cold, quick, clear—spiritualize the brain. It is a fact that the winter, when it is bright, is a season that protects intelligence; that scattered light, without smoke, weightless and tepid, produces an endless awakening of ideas. Now I pass through these streets, crowded with people, just walking along, studying the types like a true idler, laughing at the coiffures of the women, inspecting the new books, listening to the political discussions, the insipid and painful drollery of our journalists."

For the first time, Eça encounters the excruciating boredom of the provinces, and he finds a critical spirit in his writing to while away the time. It is only in Évora that he is able to penetrate and observe the constrictions of feeling and the impositions of custom and habit upon a somnolent citizenry. Social concerns, openly expressed, appear in Eça's writing for the first time. For instance, he will repeat his praise for the Portuguese folksong (as *cantigas*), but now in Évora the sustaining principle of folk art will transform itself into a critical medium—the spirit of the *cantiga* begins to eradicate a merely literary stance before the facts of poverty. "When the disconsolate, the abandoned, the poor, the oppressed have run out of everything—bread,